THE COLONY AND THE COMPANY

The Colony and the Company

HAITI AFTER THE MISSISSIPPI BUBBLE

MALICK W. GHACHEM

PRINCETON UNIVERSITY PRESS
PRINCETON & OXFORD

Copyright © 2025 by Princeton University Press

Princeton University Press is committed to the protection of copyright and the intellectual property our authors entrust to us. Copyright promotes the progress and integrity of knowledge created by humans. By engaging with an authorized copy of this work, you are supporting creators and the global exchange of ideas. As this work is protected by copyright, any reproduction or distribution of it in any form for any purpose requires permission; permission requests should be sent to permissions@press.princeton.edu. Ingestion of any PUP IP for any AI purposes is strictly prohibited.

Published by Princeton University Press
41 William Street, Princeton, New Jersey 08540
99 Banbury Road, Oxford OX2 6JX

press.princeton.edu

GPSR Authorized Representative: Easy Access System Europe - Mustamäe tee 50, 10621 Tallinn, Estonia, gpsr.requests@easproject.com

All Rights Reserved

ISBN 9780691261461
ISBN (e-book) 9780691261485

British Library Cataloging-in-Publication Data is available

Editorial: Priya Nelson & Emma Wagh
Production Editorial: Jaden Young
Jacket/Cover Design: Heather Hansen
Production: Lauren Reese
Publicity: William Pagdatoon
Copyeditor: Leah Caldwell

Jacket image: "Carte du Cap Français, côte St. Domingue et de l'étendue de son port et de ses environs" (1723). Cartes Marines (Ayer) Map Collection. Courtesy of the Newberry Library, Chicago, IL.

This book has been composed in Arno

10 9 8 7 6 5 4 3 2 1

In loving memory of Said H. Ghachem (1941–2021)

CONTENTS

Figures and Maps   ix

	Introduction	1
1	Company Colony	11
2	Colonial System	54
3	"Women, Negroes, and Unknown, Unimportant People"	80
4	Militant Slavery	103
5	The Company of Jesus	128
6	Maroons and the Military-Planter State	155
	Conclusion	182

Acknowledgments   191
Appendix: The August 1722 Royal Ordinance on Money   195
Notes   197
Bibliography   235
Index   251

FIGURES AND MAPS

1 Map of Saint-Domingue in the early 1720s. Redrawn by
Ronald Draddy from figures 7 and 8.   xiv

2 Disembarkations of west African captives at Saint-Domingue,
1685–1750. *SlaveVoyages.* https://slavevoyages.org/voyage
/maps.   29

3 Disembarkations of west African captives at Saint-Domingue,
1700–30. *SlaveVoyages.* https://slavevoyages.org/voyage
/maps.   33

4 Disembarkations of west African captives at Martinique,
1700–30. *SlaveVoyages.* https://slavevoyages.org/voyage/maps.   33

5 1721 Spanish silver piece of eight (piastre). Courtesy of
Stacks Bowers.   38

6 Nicolas de Fer, "Carte de l'Isle St. Domingue ou Espagnole,
découverte l'an 1492 par les Espagnols" (1723). Courtesy of
the John Carter Brown Library, Providence, RI.   46

7 Amadée-François Frézier, "Carte de l'isle de St. Domingue et
débouquements circonvoisins" (1724). Courtesy of the John
Carter Brown Library, Providence, RI.   47

8 Detail of the southern peninsula, from Guillaume Delisle,
"Carte de l'Isle de Saint Domingue dressée en 1722 pour
l'usage du Roy sur les mémoires de Mr. Frézier Ingénieur
de S. M. et autres" (Paris, 1725). Courtesy of the John Carter
Brown Library, Providence, RI.   48

9 "Veüe et perspective du Cap Français levé en 1723," based
on an engraving by Sartre de Saint-Laurens (1723). Courtesy
of the Newberry Library, Chicago, IL.   49

10 "Carte du Cap Français, côte St. Domingue et de l'étendue de
son port et de ses environs" (1723). Cartes Marines (Ayer) Map
Collection. Courtesy of the Newberry Library, Chicago, IL.   50

X FIGURES AND MAPS

11 René Phelipeau, "Plan de la ville du Cap Français et de ses environs dans l'Isle de St. Domingue" (1786). Courtesy of the John Carter Brown Library, Providence, RI. 52

12 Detail showing the headquarters of the Indies Company at the corner of the rue Neuve des Petits Champs and the rue Vivienne, in Louis Bretez, "Plan de Paris" [the Turgot plan], planche 14, 1739. Courtesy of the Bibliothèque nationale de France. 60

13 Bernard Picart, "Monument consacré à la postérité en mémoire de la folie incroyable de la XX année du XVIII siècle," from *Het groote tafereel der dwaarsheid* (1720). Courtesy of Baker Library Special Collections and Archives, Harvard Business School, Cambridge, MA. 68

14 French colonial copper coin (9 *deniers*) minted pursuant to June 1721 royal edict. Courtesy of www.cgb.fr, CGB Numismatique Paris. 92

15 Detail showing the western region of Saint-Domingue, from Amédée-François Frézier, "Carte de l'Isle de St. Domingue et débouquements circonvoisins" (1724). Courtesy of the John Carter Brown Library, Providence, RI. 105

16 "Plan de la Ville de Léogâne et du fort de la Pointe" (1742). Courtesy of the Archives nationales d'outre-mer, Aix-en-Provence, France. 107

17 "Plan de la Baie de St. Louis, qui représente la Ville, le fort et l'établissement de la Compagnie des Indes" (1742). Courtesy of the Archives nationales d'outre-mer, Aix-en-Provence, France. 109

18 Amadée-François Frézier, "Plan de l'aggrandissement qu'il conviendrait faire au Fort du Petit Goâve," February 15, 1723. Courtesy of the Archives nationales d'outre-mer, Aix-en-Provence, France. 121

19 "Plan de la ville du Cap, à la côte septentrionale de Saint Domingue" (1728). Courtesy of the Musée d'Aquitaine, Bordeaux. 136

20 Title and opening lyrics of Père Michel, "Au sujet de la révolte de S. Domingue" [1723]. Courtesy of the Bibliothèque nationale de France, Département des manuscrits, Ms. 13658. 138

FIGURES AND MAPS xi

21 Guillaume Delisle, "Carte de l'Isle de Saint Domingue dressée
en 1722 pour l'usage du Roy sur les mémoires de Mr. Frézier
Ingénieur de S. M. et autres" (Paris, 1725). Courtesy of the John
Carter Brown Library, Providence, RI.   162

22 Joseph-Louis de la Lance, "Carte de Bayaha représentant
la frontière terminée présentement par la rivière du
Massacre" (1728). Courtesy of the Bibliothèque nationale
de France.   164

THE COLONY AND THE COMPANY

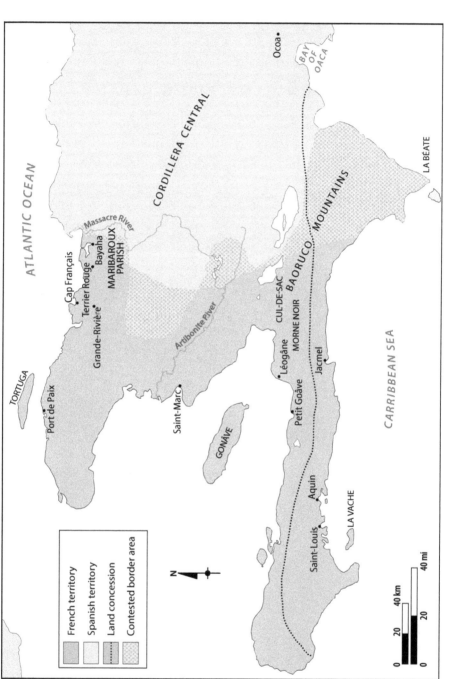

FIGURE 1. Map of Saint-Domingue in the early 1720s. Redrawn by Ronald Draddy from figures 7 and 8.

Introduction

THIS BOOK follows a previous study titled *The Old Regime and the Haitian Revolution*.[1] As in that earlier book, I am concerned here with how the colonial society known as Saint-Domingue (Haiti before independence in 1804) took on some of its fundamental characteristics and how those features of the colonial landscape shaped Haiti's subsequent trajectory.[2] The development of a militant white supremacy dedicated to the sovereignty of large-scale sugar planters is one such feature. Another is the establishment of a military-planter state at war with the resistance of enslaved persons, especially the maroons who built spaces of freedom in the time of slavery. Historians have devoted much of their energies in recent years to understanding how these twin pillars of plantation society were overthrown in the Haitian Revolution of 1789–1804. The story of how and when they were constructed in the first place is a less familiar chapter of the Haitian past. The tragedy of Haiti's ongoing political and economic crisis has persuaded me that this earlier chapter, which hinges on the decade from about 1715 to 1725 in Saint-Domingue, was no less consequential for the future of Haiti than the revolutionary decade.

The archives of the late seventeenth and early eighteenth centuries in Saint-Domingue offer far less opportunity to showcase the agency of enslaved persons and other Afro-Haitians than do the voluminous materials that document the Haitian Revolution. But by reading both against and along the archival grain, it is possible to reconstruct a narrative of this period that does at least some justice to the diversity of those who shaped the course of events at an especially tumultuous time in the prerevolutionary history of Saint-Domingue.[3] The relevant cast of characters in this study includes white women, vagabonds, free people of color, enslaved persons, and maroons. Reaching the experiences of these groups requires traveling through stories of white planters, Jesuit missionaries, and a Scotsman and convicted murderer turned theorist of public finance named John Law. But the reverse is also true: people dismissed as "women, negroes, and unknown, unimportant people" played large roles on the tragic stage of the sugar revolution in Saint-Domingue.[4]

All of these stories—subaltern, elite, and in-between—pass through the drama of the North Atlantic world's first major financial crisis, the Mississippi Bubble of 1719–20, and the "System" that John Law devised for the reconstruction of French finances following the wars of Louis XIV: (r. 1661–1715). The British variation on this theme of financial crisis and reconstruction, the South Sea Bubble, makes a guest appearance. The three capitals of European finance—Paris, London, and Amsterdam—have their say, as do other territories of the Caribbean (French, Spanish, Dutch, and British alike). Throughout, however, the primary emphasis is on Saint-Domingue, which held a remarkably important (if little known) place in John Law's plan to help France recover from the wartime debts left behind by the Sun King at his death in 1715. And that plan, in turn, played a crucial role in Haiti's early colonial history.

The study of high finance is not easily set alongside the subaltern stories that pop up at regular intervals in the archives of this period. Integrating these two narratives is necessary to understanding how the financial developments impacted Saint-Domingue and how the colony in turn impinged on decisions about money and finance. For the System was, first and foremost, an effort to respond to the twin problems of debt and money: far too much of the former for the crown to stay afloat, and far too little of the latter (especially in the form of Spanish silver) for states and individuals to satisfy their economic needs and dreams. John Law pursued Saint-Domingue as part of his own economic dream for France. His integration of the colony into the System turned Saint-Domingue into a bubble colony for the duration of the Old Regime.

The transformation of Saint-Domingue into a bubble colony, stirred by the deep early modern anxieties over debt and money, continued to shape Haiti's trajectory long after the bubble was burst in the Haitian Revolution. Money as an instrument of coercion, particularly in the form of debt, was central to the ability of European states to project their power across the globe.[5] The world we inhabit today is still structured by the monetary regimes and creditor-debtor relationships that took hold of vast parts of the globe in the seventeenth and eighteenth centuries. Arguably, no nation has been subjected to the oppressive yoke of those financial forces for as long as Haiti. The most infamous of the coercive financial instruments that have hobbled Haiti's chances at developing successful democratic institutions is the 1825 indemnity that France imposed on Haiti as a form of reparations for Haiti's success in the revolutionary war of independence (1802–3). The perverse logic of that arrangement—Haiti ultimately paid France some 112 million francs for depriving France of the opportunity to enslave its people and own its land—was

INTRODUCTION 3

aptly characterized by the *New York Times*, in a remarkable multipart investigation published in May 2022, as "the Ransom."[6]

That ransom should be seen in light of the broader notoriety of Haiti's slave past, and particularly John Law's debt-financing revolution of 1719–20. What happened when this revolution eventually arrived on the shores of Saint-Domingue in 1722 is the central story of this book. It is a political history of Haiti's early economic life at an especially fateful moment in the evolution of that nation and of the Atlantic world, told from as many vantage points as the available sources permit, and written against the grain of the abstractive dynamics of finance.[7]

———

The starting point of this story involves situating the System in the ecosystem of Caribbean capitalism circa 1715.[8] Saint-Domingue is not the milieu to which John Law is customarily assigned in the literature on financial history, but that is where his plan to rebuild the French economy on the back of a global trading empire finally ended. This ending says much about Europe's first major attempts to reconstruct national economies from the ground up. On both sides of the English Channel, the basic idea was to convert the massive government debts inherited from the wars of Louis XIV into privately held equity in either the Indies Company (for France) or the South Sea Company (for Britain). These efforts competed with one another, fueling reckless stock market speculation that culminated in the twin crashes of 1719–20—the subject of a large and growing popular as well as technical literature.[9]

The bubbles intersected with another development that, by comparison, has flown under the historical radar: the intense Franco-British competition to supply the Spanish American slave market and compete for Spanish American silver after the Peace of Utrecht in 1713 ended the long era of war.[10] That competition led both nations down the road of a dramatic expansion of and investment in the slave trade. It was in this context that France moved to subordinate the colony that was already its most prosperous overseas territory, Saint-Domingue, to the demands of reconstructing French finances. The "System" was so called because it connected one area of government policy to another until the various arms of the state had been swallowed up by a single, enormous corporation called the Indies Company.[11] But the integration of all state financial functions was merely one dimension of Law's System. The Indies Company was first and foremost a commercial monopoly, and so the System involved the further integration of royal finance with France's global trading networks. This integration of finance with trade, in turn, steered the System in the direction of becoming heavily dependent on slavery and the slave trade.[12]

Louisiana and the Mississippi Company were only starting points for the global slave-trading network that Law constructed from 1717 to the fall of 1720, and they were unable to feed the financial addictions that drove the growth of the System.[13] By the end of the second decade of the eighteenth century, Saint-Domingue had already displaced Louisiana—and all other French colonies—as the territory that promised to provide Law with the greatest amount of leverage over the profits to be made from the international slave trade. One after the other, the companies that Law targeted for acquisition had a clear role in or relationship to slavery and the slave trade, including one known as the Saint-Domingue Company that had an actual territorial foothold in the colony. Integration of this trading empire with control over the French royal bank (obtained at the end of 1718) opened the door to events that would become known as a "revolution" in Saint-Domingue.

The business of populating the various colonial territories that served as hubs of this trading empire brought new communities of the disaffected and oppressed to the New World. White women and vagabonds were deported in modest but conspicuous numbers to nearly all of France's American colonies, Louisiana and Saint-Domingue very much included.[14] The forced migration of west African captives to the French Caribbean, and the transition away from white indentured servitude, were well underway by the time John Law arrived on the scene. In fits and starts, the arrival of peace in 1713 permitted a gradual expansion of the slave trade that included opportunities for independent merchants to compete with companies. The corresponding growth of diverse communities of enslaved persons, free people of color, and maroons in Saint-Domingue transformed the colony's demographic map. Access to the contraband market in west African captives helped subsidize the emergence of large-scale sugar plantations in the north and made it possible for more and more white settlers to join the sugar revolution underway, especially in the western region around Port-au-Prince.

Even so, Saint-Domingue was not yet the hub of the international sugar business that it would become by the middle decades of the eighteenth century. In the early eighteenth century, Taiwan still produced more sugar than any other area of the world.[15] And Spanish silver, the lifeblood of the Atlantic economy, remained scarce. The demand to join the universe of large-scale sugar planters still far exceeded the supply of available necessary factors, labor and money first and foremost among them. The economy of Saint-Domingue was certainly growing, but that very growth seemed to create expectations of financial prosperity that were easily frustrated. For those who saw the large-scale sugar plantation as a path out of debt, it was particularly frustrating that debt was often the only point of entry into that very world.[16]

INTRODUCTION 5

Into this unstable demographic and economic mix stepped the Indies Company, suddenly announcing the return of monopoly commerce with a vengeance following a period of experimentation with "free trade" authorized by the Peace of Utrecht. Monopoly companies had long been a familiar feature of life in the French colony and in the business of Europe's New World empires more generally.[17] The decision to dispatch the Indies Company to Saint-Domingue in 1722 with a monopoly on the colony's slave trade ran headlong into that history, littered as it was with the traces of white settler determination to defend the right to trade "freely" in anything and everything. Enslaved persons were at the top of this "free trade" agenda.[18] So, too, were silver coins. Even for those who could not yet hope to buy into the sugar revolution, the Indies Company was the face of a wealth-power nexus designed to funnel riches away from the colony and leave only personal debt in its place.

A company that had failed catastrophically to alleviate the kingdom's public debt crisis was not in a good position to assert privileges it had first been granted in 1720. But that was exactly what the Indies Company attempted to do in 1722, after an extended period of receivership from which it nearly failed to recover. These privileges included a monopoly over the slave trade to Saint-Domingue and an export tax exemption that, by themselves, were enough to trigger a hostile reaction. But the company came to Saint-Domingue with the added burden of the System's recent attempt to substitute paper for metallic currency. As Law understood it, the success of that policy depended on withdrawing from circulation the silver coins on which everyone had long depended for commercial exchange.[19] When the monarchy issued an ordinance in August 1722 that effectively devalued the Spanish silver coins used in the colony, the settlers directed their hostility to the measure at the company. The result was a vast show of force that extended over the remainder of 1722 and well into the following year.

The settlers' sensitivity to changes in the money supply was endemic to and perhaps constitutive of the Atlantic project, which began as a quest for silver and gold. From the sixteenth to the eighteenth centuries a basic responsibility of virtually every monopoly trading company created by the monarchies was to help their home states amass more silver than rival empires.[20] Access to silver meant access to the market for west African captives, since silver was needed to purchase enslaved persons in local Caribbean markets.[21] Slaves themselves—as well as the tropical goods they cultivated, such as coffee, sugar, and tobacco—were sometimes used as money in the absence of silver. And some form of money was needed to make tax payments in this economy. Colonial administrators who took steps in the 1710s to restrict the use of colonial goods as a substitute for actual silver were simply upping the ante on everyone who owed money debts. The monarchy had moved several times in recent memory to devalue the kingdom's currency. And in 1721, the regency government attempted to introduce copper coins into the French colonies to make up for the dearth of silver specie. Few would take a currency that could not be used elsewhere in the Caribbean economy.[22]

Marginalized people and wealthier planters alike felt threatened by these changes and responded accordingly. White women and others identified as "vagabonds" took the lead, storming the facilities of the Indies Company in response to news of the August 1722 devaluation. In so doing, they were acting out on a small scale the very large drama of early modern Atlantic mercantilism that Thomas Sargent and François Velde have called the "big problem of small change."[23] Eventually coopted by the planters, the revolt against the Indies Company threatened to displace altogether what passed for a French colonial state at the time: a thinly staffed colonial administration consisting of the governor and intendant, some subordinates in the main urban centers, and a coterie of troops.

A naval armada sent to "restore order" in the fall of 1723 secured the planters' allegiance to the monarchy but paved the way for concessions on the rebellion's two principal fronts. First, in 1724 the royal ordinance devaluing local Spanish silver was repealed, thereby "liberalizing" a monetary regime that remained, in so many other ways, an instrument of coercion tied to the world of forced labor. Second, the monarchy opened the slave trade in 1725 to the independent merchants of Nantes and other French Atlantic (Ponant) ports. Open it would remain until the Haitian Revolution brought an end to French sovereignty over Haiti.

———

This dramatic reversal of company fortune is the scaffolding on which I hang another, equally important set of stories about a transformation in the domestic political and social order in Saint-Domingue. Those stories involve another early modern Atlantic drama known as the sugar revolution (or *revolution à canne* in French). That shift took place much later in Saint-Domingue—roughly 1700–30—than it had in the eastern Caribbean, where the sugar plantation complex crystallized beginning in the 1650s and 1660s.[24] The opening of the French slave trade in 1725 was a key contributor to the rise of an extraordinarily profitable complex of large-scale sugar plantations that powered Saint-Domingue to the center of the Atlantic world economy. But it was not the only factor. My concern in this book is not so much with the underlying, empirical economic causes of the sugar revolution in Saint-Domingue as with the political and social movements that accompanied it.[25] These movements would shape the destiny of Saint-Domingue in the long run no less powerfully than John Law's System.

Indeed, the transformation of the western third of the island of Hispaniola into a massive complex of intensely cultivated sugar plantations based on large-scale slave labor is, arguably, the single most defining development in Haitian history. Yet how exactly the sugar revolution unfolded in Saint-Domingue, and how it changed the colony's trajectory, remain shrouded in relative obscurity compared to the rapidly proliferating literature on the Haitian Revolution and its aftermath.[26] The rebellion against the Indies Company permits us to see the sugar revolution in Saint-Domingue as a richly textured process: a multidimensional tragedy set in narrative motion.[27] The credit that permitted planters to operate at scale, the expansion of the slave trade, and the codification of slavery in the Code Noir (or Black Code) of 1685 all have their place in the narrative.[28] The accumulation and clearing of vast plots of land suitable to sugar cultivation—facilitated by legal rules that permitted the merger of smaller parcels of land into larger domains—was indispensable.[29] The development of sugar processing and refining technologies that amplified the productivity of enslaved labor was another critical component. And the conversion of pirate nests toward more sedentary, or at least traditionally commercial, pursuits by the end of the 1720s was a source of much-needed relief for the planters of Saint-Domingue.[30]

Beyond these relatively familiar factors, several other dramas somewhat further from the historiographical center played into the tragedy of the sugar revolution in Saint-Domingue. The leadership of "women, negroes, and unknown, unimportant people" in the uprising against the Indies Company is one such drama. The evidence is limited but suggestive that at least some Afro-Haitians—whether free people of color, free blacks, or enslaved persons we cannot be sure—were part of the crowds that mobilized in the fall of 1722 in defense of the colony's silver money supply. Jesuit missionaries played an ambiguous but essential role in ministering to the newly arriving boatloads of west African captives, developing linguistic and spiritual tools that served the plantation machine in some respects but may have undermined it in others.[31] Finally, some of the colony's earliest maroon communities broke decisively with the plantation mold and mounted a challenge to the colonial order that administrators and settlers alike regarded as existential. That challenge, too, was part of the sugar revolution as it unfolded in the period from 1700–30. Maroons galvanized a panicked white colonial community to organize in defense of their way of life by creating Haiti's earliest hybrid, public-private gang system: the murderous fugitive slave patrol known as the *maréchaussée*.

All of these stories combined and overlapped to make Saint-Domingue a colony where the sugar revolution could prosper. And the overlap is clearest in the early 1720s. Multiple crises converged on the colony at that moment. The mobilization of the colony's politically marginalized communities—white women, vagabonds, people of African descent—coincided with the Jesuits' equally conspicuous entry onto the scene of public affairs. The maroon movement, led by a figure named Colas Jambes Coupées, inspired maximum fear in white communities, and a tenuous hope in Afro-Haitian communities, all along the mountainous border region separating Saint-Domingue from the Spanish side of Hispaniola. The creation of the *maréchaussée* in 1721 and the apprehension of Colas in 1723 serve as bookends to the Afro-Haitian experience documented in this book. There was a revolt within the revolt, in other words, but in the long run, the maroon rebellion may have subsumed the drama concentrated in the 1722–23 uprising against the Indies Company. Put differently, the revolt against the Indies Company captured a much broader set of political agendas than is reflected in the controversy over money and monopoly of these years. A highly divergent cast of characters interacted with each other, and with various agents of the French state, to produce a uniquely tragic, often violent, always improvised script for the sugar revolution in Saint-Domingue.[32]

White planters retain an important place in this heterogeneous narrative, but not as the inheritors or progenitors of an enduring culture of "white revolt" in the colony. Indeed, when one looks broadly at the events of the early 1720s in Saint-Domingue, "whiteness" per se seems like an incomplete label for describing the breadth and depth of changes that occurred during this period. The planter movement against the Indies Company expressed a militant commitment to protecting the sovereignty of the sugar plantation from all enemies internal and external.[33] White supremacy was written into the heart of this commitment and would remain a defining feature of the colony's political culture until the Haitian Revolution. In this book I use the phrase "militant slavery" to define this radical commitment to the sovereignty of the plantation system. Not surprisingly, that commitment was defended most forcefully by the planters themselves, who showed themselves willing at times to act against the short-term interests of the plantation system to protect its long-term prospects. The colony's administrators typically struggled to come up with coherent responses to planter militancy, but on occasion, they, too, adopted the same style of precautionary risk-taking to advance the colony's sugar revolution.[34]

The Indies Company was never the only adversary in this conversation between planters and administrators, however. The planters' militant slavery was also directed at the maroons of Saint-Domingue, who inscribed their own vision of the colony's future onto the very topography of Hispaniola. By the 1710s and early 1720s, enslaved persons had already begun to break free of the constraints to which they were subjected, and their uprising against the emerging plantation order in these years produced what administrators described as a public safety crisis of the first order. Taking advantage of the porous border with the Spanish side, maroons began to foster spaces of relative autonomy in mountainous redoubts while maintaining ties to the slave communities of the plantations. The maroons' refusal to accept the inevitability of the sugar revolution prompted a deeply racialized and militarized response in the form of the *maréchaussée* system. The fugitive slave patrol sent the entire society into a downward spiral of retributive colonial violence as an answer to the phenomenon of slave resistance. In this way, the planters and maroons of Saint-Domingue arrived at the enduring, highly unstable settlement that I call the military-planter state[35]—another tragedy from which the people of Haiti are still recovering.[36]

The emergence of a radical commitment to planter sovereignty and the establishment of the military-planter state in the early 1720s were key elements in the creatively destructive rise of the sugar plantation complex in Saint-Domingue.[37] By the time the sugar revolution was in full force in the 1730s, some of the rival visions for the colony's future at work in the previous decade had begun to recede. Commercial corporate sovereignty in Saint-Domingue was one. From 1727 onward, planter supremacy and colonial smuggling coexisted uneasily with the formal imposition of an imperial (rather than corporate) monopoly known as the *Exclusif*.[38] White women and men without property were further marginalized by the victory of the large sugar planters. The Jesuits ministered prominently to the enslaved of Saint-Domingue over the next few decades but were expelled in 1763, on suspicion of having crossed the line that separated ministry from aiding and abetting marronage.

But the movement for planter supremacy and the umbrella uniting the different forms of slave resistance persisted as twin legacies of the 1720s throughout the colonial period. The maroon rebellion, especially, proved to be a permanent feature of slave society in Saint-Domingue, and is where this study ends.[39]

How the developments addressed in this book bear on the Haitian Revolution is a complicated matter. The strident militancy of the movement for creole autonomy, which so struck observers of the 1760s–80s such as Hilliard d'Auberteuil, Emilien Petit, and Moreau de Saint-Méry, certainly fed into the impasse at which the colony arrived by 1788. There is a long-standing debate over whether marronage exercised a direct influence over the revolution.[40] And in recent years, some skeptical academic commentators have questioned the ability of the Haitian revolutionary tradition to contribute to contemporary progressive politics. David Geggus and others suggest that the content of the revolutionary movement was not particularly "republican" and find in it the seeds of postrevolutionary Haitian authoritarianism.[41] David Scott argues that the developing world has arrived a moment of postcolonial exhaustion that calls for a more supple politics freed from dogmatic assertions about the need to emancipate itself from imperial servitude.[42] But however we define or interpret the Haitian Revolution, it occupies a relatively short space on the timeline of Haitian history: a few short years of dramatic action set against a century and more of colonial slavery. That longue durée was followed by an equally long era during which the Haitian economy has been dominated by subsistence, peasant agriculture at odds with a state that sought to revive and continue the plantation export model of the colonial era.[43]

The Haitian Revolution did not entirely undo the sugar revolution that preceded it.[44] The organization of the colony around large-scale sugar cane plantation settlements still structures the nation's geography and, to a large extent, its agricultural life. The parishes formed in the early decades of the eighteenth century to recognize concentrated areas of planter activity are still the neighborhoods, towns, and regions that figure on a contemporary map of Haiti. Perhaps the most concrete ramification of the events of the 1720s, after the liberalization of the French slave trade, was the eventual relocation of the colony's capital to Port-au-Prince, away from the military and political vulnerabilities associated with Léogâne and Petit Goâve, the earliest administrative headquarters of Saint-Domingue.[45] The overwhelming majority of Haiti's population today lives in the vicinity of a city whose place on the map was effectively drawn in response to the combustible politics surrounding the Indies Company. The mountainous border between the French and Spanish colonial sides of Hispaniola, so prominent in the archives of the 1710s and early 1720s, and which remained unsettled until 1779, is still a source of much conflict between Haiti and the Dominican Republic. These topographical continuities, the geographic expression of a deeper economic continuity framed by the legacies of the "plantation machine," speak to a persistent feature of Caribbean life that is perhaps most strongly felt today in Haiti.

The story told here suggests that debt and slavery, rather than revolution, account for Haiti's ongoing tragedy. The subordination of Haiti to the demands of servicing French public and private debt goes back to the Mississippi Bubble. It was in 1720 that Haitians were first placed under the yoke, not only of the tropical plantation enterprise, but of the perverse logic that says people of west African descent must be sacrificed to satisfy the unbridled monetary appetites and financial woes of the French nation. That is an unrecognized cost of the Mississippi Bubble and of so much of the Euro-Atlantic experience of financial modernization.[46] Unlike its stock market counterpart, the bubble that was the sugar revolution did not burst in Saint-Domingue with the defeat of Law's plans for the colony. Instead, the planters internalized and privatized the financial and economic logic of the System against which they had rebelled, making of it a script for the management of plantation society. Saint-Domingue became a bubble colony. And it would continue to inflate until the Haitian Revolution.

1

Company Colony

"The sole object of companies has only ever been to establish new colonies."

—FROM THE "VERY HUMBLE SUPPLICATION OF THE PEOPLE OF
SAINT-DOMINGUE TO THE KING" (1723)

FROM THE 1660s to the 1720s, as France accumulated the massive debt needed to fund the wars of Louis XIV, corporate monopolies were a constant factor in the settlement and economy of Saint-Domingue. The colony was itself under the control of the West Indies Company until 1675, when it was absorbed into the royal domain. Thereafter, merchant monopolies controlled the colony's access to newly arrived west African captives (but not those smuggled locally from neighboring Caribbean outposts of the triangle trade). In 1698, control of the southern coast of Saint-Domingue was given to the Saint-Domingue Company as a perch for acquiring silver coin from Spanish America. For a few short years following the Peace of Utrecht in 1713 and the end of the War of the Spanish Succession, both France and Britain permitted private traders access to the west African coast. That short-lived experiment, however, was itself driven (in the British case, at least) by the desire to capitalize on Britain's acquisition of the *asiento* license to supply slaves to Spanish America, which the crown vested in the South Sea Company.[1] John Law's Indies Company would take over the Saint-Domingue Company privilege, and more, in 1720.

Saint-Domingue was therefore truly a company colony throughout this long period, a status that was relatively pronounced in the Caribbean of the late seventeenth and early eighteenth centuries. When colonists in Saint-Domingue envisioned what an economy organized along "free trade" principles would look like, they imagined, above all, the absence of companies. And when they rebelled against local authority, it was typically a company of one kind or another—not monarchy or government per se—that was the target of their ire. To remove monopoly trading companies from the local scene would not only do away with the onerous taxes from which chartered companies were, by definition, exempt. It would also expand access to (and reduce the costs of) the market for west African captives. That meant more money in the pockets of settlers as they began to move toward the large sugar plantation model that would come to dominate the life of Saint-Domingue. The nexus of companies, taxes, and money would play a major role elsewhere in the North Atlantic, and notably in the major North American commercial ports of the revolutionary era.[2] In Saint-Domingue, the high-water mark of anticorporate protest came in the early 1720s, but its origins traced back to the 1660s and coincided with the gradual extension of French control over the colony itself.

The settlers' hostility to companies, their glorification of "free trade," and their denunciation of taxation as a form of enslavement were fueled by the anxiety of debt. A lack of money rarely prevented the emerging planter sector from doing business. Instead, those wishing to join the sugar revolution went into debt to make up for the money they did not have or to make up for the weak purchasing power of the money they did have. Debt meant the absence of freedom, and monopoly companies seemed as if they had been constitutionally designed to deprive settlers of that freedom. In these circumstances, fiscal and monetary policy—indeed the supply of money itself—were strongly associated with the (real and perceived) influence of monopoly corporations. To protest that influence was the settlers' single most important strategy for maneuvering their way through the sugar revolution without ending up hamstrung by debt.

The vehemence of anticorporate crowd protest during these years attests to the power and pervasiveness of debt in a place of unusually fluid state authority and haphazard economic arrangements. The first generations of settlers and administrators in Saint-Domingue were engaged in the task of building an economy and a colonial state essentially from scratch, against a backdrop of systemic smuggling and pervasive piracy. From the 1660s to the 1720s, the colonists negotiated the extreme fluidity of state authority and economic arrangements in the Caribbean. As the French monarchy tumbled headfirst into public debt—in part to secure distant colonial territories from the threat of foreign incursion—the settlers of Saint-Domingue (and elsewhere in the French Caribbean) began to slide inexorably into private debt. With the aid of enslaved labor, they managed to create one of the world's most profitable eighteenth-century markets.

That end seems foreordained in hindsight, but the process was remarkably chaotic at nearly every stage. The disorderliness of money and the inexorability of debt stand out as the only consistent expressions and drivers of this world of fluid and evolving institutions. At one level, this was a universal dilemma of the early modern world: how to pay for one's obligations in an economy that was moving away from a reliance on informal mechanisms of barter and trust and toward a more stringent accounting of debts and credits. But in the Caribbean of the late seventeenth and early eighteenth centuries, money increasingly mattered for one reason above all: the ability to pay for the manual labor that would permit colonists to carve out their own piece of territory in a still largely unsettled colony. As the market for west African captives expanded and the demand for white indentured servants waned, the question of how to pay for slaves became the central item on the planters' agenda. Article 48 of the Code Noir—the basic law of slavery in the French Caribbean, codified in 1685—clearly reflected this enduring dilemma. That provision barred creditors from seizing adult enslaved persons except for the price of their purchase, or unless the plantation on which they labored was physically seized (in which case the enslaved had to remain part of the foreclosed plantation).[3]

Acquiring and maintaining title to enslaved persons was the key pressure point in this system, which had already been pervaded by debt relations and money struggles by 1685. Realizing that this was so, colonial administrators hitched their own need for tax revenues to the privilege of owning slaves. The result was a tight but troubled relationship between specie and taxation: money was necessary to pay for the slaves who could create wealth, but the ownership of slaves incurred additional obligations to the emerging colonial state that could only be discharged with more money. Moreover, slaves could themselves serve as a form of currency. This was true not only in west Africa, as Toby Green has shown, but also in the world of private Atlantic exchange, between planters and merchants.[4] Such was their value that, like sugar or tobacco, enslaved persons could take on the characteristics of the money that was needed to acquire them.

To reduce the uncertainty, risk, and fluidity associated with such an economy, the colonists relied on what material resources they could harness. But they also fashioned a story about the founding of Saint-Domingue as a self-starting, self-sustaining settler community from which the crown was largely absent. This narrative did work in real time by justifying the colonists' untrammeled pursuit of scarce resources without having to rely on, and thereby become indebted to, outsiders like monopoly trading companies and state authorities. That myth of independence filled the political and institutional vacuum of the early colony, and it would run headlong into John Law's vision of a tightly interconnected global economy centered in Paris.

———

The Saint-Domingue founding story is a variant of a still popular tradition that typically features tales of heroic survival and rugged determination on the shores of the New World. Colonial Virginians traced their origins back to the

Jamestown settlement, while their counterparts in the Massachusetts Bay Colony looked back to the story of the Pilgrims creating a new life for themselves at Plymouth. A good deal of creative license (and indigenous erasure) went into the development of these New World origin stories. But the generation of Saint-Domingue colonists that coincided with the revolt against the Indies Company exercised perhaps more than its fair share of that license.[5] Their story looked back to the first French pioneers in Saint-Domingue, the privateers (*flibustiers*) and buccaneers who began arriving toward the end of the sixteenth century. Using the small island of Tortuga, just off Hispaniola's northwestern coast, as their base, they launched raids on the Spanish American mainland, cultivated tobacco on a small scale, and corralled the local hog and cattle populations. Seeing in these pioneer settlers the best available means for establishing a more permanent foothold in the Greater Antilles, the French merchant marine commissioned the *flibustiers* to settle along the northern and western shores of Hispaniola. And so began the French colonial presence in the territory that became Haiti.[6]

In a Caribbean theater dominated by the threat of piracy, these early colonial denizens were eminently useful to the French monarchy's campaign to establish a frontier society that could compete with Spanish, British, and Dutch traders in the region.[7] But the ultimate goal of that campaign was to settle colonies rather than to perpetuate forms of Caribbean enterprise that, by comparison, came to take on an increasingly disreputable, even illicit character, especially at the level of state-to-state diplomacy. In the fashioning of an appropriately respectable origin story, the privateers and buccaneers of the frontier era would have to cede space, at least partly, to more compliant and less colorful agents of the French colonial mission. The result was the relatively more sedentary era of planter settlement and imported white indentured servitude around the middle of the seventeenth century.

Given the limitations of the French navy and the monarchy's capacity for imperial administration in this period, much of the actual work of colonizing initially fell to a series of chartered companies. The very earliest form of French colonial organization in the West Indies dates back to the Company of Saint Christophe and its successor, the Company of the Isles of America, which colonized the islands of Martinique and Guadeloupe.[8] Established in 1664 by Colbert (Louis XIV's Comptroller-General and chief minister), the West Indies Company would initiate in 1664 the gradual process of bringing Saint-Domingue, still predominantly a pirate and buccaneer haven that Colbert himself regarded with apparent indifference, into the orbit of the French state.[9] Through the ten-year reign of that company, Colbert's vision of corporate mercantilism in the Americas, like the eighteenth-century French empire as a whole, would come to center on the colony of Saint-Domingue.

Mercantilism as a term has fallen on somewhat hard times in recent years. Like capitalism, it is now seen as housing so many different variations and alternatives that it is reasonable to wonder whether the term does more to clarify or to confuse. The broadest notion is perhaps also its earliest meaning: the commitment to organize economic policy along national lines, with the aim of maximizing net economic benefits for the nation in the face of a zero-sum competition for scarce resources with rival powers. The competition was by nature zero-sum, according to this classic view, because the key scarce resources of the early modern era were land and metallic specie. The strategies of early modern states were driven by the imperative to acquire as much land (both in Europe and abroad) and to hoard as much gold and silver coin as possible within the territorial limits of the metropole. Mercantilist principles therefore dictated the transfer of coin from colonies to metropole, and the restriction of trade within national commercial frameworks: trading with foreign merchants (otherwise known as smuggling) was a recipe for diverting profits to rival powers. Monopoly trading companies, such as the French West Indies Company or the British East India Company, were particularly useful instruments toward this end: the economies of scale they created could facilitate the extension of territorial control abroad and the funneling of wealth back to the metropole.[10]

Colbert is (rightly) seen as one of the iconic champions of mercantilism in seventeenth-century Europe in all of these respects. But there is a world of difference between what he understood by mercantilism, and histories of economic life as told in the archives of the French Caribbean. Steven Pincus has argued that partisan politics (Whig vs. Tory) filtered understandings of mercantilism in the early modern British empire and that an alternative vision of political economy that embraced the benefits to be had by trading with other nations was always available within that ideological competition. A similar point could be made about the French empire, as John Shovlin has recently shown, except that the operative dynamics in France involved the quest for peaceful coexistence with Britain rather than parliamentary politics. Neither of these important revisionist accounts, both of which are focused on the metropole, brings us in touch with the core political-economic struggle in Saint-Domingue: the long-standing controversy over how best to supply enslaved labor for purposes of sustaining the sugar revolution.[11]

That controversy was not a matter of partisan political competition, or part of a quest for interstate peace, but rather a violent, often warlike conflict that linked the coasts of France, west Africa, and the West Indies. One by one, a series of slave-trading companies, including the West Indies, Senegal, Guinea, Saint-Domingue, and Indies companies, would rise and fall on their ability to supply a certain number of west African captives to French Caribbean colonists. From the settler perspective, mercantilism mattered primarily insofar as it limited colonial access to coin. Buyers who struggled to come up with the hard currency needed to purchase slaves were constitutionally disposed to be hostile to the chartered slave-trading companies. And those companies suffered from an additional systemic liability in the Caribbean: the prevalence of contraband trading. The term "underground" seems misplaced as a way of capturing this massive component of the intra-Caribbean economy. Smuggling of slave cargoes was a key part of an open and notorious contraband trade in the Caribbean, flourishing especially in and through the smaller Dutch and Danish islands of the Lesser Antilles. But, by its very nature as a form of exchange between colonists of different nationalities, contraband was widely practiced by French, Spanish, and British merchants as well.[12]

Chartered in 1664 to assume control of metropolitan trade with the French Antilles as a whole, the West Indies Company provided an object lesson in how to navigate the very close relationship between contraband and self-determination that would come to characterize the eighteenth-century Atlantic, including in North American commercial centers like Boston. Settler opposition in Saint-Domingue stemmed, in significant measure, from the West Indies Company's prohibition on trade with Dutch Caribbean ports, where duties on tobacco sales were half the level assessed within the French corporate orbit. But Bertrand d'Ogeron, whom the company appointed as governor of Tortuga and Saint-Domingue in 1664, also alienated the local population by seeking to regulate privateering, instituting a militia system with required training for all men and cutting down on the use of inferior tobacco leaf as a method of payment for goods imported from France. In 1665, the *flibustiers* raised the flag of mutiny after d'Ogeron ordered them to present their prizes at Tortuga (then the capital) for an orderly distribution that, conveniently, entailed a 10 percent cut for the governor himself. When d'Ogeron accepted a commission as the West Indies Company's actual agent in the colony in 1669, he seemed to be adding insult to injury.[13]

The issue of taxation inspired a second and more serious rebellion in 1670, when d'Ogeron announced that he finally intended to begin enforcement of the company's monopoly and revoke privateer commissions. The insurgents unleashed their fury by burning the governor's own plantations and claiming (in affidavits taken after the fact) that the company had reduced the inhabitants to a state of "white slavery." D'Ogeron would eventually blame all of the commotion on two Dutch merchants, Pieter Constant and Pieter Marc, who, from their base in the Gulf of Léogâne, allegedly incited the Saint-Domingue settlers to declare their independence from the West Indies Company. After d'Ogeron's men seized Constant's and Marc's vessels as instruments of contraband, the two Dutch merchants followed the vessels to Petit Goâve, where they made a prisoner of the port's commander while recapturing their ships. The conflict escalated yet further with word that the Léogâne settlers were preparing to march on the capital at Tortuga. D'Ogeron's appeal for French naval assistance was soon answered with the arrival of a squadron from Grenada, a move that undoubtedly persuaded the rebels to seek a negotiated resolution of their grievances by way of a reduction in the taxes charged by the West Indies Company and a pardon for participation in the rebellion. On October 10, 1671, Louis XIV signed an ordinance of general amnesty, declaring that "we had resolved to punish such a manifest rebellion, but . . . [Governor] d'Ogeron has given us to understand that our subjects have let down their arms and are showing visible regret for having strayed from obedience."[14]

Clemency of this ambiguous nature offered a striking contrast to the harsh repression meted out to contemporaneous revolts in the metropole, as in the case of the Breton uprising of 1673–75.[15] Accommodation against the backdrop of a show of force would prove to be the modus vivendi of the French monarchy in the face of similar creole uprisings to come. That approach did not bode altogether well for the future of chartered trading companies in Saint-Domingue, and with the writing on the wall for his inaugural experiment in corporate colonization, Colbert dismantled the West Indies Company in 1674.[16] By the time of d'Ogeron's death the following year, and largely as a result of his governorship, Saint-Domingue had been established as a territory solidly linked to the French crown and metropole—more than two decades before the declaration of formal French sovereignty in the 1697 Treaty of Ryswick.[17]

But it remained a fragile, mostly ungoverned, and sparsely settled place of uncertain direction. Exactly how sparsely settled is unclear: the first census figures date from 1681 only, and what numbers we do have for the earlier period are impressionistic at best. One historian suggests that Tortuga had a population of only 250 in the 1660s. The other major settlements were located on or near the northern coastline—Port-de-Paix (just across the Canal de la Tortue from the island capital) and Port-Margot (which counted only 150 inhabitants)—and along the western shores in the vicinity of Léogâne (which had gathered a population of 120). These figures exclude about seven to eight hundred buccaneers living at various places along the Saint-Domingue coastline, and an unknown number of freebooters. As part of his policy to domesticate these frontier groups, d'Ogeron persuaded the West Indies Company to send over a contingent of fifty "eligible girls" who, in the manner of "Amazons," learned to shoot, ride, and hunt with their new husbands. The colony's population of white women dates back to this shipment, which the company declined to repeat despite d'Ogeron's entreaties.[18]

The conflicts over company power in this fragile and uncertain environment would nonetheless establish some enduring features of the political and economic landscape in Saint-Domingue (and, later, Haiti). After the 1670 rebellion, many insurgents withdrew from the urban center of Léogâne westward to the Cul de Sac region surrounding what is today Port-au-Prince, an area that would emerge as one of the colony's major centers of plantation agriculture by the early eighteenth century. By 1692, that area had attracted eighty-one *habitants* and thirty-one indigo plantations, and indigo would remain the core of the region's economy until sugar began to take hold after 1715.[19] Other veterans of the uprising against Colbert's company converged on the region surrounding Cap Français, which was founded in 1670 as a dependency of the previously settled Petite Anse and Haut du Cap areas—and hence known, at first, as la Basseterre or Bas du Cap. The sources attribute the founding of Cap Français either to d'Ogeron or a Calvinist refugee from France named Gobin, who is said to have built the first *habitation* in the town. Gobin's initiative encouraged others to join him in clearing out the ground that would become the colony's most populous city. After the Revocation of the Edict of Nantes in 1685, Gobin's small Huguenot community would be joined by several hundred coreligionists, deported from the metropole pursuant to the aggressively anti-Protestant policies of Louis XIV's war minister Louvois. Alienated from the French monarchy, the colony's Huguenot population may have been even more prepared to foster contraband ties with English and Dutch adherents of the "alleged Reformed religion" (*la réligion prétendue réformée*, also known as RPR). In these budding hubs of disaffected white prosperity— Cap Français and the Cul de Sac region in particular—the events of 1670–71 inaugurated what Charles Frostin calls "a veritable insurrectionary tradition" that would echo in subsequent years and decades.[20]

That tradition would aim primarily at preserving the favorable fiscal regime that emerged on the heels of the 1670 rebellion. With the phasing out of the first West Indies Company, Saint-Domingue was absorbed directly into the royal domain. In theory, royal territorial status entailed subjection to the full array of taxes that applied to the metropolitan provinces. With the West Indies Company no longer around to collect those taxes, its fiscal privileges were transferred in 1674–75 to another royal monopoly corporation called the Domaine d'Occident (or Domain of the West). The name reflected the monarchy's vision of using a tax-farming company to capture the revenues flowing from the entirety of its New World empire, from Canada in the north to Guiana in the south. The Domaine thus became one of "the Five large farms," a customs union created by Colbert in 1664 (the others included the *gabelle*, or salt tax; the *octroi*, a duty on certain basic goods; and the tobacco farm). The Five farms contracted with the monarchy to handle the business of royal tax collection. Some of the taxes collected by the Domaine d'Occident were specific to Atlantic colonies, like the beaver monopoly and a duty on exports to the metropole. Others applied to French subjects generally, such as the capitation, or head tax. In

COMPANY COLONY   19

exchange for a lump sum payment to the monarchy that represented the anticipated value of these revenues, the lessor of the Domaine, like the other royal
tax farmers, received the privilege of retaining the taxes he was able to collect.
The decision to grant one of the royal tax farms a monopoly over the sale of
tobacco grown on French territory reinforced settler hostility to corporate monopolies in Saint-Domingue, where tobacco remained an important source of
revenue at this time.[21]

The key issue in the Caribbean was the same one that tax farmers in the
metropole would repeatedly confront: Which of these taxes was susceptible
to collection, and at what rate? The fluidity of state authority in the
seventeenth-century French West Indies made this question particularly
uncertain. And the perceived necessity of forced labor to clear and extract
resources from Saint-Domingue rendered the issue all the more sensitive.
In this context, minimizing one's tax burden did not mean seeking to avoid
payment of an already established tax. Rather, the idea was to prevent the
state from establishing a precedent that certain categories of goods and
transactions could be taxed in the first place. Throughout the French
Caribbean, any tax that threatened to raise the cost of forced labor, or reduce the profits that one could obtain from the sale of goods produced by
that labor, was by definition a hostile form of state action. The insertion of
chartered companies into this sensitive terrain doubled the stakes, for part
of the essence of monopoly was the all-important privilege of tax
immunity.

Perhaps the most enduring legacy of the rebellion of 1670–71 was a claim
about metropolitan fiscal authority that would become known as "the Colonial Pact" (*Pacte Colonial*). The uprising had already demonstrated that the
colonists of Saint-Domingue were not prepared to simply fork over whatever
amount was demanded of them. Taxes were a matter for negotiation (whose
way was to be paved first by rebellion). The October 1671 ordinance by which
Louis XIV accorded a general amnesty to the rebels of Saint-Domingue included an additional carrot: confirmation of the tax immunities that had been
promised by d'Ogeron at the height of the resistance. According to the Colonial Pact principle, any taxes imposed on colonial goods were levies that reduced the profits the kingdom would derive from the sale of these products in
Europe: the monarchy, in effect, would be taxing its own revenue. The theory
was too clever by exactly half, for while metropolitan goods bound for all
French West Indian colonies (not just Saint-Domingue) were indeed exempted from export duties, colonial goods exported to France were subjected
to a 3 percent export duty as of June 1671. This export duty, which would remain in effect until 1713, was to be collected upon loading in the colonies as
part of the Domaine d'Occident. In effect, it was a continuation of the fee that

the West Indies Company had charged separate traders in exchange for a license to do business on the coast of Saint-Domingue. To complicate matters still further, in August 1671 the Conseil d'État exempted all French West Indian imports to the metropole from all taxes upon reexport to European destinations and provided for a drawback of taxes paid upon entry into France.[22]

These technicalities notwithstanding, the Colonial Pact of 1671 did indeed bring Saint-Domingue a large degree of fiscal autonomy that the Leeward Islands did not enjoy. In particular, it brought immunity from the capitation that masters elsewhere paid based on the number of slaves they kept.[23] Until 1713, the only direct taxes levied in Saint-Domingue were distinctly local affairs: a tax on the leasing of taverns, butcher shops, and ferries; assessments for the support of parish priests; and a tax to support reimbursement of the owners of slaves subjected to capital punishment (*nègres suppliciés*). More than these pecuniary benefits, the Colonial Pact of 1671 affirmed the latent notion that colonial affairs were for the colonists to govern, and that the king ruled Saint-Domingue more in the manner of a constitutional monarch than an absolute sovereign. That tradition of fiscal autonomy and consent would collide with the demands of colonial defense in 1713–14, when the colony was finally subjected to an *octroi* (a grant or concession, in the form of a levy on slaveholdings) to help pay for the costs of public works in the aftermath of the War of the Spanish Succession.[24]

The 1671 deal did not remedy another of the settlers' principal grievances: procurement of an adequate supply of west African captives in Saint-Domingue. In 1680, ten years after the uprising against the West Indies Company, the Dominguans mobilized again, this time to oppose the monopoly of a reenergized Senegal Company.[25] Saint-Domingue had begun to change rapidly in the decade since the 1670 uprising. As of 1681, the colony was home to more than two thousand slaves, most of them tethered to an increasing number of indigo plantations. To cater to this growing demand for coerced African labor, Colbert had reorganized the Senegal Company in 1679, expanding its monopoly to include the entire west African coast, including the trading fort of Gorée, which had been captured in 1671. Colbert also committed the lessors of the Domaine d'Occident to pay the Senegal Company a substantial subsidy per head of slave transported to the Caribbean colonies. As Robin Blackburn notes, these policies could not protect the Senegal Company from the competition of the Royal African Company and the inroads made in Saint-Domingue by English and Dutch interlopers. Bankruptcy loomed, but not before colonists in Saint-Domingue took matters again into their own hands.[26]

The trigger of the 1680 events was the Senegal Company's exclusive, twenty-five year license to supply the West Indian colonies with slaves despite a consistent failure to meet its quotas in prior years. Complaints about the inadequacy of the chartered slaving companies were common coin in Martinique and Guadeloupe as well as Saint-Domingue.[27] But, once again, it was at Saint-Domingue that creole resistance came to a decisive head. The uprising testified to the emergence of Cap Français as the center of the northern economy in the years since its founding in 1670. As Charlevoix tells the story, the rebels were once again put to the task of mutiny by outsiders: merchants from France who persuaded the settlers of Cap that the Senegal Company intended to assume control over the colony's entire trade, not simply the commerce in slaves. "We do not want any part of the company," the inhabitants protested. After Franquenay, the *lieutenant du roi* in Le Cap, tried and failed to disabuse them of their misunderstanding, management of the uprising promptly passed to d'Ogeron's successor Pouançay in the Cul de Sac district. Realizing that the Senegal Company had several ships anchored off the nearby coast, Pouançay first arranged to have the vessels unloaded under his personal supervision. After the company's business was safely transacted, the governor made his way to Le Cap and argued directly with the rebels that they had no business interfering with the king's wishes for the Senegal Company, particularly on the basis of such a blatant misunderstanding of the company's privileges.

This sufficed to cause the protesters to retreat and disband. Shortly afterward, however, Pouançay received word that the rebels were of a mind to burn their *habitations* and take refuge in a forested area. The following morning, Easter Sunday, the governor proceeded to assemble a force of eight hundred men for purposes of deterring further agitation. As the governor's band approached the rebel assembly, Pouançay learned that an insurgent force of three hundred men had gathered only eight hundred feet away. Detaching himself from his men, the governor again placed himself in the midst of the mutinous crowd and repeated the gist of his discourse the previous day. This time, the insurgents admitted their mistaken understanding of the company's intentions before professing concern for the security of their persons, a statement that Pouançay interpreted as a plea for clemency. In his report to the naval minister summarizing these events, the governor urged that the rebels be pardoned for their actions, noting that the colonists had suffered considerable losses at the hands of the Tobacco Farm and would not take lightly to additional setbacks.[28]

While emphasizing the settlers' misapprehension of the Senegal Company's charter, Charlevoix's account points to some deeper truths about the colonial economy in which the rebels' anxiety was rooted. Slave traders, like other French merchants, were not content to traffic in goods of a particular kind. Instead, they actively sought to piggyback onto the colony's emergent export trade by bringing colonial goods back to Europe (and European goods onward to the west African coast). This basic reality of the triangle trade was impossible to separate from the company's role in Saint-Domingue. An outfit like the Senegal Company, with its fleet of twenty-one ships, enjoyed economies of scale not available to the small landholders of the Cap Français region, whose access to the market depended either on an adequate supply of Spanish silver or French merchants willing to extend credit.[29] Hostility to the chartered companies in Saint-Domingue stemmed from these pressure points in the colonial economy. As Franquenay and Pouançay discovered, the settlers' anxiety about monopoly could not be contained within the legal parameters of any one privilege.

The specifically anticorporate pattern of creole resistance in Saint-Domingue stands in suggestive contrast to the opposition that metropolitan authority encountered elsewhere in the Caribbean. In both the British and French Leeward Islands, the first decades of the eighteenth century witnessed several especially dramatic uprisings against royal administrators, including the 1710 assassination of Daniel Parke in Antigua and the 1717 Gaoulé revolt in Martinique.[30] Parke had no sooner taken office as governor and commander in chief of the British Leeward Islands than he attempted to compel the planters of Antigua to pay long-standing debts to British merchants. A former aide-de-camp to the Duke of Marlborough and protégé of the controversial North American governor Edmund Andros, Parke also charged the local elite with brutal mistreatment of their slaves and "unnatural and monstrous lusts" that had produced a "mungrell race" in the British colony.[31] In exchange, he was himself accused of abuse of office and personal misconduct, and his murder in January 1710 brought Antigua to the brink of provincial insurrection.

The Martinique Gaoulé (creole for "rising") was similarly triggered by the arrival of a new colonial administration determined to assert control of local planter society. One of the first steps taken by the governor and intendant who took office in January 1717 was to suspend construction of all new sugar plantations as a way of preventing the colonists from abandoning the cultivation of cotton, cacao, and other crops. This decision added fuel to the fire created by earlier measures of 1715–16: the introduction of an *octroi* tax on slaveholding in the French Leeward Islands and the requirement that merchants engaged in trade with foreign colonies obtain a passport from colonial administrators. The leaders of the revolt, Latouche de Longpré and Jean Dubuc, succeeded in arresting the governor and intendant and deporting them to France before order was restored with the aid of five naval companies and a near total amnesty.[32]

———

Local economic patterns of indebtedness and efforts to regulate the sugar revolution drove creole resistance throughout the Caribbean, across imperial and national lines. In Saint-Domingue, these grievances were spiked by the element of company control over access to the west African slave trade. Whether chartered companies were up to the demands of the sugar revolution, however, was itself part of a larger early modern debate over monopoly and free trade that entered the general discourse of the Atlantic world through the gateway of political economy during the seventeenth and early eighteenth centuries. In this debate, protection and free trade were not so much diametrically opposed categories as two sides of the same coin. From the point of view of imperial officials, what colonists called "free trade" was a strategy that could be used to mitigate the problems created by protectionist policies.[33] Law and ideology were also important influences: the right to engage in free trade on the high seas emerged by way of a complicated process involving both natural (unwritten) right and positive law understandings of liberty.[34]

Front and center in this debate were the great monopoly companies. As early as the late sixteenth century, the East Indies and other large trading companies had become central points of reference in the discussion of something contemporaries were already calling "free trade." In England, two institutions stood out from the rest. The Merchant Adventurers were chartered as a so-called regulated company in 1505 to handle England's wool and cloth trade with Europe. (As a regulated company, its protection extended only to qualified merchants who had passed an apprenticeship requirement or paid a special fee.) The East India Company (EIC) was chartered in 1600 as a joint-stock company in which any member of the public could purchase shares. Referencing the debates over these charters, Andrea Finkelstein observes that it is "difficult to find a single session of Parliament or a single volume of *State Papers* from the 1590s to the outbreak of war in 1642 in which there was no complaint of monopoly or call for 'free trade.'" At no point during this period, however, did such complaints go beyond demands for inclusion in the circle of monopoly privilege itself, as in the case of outport merchants in cities like Bristol or Liverpool who were cut out of the EIC's London trade. "*Free trade* (or even a domestic *free market*) as we understand it was never on the line." Indeed, it was entirely possible to advocate the "natural freedom" of trade while simultaneously defending the legitimacy of exclusive privileges. The writer Edward Misselden, for example, published several important works on English trade in the 1620s that some historians of economic thought have reduced to a straightforward laissez-faire position. In fact, these writings were tied to Misselden's position as an agent of both the Merchant Adventurers and the EIC.[35]

The contradiction was more apparent than real because the concept of privilege was itself used to defined "liberties" in the medieval and early modern world. Royal liberties were royal delegations of power or privilege to specific individuals or groups. Often used to recognize the self-rule of cities or regions, as well as corporate professional, religious, and other group identities, liberties were also used to delegate feudal functions such as landholding, tax collecting, or the execution of royal writs in a particular locality. In exchange for an exclusive charter, the holder of a royal liberty was required to perform specified services for the crown. To be sure, these privileges conferred benefits. The term "liberty" denoted the very territory, held in tenure from the king, over which nobles exercised their landed jurisdiction. But that jurisdiction was exercised on behalf of royalty. Thus, a privilege always implied a corresponding duty or responsibility to the king.[36] Misselden's defense of the Merchant Adventurers and the EIC was predicated on just such a notion. Even while denouncing monopolies generally as restraints on "libertie of Commerce" or mechanisms for the fixing of prices, he distinguished the Merchant Adventurers and EIC charters as restraints that served the public good, performing a special function for the Commonwealth that outweighed the cost of the restraint. In the case of the EIC, this function was especially critical where that company's rivalry with the Dutch East India Company (VOC) was concerned. Finkelstein suggests that it was not until the Cromwellian Protectorate of the 1660s and the rise of the Levellers that the monopoly trading company came itself to be seen as a restraint on the principle of freedom of trade. At that time, she observes, the word "liberty" began to mean something distinctly more than a particular corporate privilege.[37]

The English legal tradition afforded certain weapons that could sustain this more expansive campaign on behalf of liberty of commerce toward the latter part of the seventeenth century. But even then, the understanding of what free trade meant was bound up with merchants' lived experience of particular companies. Consider the case of *East India Company v. Sandys*, known by contemporaries as the "Great Case of Monopolies." The case was, in its origins, a forfeiture proceeding brought by the EIC in 1682 against Thomas Sandys, an interloper who was preparing to send out his own ship to the East Indies in violation of the EIC charter. His vessel having been seized pending resolution of the matter in the Court of Chancery, Sandys went on the offensive, arguing that, under the common law of England, monopolies were per se void.[38] Lord Coke's *Institutes of the Laws of England* (1628–44), treated as authoritative in the seventeenth and eighteenth centuries for its summary of statutory and case law, captured the antimonopoly principle in no uncertain terms: "All Grants of Monopolies are against the ancient and fundamental laws of this Kingdom." A monopoly, in turn, Coke defined as

> an Institution, or allowance by the King by his Grant, Commission, or otherwise to any person or persons, bodies politick or corporate, of or for the sole buying, selling, making, working, or using of any thing, whereby

any person or persons, bodies politick or corporate, are sought to be restrained of any freedom or liberty that they had before, or hindered in their lawful trade.[39]

The prohibition of such institutions was all the more sacrosanct because it drew not simply on statutory and common law, but also on Magna Carta, duly cited by Coke and counsel for Sandys alike.[40]

On the strength of such authorities, Sandys claimed a right to be free of the EIC's restraints not merely in England but also on the high seas. In this, as Philip Stern points out, the interloper and his adversary were "replaying a version of European debates over the East India trade."[41] The lawyers for Sandys reverted to the natural law theorist Hugo Grotius (and onetime counsel for the VOC), whose 1609 work *Mare Liberum* posited that "trade is as free to all men as the air, that the seas are like the highways, free and open to all passengers." In the spirit of Misselden's equally instrumental briefs on behalf the Merchant Adventurers and the East India Company in the 1620s, this Grotian postulate was a thinly veiled defense of the right of the VOC to intrude on Portugal's putative dominion over the world east of the Cape of Good Hope. Notice that the defense of commercial liberty here, which was itself prompted by a legal proceeding involving the VOC's seizure of a Portuguese ship, did not follow from a prior legal doctrine of rights. Rather, the claim of right flowed from Grotius's acceptance of the logic of reason of state, and in particular, the legitimacy of "the aggressive acquisition of wealth as a mode of national self-preservation."[42]

After circling around these and other precedents for nearly a year of trial and deliberations, the "Great Case of Monopolies" came up for decision by the Court of King's Bench in 1685. The argument that most seemed to persuade the judges in favor of the EIC was not that of Magna Carta or *Mare Liberum*, but rather the position (reflected in Misselden's writings) that the East India Company was a kind of public good distinct from mere monopolies and thus an exception to the general rule against restraints on the freedom of trade.[43] Magna Carta and the common law tradition of commercial liberty nonetheless remained as forces to be reckoned with, particularly in the 1690s when a new movement challenging the EIC monopoly emerged. Seeking incorporation of a new "National East India Joint Stock or Company" not controlled by the "very few Persons" who had reserved for themselves the profits of the old one, the opponents of the existing company argued for a dissolution of its charter. Stopping short of these demands, the crown agreed to charter a rival firm in 1698, before merging it with the existing company in 1709, to create the "United Company of Merchants of England trading to the East Indies."[44] As this example nicely captures, opposition to a particular privilege—even one "absolutely against the right of the freeborn subject of England, no mean Infringement of Magna Charta"[45]—did not entail opposition to privilege generally.

In France, too, critics of mercantilism had begun to make the opposition between commercial liberty and the intercontinental monopolies commonplace in the decades before the Mississippi and South Sea crashes. A defining moment for these advocates came in 1700 and 1701, when the merchants of Nantes, Rouen, and other Ponant (Atlantic seaboard) ports went before the King's Council of Commerce to demand abolition of the privileged companies. No area of the globe was left out of these discussions: the Ponant deputies called for the elimination of monopoly along the west African coast, in the West Indies, the East Indies, and the Levant (a trade that favored Marseille by virtue of the 20 percent duty that applied to Levantine goods imported into France through any other port). Here again, as Charles Woolsey Cole has written, "most of the suggestions that more freedom was desirable in economic matters seem to have arisen from direct criticisms of restrictions that injured a business interest." But a few of the deputies at the 1700–1 proceedings spoke in more expansive terms, evoking "liberty . . . as the soul of commerce" or opining that "as soon as one limits the genius of businessmen by boundaries, one destroys commerce."[46]

In comparison to the English debates of the 1680s and 1690s, the absence of a specifically French legal tradition that could be invoked on behalf of liberty of trade seems noteworthy. In other contexts, French critics of absolutist mercantilism did not hesitate to revert to the natural law tradition, as in the case of the dissenting aristocrat Jean de Lartigue, whose 1661 treatise *La politique des conquérans* made significant use of Grotius.[47] Pending further research into this point, one is struck by the apparent inability of French interlopers to rely on prestigious lines of ancient legal precedent of the kind cited, persuasively or not, by counsel for Sandys in the "Great Case of Monopolies." The English legal tradition seems to have offered merchants a platform on which to press their claims in courts of law. By enabling merchants to pursue commercial disputes in the legal arena, rather than on the high seas and in the colonies where those disputes arose, English law may have fostered the illusion that overseas trade was a matter of right rather than power. Lacking access to a similar legal tradition, French merchants may have been more inclined to view their grievances in political or natural-law terms.

This difference notwithstanding, by the first few decades of the eighteenth century, the call for free trade overseas had acquired something of a double character in both Britain and France. While still reflecting the instrumental logic of reason of state and the associated rivalries between competing groups of merchants both within and across national boundaries, it had also begun to take on more abstract overtones as a representation of the ideal political economy. As John Shovlin has shown, the War of the Spanish Succession had begun as an effort to restrain France from monopolizing Europe's trade with Spanish America. The Utrecht Treaty in 1713 attempted to restore the European balance of power that had been threatened by France's privileged access to Spanish silver through the *asiento* slave trade license. For Britain, above all, peace in Europe required recalibrating control over the global silver trade. And in that context, "free trade" could be secured only by an agreement between states to exercise collective restraint vis-à-vis Spanish American markets.[48]

Thus, when the curtain finally dropped on the long era of the wars of Louis XIV in 1713–14, merchants and their advocates in Britain and France could finally lay claim to the full benefits promised by unrestricted commerce within national mercantilist frameworks. That claim extended to the slave trade, and advocates for a "free trade" in west African captives consistently used the phrase without any apparent sense of irony or paradox.

The end of the War of the Spanish Succession coincided with three major developments in the British and French slave trades that both reflected and reinforced the new turn in the Atlantic political economy. The first was the phased liberalization of the British slave trade after an extended period of corporate monopolization. Like the Dutch West Indies Company, the (French) Senegal Company (founded in 1673), and the (French) Guinea Company (chartered in 1684), the Royal African Company (RAC) enjoyed a national monopoly on the trade to west Africa. Founded by royal charter in 1672, the RAC enjoyed an exclusive privilege for most of the late seventeenth century until 1698, when the English Parliament began permitting private traders to participate on condition of payment of a tax for the upkeep of the RAC's forts along the west African coast. In 1712, Parliament abandoned the permit system in theory and opened the trade to all comers.[49]

The impact of this liberalization was mitigated by a second development: Britain's acquisition of the very profitable *asiento* license after 1713, displacing France from its role as supplier to the Spanish mainland colonies. The British government placed the *asiento* in the hands of the Tory South Sea Company, which promptly contracted with the RAC to supply Spanish America with most of the requisite enslaved persons. As Nuala Zahedieh observes, the new regime was not exactly a victory for free trade, since it "placed a very substantial portion of the [British] slave trade in the hands of one monopoly company which supplied another monopoly in a competing empire at the expense of its own."[50]

The contradiction was felt most acutely in Jamaica, which served as a reexport station for South Sea Company slave cargoes bound for Spanish America. Spanish demand drove prices for west African captives 20 percent higher in Jamaica than Barbados. With private traders and privileged corporations competing for control of the trade, the volume of enslaved cargoes arriving in Jamaica increased nearly fourfold between 1687 and 1729. Increased supply and higher prices went hand in hand over the first decades of the eighteenth century. The new arrangement between the South Sea Company and the RAC threatened to cut into the profits of Jamaican merchants and planters. The colonial assembly responded in 1715 by passing a duty of forty shillings on the heads of all enslaved persons exported by the South Sea Company to the Spanish mainland via Jamaica. By the end of the decade, the situation had so deteriorated that the South Sea Company transferred its operations to Barbados. Jamaica's rebellion against corporate monopoly was over before the revolt against the Indies Company in Saint-Domingue could start.[51]

The third shift was the move by private traders in France to take over territory previously monopolized by the Senegal Company and the Guinea (or Asiento) Company. With the signing of the Treaty of Utrecht and the transfer of the *asiento* contract from France to Britain in 1713, the Guinea Company entered a long process of liquidation. Slave traders from Rouen, La Rochelle, Bordeaux, Saint Malo, and Nantes, for their part, began to push for the liberalization of the French slave trade on the grounds that the monopoly companies had failed to supply the French colonies with adequate numbers of African captives. French planters had been forced to switch from sugar to less labor-intensive indigo cultivation because of the shortage of slave imports, argued the *négociants* of Nantes. These same representatives saw no irony, tragic or otherwise, in the claim that the French slave trade should be opened up to counteract the high mortality rates on the Middle Passage. Finally, the private traders rebutted the traditional defense of the monopoly firms that having too many competing firms negotiating with suppliers along the west African coast would drive up prices for everyone.[52]

Data from the Slave Voyages project confirms that the influx of private traders resulted in a significant rise in the numbers of enslaved persons disembarked in Saint-Domingue during these years, even if the increase is part of a larger upward trend initiated by the end of war. The traders' claims hit their intended target, and in January 1716 the regency government responded with *Lettres Patentes* that effectively opened up the Guinea trade to merchants from the Ponant cities of Rouen, La Rochelle, Bordeaux, Saint Malo, and Nantes. (Le Havre, Honfleur, and other ports were added to the list soon after. The Senegal monopoly was retained only because of concerns that revoking it would compromise France's special position in the gum trade north of the Sierra Leone River.)[53] This liberalization, which would turn out to be only temporary, retained a distinctly mercantilist framework of passports and permissions. Merchants interested in outfitting slave ships were required to pay a tax of twenty *livres* for each captive imported into the colonies. These revenues were

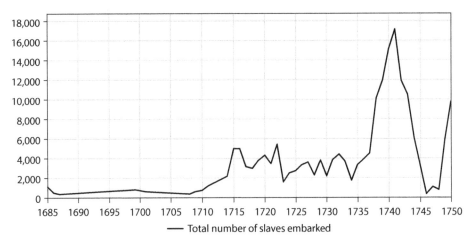

FIGURE 2. Disembarkations of west African captives at Saint-Domingue, 1685–1750. *SlaveVoyages*. https://slavevoyages.org/voyage/maps.

earmarked for the upkeep of the former Guinea Company's fort at Whydah. The arrangement constituted a quid pro quo insofar as the private traders were given the ability to finance their purchases of African captives with French metropolitan goods exported on a duty-free basis. An additional incentive came in the form of a 50 percent exemption from duties attached to the traders' subsequent export of sugar and other Caribbean goods to France.[54]

These near-contemporaneous liberalizations reflected the effects of war and the pressures of competition between the major European slave trading companies, as well as the logistical difficulties that each encountered along the west African coast. In both the French and British American contexts, moreover, colonial merchants echoed creole agitators in arguing that monopolies failed to import sufficient enslaved persons to support the production capacity of the plantations.[55]

But the apparent convergence of the British and French paths disguises some important differences. If it is difficult to agree that the deregulation of the British slave trade was ahead of and exceptional for its time, there does seem to be something distinctive about the condition of French corporate mercantilism toward the latter part of the reign of Louis XIV. As William Pettigrew has shown, the decisive factor in the dissolution of the RAC's monopoly was the ability of the separate traders to galvanize parliamentary support for the cause of "free trade" in the aftermath of England's Glorious Revolution.[56] Though amplified by influential voices in the British West Indian and North American colonies, this political campaign was fundamentally based on the

English rights tradition, and it had no real counterpart on the French side. While both Britain and France ultimately reverted to the monopoly form in the years leading up to the South Sea and Mississippi bubbles, that reversion took a significantly different form in the two cases. Britain's monopoly was not superimposed over her own colonies, but rather answered to an opportunity dangled before the RAC (and later the South Sea Company) by the Spanish monarchy. In France, by contrast, the Indies Company would become a direct constraint on the ability of French Caribbean colonists to determine and manage their own laws of supply and demand.

———

Parliamentary mobilization and the heritage of the Glorious Revolution were not the only tools by which to defeat a corporate monopoly. Creole uprisings could and did serve the same function. For all the importance of the English rights tradition in framing the campaign against exclusive privileges, the actual dismantlement of the great trading monopolies in Britain took much longer than it did in France. Even the Dutch, the leading sponsors of the early modern Caribbean contraband trade, allowed their own West Indies Company to retain its monopoly privileges until 1738. The RAC was only fully dissolved toward the middle of the eighteenth century, and the India and China monopolies of the British East India Company survived much longer, until 1813 and 1833, respectively. The persistence of these Anglo-Dutch privileges, and the demise of the French privileges, can only be explained by factors external to domestic political culture.[57]

The search for those factors takes us back across the Atlantic to the Caribbean, where long-standing patterns of colonial indebtedness and smuggling fostered rebellion across imperial and national boundaries. Smuggling enabled the dramatic growth of Saint-Domingue in the three or four decades before the arrival of John Law's company. Consistently, one after another of the monopoly companies that Colbert and his successors chartered to supply the French West Indies with slaves had failed to compete with Dutch and British interlopers.[58] The failure stemmed from factors of quantity as well as price. Dutch and British smugglers offered larger supplies of west African captives for significantly lower costs. And by resorting to contraband, French Caribbean settlers could also avoid payment of taxes attaching to the sale of slaves. From this perspective, the revolts against the West Indies Company in 1670 and the Senegal Company in 1680 appear as transparent efforts to protect a status quo that violated principles of both corporate and national mercantilism.

At the same time, it would be a mistake to see contraband as simply the economic base of a superstructure called creole autonomy, whether in

Saint-Domingue or elsewhere. Smuggling created and obeyed its own laws, and these laws were often entirely consistent with mercantilism, which tolerated and even used contraband in a manner not unlike the law of slavery's allowance of manumission.[59] Some element of freedom was necessary to maintain the fiction of mercantilist sovereignty.[60] In the most extreme situations, the monarchy explicitly instructed colonial administrators to look the other way. In 1692, for example, the crown directed Governor Du Casse of Saint-Domingue to permit the planters to obtain slaves from any available source, given the wartime constraints on the Senegal and Guinea companies.[61]

Deeply dependent on geography, smuggling also operated differently depending on the nature of the items being smuggled. In exchange for sugar, molasses, and rum, New England had become a primary source of fish and timber for the French Caribbean by the early eighteenth century.[62] To evade detection at the hands of the customs commissioners, New England merchants went to the extent of bringing coopers all the way to the French islands to assemble casks into which sugar, molasses, and rum could be poured from their original French barrels.[63]

Human trafficking created its own distinctive patterns of intercolonial smuggling in the Caribbean. For the planters of Saint-Domingue, and those on the southern peninsula especially, three Caribbean locations provided the bulk of this interstitial market: Curaçao, St. Eustatius, and Jamaica. The first of these colonies began sending slaves to the French Caribbean shortly after 1662. Between June 1664 and April 1665, approximately twelve thousand to thirteen thousand west African captives were carried via Curaçao to Martinique and Guadeloupe. During the War of the Spanish Succession, Curaçao merchants made a special point of sending enslaved persons to Saint-Domingue even though the United Provinces and France were on opposing sides of the conflict.[64] Contraband was itself an economic form of war by other means, but in this war, allies and enemies traded places as easily as the goods they exchanged.

Beginning in the late 1710s and then especially in the 1720s, a new combatant entered the arena: the diminutive but immensely important island of St. Eustatius, a critical entrepôt for both the Saint-Domingue colonists and their British North American counterparts. Whereas Curaçao merchants had traditionally concentrated on the Spanish American market (the New Granada province of Venezuela above all), St. Eustatius capitalized on its proximity to other Caribbean islands.[65] Both Dutch islands were subject to the monopoly jurisdiction of the Dutch West Indies Company, but when that company's board of directors decided to temporarily stop carrying African captives to Curaçao, St. Eustatius (also known as Statia) was designated to fill the breach. During the 1720s, roughly eleven thousand slaves were brought to the Dutch island, there to be picked up by foreign merchants for transportation to other West Indian destinations.[66] It was only to be expected that many of these captives would end up in the nearby Leeward Islands of St. Kitts, Martinique, and Guadeloupe. But planters from Saint-Domingue were also well represented on Statia. From there, French smugglers would often proceed to St. Thomas in the Virgin Islands, a neutral jurisdiction under the control of Denmark and Brandenburg, where they could take on additional slave cargos in exchange for raw goods from Saint-Domingue.[67] The illegal slave trade out of St. Eustatius witnessed a massive spike between 1722 and 1726, outpacing the normal yearly average by more than six thousand captives.[68] Although the destination of these slaves is not known, the spike corresponds exactly to the period of the revolt against the French Indies Company in Saint-Domingue.

As the Dutch West Indies Company began to lose position in the Atlantic slave trade vis-à-vis French and British traders in the 1720s and 1730s, so too did Saint-Domingue's contraband trade with Statia fade in favor of Jamaica.[69] The ties between the French and British colonies developed in the 1690s, when French planters began to derive significant numbers of enslaved persons from raids on Jamaica.[70] Gregory O'Malley estimates that by 1715, some nine thousand African captives had been taken to Saint-Domingue from neighboring English colonies.[71] The eastern tip of Jamaica is separated from the southwestern tip of Haiti by only a little more than one hundred miles. Even across this relatively short distance, illegal transport likely carried some distinctive risks for the captives owing to the need to conceal them from naval and customs officials.[72] On the other hand, that same need was well served by the many nooks and crannies that appear along virtually the entire coastline of Saint-Domingue, north, west, and south. Along with this advantage came one conspicuously lacking in the Leeward Islands: four capacious plains that permitted large-scale, intensive agricultural production, and demanded a level of forced labor to sustain such cultivation.

These considerations help to explain why Saint-Domingue overtook Martinique by 1715 as the primary market for slaves in the French empire, as figures 3 and 4 illustrate.[73] The growth in the contraband trade with Jamaica reflected an overall growth in the slave trade to Saint-Domingue during this period. The fruits of this expansion were by no means uniformly distributed across the different regions of Saint-Domingue, however. The south, in particular, suffered from a massive disruption in its trading relations with the outside world in the years after 1720, when pirates aggressively asserted control of the coastline facing Jamaica.[74] Notwithstanding that deterrent, about thirty million livres of plantation goods made their way from colonists in the southern peninsula of Saint-Domingue to Jamaica between 1720 and 1733. Such a figure suggests that, even in an era of intensified piracy, this branch of the illegal slave trade somehow managed to endure.[75]

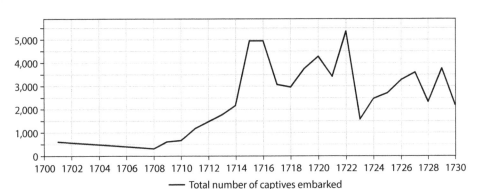

FIGURE 3. Disembarkations of west African captives at Saint-Domingue, 1700–30. SlaveVoyages. https://slavevoyages.org/voyage/maps.

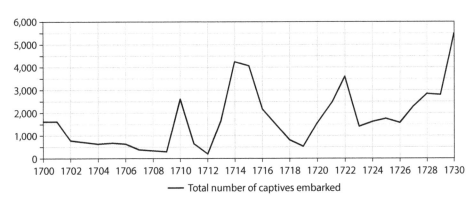

FIGURE 4. Disembarkations of west African captives at Martinique, 1700–30. SlaveVoyages. https://slavevoyages.org/voyage/maps.

The market for the illegal slave trade endured in part because it was intimately tied to another vital Caribbean market: Spanish silver. Chartered companies and intercolonial smuggling alike were driven by the need to access silver as much as west African captives.[76] Silver was necessary to purchase captives, but the enslaved could themselves serve as a form of currency in the specie-deprived markets of the Caribbean. No institution better illustrates the persistence and interdependence of these markets than the Saint-Domingue Company, the direct predecessor to the Indies Company.

The need to secure a reliable supply of Spanish silver prompted the French monarchy to charter the Company of Saint-Domingue in 1698. The institution was a throwback to Colbert's West Indies Company in most respects: endowed with a fifty-year monopoly on trade to the colony, the new company would enjoy the same rights, privileges, and duties as the West Indies Company, a clear sign that the crown had not learned the lessons of the recent colonial past.[77] The draw of silver was simply too strong, as demonstrated by the decision to grant the Saint-Domingue Company territorial jurisdiction over the southernmost slice of the colony: the area below the dotted line running across the peninsula designated as "Quartier du Sud" in figure 8.[78]

The Company's founding came exactly one year after French forces had laid siege to Cartagena on the Spanish mainland in one of the final acts of the Nine Years' War (or War of the Grand Alliance). Cartagena was one of the headquarters of the Spanish silver trade, the favored port of call for vessels flying every flag, which could obtain silver there in exchange for a variety of European and Caribbean goods, including slaves, rum, and molasses. In March 1697, the Baron de Pointis, a French naval commander with strong ties to the court, arrived in Saint-Domingue and proceeded to assemble a force of about 1,600 buccaneers and colonists, men with considerable experience in the art of capturing booty. (As James Pritchard notes, the recruits included two companies of free blacks.) With the colony's governor, Du Casse, sailing alongside him, Pointis and his men mounted their raid on Cartagena in April, an operation that brought vast quantities of Spanish silver to the shores of Saint-Domingue—only a small amount of which Pointis actually shared with the buccaneers and freebooters who carried out the raid, leading them to stage a retaliatory riot. By then, Pointis was already on his way back to France, with most of the silver from the Cartagena raid in tow. A few weeks after his arrival home, Spain and France signed the Treaty of Ryswick, granting France formal sovereignty over the western third of Hispaniola.[79]

This was the dramatic context in which the Saint-Domingue Company arrived in Haiti to implement its 1698 charter. As originally conceived, that charter would have given the company an ideal vantage point from which France could supply the Spanish American colonies with west African captives. When Spain proceeded to award the *asiento* trade to France in 1702, the Saint-Domingue Company (in conjunction with the Guinea Company operating on the west African coast) appeared to have the legal basis for a sustainable commercial position in the greater Caribbean.[80] These prospects were enhanced by what Wim Klooster describes as a "qualitative leap" in the Caribbean contraband trade, which coincided with the War of the Spanish Succession (1701–13). That conflict reduced the volume of Spanish shipping in the region to a minimum, a gap that French vessels, many of them operating via Saint-Domingue, stepped in to fill. French Caribbean authorities used the *asiento* as a front for smuggling west African captives into areas of South America, such as Buenos Aires, that were excluded from the terms of the treaty with Spain. The trade with Spanish American ports brought the French colonies mules, cacao, hides, and other goods in addition to bullion. As a result of these commercial ties, France accrued an estimated 180 million livres in revenues during the first eight years of the eighteenth century. Not all shipping to the Spanish Main involved the Saint-Domingue Company's vessels, but the company enjoyed a valuable position in the middle of this flourishing contraband traffic until the French monarchy prohibited it in 1716 out of deference to the Spanish crown.[81]

In addition to acting as a magnet for Spanish silver and a vehicle of contraband, the Saint-Domingue Company played key roles in the local economy—not all of them welcome. In the south, the company was responsible for fostering both settlement and agricultural production, and during its reign indigo, sugar, and cacao cultivation all began their upward climb. The blue dye, especially, became a beneficiary of company rule, rising to half of all exports from Saint-Domingue by 1720.[82] The company's intervention in tax policy did not endear it to the settlers. In 1716, the directors announced that they would begin collecting (and pocketing, for the company's own purposes) the full range of domanial and seigneurial taxes that applied elsewhere in the French Caribbean—including those falling under the rubric of the Domaine d'Occident. They justified this maneuver on the curious grounds that the colony's quasi-immunity from the Domaine had created a perverse incentive for French settlers elsewhere in the West Indies to migrate to the tax-free territory of Saint-Domingue.[83]

The last of the great military conflicts of Louis XIV's reign proved to be a double-edged sword for the company, taking away with one hand what it gave the company with the other. By 1704, English, Dutch, and Portuguese contraband slave traders, acting with the collusion of local administrators in Saint-Domingue, had begun to eat away at the company's putative monopoly. Taking advantage of interruptions to the company's own shipping caused by the War of the Spanish Succession, these foreign interlopers became familiar visitors to the colony's coastlines.[84] The company's fate was formally sealed in April 1720, when the monarchy revoked the charter of the Saint-Domingue enterprise, citing the growth of a southern settler community whose trading needs could no longer be satisfied by the small size of the company's merchant fleet.[85]

The Saint-Domingue Company's experience at the intersection of Spanish silver and the contraband slave trade was emblematic of a larger dilemma in the period before and after Utrecht. This was the problem of how to pay for newly arrived African captives in a Caribbean world with steadily declining access to Spanish silver, the coin of the Atlantic colonial realm, from Spanish America to the south all the way up to French Canada in the north.

For as long as Saint-Domingue was a colony of France, the problem of securing a viable money supply for both local and external market transactions proved an insoluble quandary (one that Haiti continues to struggle with even today).[86] In some ways, the troubles of the early 1720s were the first warning sign of the many less visible (and less audible) crises to come. The only constant in the colonial chapter of this history was a reliance upon silver specie, drawn from the same Spanish mainland territories, Mexico and Peru, that provided the engine of Iberian imperial expansion for most of the sixteenth and seventeenth centuries.[87] Silver and, to a lesser extent, gold were not simply media of exchange throughout the New World (as well as the East Indies). They were at the heart of the doctrine of mercantilism itself, defined to a very large degree by the notion of bullionism, according to which a nation's wealth corresponded to the amount of precious metals in its coffers. The allure of these metals, presumed finite in supply, led metropolitan governments to see their Atlantic colonies as instruments by which Spanish silver could be made to flow into the coffers of continental treasuries. And that policy of extraction, in turn, constituted the nub of the money problem in most areas of French America under the Old Regime.

Saint-Domingue in the latter part of Louis XIV's reign affords an especially dramatic and revealing example of what the economists François Velde and Thomas Sargent have called the "big problem of small change" in medieval and early modern Europe. For our purposes, the key feature of the Velde/Sargent model is its explanation of the depreciation and devaluation of small coins. Currency made of precious metals could be valuable to its owner either as money (a medium of exchange) or as metal (a commodity in and of itself). If the coin was worth more as metal, the holder could profit by having it melted. When currencies depreciated, the only way governments could avoid converting coin into metal was to adjust the point at which it became more profitable to hold silver in one form or the other—that is, the melting point for small coins. Velde and Sargent argue that the repeated devaluations of metal currency over the medieval and early modern periods were a response to this problem. In what amounted to a perverse feedback loop, it seemed to monetary authorities that shortages of small change could be cured only by debasing the coins themselves. This vicious cycle of depreciation and devaluation unfolded, moreover, within the context of a system, known as seigniorage, by which the crown traditionally reserved for itself a percentage of the bullion brought to the mint for coining. Both the initial making of metallic money, and the subsequent adjustment in its value, were therefore profit opportunities in and of themselves.[88] The French monarchy took liberal advantage of those opportunities in the years leading up to the crisis of 1719–20. Between December 1713 and September 1715, for example, the crown ordered no less than eleven currency diminutions in a vain effort to bring hoarded specie back into circulation.[89]

John Law's System was, among other things, an effort to solve this big problem of small change. The solution that Law fixed upon was not to devalue silver and gold coins but to displace them altogether with paper money. In this, he was following in the footsteps of a colonial precedent. In French Canada, the dearth of silver coin prompted the first experiment in paper (card) money, as early as the 1680s—preceding a similar, more well-known experiment in Massachusetts by a decade.[90] To induce holders of small coin to switch over to the paper notes of the Banque Royale, Law initially resorted to a voluntary conversion scheme, and then, when that proved insufficiently persuasive, to a prohibition on the use of metal coin as legal tender. When the banknote experiment itself began to founder on the shoals of overprinting (in order to subsidize speculation in the inflated shares of the Indies Company), Law applied to his paper money measures traditionally used for metallic currency in the medieval and early modern periods. By turns, he tried reducing either the face value of paper notes or their total number. The latter measure entailed using coin and other assets to buy back the banknotes. And that, in turn, required that coin be perceived, once again, as having an adequate value as legal tender.[91]

Its distance from the metropole gave Saint-Domingue some relief from the incoherence and burden of these policies. To be sure, the Regency saw Saint-Domingue and the other French Caribbean colonies as extensions of the realm and moved to extend its emergency measures across the Atlantic. On July 30, 1720, the Conseil d'État sought to implement the buyback of depreciated banknotes, first by augmenting, and then debasing, the value of gold and silver coin. Moreau de Saint-Méry prints only the title of this decision in his late-eighteenth-century compilation of French colonial law, noting that because it was only registered by the Conseil Supérieur of Cap Français on December 30, 1720, there had been insufficient time to execute it.[92] Given the highly compressed time span of the Mississippi Bubble, such was the colonial fate of Law's revolution generally. As a formal matter, the Caribbean was subject to the System. But decisions that required immediate execution to have any practical effect could not meaningfully be applied to territories at a remove of four thousand miles and two to three months' crossing time from the Indies Company headquarters in Paris.

Distance also required a measure of monetary autonomy and adaptation to the conditions of colonial life that transcended questions of timing. Nearly all of these local variations stemmed from the same fundamental difference between metropolitan and colonial monetary systems: the absence of a mint in the West Indies. (The metropolitan unit of account, the *livre tournois*, was not itself minted as a circulating coin in France, but it was defined in relation to a

FIGURE 5. 1721 Spanish silver piece of eight (piastre). Courtesy of Stacks Bowers.

standard of weight: the mark [*marc*] of Troyes, or eight ounces of silver. The royal livre was double this weight, or sixteen ounces.) The French government coined only small amounts of French money for use in its overseas colonies, far too little to have any meaningful impact. In 1672, Colbert tried to compensate for the paucity of French coins in the colonies by creating a special unit of account for its colonies, the colonial livre, which was valued at 133 percent of the livre tournois. The colonial livre, in other words, traded at a one-quarter discount and would do so until 1727 (throughout the period of the events covered in this book). As Robert Lacombe explains, that solution proved to be illusory because French coins only traded for their weight in precious metal. The colonial livre became essentially an accounting unit for administrators to use in preparing their financial statements, as well as a way for merchants to compare the value of real money and market prices.[93]

As a result, the de facto or "real" currency of the French Caribbean was the Spanish silver coin known as the *pièce de huit*, or piastre. A subdivision of the piastre known as the *escalin* also circulated widely in Saint-Domingue, as did (albeit less widely) the Portuguese gold coin known as the *pistole*. By the early eighteenth century, Spanish coins were typically drawn from Mexico (where they were known as the *macuquina*, in use from the coronation of Philip III until 1732). They made their way to Saint-Domingue in the same way that most other commodities and supplies entered the island: as an accompaniment to the slave trade. Initially, the piastre trade operated out of the southern peninsula, which the Saint-Domingue Company had used as a base for importing silver coins from the Spanish American mainland in exchange for French goods and slaves. Later in the eighteenth century, Spanish merchants from the eastern side of Hispaniola and from Puerto Rico brought their piastres to Cap Français and Port-au-Prince, seeking to purchase African captives newly arrived on French slave ships.[94]

The de facto monetary system was therefore dependent on the strength of the French slave trade. In a sense, that trade served as the functional equivalent of the metropolitan mint: it made money available in greater or lesser quantities depending on the volume of transactions taking place at a given moment in the colonial economy. Relative to a mint, however, the slave trade was a very imperfect mechanism for calibrating the size of the money supply, since the supply of African labor was itself highly sensitive to the disruptions of war, anti-mercantilist agitation, and the rate at which captives survived the Middle Passage. It is therefore difficult to apply the Velde/Sargent model in any straightforward fashion to the Saint-Domingue experience, for the model presumes the availability of a mint that renders intelligible (and makes possible) the decisions of governments and individuals to convert coin into metal or vice versa.

But the biggest weakness in the West Indian system stemmed from the mercantilist commitment to the hoarding of precious metals, which drained the colonies of their silver and gold money supplies. Adapting to the persistent dearth, the colonists had recourse to two different strategies. First, they made use of alternative currencies for both intracolonial and intercolonial exchange: tobacco, indigo, sugar, even slaves. Colbert had tried to ban such in-kind or *denrée* payments as early as 1672, but the combination of necessity and local custom was strong enough to prevail over metropolitan dictate. Tobacco was the most common form of money in Saint-Domingue in the second half of the seventeenth century, often used to pay the wages of white indentured servants. It remained a viable method of payment until as late as 1715; thereafter, contracts generally substituted sugar where tobacco had once been used. Sugar's rise went hand in hand with the ability to offer slaves in payment of larger contracts. For example, in 1711 the director-general of the Saint-Domingue Company, Jean Louis Molière, offered Léonard Lavigne, a Saint-Louis contractor, "two of the first negroes to be imported" in exchange for building Molière a house of fifty-three by twenty feet.[95]

Unable to attribute the outward flow of precious metals to an abstract economic doctrine, the colonists tended to blame it on the entire merchant community that traded in and to Saint-Domingue. This assignment of responsibility was not entirely misguided. In October 1720, citing the "final extremes" to which colonists had been reduced by lack of access to the piastre, Governor Léon de Sorel and acting intendant Jean-Baptiste Dubois Duclos[96] sought to compel merchants to accept payment in kind—sugar, tobacco, or other colonial products—for essential metropolitan goods. But merchants scoffed at the injunction, insisting on payment in silver coin. The next month, the administrators effectively took monetary policy into their own hands, raising the value of the piastre relative to the (noncirculating) unit of account, from five to eight livres tournois. That measure effectively gave the colonists' more buying power with the currency they possessed, an artificial hike that the administrators justified by citing the obstinate refusal of the captains of newly arriving merchant vessels to accommodate the local shortage of silver coin. Sorel and Duclos even hinted that they might also let the other shoe drop, noting that colonial taxes—the *octroi* and other duties—were payable only in specie. But whereas the government effectively controlled the terms by which a subject could redeem his public debts, the world of private transactions was inherently not amenable to such a unilateral approach. When Saint-Domingue's planter community complained of the net imbalance in the colony's silver trade, therefore, they had in mind a merchant-driven conspiracy to deprive them of their rightful inheritance.[97]

The colonists' second strategy for dealing with the dearth of Spanish and Portuguese money was to make increasing use of clipped or diluted coins that contained smaller and smaller amounts of silver and gold. They could do this because Saint-Domingue and the other French West Indian colonies were notorious in the Atlantic world as a dumping ground for underweight silver and gold coins. Clipped or diluted coins were a problem for the Saint-Domingue colonists when they sought to have dealings with colonies that gave their own coins currency by weight—a practice also followed by the same French merchants who refused to accept payment in kind. Indeed, giving coins currency by weight was the general policy of colonies throughout the Americas, as it was the most effective strategy for countering the clipping or diluting of coins. But the French in the West Indies gave their coins currency by tale, that is, by number: one accepted another's five piastres as worth five full piastres even if the coin had been clipped.

This practice is critical to understanding the drama that followed for two reasons. First, as John McCusker explains, it made the French Caribbean a "dumping ground" for underweight Spanish silver coins. Second, unlike nearly all coins that circulate in today's world, the silver and gold coins used in Saint-Domingue in the eighteenth century did not have a face value. Instead, they had a weight (which, as we have just seen, might or might not be used to determine the exchange value of the money) and a value expressed in relation to the unit of account, the colonial livre. In 1704, one piastre was worth three colonial livres twelve *sous* (there were twenty *sous* to a livre, and twelve *deniers* to a *sou*). In 1720, the rate had increased to four livres 15 *sous*. In 1721, following the Mississippi crisis, the level jumped all the way up to eight livres, before falling to seven by August 1722, when the monarchy intervened with its fateful currency ordinance. Devaluation of the colonial livre relative to specie lagged slightly behind its depreciation relative to the livre tournois, which was itself in the process of a gradual decline.[98]

These trends were not necessarily the product or reflection of John Law's System or the Indies Company. They were rather a function of the paucity of silver coin in the colonies and only increased the premium that settlers placed on their ability to obtain such coin, a premium reinforced by the willingness of colonial merchants to discount prices significantly for those able to pay in precious metal.[99] But the long association between chartered companies, the dearth of Spanish silver, and the ruthless competition to obtain west African captives—culminating most recently in the highly unpopular twenty-year reign of the Saint-Domingue Company—made it easy for settlers to identify fluctuations in the value of money with company rule. This included changes in the purchasing power of Spanish silver. Devaluation of local currency meant price inflation across the board. And inflation prevented some settlers from claiming what they saw as their right to participate in the full benefits of the sugar revolution, even as it prevented others from entering the plantation market altogether.

———

Monetary instability in the decades before the takeoff of the sugar revolution was accompanied by profound demographic instability in Saint-Domingue. A true demographic revolution over the course of the 1660s to 1720s generated intersecting financial, legal, and racial anxieties that made the colony a volatile place at the time of John Law's System. The distinctive marginal populations— white women, vagabonds, free people of color, and, above all, the newly enslaved—brought to the shores of Saint-Domingue during these decades would shape the response of administrators and the emergent planter elite to the arrival of the Indies Company.

The fear that control of the slave trade augured a takeover of the entire colonial economy, including the value of local money, reflected the growing importance of the commerce in west African captives to Saint-Domingue. But it also testified to the magnitude of a contraband trade in slaves that had contributed, in some unmeasurable but decisive way, to the growth of the colony's population of bonded laborers. As Saint-Domingue pressed forward with the transition from frontier settler society to plantation-based colony in the closing two decades of the seventeenth century, it simultaneously began to reach out in all directions for an ever larger share of the supply of African captives.[100]

This search for a coerced labor force capable of supporting the rising number of plantations in Saint-Domingue was not confined to the African market.

The importation of white indentured servants, or *engagés*, acted as a major force in the peopling of Haiti in the late seventeenth century. Beginning in the early 1680s, the flow of *engagés* was redirected from the Lesser Antilles to Saint-Domingue. The overall numbers were significant, but not overwhelming. Between 1680 and 1715, La Rochelle alone sent 1,280 *engagés* to Haiti, among them many deportees, prisoners, galley slaves, and convicted murderers.[101]

Women and child servants were rare but not entirely unheard of during this period. By century's end, d'Ogeron's efforts to recruit French women to the settler cause had borne fruit, at least in the colony's urban spaces. As of 1700, the figures reported 449 men and 373 women (all nonindentured) in Cap Français. That population was rounded out by 241 *engagés* (roughly 10 percent of the total) and 854 arms-bearing men, a group that far outweighed all other categories of the city's residents. Léogâne's numbers for the same categories were slightly higher but proportionally similar. These urban census figures do not distinguish along racial lines, but there is good reason to believe that, by no later than 1713, women of color had already begun to constitute the predominant part of the female population in Haiti's major towns. In 1713, Paul François de La Grange, comte d'Arquian, the municipal (military) governor of Le Cap, wrote directly to Naval Secretary Jérome de Pontchartrain to complain that in Saint-Domingue one observes "only negresses and mulatto women (*mulles*) with whom their masters have swapped liberty in exchange for their virginity (*pucelage*)." Montholon, the intendant who attempted to preside over the revolt against the Indies Company, reported to Pontchartrain's successor Maurepas in 1723 that most of Haiti's landless young men "seem to regard the deficit of white women as a fair pretext to commit to remaining in a state of licentiousness (*libertinage*) with the negresses." The apparently few white women who already inhabited the colony were denounced by colonial administrators as prostitutes. In a 1713 appeal calling upon the metropole to send women more suitable for procreation (*génération*), Governor Blenac and Intendant Mithon complained that Saint-Domingue's white women had been drawn primarily from the impoverished corners of Paris, their bodies and manners alike corrupted by a vice that threatened to "infect" the colony.[102]

The consequence of these unsuccessful efforts to establish an orthodox, gender-balanced French community in Haiti was modest growth in the white population accompanied by a small but far more rapidly increasing population of freed persons (*affranchis*). Between 1681 and 1720, the white population grew by less than double: from 4,336 at the beginning of this period to 7,264 at its end. *Affranchis*, a mere 210 in 1681, numbered 1,573 by 1720—most of them the children of white planters. These disparate growth rates therefore not only reflected the inability to recruit more white women from the metropole, but also the tendency of white men to make up for that inability by the sexual exploitation of African-born women. The proportional figures are even more revealing: whereas whites constituted 65 percent of the colony's total population in 1681, they were only 14 percent in 1720. While the *affranchi* proportion of the population remained relatively stable over that same time period (at 3 percent), freed persons had a decisive impact on efforts to regulate the colonial social order. By 1711, the rapid growth in the *affranchi* population led administrators to revise the Code Noir by requiring that masters gain written approval from royal agents before they could manumit their slaves (a reform ratified by the monarchy in 1713).[103]

The racial and gender anxieties that attended the emergence of a biracial population in Haiti took backstage, however, to a more overwhelming concern with the size and suitability of the male labor force. White indentured servants were an increasingly rare commodity, and a distinctly unstable and socially mobile one at that. Their numbers were insufficient to fill the gap between the demand for and the supply of coerced labor, despite efforts to make the terms of indenture more appealing, such as a 1670 ordinance limiting the period of service to eighteen months (down from thirty-six). Some *engagés* patiently waited out their terms of service, while others escaped before their contracts had expired. One way or another, they aspired for a future not as agricultural workers, but as small landholders in their own right or, failing that, as skilled artisans, coopers, and plantation commanders: people who could help with the task of managing contingents of fifty or more African slaves on the expanding *habitations* of Saint-Domingue. After 1700 especially, the planters, many of whom had once been indentured themselves, actively encouraged these aspirations. As Gabriel Debien puts it, the *engagés* were the building blocks of Haiti's emerging plantation society; they had "made the colonists, and thus the colonies."[104]

But it was becoming increasingly clear that whites would not be able to make this colony by themselves, and that, in fact, the brunt of its making would be thrust upon the shoulders of racially defined others. With the flow of incoming *engagés* slowing to a trickle, Saint-Domingue's planters wasted little time in shifting their gaze toward the west African coast. Between 1681 and 1713, the slave population of Saint-Domingue grew by over 1,000 percent, from 2,102 to 24,156. A mere seven years later, in 1720, that number had doubled, to 47,528—and by 1730 it would double again, to nearly 80,000. The proportional figures are even more striking: only 31 percent of the colony's total population in 1681, the enslaved had risen to two-thirds of the total by 1700, and to an overwhelming 83 percent by the time of the Mississippi Bubble. These numbers highlight the dramatic role of the decades just before and after 1720 in paving the way for the Saint-Domingue sugar revolution.[105]

The number, size, and variety of plantations in Saint-Domingue all show a corresponding increase over the same period. By 1713, the colony boasted 1,182 indigo works and 138 sugar plantations. As of 1730, the number of indigo plantations had risen to 2,744—a useful reminder of the importance of the blue dye to the French Caribbean, especially in this early part of the eighteenth century, but perhaps also evidence for the claim that monopoly companies had failed to supply Saint-Domingue with slaves on a scale sufficient to sustain the work of the larger, more labor-intensive sugar plantations. Sugar nonetheless began to conquer a growing portion of the colony's business, owing in part to a blight that, in 1715–16, destroyed all of the colony's cacao trees. Between 1713 and 1730, the number of sugar plantations more than doubled, from 138 to 339. Mills were not yet a standard feature of these plantations, but they were becoming so: whereas in 1717 the colony as a whole was home to one hundred sugar mills, by 1727 that number had risen to two hundred in just the area of the Plaine du Cap. Increasing technological sophistication went hand in hand with larger scale production: many of these sugar plantations comprised upward of one hundred *carreaux de terres* (a *carreau* is a unit of land equivalent to 3.2 acres). Typically formed by the joining of smaller terrains into one, the trend toward more extensive sugar plantations closed off opportunities for smaller, less wealthy landholders and helped give rise to the creation of a community of so-called *petits blancs*.[106]

The growth figures for the southern peninsula (where the Saint-Domingue and Indies companies exercised territorial prerogatives) are similarly striking. By 1713, 644 white immigrants and 2,947 slaves had arrived. By 1720, the south had 797 free inhabitants and 4,818 enslaved persons. Sugar cultivation increased from six plantations in 1713 to twenty-three sugar works in 1720, and sixty by 1727. Planters in this region occupied a position somewhere between dependence on and outright competition with the company, from which they leased their properties. But it also gave them closer access to the contraband networks that operated out of the south than their counterparts in the west and north.[107]

———

Saint-Domingue by the 1720s was already in the throes of the sugar revolution. The signs of social and political dislocation that attended the turn to large-scale sugar plantations were everywhere to be seen. A pervasive settler anxiety about company control of the market for west African captives kept alive memories of the insurrections of 1670 and 1680, as well as the more recent uprising in Martinique.[108] Monetary instability provided an additional reminder that the French state and its corporate representatives were powerful enough to wreak havoc on the local economy, if not powerful enough to support the planters' growing economic ambitions. Similarly, widespread smuggling and piracy testified both to the limits of state authority and to the state's creativity in adapting local practices for its own ends. Finally, the colony's demographic transformation into a slave society, still in its early stages when the Code Noir was framed in 1685, had by the 1720s begun to reveal the basic patterns of racial antagonism and oppression that characterized the sugar revolution.

Cartographic evidence from this period illustrates the impact of these changes in Saint-Domingue. The rebellion against John Law's monopoly coincided with the creation of some of the colony's earliest maps. The quality and level of detail of these maps, which cluster around the years 1722–25, vary widely, which makes it difficult to read them as objective measures of the settlement patterns or topography of early Saint-Domingue. Perspective and distance appear highly distorted relative to later maps of Haiti. Still, these early cartographic representations give an indication of the groups, places, and institutions that contemporaries believed carried the most weight in their society.

Nicolas de Fer's eccentric 1723 map gives the impression of a thinly settled island dominated by a handful of emerging urban centers on the coastline. With its cartouche featuring a person of African descent smoking a tobacco pipe, de Fer's work conveys a distorted picture of Saint-Domingue in more than one respect, including its depiction of the colony's boundaries as demarcated by the 1697 Treaty of Ryswick that divided the island between French and Spanish sovereignty (figure 6). In de Fer's generous reading, the western third under French control appears significantly larger than its actual extent relative to the more expansive Spanish territory to the east. Other details suggest a less than intimate familiarity with the colony's interior topography. The Artibonite River, for example, is drawn as an essentially horizontal flow from the boundary with Spanish Santo Domingo to the western coastline, whereas the main Haitian stretch of the actual Artibonite flows in a generally northwest direction from what is now Mirebalais toward a point on the western coast about halfway between Saint Marc and Gonaïves.

Although defective in these and other respects, de Fer's rendering of settlement patterns on the French side is suggestive of the orientation of the colony's political and commercial life at this time. Using the symbol of a church building or other large structure, the cartographer marks only a handful of port cities as sites of meaningful settlement: Le Cap in the north, and Léogâne, Grand Goâve, and Petit Goâve in the west. In the south, Fort Saint-Louis is indicated, in the vicinity of an offshore anchor that implies de Fer's awareness of the Indies Company's presence in an otherwise largely uncleared area of the colony. Port-au-Prince—the city that would become the colony's capital at

FIGURE 6. Nicolas de Fer, "Carte de l'Isle St. Domingue ou Espagnole, découverte l'an 1492 par les Espagnols" (1723). Courtesy of the John Carter Brown Library, Providence, RI.

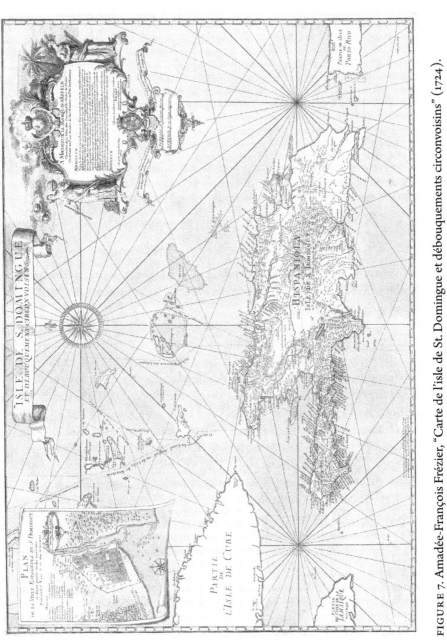

FIGURE 7. Amadée-François Frézier, "Carte de l'isle de St. Domingue et débouquements circonvoisins" (1724). Courtesy of the John Carter Brown Library, Providence, RI.

FIGURE 8. Detail of the southern peninsula, from Guillaume Delisle, "Carte de l'Isle de Saint Domingue dressée en 1722 pour l'usage du Roy sur les mémoires de Mr. Frézier Ingénieur de S. M. et autres" (Paris, 1725). Courtesy of the John Carter Brown Library, Providence, RI.

mid-century (and is, by far, its most populous urban center today)—is entirely absent from the map, the only hint of its eventual location being the islets du Prince sandwiched inside what would become the Bay of Port-au-Prince (and from which islands the city would take its name).

In May 1724, one or two months after Champmeslin concluded his mission to pacify the insurrection against the Indies Company, the colony's director of fortifications, Amadée-François Frézier, completed a map that was clearly designed to expose de Fer as an amateur in the cartographic business (figure 7). Without mentioning de Fer by name, the cartouche refers to some recent maps "in which there is neither detail nor a relationship to truth." As befits the work of someone responsible for identifying and shoring up vulnerabilities along the Saint-Domingue coastline, Frézier's map, begun in 1721, provides what seems like an exhaustive account of every known topographical detail and area of settlement in the colony. And it was the source of the precision reflected in other representations of Haiti during this period. In a 1722 map by the royal geographer Delisle that was based on Frézier's research, one feature is particularly relevant to our purposes: the dotted line running across the southern peninsula, which denoted the territory, south of this line, that the Indies Company would inherit from its predecessor, the Saint-Domingue Company (more on this in chapter 2) (figure 8).

The overall effect of the coastal detail in the Frézier and Delisle maps is misleading in its own way, for many of the locations identified by Frézier were sparsely populated, if at all. At this time, even the major towns of Saint-Domingue were years, if not decades, away from the densely settled, highly built-up cities of the later colonial period. To be sure, the northern port town of Cap Français

FIGURE 9. "Veüe et perspective du Cap Français levé en 1723," based on an engraving by Sartre de Saint-Laurens (1723). Courtesy of the Newberry Library, Chicago, IL.

was already emerging as one of the colony's principal commercial centers, to judge from the cartographic attention accorded it in 1723. But those estimations must be viewed relative to the more modest baseline suggested by de Fer's overall picture of Saint-Domingue. In one image (based on an engraving by Sartre de Saint-Laurens) showing a view of the Cap harbor from the east, the town appears as something closer to a hamlet or village than a city: an upstart collection of only a few built-up structures surrounded by mountains that still retained their forest cover (figure 9). The only edifices judged worthy of highlighting in this image included the town church, the Jesuit compound, the clock tower, various military installations, and the *habitation* of the Indies Company. Indicated by the letter "H" at far left, the company's plantation was a short distance from the center of town, at La Fossette, on the edge of a dirt path leading upward to the Haut du Cap area overhanging the city. Even though Le Cap had a Conseil Supérieur by this time, as well as a local governor and commandant, no buildings housing a government function of any kind are designated.

A bird's eye view of the town, also from 1723, gives the impression of a more densely populated but still fledgling urban space (figure 10). In contrast to the

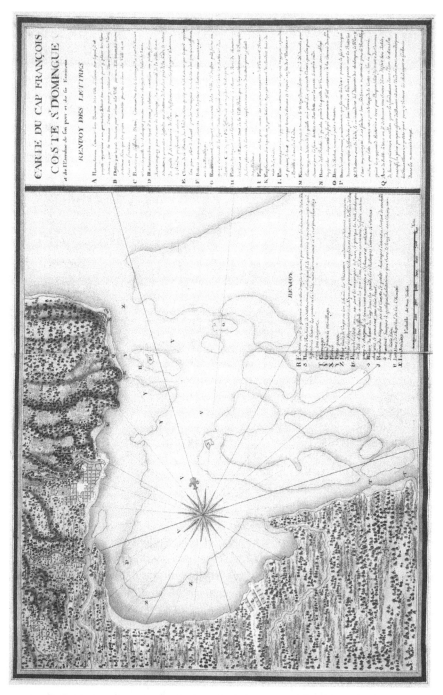

FIGURE 10. "Carte du Cap Français, côte St. Domingue et de l'étendue de son port et de ses environs" (1723). Cartes Marines (Ayer) Map Collection. Courtesy of the Newberry Library, Chicago, IL.

previous image, with its purely illustrative depiction of ships moored in the Cap Français harbor, this map was clearly designed to provide practical guidance to ship captains as they entered the bay. In addition to marking out the location of reefs and sandbanks, the map served to project a vision of the city Cap Français might soon (but had not yet) become. Most of the letters in the right-hand column of the legend indicate locations where improvements to military fortifications could be made or new installations erected. Others designate spaces that could be turned to the advantage of the emerging plantation economy. The letter "A," for example, indicates an entrenchment and wall running westward from near the mouth of the Haut du Cap River up into the mountains above the town. This wall, located on privately owned land, marked the outer limits of the town of Cap Français. According to the mapmaker, that area would be an ideal space for situating newly arrived slaves, who could occupy themselves by cultivating crops pending assignment to a works project (*travaux*).

Like the colony whose trade it served, Cap Français was thus depicted as an entrepôt in the making, a work in progress, full of possibilities that required the labor of west African captives. And those possibilities required, for their realization, attention to such mundane details as the location of reefs, the strengthening of coastal fortifications, and the development of a local food supply. In the meantime, the major landmarks of the settlement remained religious establishments: the Jesuits, with their vast compound at the upper western edge of the town (designated by the letter "X"), and the missionaries of the Charité hospital, headquartered in the Haut du Cap area that was the site of the earliest planter settlements in the region (indicated by the letter "U," near the top left corner of the map).

One other location destined to play a decisive role in the colony's future lay at the southern edge of the harbor, a "swampy, salty, insalubrious" site that provided "nearly the only landing pier" in the entire bay (indicated by the "&" sign). In this inauspicious but critical stretch of the coast, known as the Petite Anse, three rows of warehouses stored the sugar that had already begun to fuel the dramatic eighteenth-century rise of the Haitian economy. Although not mentioned by the cartographer, it was here that the Indies Company maintained some of its most important facilities in the entire colony—facilities that would attract special attention from the rebels of 1722.

Instructive in their own right, these images reveal even more about the colony of 1723 when juxtaposed with the fine-grained maps of Saint-Domingue that appeared in the final years of the Old Regime. To get a sense of the transformation of Cap Français from a town into one of the New World's largest cities, one has only to glance at the 1786 map by René Phelipeau that Moreau de Saint-Méry published in 1791, part of a collection of colonial sites and scenes engraved by Nicolas Ponce and widely used by historians of Haiti

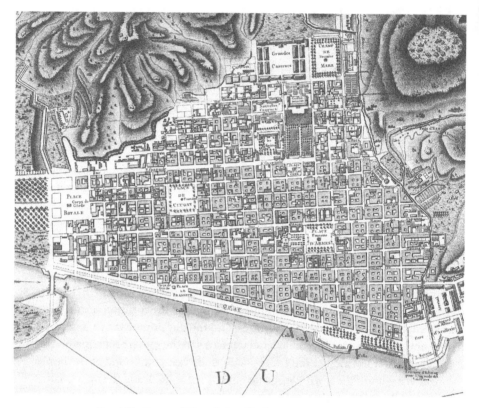

FIGURE 11. René Phelipeau, "Plan de la ville du Cap Français et de ses environs dans l'Isle de St. Domingue" (1786). Courtesy of the John Carter Brown Library, Providence, RI.

(figure 11).[109] Phelipeau's map shows the densely populated, neatly laid-out urban center that dominated the colony's commercial life from the late 1720s onward. At the upper tip of the city, in the space formerly occupied by the extensive Jesuit compound (the Jesuits having been expelled from Saint-Domingue in 1763), lies Government House: an administrative complex that housed one of the colony's two high courts, among other tribunals and official functions. But, in this map from the eve of the French and Haitian revolutions, one absent detail stands out for our purposes: there is no reference to any property or facilities owned and operated by the Indies Company. La Fossette is still there, above the mouth of the Haut du Cap River. But, on the 1786 map, it is now marked as the site of the bazaar for the sale of newly arrived slaves rather than the location of the company's plantation. The anonymous 1723 cartographer of the bay of Cap Français had correctly foreseen that this area, just outside the wall and with entrenchments protecting the city's southern boundary, could serve as a transit point for enslaved persons suspended between the horrors of the Atlantic slave trade and those of the plantations. The problem of finding the specie to pay for these enslaved persons remained an intractable one even as Phelipeau drafted his map.[110] But the city had experienced unforeseeable growth in its density, scope, and organization. And this growth was itself the most powerful testament to the impact of the sugar revolution on a colony that, even in 1786, had little idea of the dramatic events about to unfold on the western third of Hispaniola.

2

Colonial System

A COLONY undergoing a massive economic and demographic transformation since the 1660s, Saint-Domingue was well on its way to capturing the benefits of the sugar revolution by the end of the reign of Louis XIV. But it would finally join the rest of the Caribbean in this revolution on its own terms. John Law's System and the Mississippi Bubble provided a final jolt that sealed the fate of Saint-Domingue and gave it a distinctive character in the world of the leading American plantation societies. From the vantage point of the settlers there, Law's System and the French Indies Company appeared on the horizon as another in a discredited line of corporate monopolies coming out of France. Neither the colonists nor the System's architects in France, however, had any idea of what would ensue from this encounter. On both sides of the Atlantic, they would improvise their way toward a massive expansion of the slave economy of Saint-Domingue, collaborating in the process with a host of more marginal actors who left their own distinctive imprint on the colonial System. These actors were not all men, but they all acted in the spirit of Marx's famous dictum in "The Eighteenth Brumaire of Louis Bonaparte": "Men make their history, but they do not make it just as they please; they do not make it under circumstances chosen by themselves, but under circumstances directly encountered, given and transmitted from the past."[1]

The decisive circumstance transmitted to Saint-Domingue from the North Atlantic world of the late seventeenth and early eighteenth centuries is that the System was a colonial enterprise. Historians of the System disagree on this point in part because they write of these years from different vantage points, both geographic and methodological. An emphasis on financial, administrative, and intellectual history tends to go hand in hand with a focus on Paris, London, and (to some extent) Amsterdam. The South Sea and Mississippi bubbles are thus often seen as essentially metropolitan affairs in terms of their causes and consequences. In this interpretation, which goes back to some of the earliest writing on the subject, a fantastical portrait of the profits to be reaped from the vast Louisiana territory or the *asiento* contract helped to promote investment in the South Sea and Indies companies. But the colonies themselves are typically seen as external to the origins and unfolding of the metropolitan financial crisis.[2]

This emphasis on the metropole sits awkwardly with another widespread verdict on the System: its failure to transform the structures of French finance. After a crash so spectacular that it led John Law to abscond to Venice to avoid criminal punishment, the French government reverted to most of the same methods of tax farming, debt management, and monetary policy that were in place before Law's arrival. If anything, the bubble may have reinforced preexisting hostilities toward financial innovation, ensuring that France would not experiment again with central banks, paper money, and credit creation until the Revolution.[3] This verdict, too, echoes the views of the earliest commentators on the crisis of 1719–20, who very quickly came to see that episode as an aberration from a natural order of self-correcting, self-organizing credit and trade.[4] The Marquis d'Argenson (1694–1757), for example, wrote that "the finances of France were soon reestablished, notwithstanding the catastrophes of the bank and the *Visa*," in illustration of a natural law whereby "finance, public credit and circulation find their own level, like the water of the sea, after storms and tempests."[5]

We need not settle whether this legacy was itself a kind of transformation, for continuity is always competing with change as a driving force in human history. Taking a broader perspective on the years from 1715–22, however, makes clear that the bubble (and the System of which it was a part) were far from purely metropolitan affairs. They were key chapters in French colonial history, and in the history of Saint-Domingue in particular—not just Louisiana. The System exerted a visibly transformative effect on Saint-Domingue, making the French West Indies a crucial theater of what is commonly identified as the first major financial crisis of modern times.

The System played out so differently on either side of the Atlantic, above all, because of slavery and the slave trade. And slavery and the slave trade helped to make the System what it was. This is a large story, far transcending the borders of a single colony. With the Treaty of Utrecht and the coming of peace in 1713, France and Britain quickly came to see the west Africa trade as one of the keys to solving the public debt crises they had inherited from the dynastic conflicts of the reign of Louis XIV. As we saw in chapter 1, both nations effectively liberalized their slave trades despite the persistence of state-sponsored slaving companies that went back to the 1670s. And then, just as the era of monopoly commerce and colonization in the French and British Atlantic seemed on the verge of a permanent demise in the 1710s, it made a sudden and decisive comeback. As quickly as they had moved to open up the slave trade in the earlier part of the decade, France and Britain reverted to the seventeenth-century tradition of corporate mercantilism at its end.

The seesaw motion reflected France's imperial and financial insecurity in the face of Britain (and vice versa), but the shifts appeared nowhere more contradictory and unstable than in the context of the slave trade. The years leading up to the bubbles mark the moment at which France and Britain, in competition with each other and with Dutch interlopers to supply the Spanish American slave market through control of the *asiento* contract, committed themselves to a decisive expansion of and investment in trade along the west African coast. What unites the near-simultaneous French and British experiments in financial engineering is not simply their reliance on overly optimistic strategies for converting state debt into corporate equity, but also their investment in slavery and the slave trade. It was this investment that brought the Indies Company and, with it, John Law's System, to the shores of Saint-Domingue. There, the System would produce a crisis that unfolded according to a colonial logic of its own, several years after the measures that originally authorized the Indies Company to operate in Saint-Domingue had been enacted.

The implementation of the System in Saint-Domingue was part of an effort to help France recover from the debts of Louis XIV. The integration of the slave economy into the heart of the System committed France to a path that entailed conflict and violence. War was the path by which France initially fell into debt, and the colonial System was a key part of the strategy by which it would hope to exit from debt. However much John Law intended his scheme as a substitution of trade for war that would bring peace to Europe, the implementation of this scheme entailed forms of exploitation and domination abroad that are obscured by the dramatic twists and turns of the bubble.[6] Put differently, the line between trade and war as instruments of state is not always clear. The line seems particularly fuzzy when the story of the System is seen in its Caribbean theater. During the Regency period, Saint-Domingue was made a colony of the bubble, in a moment of financial and commercial hubris that would define its future as a bubble colony.

———

It is an extraordinary and little-known fact of Haitian history that a Scottish financial theorist and convicted murderer turned controller general of France came to exercise such an outsized influence on the colony's history. John Law, who never came close to setting foot in the Caribbean, appears in the indices of very few books about colonial Haiti, just as Saint-Domingue figures rarely, if ever, in the literature on John Law. There is some irony in this, for Law's criminal background associated him with the many forced emigrants driven into exile by his own System and destined to form part of the vagabond community of early-eighteenth-century Saint-Domingue and Louisiana. Instead, John Law oversaw the western third of Hispaniola in the way that many foreign heads of state and business leaders have ever since: while presiding, in government offices and corporate boardrooms, over large enterprises in which Haiti itself seems to figure only as one of several moving pieces of a larger puzzle.

The story of how Law's System came to include Saint-Domingue in its purview begins with Law himself, even if it finally encompasses a host of less visible characters. The colorful incident of 1694, which brought Law to a Bloomsbury Square duel with Edward Wilson over the affections of a woman who had captured the attention of both men, is a staple of biographical accounts. After killing Wilson, Law was charged with murder and imprisoned in London's Newgate Prison. Although his death sentence was commuted, Law escaped from prison (with the connivance of the authorities, according to Antoin Murphy) and eventually made his way to the other capital of the financial revolution, Amsterdam. Seeing a chance to influence economic policy in England and Scotland, Law returned to Edinburgh several years later and produced a pair of pamphlets in 1704 and 1705 that one scholar describes as the first articulation of demand and supply in modern economics.[7]

The gist of his theory—clearly reflected in the title of the 1705 pamphlet, *Money and Trade Considered, with a Proposal for Supplying the Nation with Money*—was that the amount of trade in a given nation depended crucially on the availability (supply) of money. Law's pamphlets sought to persuade the English and Scottish parliaments (prior to the 1707 Act of Union that created Britain) to establish land banks. According to Law, history taught that commerce flourished where money was freely available. In particular, fiat paper money offered an answer to the persistent shortcomings of a specie-based, commodity money system. Law made the case for land banks as institutions that could solve the problem of money's scarcity by injecting paper money (banknotes) into the economy. By 1705, then, one of the central intellectual premises of what would become the System was already in place. It remained for Law to identify a sovereign willing to put his theory to the test.[8]

After his proposals failed to command a receptive audience in either London or Edinburgh, Law again crossed the channel in 1706 hoping to pitch his ideas to continental ministers of finance. Louis XIV's death in 1715, which brought to power a regency government headed by the late monarch's younger brother, the Duc d'Orléans, created the political dislocation that Law's approach seemed to require. Law managed to persuade the regent to hand him, one by one, the levers that amounted to near-total control over the French economy and state within the space of a few short years. Although Law may have had a grand conception of his ultimate design from the very beginning, the pieces of his plan were put into place only gradually. In May 1716, he received approval from the regent for a chartered, privately owned bank that would have a monopoly on the issuance of currency. Between the spring of 1716 and December 1718, Law's private Banque Générale was effectively nationalized and became the official (royal) bank of France, with exclusive control over the issuance of new money.[9]

From these banking origins, Law then branched out into the intertwined worlds of overseas colonization and international trade. He founded the Company of the West in 1717 by taking over its predecessor (Mississippi) company from the financier Antoine de Crozat. Both the South Sea Company, founded in 1711, and Crozat's company, chartered in 1712, anticipated Law's scheme of converting state debt into the private equity of a corporate monopoly—just as both enticed investors with images of the riches to be reaped by investing in the slave economy. Aiming to use the new Company of the West to catapult himself into the Louisiana tobacco industry and the Canadian fur trade, Law was granted a twenty-five year monopoly over the Louisiana and beaver trades and a dispensation to colonize and develop the lower Mississippi Valley. Colonization required colonists, however, and these were in especially short supply in 1717—notwithstanding a vigorous effort to paint the Louisiana territory as a resplendent paradise of unclaimed, fertile land, vast stores of gold, and cooperative natives. That few were actually tempted by the "vocabulary of the marvelous" (in Arnaud Orain's phrase) is clear from the phenomenon known to historians as the forced emigration, or transportation: the deportation of gens sans aveu (vagabonds or vagrants) and criminals to the colonies.[10]

Forced emigration was designed to purge the metropole of its most "troublesome" and disadvantaged elements: the errant (because homeless and unemployed) poor, defined in terms of their propensity to engage in conduct classified as criminal. Beginning in the late seventeenth century, thousands of vagrants came to Paris from the surrounding countryside, often fleeing poor harvests and famine. As of 1702, the city's mendicant population had reached nine thousand. Royal authorities responded by resorting to the traditional instruments of criminal punishment: prison and, for those repeatedly convicted of capital crimes, galley slave labor. Men whose death sentences had been commuted under the galley system were bound to each other by foot and marched from Paris to Marseille, where they were put to hard labor rowing the vessels that departed from France's southern port. By the end of the reign of Louis XIV, it was clear that the criminal justice system alone could not provide an answer to the problem of migrant poverty. Rather than address the problem of poverty itself, the monarchy turned to colonization as an alternative to incarceration.[11]

Louisiana offered an opportunity to solve two problems at once: the swelling vagabond population of the metropole and the dearth of willing applicants for the Mississippi colony. Between 1716 and 1720, hundreds of *gens sans aveu* and indentured criminals, including beggars, alleged prostitutes, salt smugglers, thieves, and others, were sent on company ships to help populate and provide menial labor in New Orleans. By 1720, the Louisiana colony had been so thoroughly defined in the popular imagination as a site of depravity and hopelessness that violent protests against the recruiters of forced emigration broke out in Paris and elsewhere. The monarchy responded by ordering the flow of unwanted persons to be redirected to the Antilles rather than the North American mainland. The years 1720–22 saw the apex of the forced emigration of indentured prisoners to Saint-Domingue. These deportees undoubtedly included some of the white women who would figure in the rebellion against the Indies Company.[12]

The effect on the social order in Saint-Domingue was soon apparent. In July 1722, the monarchy ordered an end to the transportation of "vagabonds and *gens sans aveu*" to the colonies. The latter's "indolence and bad mores," the royal declaration stated, had become incompatible with the "great number of families" that now voluntarily chose to take up residence in Saint-Domingue.[13] As in France, concern over vagabondage became a frequent refrain of administrative discourse in early-eighteenth-century Saint-Domingue.[14]

The Regency's willingness to gamble with these marginal lives for the sake of an unproven colonial experiment was of a piece with the ruthlessly acquisitive character of the System. In Law's conception of the System, only sudden, spectacular growth could bring its promise to fruition. And it was necessary to enact that growth along several different axes simultaneously—monetary, commercial, colonial, and financial—to achieve the immediate goal of dissolving the monarchy's debt and catapulting France into a position of unrivaled supremacy in Europe. The takeover model of mergers and acquisitions by which Law had come into the possession of Crozat's company was clearly the modus operandi of Law's new empire. But the sequence of takeovers, and their role in the inflation of the bubble, reveals a more distinctive pattern than is suggested by the image of random accumulation resulting in a "global" trading network.

Law correctly saw that by stitching together the various regional economies of the slave trade, he could create a behemoth that would appear to investors so profitable that it could not be resisted. And the only way to unite the slave trade was to transcend the old division of the world into an "east" and "west" Indies that had structured imperial thought since 1493, when the Treaty of Tordesillas sliced the globe into rival Spanish and Portuguese spheres of influence. The very name with which Law rechristened his enterprise in 1719—the "Indies" Company—defined the ambition. This was not to be a mere association of adventurers to either the East or West Indies alone, but a unification of

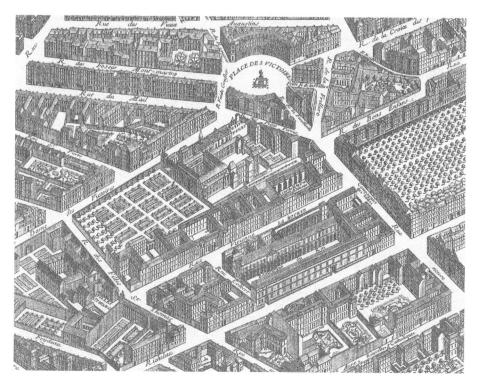

FIGURE 12. Detail showing the headquarters of the Indies Company at the corner of the rue Neuve des Petits Champs and the rue Vivienne, in Louis Bretez, "Plan de Paris" [the Turgot plan], planche 14, 1739. Courtesy of the Bibliothèque nationale de France.

the "two Indies" (to use the phrase the Abbé Raynal would later coin in the 1770s). From the vantage point of its headquarters on the rue Neuve des Petits Champs in Paris (figure 12), this corporate conglomerate would become the first truly global corporation.[15]

However global in nature, slavery and the slave trade remained integral to the overall design. One after the other, the companies that Law had targeted for acquisition were tied to slavery and the slave trade in some way. The institutions of the Atlantic economy—the Mississippi Company, the Senegal and Guinea companies, and the Saint-Domingue Company—clearly fall within this category. But the slave trade was also a critical component and extension of the East Indies trade. Law's investments in the coffee trade of Yemen, French trade in South Asia, and even trade with China were linked to the slave economy for at least two reasons. First, the French slave trade also operated on the east African coast. Second, French ships funneled Spanish silver around the

Cape of Good Hope to Asia in exchange for spices, cotton textiles, and cowry shells—which were then used along the west African coast to finance the Atlantic slave trade. When investors put their money into the Indies Company, therefore, they were betting on the future of Saint-Domingue as part of a larger bet on the future of the slave economy.[16]

In the early eighteenth century, global networks were no greater than the sum of their parts. Law placed a heavier emphasis on one node of the global slave-trading network—Saint-Domingue—than historians of the so-called Mississippi Bubble have recognized. The Mississippi Company itself was a mere starting point, one that, moreover, remained mostly inactive after its flotation in 1717.[17] Louisiana might have remained more integral to Law's vision of empire had it been capable of feeding the financial addictions that drove the growth of the System. By the end of the second decade of the eighteenth century, Saint-Domingue had already displaced Louisiana—and all other French colonies for that matter—as the territory that promised to provide Law with the greatest amount of leverage over the profits to be made from the international slave trade.

Saint-Domingue was the culmination of a process of building out the Mississippi venture that unfolded from late 1718 to the fall of 1720. During that period, Law added one corporation after another to his original entity, following the paths laid down by the divergent trade routes that linked the coasts of Africa to the rest of the world. Vertical integration of monetary, financial, and fiscal functions accompanied this horizontal commercial integration of the globe. In December 1718, Law acquired the Senegal Company, which enjoyed a monopoly on the slave trade along the west African coast north of the Sierra Leone River. By June 1719, the portfolio had expanded to include Colbert's former Company of the East Indies, the Company of China, and the Company of Africa (the latter chartered with a monopoly over the French trade with a pair of North African outposts located in what is now Algeria and Tunisia). In July, Law obtained a nine-year monopoly over the minting of new money. And in August, Law committed his Indies Company to the buyout of the entire French national debt, which had the additional, closely related consequence of making him the monarchy's tax collector in chief, responsible for roughly 90 percent of the nation's total revenues.[18]

The slave trading companies could not alone sustain the System, even when added to the profits to be derived from the tobacco and fur trades. And yet they were critical components of Law's larger design since they permitted him to crowd out the private slave traders of Nantes and other port cities of the Ponant. The acquisition of the Senegal Company's monopoly had accomplished this purpose for the region north of the Sierra Leone River, but not south. The aggressive lobbying campaign that Law mounted for the rights to the Guinea Company, which would shut out the Nantais merchants from the vast coastal region to the south, brought the process to a culmination in September 1720. With the monopoly on the entire French trade to the west coast of Africa, Law had not only secured a lock on the full profits to be reaped from the slave trade, he had established a bridge between the West and East Indies spheres of his empire.[19]

To finance the purchase of these privileges from the monarchy, Law carefully targeted Saint-Domingue as the commercial pivot on which his scheme depended, and the French royal bank as its financial engine. By the time Law's attentions came to focus on Saint-Domingue in the fall of 1719, the stock market was at the height of its speculative fever, and Law felt intense pressure to make these gains available to the largest possible number of subscribers. On September 13, he announced the first of two spectacularly large share offerings: one hundred thousand shares at a nominal value of five hundred livres (or fifty million livres in total) but a market price of five thousand livres (for a total of five hundred million livres). Law directed that payment for the September 13 issuance be received only in *billets d'états* (the bonds the monarchy had issued under the reign of Louis XIV to raise money for wartime expenses). The restriction had a dual purpose: furthering the conversion of high-interest-paying royal debt into corporate stock, and limiting the audience for the new shares to those who were already creditors of the monarchy. When demand for such a large volume of shares paying 4 percent dividends continued to prove robust, the company announced a second issue on September 28 of one hundred thousand shares on the same terms as the September 13 issue, again requiring payment in *billets d'état* unless the buyer was willing to pay a cash premium.[20]

This extravagant expansion of the market for Indies Company shares was tied to Law's expectation, or hope, that Saint-Domingue and the Royal Bank would vindicate and sustain the bull market. As Thomas Crawford, the secretary to the British ambassador to Paris, explained in a letter to James Craggs, the secretary of state for the Southern Department at the end of September, Law had been "[h]arassed by petitions and solicitations from all parts of the kingdom and from all sorts of people to be allowed to subscribe." By continuing to stoke this fever, Crawford correctly perceived, Law was entering into territory from which it would be difficult to recover. The market value of the original shares had now increased to five thousand livres, representing enormous capital gains for buyers who had entered the betting at only five hundred livres. To continue to attract more investors at the radically inflated September price, Crawford observed, Law

> will certainly be obliged at this occasion to throw in some new thing into the company by which it may appear that a great profit will arise to it,

otherwise the actions must certainly fall. By what I can judge from his discourse it will probably be the Banque and the island of St. Domingo which he'll get from the King. It if is so, they will acquire a great credit and really a great power, which ought to put all their neighbors upon thinking seriously of putting their affairs likewise in order, that they may not lie at the mercy of France which will in all human probability be more powerful in two years hence, then ever it was since it has been a kingdom.

This evocation of a dominant, debt-free French monarchy, capable of doing "easily things that appear to other nations miraculous," was of a piece with the zero-sum vision of Franco-British great power rivalry that dominated thinking on both sides of the English Channel at this time.[21]

And on both sides of the channel, that anxiety was wrapped up in expectations about the future of Saint-Domingue, in addition to the possibility that France might gain for itself a credible rival to the Bank of England. Crawford's information on this point was more than speculative. A native of Renfrewshire in western Scotland, he was not only a key member of the Scottish diaspora in Paris, but a British power broker who had Law's ear (and was personally indebted to him). In the same letter, Crawford reported a conversation directly with Law in the regent's box at the *Comédie Italienne* the previous week that, by contemporary standards, would almost certainly amount to insider trading. Indeed, Crawford had himself invested in the Indies Company, as had Secretary Craggs (whose father, Craggs the elder, would be altogether ruined by the Mississippi affair).[22]

In any case, investment in the Royal Bank and Saint-Domingue proved to be far more than the reflection of a Scottish diasporic rumor mill. In February 1720, with the incorporation of the bank into the Indies Company, Law was able to unite a fiscal quasi-monopoly with sole control over the French money supply, now denominated in units of account rather than silver coins and issued in notes of the Banque Royale. Law's position at the top of the nation's financial and economic pyramid was made official by his appointment the month before (January 1720) as controller general, or finance minister, of France, immediately following his conversion to the Roman Catholic rite.[23] Then, in September, came the culminating effort to fortify the System: the acquisition of the former Saint-Domingue Company and the Guinea Company. The latter meant that the Indies Company now had an exclusive privilege to the west African slave trade south of the Sierra Leone River all the way down to the Cape of Good Hope, and thus deep into what had traditionally between predominantly Portuguese slave trading territory. In conjunction with the Saint-Domingue privileges, this amounted to a full-scale embrace of the Atlantic slave economy. John Law's scheme to rescue the French monarchy from the debts of Louis XIV had now evolved irreversibly in the direction of a colonial System.

———

Speculative fever and a desire to capitalize on the riches to be made from the slave economy blinded the Indies Company to the difficulty of the path it faced in Saint-Domingue, strewn as it was with the cadavers of failed commercial monopolies. Before the final crash of late 1720, a timely implementation of Law's vision may still have seemed within reach. According to the original schedule, the company would have assumed control of Saint-Domingue and French commercial outposts along the entire west African coast before the end of 1720. This was the Afro-Caribbean linchpin of the scheme to unite the two Indies into a single commercial network. On September 10, 1720, the Conseil d'État approved Law's proposal to buy out the rights and settle the debts of the existing Company of Saint-Domingue for approximately six million livres tournois.[24] An independent group of private investors, acting on behalf of the Indies Company, was to pay six million livres to the notary Lefevre, who would distribute that amount among the directors and shareholders, with the balance used to pay off any of the company's remaining private debts incurred in France and elsewhere.[25] The Indies Company would also pay roughly fifty thousand livres directly to the crown for purposes of extinguishing the Saint-Domingue Company's royal debts.[26] These provisions foreshadowed the imminent bankruptcy of John Law's own company, as well as the plight of its reign in Saint-Domingue.

But the company had some bona fide reasons for banking on the success of its gamble in Saint-Domingue. First, where the Saint-Domingue Company had lacked a fleet of vessels sufficient to sustain an expanding trade in both slaves and Caribbean raw goods, the Indies Company would bring economies of scale, vast resources, and a seamless network of interconnected hubs.[27] These assets were premised on a new and special relationship with the French state. Granting the Saint-Domingue monopoly to the Indies Company made sense not only because of the "considerable funds" at its disposal, but also because it was fair to give preference to a "public Company" over private individuals (*particuliers*), a company in which "the majority of His Majesty's Subjects are invested, and which His Majesty regards as the most important institution (*établissement*) of the State."[28]

Second, the new company was exempt from export duties for any goods generated by the labor of slaves brought to Saint-Domingue by the company. This arrangement effectively incorporated into the company's tax advantage an incentive to expand the scope of its participation in the slave trade.[29]

Third, the company would enjoy an "exclusive privilege" in Saint-Domingue. The term "monopoly" is of limited use in capturing the company's new position. Strictly speaking, its exclusive privilege to trade with the French colony was limited to the southern territory that it controlled outright. That is, the company had the authority to prohibit private French traders from landing ships on the southern coast and to ban planters in the southern territory from exporting colonial goods on any other than a company ship. The territorial character of this authority was conspicuous. As the creole jurist Moreau de Saint-Méry reminded his readers at the end of the eighteenth century, the *arrêt* of September 10, 1720, gave the company the authority to sell for its own profit any terrain not previously conceded to local planters by the Saint-Domingue Company. Moreover, the privilege vested the Indies Company with the right to enter and occupy any uncleared lands. These commercial and territorial powers flowed from the act subrogating the Indies Company to the rights and privileges of the Saint-Domingue Company as formalized in its 1698 charter.[30]

The resentment created by these prerogatives remained alive and well even after the Saint-Domingue Company had ceded them to John Law. In April 1721, arsonists set fire to the warehouses of the defunct Saint-Domingue Company in the southern port of Jacmel.[31] That same month, the head of the Conseil de Marine, Louis-Antoine de Bourbon, the Maréchal d'Estrées, ordered the administrators of Saint-Domingue to provide "all manner of protection" to one of the Indies Company's incoming agents, a ship officer by the name of Gaultier. Alluding to the company's new charter, the Maréchal explained:

> The changes that have occurred give reason to fear that the Company's ships may be exposed to a lack of assistance (*secours*) upon putting in to port at Le Cap, assistance that they may need all the more given the Conseil has been informed that the inhabitants of this place are ill intentioned toward the business of the Company.

To provide local residents with an incentive to cooperate with Gaultier, the commissioners of the reorganized company in Paris assured the minister that colonists who agreed to supply the arriving ships with their needs "will be well paid." These precautions show that, by 1721 at least, royal officials and company administrators were becoming more realistic about the company's prospects, even if they could hardly have anticipated the full scope of the storm to come.[32]

Control of the slave trade to Saint-Domingue—the company's fourth and final advantage compared to its predecessors—proved to be the decisive factor in the new regime. Law's acquisition of the Guinea Company, less than three weeks after acquiring the Saint-Domingue privilege, would give the Indies Company permanent authority over a newly unified French slave trade, one no longer divided between different companies and territories or dependent on the largesse of the Spanish crown.[33] More than any other area of colonial policy, the slave trade reveals that even as the French state was yielding ever greater control of the economy to John Law, it was not abandoning the tenets of mercantilist capitalism altogether. In the tradition of Richelieu and Colbert, the French monarchy had empowered commercial companies not simply to enrich themselves, but to expand the nation's economy and enhance the state vis-à-vis its major competitors, Holland and England.[34]

The terms of the license reflected both the mercantilist legacy and concern to satisfy local planter demand for an adequate supply of forced labor. The heart of the company's "exclusive privilege" was the right to import thirty thousand Africans (*nègres*) from "foreigners" on a tax-free basis for a period of fifteen years. The privilege was good for the entirety of Saint-Domingue, not just the southern peninsula, but it was limited to the island of Saint-Domingue only (a gesture to the concerns of planters in other French Caribbean islands). At two thousand enslaved persons per year, this was not, according to the expectations of the local planter community, an especially demanding quota. But the privilege also had a sunset clause attached to it: if the company reached its cap of thirty thousand imported Africans before fifteen years had passed, its right to import slaves on an exclusive basis would expire and private traders could step in to fill the gap.[35] In a sign of just how closely the colonial administration sought to monitor the ongoing contraband slave trade to Saint-Domingue, the privilege also included a condition on the resale of Africans imported by the Indies Company: no such resale could occur without the seller producing an invoice showing that he had payed the company full price for the slave. And the company itself was required to pay for all imports of African captives either in metropolitan merchandise legally imported from France or in molasses produced in Saint-Domingue. In short, the company enjoyed, as of September 1720, what we might call a privilege to provide: a right coupled with a duty that local colonists would have no trouble understanding, by the fall of 1722, as a simple, perfidious monopoly.[36]

———

Many North Atlantic hopes evaporated during the years between 1720 and 1722, but somehow, the notion that the Indies Company would play a major role in the future of Saint-Domingue remained. What happened during these years is, in part, the story of a massive reaction to the bursting of the Mississippi and South Sea bubbles. The recriminations and the alienation unfolded in Paris and London, where efforts to hold those responsible for the crash were protracted and fraught. But the reaction took hold also in Saint-Domingue, Louisiana, Jamaica, and a host of other overseas territories that have not conventionally been understood as part of the first major financial crisis of the

North Atlantic. The financial wreckage not only delayed implementation of the System in Saint-Domingue; it radicalized opposition to the rule of the Indies Company and the monopoly joint-stock company generally.

Metropolitan intellectual reactions fed directly into some of the great motifs of the Enlightenment. A very small part of this early Enlightenment reaction centered on the Indies Company's complicity with slavery. The Abbé Joseph Lambert, a priest and lecturer at the Sorbonne and Prior of St. Martin de Palaiseau (near Versailles), wrote a scathing denunciation of Law's enterprise just as speculation in Indies stock was rising to feverishly high levels in the early months of 1720.[37] Lambert dutifully subjected the bubble to a "theological decision" condemning both its "injustices" and "inequities" in ancient Christian terms that evoked the sins of luxury and financial excess.

The key to this critique was its emphasis on the share itself as an expression of complicity with the slave trade, a theme that lends Lambert's text a distinctly modern note. "[I]n the language of commerce," Lambert explained, a share (*action*) is "a right that one acquires to share the profits that can flow from a particular business; whence it is apparent that a share places us in society with a number of persons who acquire, with us, one or more actions."[38] The share, in other words, draws the investor into a relationship of profit and loss with the company's business. And that relationship had especially pronounced moral implications where the business in question encompassed the commodification of human beings. Lambert's discussion of the slave trade opened by referencing the December 1718 and May 1719 edicts merging the Senegal, East India, and China companies with the Company of the West (to form the new Indies Company). Such a combination permitted France to extend its trade "to the four corners of the world," in the words of the preamble to the May 1719 edict.[39] But it was felt most powerfully by the people living in one particular region (west Africa) who were subjected to this commerce:

> The buying and selling of men . . . accord poorly with the Christian religion. The invasion of lands and countries occupied by other men, the violence, the extortion, the fraud and shock inflicted by the Company's clerks is the profit that reverts to the Company.

Investors with the fear of God in them would recognize that, just as they were liable as shareholders for any embezzlement that occurs within the company, they were responsible for renouncing any dividends derived from such injustice and theft. Thus, although a potential investor had multiple reasons to abstain from the Indies Company craze, avoiding complicity with slavery was an independent and sufficient reason for putting one's money elsewhere.[40] Lambert's brand of socially responsible investing did not merely reflect a set of theological commitments. Other forms of Judeo-Christian theology could just as easily be used to defend slavery and social hierarchy.[41] And

FIGURE 13. Bernard Picart, "Monument consacré à la postérité en mémoire de la folie incroyable de la XX année du XVIII siècle," from *Het groote tafereel der dwaarsheid* (1720). Courtesy of Baker Library Special Collections and Archives, Harvard Business School, Cambridge, MA.

some critics of the System saw the crash as a revelation of the dangers of a society based on absolute faith—whether faith in monarchy, money, or the church. In this view, the bubbles were more than a financial crisis in the narrow sense of the term. They were revolutions in a social order that had hitherto seemed permanent. After the crash, the rich were not destined to remain forever rich, and the poor could hold out hopes of escaping the ranks of the destitute.

A case in point is the famous 1720 engraving based on a print by the French Huguenot publisher Bernard Picart titled "Monument Consecrated to Posterity in Memory of the Incredible Folly of the Twentieth Year of the Eighteenth Century." Picart had invested heavily in bubble companies, but he cashed out his shares just in time to avoid going bust in the crash. His image appeared anonymously in *Het groote tafereel der dwaarsheid* (*The Great Mirror of Folly*), a widely distributed 1720 collection of Dutch engravings lampooning John Law and the South Sea Company (figure 13). The lengthy caption (written in French and in Dutch) explains that the scene depicts Fortuna, the goddess of shares (*actions*), standing on a cart driven by Madness (*folie*, represented by a clown). The cart is pulled along by a group of variously costumed individuals symbolizing the different companies responsible for "this pernicious trade," including the South Sea and Mississippi companies at the head of the parade (the latter represented by an Indian figure). At the top center, Satan presides over the chaotic scene, blowing soap bubbles that mix with the disastrous stocks and options held out by Fortuna. From the overhanging clouds descend snakes representing "fevers," "despair," "debt," and "sadness." Beneath the weight of Fortuna's cart, meanwhile, "true commerce" (*le véritable Commerce*) lies with its books and merchandise, "overthrown" and "nearly crushed" to death. Oblivious to the warning signs, Fortuna leads the entire assembly toward one of three doors in the rear left background that denote hospitals (*hôpitaux*) for the mad, the sick, and the destitute (*gueux*, or beggars). At top right, the label "Quinquenpoix" (a Dutch variant of Quincampoix) removes any doubt that we are indeed witnessing a society undergoing the moral meltdown that is John Law's System.[42]

Montesquieu's great portrait of Law in the *Persian Letters* (1721) evoked a similar fate while amplifying the image of a social order turned on its head. In his fictional letters on the System, written in the voice of two Persian visitors to Regency France named Rica and Usbek, the Bordeaux magistrate has Rica profess shock at seeing rich and poor trade places with one fell swing of the stock market. "Everyone who was rich six months ago is now in poverty, and those who had no bread then are gorged with riches. Never have the two extremes been so close." Such a radical reversal of the traditional hierarchy was all the more astonishing for having been the work of a "foreigner," John Law, who managed, essentially single-handedly, to "turn [the state] inside out and put the top to the bottom." If the fall of the wealthy from grace was perhaps the most conspicuous feature of this upheaval, the prospect of valets being served by their former masters added insult to injury. "The effects of all this are quite extraordinary. Footmen who made their fortunes under the last reign nowadays boast of their lineage."[43]

Other accounts championed vengeance and commercial liberty as answers to the sins of monopoly and speculation. In a series of newspaper essays between the fall of 1720 and the end of 1723 known as *Cato's Letters*, John Trenchard and Thomas Gordon mounted a direct, bloodthirsty assault on the directors of the South Sea Company. Only the ultimate sanction for "blood-suckers and traitors" could restore the public credit of Britain. In August 1722—nearly two years after the South Sea experiment had reached its disastrous denouement—Trenchard penned two missives denouncing "[m]onopolies and exclusive companies" as "pernicious to Trade" and injurious to the British constitution. Great combinations of merchants distorted the social and political equilibrium of a free state—none more so than the South Sea Company.[44]

In all of these accounts, the story of imperial decline had an unmistakable institutional nexus in the giant monopoly enterprises—the British East India, South Sea, and French Indies companies—with which the generation of Lambert, Picart, Montesquieu, Trenchard, and Gordon had come of age. The result was an understanding of despotic commercial and political power that circulated widely on both sides of the eighteenth-century Atlantic economy. The dysfunctional examples of John Law and the South Sea experiment set the tone and defined the agenda for radical opponents of monopoly trade everywhere from Saint-Domingue in the 1720s to North America in the 1770s and France of the 1780s.[45]

In the immediate aftermath of the crash, the key challenge centered on how to assign responsibility for the financial cataclysm wrought by these monopolies. The earliest answers to this challenge came out of Britain, even before the South Sea Bubble had burst (and where the crisis caused comparably less devastation than in France). The so-called Bubble Act, which received the royal assent on June 11, 1720, required parliamentary authorization for the formation of new joint-stock companies. The purpose was to protect the company's privileged place on the London stock market in the face of a flurry of new joint-stock companies hoping to partake of the bull market. The popular outcry that followed the bursting of the bubble led Parliament to appoint a secret committee to investigate the actions of the South Sea Company's directors and officers, of whom the most notorious were the former cashier Robert Knight (who took flight and would be arrested as a fugitive from justice) and the director John Blunt, whose flagrant bribery of government officials and shameless boosterism of the company's prospects even after the tide had turned had made him a special target of popular ire. Parliament eventually enacted a statute providing for the confiscation of the profits made by the company's directors during the course of the bubble.[46]

On the other side of the channel, John Law's flight from France made accountability a more complicated matter. For the second time in his life, John Law had managed to escape from the scene of the crime with the connivance of the authorities. At the beginning of December 1720, Law held his final meeting with the Duc d'Orléans, this time to request safe passage out of France. Although denouncing Law to courtiers as a "scoundrel who had tricked him," d'Orléans agreed to provide the passport, and Law promptly made his way to London. There he began to plot his political resurrection by asking for (and receiving) a royal pardon for the 1694 killing of Edmund Wilson. From London it was on to Venice, where the disgraced controller general arrived in January 1721, and where he would live, on and off, until his death eight years later—not before boldly conspiring (in 1723) to return to power in France.[47]

The French Indies Company, for its part, was placed under an extended period of royal receivership following the crash, from April 1721 to March 1723. To stem the tide of popular outrage and restore the credibility of the public debt, the regency government enacted a massive, remarkably ambitious effort known as the Visa of 1721. Placed under the leadership of the Paris brothers— longtime royal financiers and rivals of John Law with strong connections to the court in Versailles—the Visa aimed to discount the various liabilities and instruments issued under the System and then exchange them (at their reduced value) for government bonds. Since the government would now have responsibility for the interest payments on these liabilities and instruments, it was critical that the overall debt level assumed by the monarchy at the end of the Visa not exceed the government's ability to cover interest payments on that debt. The Paris brothers satisfied this requirement by capping the debt at the level of service that had obtained as of 1718, before the System, to wit, forty million livres in annual interest.[48]

From the individual investor's side of things, the liquidation process could look very different depending on the particular financial instrument at issue. The Visa subjected three broad categories of assets to the revaluation process (corresponding to the three institutions at the center of the System): notes of the Banque Royale, shares in the Indies Company, and crown bonds issued in June 1720 in an attempt to reverse Law's debt conversion scheme. Accordingly, holders of Banque Royale notes and Indies Company shares could present their titles to one of the eight liquidation *bureaux* installed in the royal palace at the Louvre. (Provincial asset holders were directed to present their claims to agents of the intendant appointed in the relevant province.) In exchange for her original notes and shares, the claimant would receive a liquidation certificate worth some percentage of the initial investment—usually a significantly reduced percentage—that varied depending on the circumstances in which the instrument was first acquired. Not every investor was happy with the results, unsurprisingly, and to appease some in this group, the Paris brothers authorized a supplementary process that two of the twenty-four liquidation commissioners exploited to fabricate false certificates for sale on the secondary market. All documentation relating to the Visa was placed into a massive bonfire in October 1722 so as to preserve the "secret of families."[49]

By this means, the extant royal debt, which had been entirely consolidated in Law's System, was partly written off and set on a new footing that allowed the wheels of the French financial system to move forward once again. As to the Indies Company itself, the government followed a less decisive path. Initially, the company was made liable for the debts of the Banque Royale (which had been merged with the company in 1718). The regency later reversed course once it became clear that the company would not survive under such a burden. For even after redeeming its liabilities with the government under the Visa of 1721, the company remained indebted to the monarchy for 580 million livres, an amount that would later (in 1725) be forgiven in its entirety. On these reconstructed terms, and under royal receivership, the Indies Company was allowed to resume its path as a commercial rather than financial company. This left the company active in all of the markets to which it had been granted exclusive access under John Law, from Louisiana in the west all the way to Canton in the east.[50]

That very much included Saint-Domingue. There and elsewhere in the French Atlantic world, investors willing to overlook the company's vices when it flourished were less tolerant of Law's excesses when they translated into personal indebtedness. The crash that brought the System tumbling down over the course of the second half of 1720 reverberated not only throughout the metropole but also overseas. Just as the System was deeply invested in slavery, the economy of slavery was heavily invested in the System. Through familial, commercial, and financial ties, the planters of the French Caribbean colonies were already assuming that intimate relationship to the towns of the Ponant that would define the colonial agenda for the rest of the eighteenth century.

Using the wealth they had accrued from the rise of the sugar industry in Saint-Domingue during the opening decades of the eighteenth century, these planters had managed to become significant investors in the Indies Company. Charlevoix's 1730–31 history was perhaps the first published account to note the impact of the crash on the French Caribbean planter elite.[51] Some of these planters, he suggested, had managed to take up residence in France during the upswing of Law's System, only to find themselves unable to support a metropolitan lifestyle on the down cycle. Having made their way back, in desperation, to Saint-Domingue, these erstwhile colonial grandees, many of them at an advanced age, found themselves lucky to find work as mid-level employees on plantations they once might have owned. Charlevoix implied that these economic and financial refugees from the System formed part of an increasingly disgruntled and restless population that was in no mood to commune further with the representatives of Law's failed experiment in financial engineering.[52]

Charlevoix's suggestive remarks about the impact of the bubble in Saint-Domingue find some empirical support in modern scholarship produced in the 1950s. This body of work emphasizes the quite temporary but massive increase in liquidity ushered in by Law's System. The most conspicuous mechanism of this increased liquidity was the proliferation of banknotes that Law hoped would give France a widely circulating paper currency for the first time. As a result of this newly available credit, imports from Saint-Domingue to France tripled between 1718–20, in many cases without corresponding returns of metropolitan goods and supplies. Indeed, even after the crash of 1720, colonial trade continued its upward march unperturbed for some time. As Robert Lacombe explains, the resulting imbalance of payments was an exceptional situation; at nearly every other moment of the eighteenth century, Saint-Domingue planters were the debtors and French merchants the creditors.[53]

The mechanism for mediating and ultimately resolving this imbalance of payments was Law's Banque Royale. Headquartered in Paris, the bank had established five branches in different parts of the kingdom, including one (founded in December 1718) in La Rochelle, a major Atlantic trading port beginning in the second half of the seventeenth century. Although the bank's archives have been lost, notarial documents have survived that reveal the nature of the commercial relationships handled through this branch, which included critical transactions with the French Caribbean islands. Marcel Delafosse has patiently reconstructed the story that these documents tell of the flow of payments between Saint-Domingue and the metropole. When public confidence in Law's System began to crumble in early 1720, Rochelais merchants, seeking to forestall losses, suddenly sought to pay off their Atlantic debts by redeeming their holdings of Banque Royale notes at the La Rochelle branch in payment of their obligations to Saint-Domingue planters. Residing as they did at such distance from the scene of the metropolitan financial cataclysm, colonial planters were all too unaware of the precipitous collapse in the value of Law's banknotes. They suddenly found themselves creditors of large sums expressed in banknotes held on the books of the La Rochelle bank. Denominated in the *écu* units of Banque Royale money, these notes had lost a quarter of their face value and now paid only trivial amounts of interest.[54]

The reactions ranged from resignation and despair to anger and nonimportation (a tactic that the American colonists would take up in the years after the Stamp Act of 1765). On the one hand, Caribbean planters were in no position to seek immediate legal or financial redress in the metropole for their losses. As Charlevoix's account of forlorn planters returning in tatters to Saint-Domingue in 1721 reminds us, for many of these men the immediate task was simply to find gainful employment:

> After twenty or thirty years of labor in a boiling climate, having flattered themselves that they would be able to enjoy wealth in their homeland,

which they had acquired by the sweat of their brow, [they] found themselves forced to return poor to a colony from which they had departed most opulent, and all too happy to find at the age of sixty years a position as bursar or steward.

At the same time, the colonists believed themselves to have been hoodwinked by metropolitan merchants with much easier access to the banking system and greater ability to manipulate notarial services. Saint-Domingue planters laid low by the Mississippi Bubble, seeking revenge in the only way left to them, managed to organize a boycott of metropolitan goods that lasted several years and succeeded in triggering a number of significant French mercantile bankruptcies. Blaming Ponant merchants for the sins of John Law and the regent who had so cavalierly enabled him was the understandable response of those who, cut off from the legal machinery of reparation in France, faced a limited set of options to assert their interests.[55]

———

For all of these reasons, the arrival of the French Indies Company at Cap Français in the late fall of 1722 could not have come at a "less favorable conjuncture," as Charlevoix put it.[56] The writing was indeed on the wall of any attempt to implement a monopoly on the slave trade to Saint-Domingue at this late date, given all that had transpired over the preceding years and decades. But how exactly was a monopoly in the area of the slave trade supposed to work as a matter of institutional practice? And why the delay between the initial grant of the privilege and its enactment in Saint-Domingue?

Research by Robert Louis Stein and, more recently, Robert Harms on the early-eighteenth-century French slave trade sheds light on these questions. The disarray introduced by the collapse of the System, followed by the experience of liquidation and corporate reorganization, undoubtedly account for at least some of the time lag between 1720 and 1722. The lack of financial resources may have been compounded by concern that the company would likely receive a hostile reception from the Saint-Domingue colonists.[57] But another part of the answer—perhaps the major part—has to do with how and why the Indies Company continued to negotiate with and rely on private traders even in the era of the new privilege.

John Law's acquisition of the Senegal and Guinea privileges augured a restoration of the monopoly era following the short-lived decision to open the French slave trade to private merchants beginning in 1713. Indeed, the Guinea privilege brought with it not only an exemption from the private trader tax of twenty livres per captive, but also an affirmative bonus of thirteen livres for each captive successfully delivered to the French Caribbean colonies.[58] That a return to the pre-1713 regime did not result has much to do with the limitations on the Indies Company's own shipping capacities and the effectiveness of the private traders' lobbying campaign. In 1718–19, the company resorted to commissioning merchants from Saint Malo and La Rochelle to help it fit out its slave ships.[59] The collapse of 1720 did not entirely negate the company's capacity to engage in slave trading or merchant shipping more generally. Between January 1 and April 15, 1721, the company dispatched from Lorient seven ships to make the Senegal-Antilles-Louisiana circuit, two for the East Indies, and one for China.[60] In total, thirteen slave ships were sent out during the company's first two years. But these numbers were clearly inadequate to meet the quota of two thousand slaves per year specified in the Guinea privilege, and they were made to seem all the worse in light of the ongoing campaign of the private traders. The company was therefore compelled to issue permissions to the *négociants* (and to those of Nantes especially) to help fill the gap in supply. The arrangement required the private traders to pay twenty livres for each captive delivered to the islands, an amount that was cut back to ten livres in 1720. Nantes alone supplied seventeen expeditions in 1720, another twenty-four in 1721, and twelve in 1722.[61] In this way, by fits and starts, a hybrid public-private slave trading operation had resumed the course that the regency had begun to set with the return of peace to Europe after 1713.

Meanwhile, the company's monopoly privileges in West Africa and the Caribbean remained on the books, there to be activated if and when the right moment arrived. That moment came in the late fall of 1722, by which time the company had managed to increase its shipping capacity to the point that it could fulfill independently the quotas envisioned in the September 1720 Guinea privilege. The company's slaving voyages increased by orders of magnitude after January 1, 1723, when the directors stopped issuing permissions to private traders. On the order of sixty company slave vessels departed France for west Africa, the Caribbean, and Louisiana over the next few years.[62] These were, indeed, the peak years of the slave trade to Louisiana, whose slave population grew during the 1720s at a rate not paralleled either before or after.[63] The ships that carried out this belated implementation of the company's monopoly were not just any vessels, moreover: averaging about three hundred tons, they held more than double the cargo of the typical private ship.[64]

Charlevoix was therefore entirely correct when he observed that the arrival of the Indies Company in the fall of 1722 could not have come at a more unstable time. But, in fact, there was an additional reason for the colonists to resent the coming of Law's System, and it turned out to be perhaps the most important one.

On August 3, 1722, the regency attempted once again to step into the fray of the colony's money troubles. In what amounted to an act of extraordinarily inept timing, the ordinance (translated and reproduced in full in the appendix) diminished the value of the silver and gold coins in use in the French West Indies. Unlike the company's slave trading privilege, the money ordinance was not part of the System per se. But it followed in a long line of previous state efforts to manipulate the value of money. And Law's program of substituting paper money for coin created an environment in which the new measure quickly became identified with the company's special dispensation in Saint-Domingue.

How exactly the ordinance worked made all the difference in this respect. First, the measure specified that full-weight piastres and pistoles would trade for seven pounds ten sous and thirty pounds, respectively. By itself, this was not particularly disturbing from the colonists' point of view. The eight livre value of 1721 was already a bit of an outlier artificially stimulated by the rise and fall of John Law. Nor were the next two articles necessarily controversial on their own terms: the full-weight piastre was defined as nine to the mark of Troyes (or 0.89 ounces of silver per piastre) and the full-weight pistole as thirty-six and a quarter to the mark (or 0.22 ounces of silver for one gold pistole). But why the need for all these references to weight given that Saint-Domingue gave its coins currency by tale? Articles 6 and 7 contained the explosive answer to that question: piastres and pistoles that were not full weight "will also trade, but only for the value of the (metal) material that they contain," in light of the prices set in the previous articles for the full-weight coins. The monarchy had suddenly outlawed the local practice of giving silver and gold coins currency by tale (i.e., by count), in a colony whose only real access to these coins was in their clipped or diluted forms. Immediately, the buying power of the colonists had been drastically diminished.[65]

The distinctiveness of this manner of diminution is worth placing in context. Even setting aside the extreme shifts of the John Law period, monetary revaluations were nothing new in late-seventeenth- and early-eighteenth-century France. Guy Rowlands has tracked some forty-three revaluations in the three and a half decades following 1689. Over these years, the metropole's own total silver supply declined from about 18 million *marcs*, the equivalent of 500–550 million livres, to 13.5 million *marcs* (about 474 million livres). At least some of this decline was owed to speculative and fraudulent coin movement into and out of the kingdom. As the Velde/Sargent model predicts, the government of Louis XIV responded to depleting silver stores with an effort to augment the unit of account, the livre tournois, by devaluing the silver coin in circulation within France itself. These measures were corollaries of the mercantilist practice of seigniorage—the charge the government earned for reprocessing coins at the mint—but they also aimed to reduce the de facto size of the royal debt (insofar as the king's liabilities were contracted in livres).[66]

On occasion, the monarchy picked an especially bad moment for such adjustments. In 1740, for example, an ill-timed currency manipulation had the effect of multiplying unrest caused by food shortages of that year.[67] But the very frequency of these monetary debasements in the years after 1689 gave them an almost routine character, as if they were part of the general economic background rather than exceptional adjustments designed to keep the ship of state afloat. The terms of transactions were being blown apart throughout Louis XIV's realm during this period, eroding the foundations of trust in government and in the value of contracts.

The August 1722 ordinance was nonetheless quite distinctive in purporting to eliminate the autonomy the colonists enjoyed over their local currency and rendering that currency nearly worthless. If small change was a big problem even in a large kingdom, it was an altogether more daunting challenge in the tightly concentrated space of Saint-Domingue, where the problem of how to pay for enslaved persons produced an especially brittle and volatile economic climate. That climate had much in common with other Caribbean and metropolitan societies of the time. But one aspect of it remains unexplained: Why, exactly, were French merchants so insistent on taking payment in metal coin?

Elsewhere in the Atlantic world, as Jacob Price reminds us, "cash purchases" did not necessarily entail the use of coin. They could also involve colonial commodities or, especially, letters of exchange (*lettres de change*). As we have seen, for purposes such as paying the wages of indentured servants, tobacco and other goods were widely used as currency in Saint-Domingue until 1715. But French merchants mostly rejected payment in kind when it came to slaves, despite administrative efforts to force them to accept it. As for letters of exchange, which were widely used in the late-seventeenth- and early-eighteenth-century British slave trade, there is some evidence of French slave traders using them on an experimental basis. Because of the letters' high nonacceptance rates in the metropole, however, French merchants soon came to avoid their use.[68]

These logistical concerns were amplified by the complicated legal framework for debt collection created by the 1685 Code Noir. Although the code defined slaves as movable property (*meubles*) and thus subject to seizure in payment of debt, the code and related legislation also created a number of exceptions to this general rule. Wives could not be separated from their husbands or children, and individual slaves between the ages of fourteen and sixty could not be seized unless the entire plantation on which they worked was seized as real property— unless the enslaved person was being seized for nonpayment of his or her purchase price (*prix de leur achat*). As Price explains, in theory that last exception protected the vendors of newly acquired slaves in Saint-Domingue, but in practice it was rarely enforced. This made French merchants less willing to extend credit in connection with the sale of enslaved persons.[69]

Credit was undergoing a major shift in Saint-Domingue at the time of the 1720 crisis. In the run-up to the Mississippi Bubble, it was planters rather than metropolitan merchants who held the upper hand in most commercial transactions. The crash reversed the creditor-debtor relationship between colonists and French merchants, making debtors out of the former and creditors out of the latter. Given the limitations of specie in Saint-Domingue and the profit incentives of the slave trade, reliance upon credit in some form was inevitable.

Indeed, in the years after 1720, credit became one of the great engines of the expansion of the eighteenth-century plantation system in Saint-Domingue. But the mechanics of this credit system remained primitive relative to British methods, which came to center on the use of factors (merchants who received Caribbean produce in the metropole and sold it on commission for planters in the colonies). French merchant houses, by contrast, favored using ship captains rather than factors to execute sales of captives. The typical slaving vessel would often leave one of its two captains behind in Saint-Domingue for more than a year to attend to the messy work of collecting planter debts. Debt collection became a pervasive problem, but the profits to be made from the slave trade sufficed to make the inconveniences and the potential for default seem like a part of the overall cost of doing business in Saint-Domingue.[70]

———

The System failed for many reasons, but above all because it could not solve the problem of debt. In fact, it greatly magnified the scope of debt in France and its empire, for the state and individuals alike, in the process making debt a permanent legacy of the Old Regime. The colonial nature of the System was central to this fate. In conjunction with the other nodes of the System, Louisiana and Saint-Domingue were supposed to jumpstart the French Atlantic economy and subsidize the financial revolution in the metropole. Ultimately, Saint-Domingue, at least, would do just this—but not on John Law's timeline. In the early 1720s, the effort to harness the colony to a debt-relief scheme for the French monarchy served primarily to accelerate the sugar revolution in Saint-Domingue.

That revolution itself was fueled by the debts of many individual colonists, many of them incurred in the cause of accumulating sufficient forced labor to reap the benefits of large-scale sugar cultivation. Debt signified dependence, and the problems associated with the colony's money supply aggravated that sense of subordination to the interests of the metropole. A series of uncoordinated measures that sought to stabilize the economy of Saint-Domingue left settlers there with the impression of a concerted conspiracy to perpetuate debt in the name of monopoly.

The reception of these measures in Saint-Domingue involved a society undergoing sudden demographic change. The System's own effort to remake the demography of France had injected a disaffected population of white women and vagabonds in the colony on the eve of the Indies Company's arrival. These very recent immigrants, along with a rapidly expanding group of free people of color and a growing Jesuit community, amplified the instability associated with the racial transformation of Saint-Domingue into a full-fledged slave society. The result was a colony poised for several kinds of revolt at once, not all of which could be easily distinguished from the others.

3

"Women, Negroes, and Unknown, Unimportant People"

IN HIS 1960 book *Crowds and Power*, Elias Canetti analyzed money's profound capacity to stir crowds to action. His primary point of reference was the 1923 hyperinflation in Weimar Germany, which, he argued, led the people of Germany to feel that they themselves were depreciating. Personal identity became an extension of the decreasing value of money. In that context, joining a crowd was a way to overcome the diminution of one's worth as an individual. Tragically, these crowd movements ended up targeting Jews—as if they were somehow specially exempted from the effects of hyperinflation—and ultimately facilitated the collapse of the Weimar democracy. Classifying the crowds that have formed over the course of human history in the shadow of inflation and monetary devaluation according to their prevailing emotions, Canetti identified baiting and flight as the dominant psychological responses.[1]

Canetti's analysis captures some important aspects of the story of monetary devaluation in Saint-Domingue in the 1720s. Historical events like the storming of the Bastille or the mass protests in Weimar Germany are indeed characterized by heightened emotion of one sort or another, as William Sewell has observed.[2] In the administrative parlance of Old Regime France, however, an event like the attack on the Indies Company in 1722 was seen as an *émotion* in itself.[3] To encourage the "unimportant people" (*menu peuple*) in their agitation against the Indies Company was to "move" or incite (*émouvoir*) the people.[4] This evocative terminology has a long history of association with popular revolt. The word *émotion* was derived, around 1475, from *émouvoir*, itself a derivative of the Latin *motio*, which connoted both movement and "trouble." By the early sixteenth century, emotion had come to signify trouble in the sense of "sedition"; Furetière's dictionary of 1690 indicates that the term designated especially the beginning of a seditious movement or uprising. The French word for riot—*émeute*—bears the traces of this etymology, and indeed it, too, became part of the conversation around the events of fall 1722, used by none other than the settlers of Cap Français.[5]

A now extensive historical literature on popular riots in early modern France emphasizes the role of women as "moral guardians of the community, egging on the men by screaming 'this isn't right.'" The large contingents of women in early modern riots, William Beik writes, were "less recognizable to the authorities and less subject to serious prosecution."[6] As such, they tended to leave few traces in the archives. That very archival invisibility is, in a way, the historical marker of those denigrated as "unimportant people" in prerevolutionary France. The crowd emotions of which they were a part left a large mark; the individuals themselves, not so much.

One such individual, a woman known only as La Sagona, entered the pages of French history on the night of November 21–22 in a remote corner of the Bourbon empire. Soon to be solemnized in song as a new Joan of Arc, she was a former *comédienne* who had left France with her husband to pursue a fortune in Saint-Domingue.[7] In eighteenth-century France, the term *comédienne* held a range of meanings, from professional actress at one end to prostitute on the other.[8] In Cap Français, she took up work as a tavern keeper. On November 21, she spearheaded a march of "women, negroes, and unknown, unimportant people" on the Africa House, the name that local residents gave to the headquarters of the French Indies Company in Cap Français.[9]

La Sagona's obscurity before and after that event is partly the obscurity of those who led lives on the margins of French institutions. But the oblivion to which La Sagona was consigned after her sedition was also a function of deliberate design. The monarchy ordered her exiled from Saint-Domingue after the revolt was pacified and expunged documents memorializing the rebels' grievances from the colony's court registers. She was supposed to disappear from the colony and the pages of history alike.

The rupture that she initiated preserved her from this anonymous fate and tied her to the global struggles of the late seventeenth and early eighteenth centuries over monopoly trade. Like other rebellions before and after, this movement appealed to the language of enslavement and liberation.[10] "Slavery" connoted the inability to trade freely in west Africa captives. "Liberty of commerce" meant exchange between the planters and merchants of Saint-Domingue and nonchartered French traders or with contraband factors in the Dutch and British Caribbean.[11] But the "unimportant people" who led this movement prioritized an issue that seemed at first secondary to the monopoly threat: money. As a result, like the Boston Tea Party, the revolt consistently threatened to escape its boundaries as a protest against corporate monopoly.

The marginal characters of the uprising against the Indies Company belonged to a creole society that was supposed to offer its white population freedom from the Old Regime world of rigid status hierarchies and hereditary corporate privileges.[12] In that context, "unimportant people" threatened to undermine the markers of personal and social status, including lines separating rich and poor, men and women, insiders and outsiders, and free and slave. This dynamic of reinforcing ruptures helps to explain the insurgents' mantra: "Long live the king, without the company." To disavow seditious motives was especially important given that some persons of African descent, probably enslaved but likely also including at least some free people of color, played a role in the rebellion. Their presence alongside women and vagabonds was especially emotive and complicates an influential account of the November 1722 insurgency as a "poor white" (*petit blanc*) movement, in contrast to the white planter (*grand blanc*) phase that followed.[13]

One scholar observes that free people of color were the most "belligerent" supporters of the uprising.[14] The evidence does not permit us to establish this with any confidence. But the revolt had broad ramifications for the entire colony of Saint-Domingue. It was not simply a "white revolt," still less a "failed" movement for independence along later eighteenth-century lines. The uprising yielded dramatic change in its own time and on its own terms. However much that change was disguised as a return to the status quo ante, it had the effect of making Saint-Domingue home to a particular version of the sugar revolution that has marked its destiny ever since.

———

In the overwhelmingly water-based environment of the Caribbean, the movement of ships was not only a vital thread of commercial life in Saint-Domingue, it was also often a trigger of political unrest.[15] A rough but revealing chronology of the major turning points of the revolt can be established simply by tracking the dates on which Indies Company vessels entered the harbors of Cap Français and the colony's administrative capital in Léogâne.

The circumstances that brought La Sagona and her band of women to the doors of the Africa House involved two such ships and an unfortunately timed announcement about money. In June 1722, the company's receivers dispatched three newly appointed directors to implement the September 1720 privilege in Saint-Domingue: Buzé de la Ferrière for Cap Français, Lesgut for Léogâne, and Grenon, the former inspector of the company's books at its Paris headquarters, for Saint-Louis.[16] The three directors, their subdirectors, and clerks departed Lorient on July 26 aboard the three-hundred-ton frigate the *Philippe*, with a crew of sixty-six, bound directly for the Antilles.[17]

As the *Philippe* was making the long crossing from Europe, a second Indies Company ship, the *Pontchartrain*, which had departed Lorient for the Senegal coast in May, found itself anchored off the west African shoreline. For most of the summer, first at Senegal and then at the island of la Gorée, the two-hundred-ton vessel with a crew of sixty waited patiently to fill its hold with a sufficient number of captives to justify the journey to Saint-Domingue.[18] With these two vessels, one carrying a group of exclusively white passengers, the other packed to its limits with a cargo of west Africans awaiting the Middle Passage, the company would inaugurate its rule in Saint-Domingue.

As the *Philippe* and *Pontchartrain* were in transit, the monarchy issued its ill-timed decision on money. The ordinance of August 3, 1722, devaluing the piastre to seven livres ten sous and requiring that it be received in payment only at its actual weight, would itself have to be carried by ship. Meanwhile, the seeds of the discontent that this announcement would aggravate had already sprouted in Saint-Domingue. In March 1721, Governor Sorel had written to the secretary of state for the colonies, Joseph Fleuriau d'Armenonville, to update him on the colony's desperate economic state. "[W]e are reduced in this island to the last extreme," explained Sorel, "absolutely lacking in wine, flour, and generally in all other needs indispensable for the life of the colonists and their negroes." These needs emphatically included Spanish silver, whose availability in the colony had been reduced to no more than a few *escalins*. The piastre was nowhere to be found, Sorel reported, courtesy of the merchants who were believed to have carried the last such coin away. And with the *asiento* treaty now a thing of the past, there was no hope to be found in Saint-Domingue's Spanish neighbors, who were dealing exclusively with the English and the Dutch. "We will never see a penny in this country," the governor despondently concluded.[19]

Such was the state of the colony at which the *Philippe* and the *Pontchartrain* arrived on October 16 and 17, respectively. This timing was purely accidental but neatly symbolized the nature of the company's new pact with the Caribbean plantation economy. In one sense, the more important arrival was that of the *Pontchartrain*, which, after its nearly two-month wait at Gorée island, had managed to embark 290 captives—slightly under the average figure of 320 slaves on an Old Regime slave ship. Only 268 were accounted for when the vessel pulled into the Le Cap harbor on the seventeenth, which made for a loss of about 9 percent of the slaves embarked, as compared to the average 17 percent death rate for the French slave trade during the first quarter of the eighteenth century.[20] Cargoes leaving west Africa with 300 slaves, for example, would not uncommonly arrive in the Americas with only 250 or even 200 slaves.

The earliest sign of protest against the physical presence of John Law's company in Saint-Domingue appears to date from the period immediately following the arrival of the *Philippe* and *Pontchartrain* at Le Cap. Charlevoix and other sources report that, with d'Arquian, the municipal governor of Cap

Français, temporarily absent from the city, Febure, the ranking military officer (*major*) in town, received the directors at the docks on October 16. From there, Febure accompanied the agents to the company's townhouse in Cap Français, known as the Maison d'Afrique.[21]

As the colony's symbolic portal to west Africa, the Africa House was not entirely unique. The Royal African Company's headquarters in London, located on Leadenhall Street along with the offices of the British East India Company, bore the identical designation.[22] Built in the image of these British institutions, the French Indies Company would acquire their same, broadly dispersed reputation for political corruption and commercial oppression. In Saint-Domingue, that reputation quickly came to settle on the structure that housed the company's business office and personnel. The Maison d'Afrique may well have been one of the facilities left behind by the Saint-Domingue Company. Its exact location is unknown: no physical traces of the building appear to remain in Cap Haïtien today, and the house is identified on neither the 1723 maps of Cap Français nor on a more detailed plan of the city drawn up in 1728. Maps of the 1740s indicate a set of structures belonging to the Indies Company near the waterfront, just above the opening of the Haut du Cap River. But these structures may have been built only after the events of 1722–24, and in any case they seem more likely to have served as a set of transit and storage facilities rather than as a place for the company's personnel to sleep, eat, and manage their affairs. At this early stage of the company's tenure in Saint-Domingue, the Africa House seems to have doubled as a temporary storage space for incoming metropolitan goods, given La Ferrière's instruction to unload and stow the merchandise aboard the *Philippe* there. Because the house was not yet in a state to receive so many visitors, La Ferrière and his team took their first meals at a nearby *auberge* (inn).[23]

Their fate was signaled by the appearance of a mysterious poster, nailed to the main doors of the church in Cap Français one day after a small Indies Company vessel entered the harbor bringing food and water relief for the larger ships. Written in a marginally literate vernacular and hard to interpret even in the original French, the message warned an individual identified only as "Philippe": "[T]hink of yourself . . . you are risking your life . . . no goods from the [damned] Company, or we will set fire there . . . Notice to the reader." The "Philippe" in question was likely the *trésorier de la marine* by this same name, essentially the naval ministry's cashier and chief financial clerk in Cap Français. His job was to keep track of government funds sent from the metropole to cover the costs of royal administration in the colonies, such as the upkeep of troops, military fortifications, and the salaries of officers appointed by the governor and intendant. He also tracked reserves of specie sent to the colonies, but since these were often in such short supply, the cashier sometimes extended letters or bills of credit to the local *habitants*. These functions required the cashier to supervise the unloading and disposition of the cargoes of arriving vessels. In February to March 1723, for example, this same Philippe was charged with overseeing the sale of captives aboard a company slaver. In short, the position was a flashpoint of controversy where matters of money and colonial finance were concerned. The threat to Philippe sufficiently disturbed Châtenoye, the royal lieutenant in Le Cap, that he transcribed it verbatim, possibly anticipating its use in a criminal proceeding.[24]

By far the greatest hostility seems to have been reserved for the company's newly arrived directors. One of several anonymous manuscript accounts of the revolt, probably penned in 1723, refers to "some ill-intentioned speechifiers" who, from shortly after the directors' arrival onward, "secretly sowed falsehoods against the Company's administration."[25] According to a widely circulated rumor, the directors seem to have conducted themselves with a distinct lack of diplomacy and tact during their first week in the Caribbean. Charlevoix gave a provocative version of the story. A few days after disembarking, La Ferrière and his subordinates were overheard at dinner at the local inn saying that the settlers seemed "proud" and were going to be "humbled." The company would sell enslaved persons only for properly weighted Spanish silver (*piastres de poid*)— words that squarely implicated the directors in the colony's monetary woes. Conceding that there was reason to be skeptical of the exact phrasing of these statements, Charlevoix doubted that the rumor was entirely imagined.[26]

As Arlette Farge and Jacques Revel have shown, rumors tended to play a decisive role in popular riots when they resonated with local experience and tradition.[27] In mid-November, Sorel and Montholon, the newly appointed intendant, complained to their superiors that the company's arrival would permit the Indies Company to "take away all of the country's goods such as sugar, leathers, and indigo without paying any taxes."[28] Sorel and Montholon observed that the effect of the September 1720 privilege would be to empty the colonial treasury of nearly all revenues, including those needed to support military expenses and fortifications. This decimation of the *octroi* regime was especially threatening because, unlike the erstwhile Saint-Domingue Company, the new Indies Company planned to extend itself beyond the limits of its southern territorial jurisdiction into the "royal areas," where it would assert a sole right to trade exclusive of all of the kingdom's merchants. Taking a stand that would become all but indistinguishable from the insurgents, the administrators joined in the demand to suppress the company's privilege.[29]

That such demands were already circulating by November 18 is not surprising. But nearly every observer, Sorel and Montholon included, seems to have been caught off guard by the explosive impact that word of the August 1722 devaluation would produce. Publication of the new measure compounded the existing rumors about price fixing with a new one predicting the hoarding and manipulation of the colony's money supply by callous corporate agents. By mid-November Sorel and Montholon had their hands on the fateful document, perhaps by way of a ship passing through Saint-Domingue en route to another French Caribbean island or Louisiana. On November 15 they sent a courier with a copy of the ordinance to their subordinates in Cap Français. In what would prove to be a critical variable in the unfolding of the revolt, land-based transport faced its own logistical hurdles in Saint-Domingue. The administrators' letter reached Le Cap on November 20 at nine o'clock in the evening.[30]

Meanwhile, the center of controversy had shifted temporarily to the colony's administrative capital, Léogâne, where (in contrast to Le Cap) planters were at the forefront of the protest from the start. The *Philippe*, carrying Lesgut, Grenon, and their employees to open the company's Léogâne and Saint-Louis operations, departed Cap Français on October 24. It was followed the next day by the *Pontchartrain*. Shortly after their arrival in Léogâne on October 30, the directors presented themselves to the judges of the Conseil Superieur for registration of the company's September 1720 privileges.[31]

Delayed now by more than two years, that registration would continue to wait. The *Pontchartrain* and its cargo of unsold captives pulled into the Léogâne harbor the day before, creating what one anonymous chronicler called, with dry irony, "a very good effect" in the city.[32] Lesgut captured the heart of the dispute in a letter to corporate headquarters in Paris:

> The exclusive trade in slaves and the privileges of the Indies Company are regarded as novelties that lead [the colonists] to anticipate troubling consequences . . . in that they imagine being able to own blacks here only through the channels of the Company, which will be able to raise the price at will.

Notwithstanding his protestations that the company's intention toward the colonists was "none other than to provide them with blacks and other merchandise at prevailing prices," the director reported that the local populace could not be appeased.[33]

Lesgut was able to arrange for the sale of the cargo only by assuring his buyers that prices did not exceed those recently charged by other slaving vessels still anchored at that time in the Léogâne harbor. He also agreed to pay export duties on the *Pontchartrain*'s return cargo of colonial goods.[34] Even then, it would be many months before the *Pontchartrain* would be in a position to depart Saint-Domingue for France.[35] Although Lesgut's agreement was contrary to the terms of the 1720 privilege, the company's tax exemption could not formally take effect until registered by the Léogâne conseil.

"WOMEN, NEGROES, AND UNKNOWN, UNIMPORTANT PEOPLE" 87

That prospect had become altogether more unlikely with the awakening of settler anxieties over money and debt. The August 1722 currency devaluation was published sometime between November 8 and 17 in Léogâne.[36] On November 17, the Léogâne conseil declared its refusal to register the company's new privileges, singling out in particular the company's exemption from export duties for colonial goods shipped back to France.[37] Grenon's submission of the company's privileges for registration had included an *arrêt* of the king's Council of State authorizing a local functionary named Boismorand to recover, on behalf of the Indies Company, debts owed to the former Saint-Domingue Company.[38] That element of the company's new regime seems to have been no more popular with the planter community than the export tax immunity.[39]

From their base in Léogâne, Sorel and Montholon could read the temperature of the local planter community as reflected in these initial protests.[40] On November 19, they took the extraordinary step of suspending execution of key provisions of the king's August 1722 ordinance on money, citing petitions from "all of the notable inhabitants and traders of this colony" and evoking the long-standing dearth of silver money in Saint-Domingue. The administrators' account of these petitions conveys a feel for what was happening to the money supply on the ground in Saint-Domingue. The merchants tended to "make off" with the local supply of piastres. This placed the colonists in the difficult position of having to trade their hard-earned plantation produce for basic necessities of life at arbitrarily imposed rates of exchange—a situation that could only result in the "general loss of this colony." Sorel and Montholon left in place the provisions of the ordinance devaluing the piastre and *pistole de poids* (to seven livres ten sous, and thirty livres, respectively). But they insisted that the articles forbidding use of Spanish coin except at their weight in silver would have the effect of "wiping out trade" in Saint-Domingue.[41]

This administrative override of a royal mandate was itself risky because it required Sorel and Montholon, at least temporarily, to place themselves above the monarchy.[42] For the time being, their chief misfortune involved a stroke of bad luck more than a violation of absolutism. The administrators had already dispatched a courier to Cap Français on November 15 with a copy of the ordinance—two days before the showdown over the company's monopoly before the Léogâne conseil was resolved. Having then decided to revoke key portions of that ordinance, the administrators' hopes for the peace of the colony now turned on which of two couriers would be quicker to their destination. The royal ordinance reached Arquian and Duclos (the *commissaire ordonnateur* of Le Cap) on November 20 at nine in the evening. The following morning, they posted the ordinance in Le Cap. Sorel and Montholon's suspension order would not arrive until November 24. When it did, d'Arquian and Duclos were happy to post it, but they also felt bound to explain to their superiors that the new order was too little, too late.[43]

In the space of those four days, the already fragile social order of Saint-Domingue came unglued, in large part because of the woman named La Sagona.[44] On the evening of November 21, La Sagona's band of women ransacked the Africa House, demanding the immediate evacuation of the company's directors from Saint-Domingue. By the following night, the company's plantation at La Fossette, on the outskirts of the town in the Haut du Cap area (see figure 9), was in flames.

———

That we know anything at all about La Sagona is due in part to Nicolas-Louis Bourgeois, a colonial lawyer who lived in Le Cap from roughly 1740 to 1770 and served as secretary of the city's Chamber of Agriculture and Commerce. At some point during his tenure in Saint-Domingue, Bourgeois recorded notes about the 1722–24 revolt that eventually made their way into the hands of his nephew, who edited and published them in 1788.

This secondhand account is quite thin on many aspects of the rebellion and provocatively revisionist, if not downright paranoid, about others.[45] It also contains what may be the only known description of La Sagona's life.[46] According to Bourgeois, La Sagona was born in France, became an actress, and married a man whose family seems to have been resolutely opposed to the union. Disowned for his determination to proceed with the marriage, La Sagona's husband concluded that his best chance of finding a secure living lay in the colonies, and he traveled to Saint-Domingue "in search of fortune." That much is indeed consistent with what we know of Saint-Domingue as a place of second chances for white French men shut off from avenues for upward mobility in the metropole. Transplanted to the Caribbean, he became a merchant and shopkeeper in Cap Français. La Sagona, for her part, settled into a new role as a tavern keeper (*cabaretière*).[47] (Bourgeois reports, without any further explanation, that her husband died at some point during the rebellion. After La Sagona was exiled to France for her role in the uprising, she was taken in with pride by the in-laws who had once rejected her and who now apparently regarded her as a heroine for her role in beating back the Indies Company.)[48]

Neither of these roles—actress and tavern keeper—would have been accidental to the direction of La Sagona's life in the 1720s. Like theaters in Old Regime France, taverns in Saint-Domingue were under a kind of political spotlight because they were believed to promote unruly forms of urban sociability.[49] Throughout the eighteenth century, colonial officials adopted measures cracking down on the ability of taverns to serve rum, provide shelter, or make gambling tables available to people on the margins of the colonial social order. A 1721 ruling to this effect specifically targeted vagabonds (*gens sans aveu*) of varying backgrounds, including poor whites, free people of color (*mulâtres*), and free blacks (*nègres libres*), suggesting that taverns played a special role in undermining the rules of racial hierarchy.[50]

In addition to hosting marginal characters, taverns served basic needs in towns like Le Cap that buttressed the public profile of their owners. A municipal ordinance dated October 1721—shortly before the events at issue here—introduced caps on the prices of bread sold by bakers and wine by tavern keepers.[51] That regulation suggests not merely the everyday importance of individuals like La Sagona in the life of colonial urban communities, but also hints at some of the tensions that affected their relationship with officialdom. La Sagona was likely to have known a good deal of the planter and merchant community in Cap Français and to have been familiar with their grievances against the royal bureaucracy in Saint-Domingue. She was, in Bourgeois's words, a person of "sociable and likable character," an "extraordinary woman" who had already begun to advance in years when she "took charge of responsibility for intimidating the director of the company and his clerks."[52]

The colonial archives reveal multiple accounts of the exact nature of that intimidation, illustrating the range of competing interests with a stake in the outcome of La Sagona's movement. These accounts highlight how marginal actors intersected with comparatively more established figures in the colony to expand the potential meanings of the unfolding action.[53]

The documents closest to the original scene of the riot are two letters dispatched by d'Arquian and Duclos from Cap Français on November 23 and 24 to the administration in Léogâne. At one level, these letters record the travails of two men taken completely by surprise, overwhelmed by superior force, and improvising whatever measures they deemed necessary to restore a local calm. They were not inexperienced figures. Duclos had recently finished serving a two-year term as interim intendant when Montholon replaced him in March 1722, and during that period he enjoyed a direct line of communication with the Naval Council in France. For his part, d'Arquian had held the post of interim governor of Saint-Domingue during the latter years of the War of the Spanish Succession.[54] But little in this background had prepared them for what they were about to encounter.

The first letter, especially, has a breathless, almost real-time quality, written at two different moments on the night of November 23 that correspond to interludes in the simultaneously unfolding action of the uprising. At seven in the evening, d'Arquian recorded that he had just escaped a "great risk" to his life in trying to save the subdirector, Desnos, from being set upon by the crowd at the Africa House. Following the evacuation of the "imprudent" La Ferrière aboard the company's ship in the Cap Français harbor (the *Bellonne*), d'Arquian acknowledged that Desnos would also have to clear out in order to spare the city from being torched "just as [the company's plantation at] La Fossette had been." Even as he wrote, five hundred men were preparing to descend from the plains above Le Cap to "raze" the buildings of the company and "get their hands on their opponents." The letter broke off at this point only to be resumed at six the following morning (November 24).[55]

D'Arquian's fragmented account combines convincing details with an almost complete lack of clarity as to who was in the crowd. Resuming his letter in the morning, he reported that "a nefarious storehouse (*mauvais magasin*) that I did not know the company kept at Petite Anse was demolished last night, torched, and reduced to ashes." (The company's waterfront facilities at Petite Anse were located several miles to the southeast around the bay of Cap Français, as shown in figure 10.) Having risked his life that night trying to save the Africa House from a similar fate, he wrote that the "people say they are hardly rejoicing at having failed to kill me when I charged the crowd with sword in hand." With neither the doors nor the windows of the Africa House secured, d'Arquian decided to spend the night there to ward off further mayhem. The threat emanated not solely from the crowd outside but also from the assembled troops of the Le Cap garrison, one of whom seems to have whispered in d'Arquian's ear the ominous news that "two hundred men in arms at La Fossette were awaiting the signal to come" to Le Cap. "[A]ll would be lost" were his men to fire on the "rebels" (*les séditieux*) without his word.[56]

The ambiguity as to the identity of the participants was engineered by the crowd itself. D'Arquian's sources for the violence at La Fossette were two militia officers, de Breda and d'Héricourt, whose efforts to identify the insurgents there met with the response: "It's the colony." The assembly threatening to sack Le Cap was large enough only to say that "prudence must stand in for the lack of sufficient forces." An equally nameless group of settlers, meanwhile, was requesting permission via d'Arquian to send its own deputies to the governor and intendant in Léogâne—a manner of proceeding that implies the group comprised relatively established planters. Between the militants at La Fossette and the anonymous planters, the need to "calm spirits" by publicizing the November 19 suspension of the money ordinance was paramount.[57]

After the initial dust had settled, d'Arquian and Duclos explained that rumors about the company's intentions in Saint-Domingue derived from statements by the newly arrived directors overheard by residents of Le Cap:

> [W]ith an air of haughtiness and self-sufficiency that one would have thought little suited them in any way, they saluted no one [upon arriving] and then spread talk among the public that left people's minds extremely

embittered toward them. On some occasions they let loose that they had need of no one and that everyone would have need of them. At other times they said they would only sell their negroes for the small pieces of money known as piastres, which would be counted by weight. On yet other occasions they remarked upon seeing women dressed in taffeta who in short order would be quite happy to have Welsh cloth to cover themselves, or they said that the inhabitants would be so at ease in their lifestyle that they would wish to take their flour through the counter hole. But throughout they made known that they were under nobody's orders at all, that no one had the right to get involved in matters concerning them, and that they were so well supported that they feared neither governors nor intendants in this land.

These statements passed "from mouth to mouth, with perhaps some ornamentation," creating a volatile context for the publication of the money ordinance on the morning of November 21. These circumstances persuaded the people of Cap Français that "the company's design was to withdraw all weighted specie from the country in order to substitute others" that were useless on the market. Even in such a fraught environment, d'Arquian and Duclos simply posted the money ordinance at dawn on the twenty-first, "without thinking that it could have such immediate consequences."[58]

In this account of their admittedly naïve conduct, d'Arquian and Duclos left the role of La Sagona herself altogether unmentioned—in contrast to all later narratives of the uprising. But the women of Cap Français assumed center stage all the same, surrounding the Africa House and using stones to break into its doors and windows. Seeing no sign of La Ferrière, the women made their way to the home of the despised tax collector in Cap Français, Langot, where the director was said to be dining. Langot quickly ushered his guest out the back door just as La Sagona arrived. Upon returning to the Africa House and observing the havoc wreaked upon the company's offices, La Ferrière announced that "the damned Colony would pay him for all of these disorders." This was the first indication of a claim for indemnification of the kind that the British government would press on behalf of the East India Company following the Boston Tea Party.[59]

The appointment of fifteen bodyguards to surround the Africa House appeared to stabilize the situation sufficiently. But the following day, the twenty-second, word spread that the women who had laid siege to the company's headquarters had discovered several copper coins with the words "French colonies 1721" stamped on them. That charge revived suspicions that the company was plotting to extract Spanish silver from Saint-Domingue and replace it with new copper money imported from the metropole.[60]

FIGURE 14. French colonial copper coin (9 *deniers*) minted pursuant to June 1721 royal edict. Courtesy of www.cgb.fr, CGB Numismatique Paris.

The rumor was almost certainly true in at least two respects: it is very likely that copper coins stamped "French colonies 1721" were found at the Africa House and equally likely that the Indies Company brought them there. In 1721, as part of an effort to remedy the shortage of specie in the colony, the regency had authorized the mints of Bordeaux, La Rochelle, Nantes, and Rouen to issue a supply of copper coins for the colonies corresponding to a total weight of 150,000 marks, or 75,000 livres tournois (see figure 14.) The coins were denominated in four, eight, and nine *denier* variations. The Indies Company was charged with transporting these coins to Louisiana and the Caribbean colonies, where they met with a predictably hostile response. In 1722, the company tried to unload them on the inhabitants of New France, who shared a similarly low opinion of coins that weighed considerably more than their intrinsic value and could not be used outside of the French colonies. In 1726, the company surrendered the venture and returned most of the money to La Rochelle, from whence the hapless tokens were sent once again to Louisiana.[61]

Recognizing the contagiousness of the allegations against the company, the beleaguered director fled to the expansive Jesuit compound atop the town. There, La Ferrière reluctantly concluded that the risk of his continued presence in the city was too great. Under disguise, he boarded a rowboat to find shelter on Captain de Chilly's vessel in the town harbor. (D'Arquian intercepted Desnos as he tried make the same escape later that same evening, returning him to the Africa House on the understanding that the subdirector would enjoy the governor's personal protection there.)[62]

Even as he piled on such telling details about the maneuvers of the company's hapless agents in Saint-Domingue, d'Arquian remained curiously abstract about the participants in the violence of the night of November 22: the second siege of the Africa House and the torching of the company's plantation at La Fossette. The crowd outside the Africa House that night consisted of "large numbers of women and among them several men disguised as women." D'Arquian identified these insurgents collectively as "the inhabitants, that is to say the *gens sans aveu*"—a revealing conflation of the city's residents as a whole with the vagabond population. Taking up the municipal governor's invitation to retreat, the crowd marched on the company plantation at La Fossette and promptly set it aflame. D'Arquian then dispatched an emissary, Captain Fourment of the Le Cap militia, to reason with the insurgents, who appeared to Fourment as a shifting mass of sixty armed men in disguise and more than three hundred women. Their faces caked with flour and painted with *faux* black mustaches to disguise their identities, the protesters shouted "Long live the king, without the company" before eventually dispersing. The following morning, November 23, reports reached Le Cap of a "large number of people, apparently also vagabonds," assembling in the surrounding plains.[63]

The very essence of such an anonymous crowd was that it lacked identifiable members of the planter elite. "[U]ntil now there still have not been any known or noteworthy persons in this entire riot, which has been caused entirely by women and vagabonds," the municipal governor explained. At some point in the course of their insurrection, however, they managed to "force the leading inhabitants into joining them, and to oblige someone to serve at their head as they did in Martinique, which then would amount to a broad-based feud [*querelle générale*] that would be difficult to resolve." This reference to the 1717 Gaoulé uprising in Martinique underscored a theme that would take on great significance in subsequent efforts to calm the storm: the transformation of a local "riot" into a more "broad-based feud" depended on the ability of the crowd to coerce the "leading inhabitants" of the Cap Français region. The expanding sphere of sedition meant that d'Arquian and Duclos had arrived at the limits of their ability to contain the uprising. "We await your orders as to all of this with great impatience," they ended their letter to Sorel and Montholon.[64]

———

This elusive report implied d'Arquian's power to lift the veil of anonymity that covered the "known" and "noteworthy" persons. That he refrained from doing so may have only partly to do with their status as unwilling participants in the seditious events of November 21–23. For one thing, it is not entirely clear how unwilling these elite figures were. Another reason may have to do with d'Arquian's omission of some key participants: the woman identified by name as La Sagona, and persons of African descent. Subsequent accounts highlight the ambiguous gender and racial dimensions of the riot while amplifying the sense of an anonymous crowd moving with inexorable force to stop the Indies Company in its tracks. In particular, these later narratives dramatize the participation of La Sagona, who emerges as not only a distinct character in her own right, but as the central figure of the entire uprising.

Perhaps not accidentally, La Sagona and the issue of gender come into somewhat clearer focus in the anonymous accounts of the rebellion found in Moreau de Saint-Méry's collection of miscellaneous Saint-Domingue materials. A 1723 "Account of What Happened at St. Domingue" confirms that La Sagona's movement drew from an unlikely source: cross-dressing men. The account observes that the company intended to "take away all of the country's specie and replace it with others or perhaps Company notes." In the left margin of a passage describing the band of Cap Français women who stormed the Maison d'Afrique, however, a note written by another hand states: "Madame La Sagonna was always at the head of this riot." By the following night, with d'Arquian back in the city and bodyguards posted at the Maison on his order, the gender makeup of the insurgents had shifted. "A large number of women, among them several men disguised as women," appeared at the house at 9 p.m. and attempted to force themselves in through the side unprotected by d'Arquian's men.[65]

The instruction itself captures both the tenuous nature of state authority in Saint-Domingue at this time and the character of the anonymous insurgency it was supposed to confront. According to the "Account of What Happened," after the insurgents had advanced on their next target at La Fossette, Captain Fourment's mission was to try to "recognize someone and make him withdraw." Instead of directing Fourment to defeat or pacify the mob, d'Arquian dispatched him to undertake the more basic but critical task of recognition: identifying someone, anyone, who could be reasoned with and held to account. The job was made no easier by the crowd's use of flour and stenciled black mustaches as disguises. Upon being ordered by Fourment to disperse "on behalf of the King," the insurgents responded that they "would always obey the King and cried 'long live the King without the Company' while firing several musket shots."[66]

These scenes of gender and ideological disguise were core elements of the disorder that administrators associated with La Sagona's actions. The way to avoid recognition was to mask one's sex, whether by caking one's face with flour to pass as a woman or painting a fake mustache to resemble a man. Like the "women's march" on Versailles in October 1789, the action against the Africa House was not restricted to women.[67] Indeed, by this "Account," the mixing of women and men, and the playful, almost theatrical manipulation of their

"WOMEN, NEGROES, AND UNKNOWN, UNIMPORTANT PEOPLE" 95

physical appearances, were themselves deliberate tactics of the protest. The riot was an eminently public act, but staged so as to preserve a wide realm of privacy.

The only limit to the transgressive character of this riot was an ideological one: the king's authority was to be respected. Even on that score, however, the insurgents' declaration of allegiance was ambiguous, precisely because it depended on a distinction between the king's mandate and the company's authority. That distinction was difficult if not impossible to draw as a legal matter: the company was in Saint-Domingue pursuant to a royal charter. As a practical matter, however, the initiative was almost entirely in the hands of the crowd, as suggested by its ability to force the company directors back onto their ship notwithstanding the protestations of the administrators in Cap Français.[68]

If gender disguise and the commingling of women and men were one sign of political rupture, the involvement of nonwhites was another. Slaves and slavery—both real and metaphorical—also appear in a second anonymous 1723 report, titled an "Account of What Happened toward the Indies Company." Here, the attack of November 21 was the work of a "troupe of women, negroes, and unknown, unimportant people [*menu peuple inconnu*]." Depicted as a pack of "furious lions," and convinced that the company's directors had personally instigated the money ordinance, this multiracial crowd of men and women carried on a general scene of "tumult" until 2 a.m. Then, they retreated to the cry of "Long live the King and the Colony, and to hell with the Company that wants to make slaves of us. We must exterminate it so that it is no longer spoken of."[69]

This was not the only reference to persons of African descent, and their campaign against metaphorical enslavement, in the "Account of What Happened toward the Indies Company." Throughout the day of November 22, the "unimportant people" persisted in their verbal harassment of the Indies Company, whose only objective (in their minds) was to "render them more slave than the negroes." To contemporary readers, the contrast between these apparent references to actual enslaved people and the rhetoric of political enslavement may suggest a near-total lack of irony, not to mention a basic contradiction in the ideology of the revolt. To highlight the presence of "negroes" among a crowd in Saint-Domingue in 1722 was to attempt to discredit that crowd as a threat to racial hierarchies. Far from a neutral act of description, highlighting the presence of "negroes" among the crowd was perhaps the ultimate form of condemnation.[70]

This observation is entirely consistent with the near certainty that some persons of African descent did in fact participate in La Sagona's insurgency. Summarizing the scene at the Africa House on the second night of rebellion (November 22–23), the "Account of What Happened toward the Indies

Company" refers to a "troupe of women, negroes (*nègres*), and several other persons disguised as women, their faces smeared with flour and a black mustache." Numbering some 250 to 300, the cross-dressing crowd depicted here echoes the description in the previously discussed "Account of What Happened at St. Domingue" but adds one crucial detail: the presence of "negroes."[71] The term *nègres* probably denoted an enslaved person. On the other hand, the usage *nègre libre* ("free negro"), while not absent from the records of this era, does yet not seem to have been widely used, and so we cannot assume from the absence of the adjective "free" that the persons described in the account were held as slaves. There were already 1,573 freed persons in Saint-Domingue by 1720, many of them likely concentrated in the area in and around Cap Français. Free people of color were a familiar part of the urban fabric at this time, and it is hard to imagine that a commotion at the scale of La Sagona's uprising would have escaped their attention. Slaves, too, were both residents of and regular visitors to Cap Français. Their demographic predominance (at nearly fifty thousand, already 83 percent of the colony's population in 1720), concentration in the Cap Français region, and centrality to the Indies Company would have made them even more likely witnesses to some or all of the events described in these narratives. And just as the line between voluntary and involuntary white participation in the uprising may have been hazy in some cases, so too persons of African descent may have found themselves caught up in the agitation for an array of different reasons, or for no reason at all.

On balance, the "Account of What Happened toward the Indies Company" suggests that persons of African descent were part of the same political mobilization that had engulfed the white population of Saint-Domingue. And why would they not have been? Both free people of color and slaves would have used Spanish silver in the urban economy of Cap Français: in town markets and for other commercial transactions. And free people of color had already joined the planter and slaveholding community at this time. In that capacity, Spanish silver was altogether even more indispensable, just as the company's monopoly on the supply of west African captives would have forged common cause between white and nonwhite planters.

———

A similar set of considerations applies to the women who, by all accounts, were lead architects of the insurgency. In that context, however, we have the evidence of a specific figure: La Sagona. The accounts that relate her story at any length postdate the actual time period of the revolt and must be read in light of a tendency to dramatize and perhaps even embellish La Sagona's role in the confrontation at the Africa House.

"WOMEN, NEGROES, AND UNKNOWN, UNIMPORTANT PEOPLE" 97

Perhaps the first post hoc account of the uprising was written by the Jesuit missionary Jean-Baptiste Le Pers, who was based in the Cap Français region and present there throughout the years 1722–24 but out of town on the night of November 21–22, 1722. Exactly when Le Pers composed his manuscript on the history of Saint-Domingue is unclear; internal evidence suggests that it was written (in whole or part) by 1726–27, though Le Pers may have drafted it earlier in the 1720s. In his rendition, the insurgents appeared as a fearless "army of women," partly composed of "men dressed as women," who marched with beating tambour drums on the Africa House, pistols in hand, sabers at their sides, and La Sagona at their head. Bursting into the company's residence, La Sagona discovered a startled La Ferrière in the middle of dinner, drinking glass in hand. She took a pistol to his neck and delivered the immaculate line: "Drink, traitor, it will be the last shot of your life." "Scatterbrained" by La Sagona's entry, the director dropped his glass and fled the Africa House to find temporary refuge at the Jesuit compound.[72]

This almost cinematic, if secondhand, account is worth taking seriously if only because it served as a principal source for Charlevoix's *Histoire de l'isle espagnole ou de St. Domingue* (1730–31). Charlevoix combined original research into the papers of the Dépôt de la Marine in Paris with a timely stint in Saint-Domingue in the fall of 1722. He came to the colony at the end of a long journey from Québec down the Mississippi River through Illinois country and then to various points along the Gulf Coast all the way to Florida. At Biloxi, he boarded a company ship, the *Bellone*, that brought him to Cap Français in September 1722 (and that later harbored there during the uprising). Charlevoix was therefore present in the French colony at the time of the arrival of the *Pontchartrain* and the *Philippe*. He would have witnessed firsthand the unrest triggered by the appearance of those vessels from his base at the Jesuit residence in Cap Français. By late October 1722, however, he had departed Saint-Domingue for France.[73]

Charlevoix's portrait of La Sagona somehow included details for which there seems to be no archival authority, though he evidently consulted many of the sources discussed above. La Sagona is now the widowed head of a "troupe of Amazons." The plantation at La Fossette has become a kind of company "pleasure house." The sabers, pistols, and tambours of Le Pers are all there, but La Sagona and her comrades find nobody present at the Africa House. After laying waste to the residence, they seek out La Ferrière at Langot's home (consistent with the report of d'Arquian and Duclos, to which Charlevoix evidently had access). According to Charlevoix, Langot and his guests had already evacuated the premises by the time the Amazons arrived. But the Jesuit historian notes "some memoranda" to the contrary (one of which, presumably, was the Le Pers manuscript) and proceeds to recount the alleged confrontation at the

Africa House essentially as Le Pers described it—complete with La Sagona's fiery directive to La Ferrière to enjoy his last mortal drink.[74]

It is hard to avoid the impression that these Jesuit accounts sought more to entertain the reader than to take seriously what white women brought to the revolt and how they experienced it.[75] The titillating character of stories about La Sagona and the white women of Saint-Domingue carried a clear implication of racial transgression. Such titillation reached a crescendo in the writing of Nicolas-Louis Bourgeois. Bourgeois, the lawyer who resided in Cap Français from the 1740s to the 1770s, provided the only known account of La Sagona's early life in his *Voyages intéressants* (published posthumously in 1788). There, he argued that Charlevoix had misidentified the true author(s) of the uprising. The actual driving force behind the attack on the Indies Company, according to Bourgeois, was none other than d'Arquian. Identified only as "le Comte d'A. . . . . . . ," the municipal governor of Le Cap figured in Bourgeois's narrative as a former naval officer who had timidly surrendered "one of our navy's most beautiful vessels" in a 1712 battle with the British while serving in the Leeward Islands. Exiled to Saint-Domingue for his incompetence, d'Arquian became governor of Le Cap and commenced a reign of "despotism" typified by the pursuit of "delicate pleasures." Chief among these was his nightly habit of taking to the streets of Cap Français, and sometimes venturing even into the surrounding plantations, to consort with "girls or women of mixed blood (*sang mêlé*)." Such *rendez-vous*—the word obfuscates the role of power in colonial sex—brought the municipal governor into frequent duels with the husbands and lovers of these women.[76]

In the late 1780s, when the *Voyages intéressants* was published, the sexual exploitation of women of color by white men in Saint-Domingue was not just commonplace but also provided a favored subtext for denouncing one's political rivals. Predictably, Bourgeois did not disclose the sources that revealed d'Arquian's propensity for sexual conquest. But he insisted that an "infinite number of persons still alive [around 1750] have certified" that the municipal governor was indeed the chief factor behind the November uprising. "He encouraged the inhabitants [and] secretly moved all of the springs of this grand affair."[77]

The "famous" La Sagona appeared in this interpretation of the sexual and racial politics of the uprising, but she was accompanied by other, apparently equally consequential women. Aiding and abetting La Sagona's every move was the "dame R. . . . . ," widow of the royal *procureur* of the Conseil Supérieur of Le Cap. It is unclear why Bourgeois and/or his nephew and publisher Nougaret chose to adopt this coy manner of identifying the revolt's ringleaders, using the first initial of the last name. It is not difficult to identify the widow in question as the dame Robineau, maiden name Françoise Féron. An inheritance lawsuit in which Féron was involved in the 1720s enables us to reconstruct the basic outlines of her life, at least as they involve her marriage to Antoine Robineau. Monsieur Robineau's passage to prominence in Saint-Domingue is a portrait in miniature of the transition of Saint-Domingue from pirate and buccaneer haven to settler colony. Born in Saint-Christophe, Robineau was exiled from that island in 1660 after the British invasion and joined the stream of refugees who made their way first to Martinique and Saint-Croix before moving on to Saint-Domingue, where their numbers lent a considerable boost to the colony's settler population. Robineau survived at first by taking up the local tradition of freebooting before being appointed seneschal (a lower court magistrate) in 1684. In 1703, shortly after the establishment of a Conseil Supérieur in the north of Saint-Domingue, he was promoted to *procureur général* of the high tribunal.[78]

Even as he was building a career in the judiciary, Robineau was also laying the foundations for private prosperity as a member of one of the colony's earliest planter cohorts. The magistrate initially owned a plantation in Quartier Morin, near Cap Français, as well as a townhouse in Le Cap. By the time his first wife, Cathérine Leroy, died in 1706, Robineau had added an indigo and sugar plantation in the area of the Petite Anse (where the Indies Company would later have its storage warehouses). He waited only a few months after Leroy's death before marrying Féron. According to the lawsuit brought against Féron by the children of Robineau's first marriage after his death, Féron came to the marriage with little by way of a dowry: only a single slave, a horse, and a bed. She had no sooner secured Robineau's hand in marriage than she persuaded him to sell his property in Le Cap and abandon his children from Leroy to the cares of a woman of African descent named Babette. As a final offense, Féron allegedly steered all of the revenues that had begun to flow in from the Petite Anse plantation toward her own children with Robineau. When the *procureur* took leave of the colony to attend to affairs in France in 1722–23, Féron was effectively in sole control of her husband's estate—just in time to assume a position of leadership in the uprising against the Indies Company that Bourgeois attributes to her.[79]

Returning to Saint-Domingue when the rebellion was in its final stages, Robineau had little time left to settle the simmering dispute within his family. By August 1724, he had fallen seriously ill, naming Féron from his deathbed as his sole beneficiary while adding a provision to his will that granted each child of both marriages a male and female slave of his or her choosing. Death followed shortly thereafter.[80]

A woman of dame Robineau's position and circumstances had an obvious reason for joining forces with La Sagona. As the de facto proprietor of two plantation properties in Saint-Domingue during her husband's sojourn in France, she had the same incentive as any other planter to worry about the impact of the Indies Company's monopoly on the local economy. Her story may also suggest that other women involved in the uprising had their own personal stakes in the plantation economy, whether as widows who had inherited properties from their husbands, or simply as spouses whose livelihood depended on the profits to be made from sugar.

We can only speculate about these possibilities, as it is difficult to draw definitive conclusions from a narrative so apparently invested in its own sexual and racial politics. Perhaps the point was partly to stir the pot of suspicion: in the case of Féron, not so much by casting doubt on Charlevoix once more, but rather to suggest that the monarchy had not quite gotten to the bottom of things when it assigned La Sagona responsibility for the uprising. As Bourgeois writes, "these two women were the leaders of the mission; but the one who spoke most affirmatively, and whom the [Royal] Court considered to be the head of the undertaking, was [La Sagona], who has been accorded too much honor by virtue of the exile to which she was condemned."[81]

Although he considered her a person of "great resolution" and an "extraordinary woman," Bourgeois denied that she could have exercised any real agency in the rebellion. The uprising over which she presided turns out, in his reading, to have been the product of an elaborate plot that joined public officials (notably d'Arquian) and private colonists. Recounting the storming of the Africa House, Bourgeois pointed out that Langot, as La Ferrière's dinner host, was secretly part of the scheming against the company, even as he pretended to assist the startled director in escaping. In short, the heralded rebellion against the Indies Company was the product of a highly coordinated "conspiracy" (*complot*) rather than a spontaneous crowd action as described in the November 23–24 letters of d'Arquian and Duclos. The political implications of this quirky interpretation are clear enough: as a plot engineered by those in a position of relative power, drawing on the brute force of the "unimportant people" of Saint-Domingue, the uprising against the Indies Company expressed the will of an entire colony.[82]

This conspiracy theory, and its diminution of La Sagona's role, had little influence over subsequent accounts. In 1847, another creole lawyer-historian, Adrien Dessalles, grandson of a magistrate who served on the Conseil Supérieur of Martinique in the later eighteenth century, closed the circle on the shifting colonial-era portraits of La Sagona. With Dessalles's narrative—part of a larger history of the French Caribbean—the transformation of La Sagona from nameless figure at the head of an anonymous crowd into an Amazonian symbol of feminine courage in the face of corporate tyranny was complete.[83]

Though he built clearly on the sexually politicized imagery of Le Pers, Charlevoix, and Bourgeois, Dessalles left behind a vision of the women's movement that can only have come from inside his own imagination. The crowd that converged on the Africa House on November 21, he wrote, consisted of "drunk, bare-breasted women, pistols in hand, their hair blowing freely in a breeze that cooled the steaming heat of a scorching day." These "new Amazons" were a force of nature, but they were not beyond listening to d'Arquian, whose calming words defused the situation and persuaded the "feminine conspirators" to moderate their attack. By this time, the damage had been done, for rumor had already begun to spread that La Sagona's band had uncovered a supply of copper coins in the company's warehouse embossed with the words "Colonies Françaises." As Dessalles characterized the mood in Le Cap, this served as an unmistakable sign that the Indies Company was not only privy to the August 1722 monetary reforms, but was in fact spearheading the effort to introduce a new, alien currency into the colony. "True or false," that "revelation" carried the insurgents to a new level of determination to rid the colony of the Indies Company. His use of poetic license notwithstanding, Dessalles was largely consonant with earlier narratives.[84]

In one critical respect, however, Dessalles departed from every previous chronicler of the uprising by slipping a brief but unmistakable critique of the slave trade into the overall story. Referencing the colonists' designation of the Indies Company residence as the "Africa House," he observed that the name itself

> encapsulated so many sorrows, so many plans for making a fortune, so many disappointments based on the hope that metropolitan traders (*négociants*) had nourished in selling the product of their human speculation.

At the time he published these words (in 1847), France was in the midst of a heated debate over slavery that would lead to the second abolition one year later, in 1848. Dessalles himself was no abolitionist. To the contrary, as Catherine Benoît has observed, he appears to have intended his history to serve as a dispassionate brief in support of the proposition that France had no choice but to maintain plantation slavery in the Caribbean. The connection that Dessalles drew between the Africa House (and, by association, the Indies Company) and the French slaving industry applied only to the perpetrators of the trade itself, which France had banned for the third and final time in 1831. Still, by making that connection, Dessalles underscored the gap that separated his own vantage point from the perspective of those writing closer to the events of the 1720s. Dessalles highlighted that the divisions exposed by the revolt against the Indies Company were rifts between groups sharing a fundamental commitment to the future of Saint-Domingue as a slave society. If there was room for this commitment to coexist with a distinction between the morality of plantation slavery and the immorality of the slave trade, that distinction was not yet available to those inside or outside the Africa House in 1722.[85]

In subsequent months, the insurgency would continue to hit the company in its physical body, most notably the arriving slave vessels. At the same time, the ideological targets of the uprising continued to expand and become more diffuse, stretching outward from issues of money and monopoly trade to taxation and representation—in short, to the stuff from which white self-determination in the eighteenth-century Atlantic world was being made. This shift coincided with an increasingly large role for the planter elite in the conduct of the insurrection: the world not of La Sagona, but of women like dame Robineau, and the men to whom they were connected.

The path to this more aggressive assertion of planter sovereignty passed through the "unimportant people" who feared becoming "more slave than the negroes."[86] Planters who stood far above the vagabonds and other marginal characters of Saint-Domingue did not share this anxious position on the colony's social ladder. But they were happy to capitalize on such fears in the service of their own interests. The appropriation of the rebellion and its rhetoric of political enslavement by the colony's elite entailed a radical form of self-determination that fused republican aspirations for the few with a relentless white supremacy.[87]

4

Militant Slavery

IN A pair of articles published in 1937 in the *American Political Science Review*, Karl Loewenstein analyzed the challenges facing democracy from the rise of fascism in Europe. The dilemma of a democracy, he observed, is that it is "legally bound to allow the emergence and rise of anti-parliamentarian and anti-democratic parties under the condition that they conform outwardly to the principles of legality and free play of public opinion." To contain this threat, European democracies began to enact antifascist legislation in tension with democratic norms, such as suppression of fascist speech and political parties. "[A] political technique can be defeated only on its own plane and by its own devices," wrote Loewenstein. "Democracy becomes militant."[1]

Something analogous to this process unfolded in the context of slavery in Saint-Domingue in the winter of 1722–23. As the rebellion against the Indies Company turned to increasingly aggressive tactics, planters and administrators adopted measures that, on their face, were at least in tension with the preservation of a plantation economy, if not altogether inconsistent with it. The planters organized a boycott of an arriving Indies Company slaving vessel, subjecting its already suffering occupants to yet more deprivation in the campaign against monopoly trade. Pushed to their own limits, administrators contemplated emancipating the enslaved population of Saint-Domingue to counter the risk that the planters would mobilize slaves in the service of the insurrection. Neither of these episodes involved an effort to undermine slavery per se; that kind of resistance would come only from Afro-Haitians (and it was, in fact, already underway at this time). To the contrary, in their proponents' minds the measures at issue entailed short-term risks to the plantation system designed to preserve its long-term prospects. In the case of the administrators' manumission proposal, that risk was altogether extraordinary for its time. This willingness to endure risk to defeat interests deemed adverse to the sugar revolution defined the increasingly militant form of plantation slavery taking shape in Saint-Domingue at this time.

The rise of militant slavery marked a shift in the nature of the insurgency, from a series of riots associated with women and "unimportant people" to a planter-led "general affair" that affected the entire colony and sought to institutionalize a radical form of creole self-determination. As the planters emerged from beneath their veil of anonymity, they pushed for constitutional reforms in Saint-Domingue that included a claim of no taxation without representation. The republican element of this campaign for self-determination would become absorbed in the larger struggle for a military-planter state that guaranteed the perpetuation of white supremacist privilege in the colony.

Planter sovereignty and a militarized form of racial hierarchy may seem like obvious endpoints for a society deep in the throes of the sugar revolution. But they were in fact part of a historical process whereby racial hierarchy and planter slavery increasingly displaced silver as the bedrock of mercantilist supremacy in the eighteenth-century Atlantic world.[2] That process did not culminate in the 1720s in Saint-Domingue, and silver remained important to the colony's future. But, as the next stages of the rebellion against the Indies Company would show, the initial emphasis on silver now gave way to something that is only thinly described as a struggle against monopoly. The core of that struggle involved an assertion that the future of Saint-Domingue was now irrevocably in the hands of the planters. And sugar, rather than silver, would become the preeminent symbol and object of this new age.

If one mark of the shift in the insurrection was the growing involvement of colonial notables, another was geographic scope. In mid-December, the north again seemed on the brink of chaos, as hundreds gathered in the hills above Le Cap and threatened to lay waste to the city while the plantation of a colonist notorious for his service to the company was burned to the ground. The news that La Ferrière and Desnos had departed Saint-Domingue on a ship bound for France restored a temporary tranquility to the north. But the rebellion picked up in the western region, where flyers appeared calling for a general march on the colony's capital at Léogâne. In the waning days of 1722, the mobilization in the west forced Sorel and Montholon to sign a striking agreement known as the Cul de Sac Treaty, which effectively canceled the company's privileges and called for elections that would give the planters control of colonial taxation and spending.

Over the course of 1723, opposition to the company's commercial power over the slave trade increasingly merged with hostility to the policies of the colonial governor and intendant. Even as the insurgents escalated their political rhetoric and made increasingly direct threats against the administration, they continued to disavow any intention to challenge the king's authority. The forced evacuation of the administration from Léogâne in early March put an end to the illusion that company and empire could be fully disentangled

FIGURE 15. Detail showing the western region of Saint-Domingue, from Amédée-François Frézier, "Carte de l'Isle de St. Domingue et débouquements circonvoisins" (1724). Courtesy of the John Carter Brown Library, Providence, RI.

from one another. This drama led the monarchy to intervene in the fall of 1723. The pacification of the revolt pretended to restore the absolutist status quo ante, but the crown eventually, if tacitly, ratified many of the insurgents' key demands, including, most notably, liberalization of the slave trade.

In contrast to the American Tea Crisis, which spiraled out of control primarily because key British leaders were unwilling or unable to broker a compromise, the creole vision of the 1720s did not require secession. The colonists ultimately found that they could achieve self-government within the constraints of their attachment to the metropole, so long as those constraints permitted local control of plantation slavery and the slave trade. This settlement wrote a new script for the sugar revolution that would help foster the explosive rise of the Saint-Domingue economy in the years to come.

———

The western region of Saint-Domingue propelled these changes. Three areas proved to be especially important as concentrated repositories of insurgent activity: (1) Léogâne; (2) the Cul de Sac plain east-by-northeast of Léogâne, surrounding what is now Port-au-Prince; and (3) the Artibonite plain, an area north of the Cul de Sac, traversing the Artibonite River as it snakes in a generally northwest direction from Mirebalais to a point about halfway between Gonaïves and Saint-Marc on the western coast. Figure 15 is a detail from the May 1724 map of Saint-Domingue by Frézier that shows all three locations, which were separated from each other by significant distances. In today's terms, the Cul de Sac plain is a good hour's drive from Léogâne, and from the Cul de Sac to the heart of the Artibonite valley is several hours more. Nonetheless, these three communities formed a loosely connected, "western" insurgent movement that would unite at critical points in late 1722 and the first months of 1723.

The region's capacity to shape the course of political events reflected its growing economic dynamism. The Cul de Sac plain had become the site of one of the colony's major clusters of plantations by the late seventeenth century, with indigo predominating over sugar until at least 1715. The colony's administrative capital moved around in the later seventeenth century (La Tortue, Port-de-Paix, Petit Goâve) before finally settling on Léogâne in 1695 in recognition of the increasingly intense cultivation of the Cul de Sac region.[3] That designation had one institutional consequence of great significance for the unfolding of the revolt: it meant the transfer of the second of the colony's two high courts from Petit Goâve to Léogâne.

As of the early 1720s, the colonial courts were, in their essence, mouthpieces for creole settler interests, and they would press at the limits of their ill-defined institutional role in defending those interests. The Conseil Supérieur was a variation on the metropolitan provincial parlements, installed in each of the conquered provinces acquired in the second half of the seventeenth century— Artois, Roussillon, Flanders, Alsace, the Franche-Comté—as well as in the overseas colonies.[4] Like early modern courts generally, they served both legislative and judicial functions, registering royal edicts as well as sitting over appeals from the lower tribunals (known as *sénéchaussées*). About a decade before he served as line of first defense against the insurgents, the Comte d'Arquian observed that the colonial councils expressed a "rustic vision" of legal procedure consisting of "pipe-in-mouth" rather than learned judgments.[5] That would change over the course of the eighteenth century, as the conseils

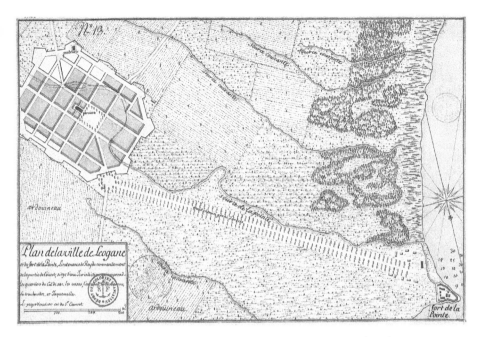

FIGURE 16. "Plan de la Ville de Léogâne et du fort de la Pointe" (1742). Courtesy of the Archives nationales d'outre-mer, Aix-en-Provence, France.

were gradually professionalized and brought more into line with the standards of their metropolitan counterparts.[6]

Legal informality did not preclude the Léogâne Council from asserting a settler version of natural right. That assertiveness was on full display in late November 1722, when Lesgut, the company's director in Léogâne, wrote to warn company headquarters in Paris of the prickly, restive mood in Saint-Domingue. The colony "is inhabited by people who are very jealous of their privileges, and who will make their utmost efforts to maintain them." "It is very dangerous to want to introduce novelties there," he signaled, emphasizing local fears about the effect of the company's imminent takeover of the Saint-Domingue slave trade on the price of plantation labor.[7]

The Léogâne director highlighted the Indies Company's export tax exemption for its potential to disrupt the colonists' fiscal arrangement with the king, which dated back to the 1670s. Taxes were the other major point of contention. In the aftermath of the tenuous compromise reached in 1713–14, colonists and administrators had continued to work out the mechanics of the *octroi* slaveholding levy. Conflicts arose over such questions as whether smaller plantation owners—those holding fewer than five slaves—ought to enjoy a break from the *octroi*, or whether the "larger planters" should be able to claim an exemption for small numbers of enslaved persons maintained in urban dwellings.[8] The arrival of the Indies Company in 1722 on terms of absolute immunity from all taxation (whether on the sale of slaves or the export of goods) renewed prior controversy over attempts to collect the taxes of the Domaine d'Occident. This prompted even Sorel and Montholon to denounce the new charter on the basis that it threatened the colony's ability to support the costs of military defense.[9]

By immediately slashing public revenues in half, the Indies Company monopoly thus signified an evisceration of the colony's tax base in addition to higher commodity and labor costs.[10] Compressing a complicated fiscal history that he may not have fully understand into a few sentences, Lesgut counseled accommodation. "[T]his land loves and maintains its liberty," he explained, "and however much the people who inhabit it are faithful servants of the king and state, one must extend them a great deal of consideration in order to succeed." Lesgut must have already received word (perhaps through company channels) of the attack on the Africa House by the time he wrote these words, for he emphasized the necessity of a distinctly conciliatory approach to the opposition. "[W]e will become the innocent victims of the furor of the rabble (*populace*) if these actions are followed by others." And the only way to accomplish that objective was to renounce the company's export tax immunity and assure the local planters that they would be able to purchase west African captives at "reasonable, current market prices." In short, the company had no choice but to find the "real interest" that it shared with the colonists in the profits to be had from the trade in "negroes and other goods."[11]

———

Accommodation was not in the cards up north, with La Ferrière and Desnos now both holed up aboard the *Bellone* after the events of November 22–23. D'Arquian and Duclos dispatched news of the uprising to the administration in Léogâne, along with a request to revoke the ordinance on the piastres. The publication of the suspension the following day, at 6:30 p.m., produced only about a week's worth of relative peace in the north. By the beginning of December, the women of Le Cap had begun to organize a new march on the false rumor that La Ferrière and Desnos had been returned to the Maison d'Afrique.

The instructions that the beleaguered d'Arquian and Duclos were desperately awaiting from the administration only further aggravated the situation. In a letter dated December 4 at Saint-Louis, Sorel and Montholon denounced the "sedition" of the north. They then advised the Cap Français administrators to share their letter with "leading colonists" in order to "open [their] eyes" to the distinct possibility that the king might unleash his full wrath upon Saint-Domingue if the current disorders were not quickly resolved. A satisfactory

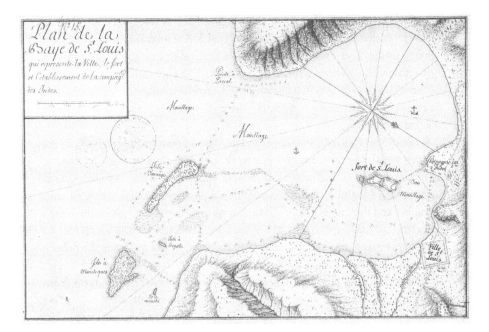

FIGURE 17. "Plan de la Baie de St. Louis, qui représente la Ville, le fort et l'établissement de la Compagnie des Indes" (1742). Courtesy of the Archives nationales d'outre-mer, Aix-en-Provence, France.

outcome required, at a minimum, that the directors of the Indies Company be returned to the Africa House and their goods restored to them.[12]

Forcing a return of the company's directors to the Africa House might cause the "mutiny" to "spread from the people to the *habitants*"—a distinction that made clear the term settlers (*habitants*) referred to planters only. But the administrators did not in fact see the uprising as a genuinely popular or widespread phenomenon. The true authors of this "tumult," they observed, were

> the merchants (*commerçants*), jealous of the establishment of a Company that excludes them from their trade, since the settlers do not care who provides them with the slaves they need to develop their lands so long as they are never lacking.

While not going so far as to call them smugglers, Sorel and Montholon made clear that these self-interested traders were manipulating La Sagona's movement to preserve a commercial status quo.[13]

Viewing the opposition to the Indies Company as a merchant conspiracy in disguise, Sorel and Montholon proposed to make use of the colonial rumor mill to defuse the situation. First, they suggested transferring a controversial threat attributed to La Ferrière—a boast that French naval ships would soon arrive to pound Cap Français with cannon fire and burn it to the ground—to the captain of the *Bellone*, Monsieur de Chilly.[14] The administrators then concocted a plot to have de Chilly removed from the scene and punished as "a favorable opportunity to appease the rebel movements, and to render a satisfactory justice."[15]

Second, Sorel and Montholon urged that the women and vagabonds of Cap Français who had originated this rumor about La Ferrière be made to take the fall in place of the "merchants and traders of your city [who] have fomented" the ruckus. "[T]hrow all the regrettable consequences that have unfolded onto the rabble and the vagabonds, until such time as we are able to assert the King's authority." To accomplish this, the town administrators should undertake to "divide this party in two and to separate the upright people from the others, in order to fortify the King's party to that extent."[16]

This convoluted analysis suggested that Sorel and Montholon, far from being capable of penetrating through the fog of the revolt, were becoming caught up in its very logic. They clearly recognized that merchants were indispensable to the colony's economic life and could not be punished for that reason. But the administrators' conviction that "merchants and traders" were behind the commotions of Cap Français was itself nebulous. What was the distinction between "merchants" and "settlers" (*habitants*), "traders" and "planters" in this context? Sorel and Montholon were also in the odd position of having supported the petition to abolish the company's privilege because of the threat that it would "annihilate" the colony's tax base.[17] Moreover, they claimed to empathize with colonists who had placed valuable stores of processed sugar aboard the *Bellone*, only to learn that La Ferrière was threatening to have their cargoes seized upon arrival in France to indemnify the Indies Company for the damage wrought to its facilities. These anxious settlers were none other than dame Robineau (La Sagona's unidentified coconspirator, according to Bourgeois) and a planter named Castaing, who would become a key actor in the Cul de Sac movement in late December.[18]

The core of the difficulty was the need to separate the respectable participants from the contemptible rabble, a task made impossible by the very terms in which it was framed. In a second letter to d'Arquian and Duclos on December 6, Sorel and Montholon lamented seeing "honest people . . . mixed up with an indocile and seditious people." These honest types "are passing for the dregs of the people in revolting against the intentions of their master as if they have nothing to risk, nothing to fear, and as if they have neither judgment nor a sense of right conduct." After all, asked the governor and intendant, what do "upright persons [*honnêtes gens*] . . . have to fear from the establishment of a company?" They ought simply to remember "all of the good that the [former] Company of Senegal procured them"—a tone-deaf reference to the institution that had occasioned the earlier "mutiny" of 1680.[19]

Unable to isolate the rootless rabble from the *honnêtes gens* who seemed to be rousing it, the administrators were at a loss as to how to proceed. They were not the first administrators to be stymied by the issue of what to do with persons known as *gens sans aveu*. Derived from a feudal custom that referred to the act (*aveu*, or avowal) by which a vassal pledged fealty to the lord whose land he possessed, the term had come, by the fifteenth and sixteenth centuries, to mean one who was without a lord or other social guarantor.[20] Charlevoix describes the Saint-Domingue administrators as determined to keep La Sagona's band out of Cap Français in late November and December 1722 because it included "a considerable number of *gens sans aveu*, who had nothing to lose, and were only looking for opportunities to pillage."[21]

The best Sorel and Montholon could come up with was to sweep matters under the rug with a modest display of fortitude. The monarchy was likely to respond to "the mutiny of this people" with a heavier dose of "anger" than "clemency." But there might still be time to "repair the past" by arranging matters so as to leave "not the least trace of what has happened," so that "only the faintest and softest news" manages to reach the court in Versailles. Meanwhile, the company's officers, exiled in the Cap Français harbor, ought to be immediately restored to land and to their rightful properties, in what Sorel and Montholon described as the only "remedy" that could "avert the storm" at hand. Pending an official response to their remonstrance against the money ordinance, the administrators promised to "render an account to the Court" that would "lead nobody to be punished and even spare the guilty ones."[22]

The administrators' awkward maneuvering and political paralysis produced only more upheaval. Their letter arrived at Cap Français on December 11 and, as d'Arquian and Duclos had been invited to do, was promptly shared with the region's leading planters. For the second time in less than a month, a communication from Léogâne succeeded in producing conflagration in the north. On the night of December 17, cannon fire announced the beginning of another general uprising of the northern quarters and a new march on Le Cap. According to Charlevoix, an "unknown negro" carried flyers signed "La Colonie" to the settlements surrounding Cap Français, calling on the inhabitants to gather at Haut du Cap on the evening of December 17.[23]

At their wits' end, d'Arquian and Duclos took matters directly to the Naval Council on December 18, bypassing Sorel and Montholon. According to d'Arquian and Duclos, at least some colonists managed to persuade themselves that the December 4 letter had in fact been written by Boismorant, the company's commissioner at Saint-Louis and, as of September 1720, a magistrate on the Conseil Supérieur of Léogâne: a man who had become the very personification of the wealth-power nexus.[24] Yet another rumor held that the Conseil Supérieur of Le Cap was about to hold an extraordinary session to register the company's privileges of September 1720. Following a night of cannon fire heard throughout the city, word arrived in the northern capital on the morning of December 18 of an approaching armed force of eight hundred colonists from districts to the east, between Le Cap and the Spanish boundary. Châtenoye, dispatched to persuade the militants to disband and return to their plantations, reported that the band grew in size by "forcing" the inhabitants of other districts encountered along the way to assemble that evening at Haut du Cap or risk having their plantations burned to the ground.[25]

It was in this context that d'Arquian and Duclos proclaimed the arrival of a new and more expansive phase of the rebellion that combined anonymity with coercive tactics. "A women's riot has become a general affair," they told the council, "and nobody is named in this entire affair." The handbills circulated in the hills above Le Cap stated: "At Haut du Cap, Thursday, on pain of being torched."[26] The alarm these handbills generated reflected their threat of physical violence. But the messengers, at least, were not entirely anonymous in one fundamental sense. In a passage of his history of Saint-Domingue, Charlevoix attributed the handbills to an "unknown negro" and related that, when asked by Châtenoye "to whom he belonged, the negro responded 'TO THE COLONY.'" Although it does not figure in the report of d'Arquian and Duclos, this striking anecdote about the participation of a (presumed) enslaved person is consistent with other primary sources from late 1722. Charlevoix's account seems to place as much emphasis on the anonymity of the unidentified slave as on his "negro" or slave status.[27] The combination of the two characteristics signaled a special challenge to the slave society of Saint-Domingue that Sorel and Montholon would soon be forced to confront.

Putting colonists to the choice between keeping their plantations and participating in the march on Le Cap meant that everyone was now effectively a part of the insurgency. Recognizing that an army driven by such mixed motivations would spell disaster if allowed to enter Le Cap, d'Arquian once more took matters into his own hands and made his way to the front lines of the approaching forces. Overcoming great "resistance and difficulty," the municipal governor managed to make headway only after giving his personal assurance that the directors aboard the *Bellone* would leave Saint-Domingue by the following day (December 19). Appeased by this offer and by the torching of

Boismorant's plantation at Petite Anse, the "wolf" of seven or eight hundred men was finally persuaded to retreat.[28]

———

The departure of the *Bellone* for France on December 19, 1722, bearing La Ferrière, Desnos, and their staff, returned the northern region to a period of relative calm. But the events of December—divulged to the ministry from Cap Français with more than a hint of insubordination—permanently buried the possibility that the upheaval in Saint-Domingue could be kept hidden from metropolitan eyes. Given what was about to unfold in the western region, that possibility would have been remote in any case. On December 16, flyers appeared calling for the inhabitants of the Artibonite valley to assemble at the Bac de l'Artibonite at eight o'clock on December 26, in preparation for a march southward on the capital, via the Cul de Sac plain. (The Bac, which is identified in figure 15, was the site of a flatboat by which residents of the Artibonite plain could cross the Artibonite River.)[29]

The western planters very quickly brought pressures for changes in the colony's governance. Their ability to do this stemmed from an unintended decision to introduce the question of representation into the politics of the revolt. With the march on the capital underway, Sorel and Montholon appointed four militia officers from the Cul de Sac plain—Dubois, Meslier, Pommier, and Deslandes, men "whom the inhabitants trust"—to serve as intermediaries between the administration and the insurgents. In authorizing these delegates to take such "measures toward the people as will calm them, by granting them what they demand without injuring the King's authority," Sorel and Montholon effectively tied their own hands in advance of an actual face-to-face negotiation.[30]

The insurgents of the Artibonite and Cul de Sac plains exploited this concession as an opportunity to organize a rudimentary political assembly and formulate a set of constitutional demands. At an assembly on December 28, they "elected," by a voice vote, "twelve of the most notable among them"—led by an Artibonite valley planter named Villaroche—to draw up a document that would soon become known as the Cul de Sac Treaty. With this decision, the western colonists steered the rebellion toward one of its most radical and controversial moments.[31]

The controversy over the treaty began with how it was recorded on paper. In its final, fully executed form, this extraordinary document consisted of two columns: on the right, a set of nine demands, on the left, carefully crafted responses to each by Sorel and Montholon. In some cases, the responses went no further than a promise to pursue the matter up the chain of command. This was true of articles 1 and 4, calling for suppression of the Indies Company in Saint-Domingue and "a free trade in negroes as well as goods." In responding to the demand for an end to the company's monopoly on the trade in west African captives, Sorel and Montholon parsed their words with particular care, promising only to petition the king to "limit the trade to the merchants of France."[32]

Not all of the colonists' grievances could be deferred or finessed in this way. Article 6 forced a decision on the critical issue of whether the inhabitants should have the right to participate in deliberations of the Conseil Supérieur relating to the imposition of new taxes:

> In order to ensure that nothing transpires at the colony's Sovereign Council to the prejudice or at the expense of the inhabitants, [His Majesty shall] ordain that where the affairs of the Colony are concerned, the councils will be required to call before them two prominent inhabitants deputized and chosen annually by each district with voting rights (*voix délibérative*) for this purpose only.

This call for representation distilled newfound concerns that the tribunal was at risk of being co-opted by the Indies Company and other obstreperous interests.[33] Sorel and Montholon responded in the margin that they believed the king would keep his promise to impose no new taxes. But they agreed all the same to add the issue to the list of grievances they would raise with the king. As for voting rights on the conseils supérieurs of Cap Français and Léogâne, Sorel and Montholon promised to petition the monarchy to allow "one or two persons" per district (*quartier*) to attend the court sessions. Pending a final decision, the colonists could immediately name "one or two settlers from each district" to attend the councils "with voting rights where the affairs of the Colony are concerned."[34]

This was a remarkable, even if temporary, concession. For all of their negotiating audacity, however, the insurgents recognized that they, too, were treading on delicate territory at Cul de Sac. In their final claim, they asked Sorel and Montholon to "implore His Majesty's clemency for the entire colony . . . which had been and always would be submissive and faithful to the King." The protests against the Indies Company were designed to no other end than "the well-being of his state." The governor and intendant promised to bring this request before the monarchy, recognizing that the events of the past two months had been prompted "purely by [the colonists'] fear that they would be oppressed by this company, all the more since they believe it to be contrary to the good of the state, and to the liberties that His Majesty has agreed to promise them."[35]

This plea for mercy demonstrates just how much the colonial revolt against the Indies Company had diverged from the pattern of communal tax revolts so characteristic of urban life in seventeenth- and eighteenth-century France.[36] The family resemblance was certainly there. The insurgents' mantra—"Long live the king, without the company"—sounded suspiciously like the cries of *"Vive le Roi sans gabelle* (Long live the king, without the salt tax)" that animated contemporaneous riots against the Farmers General in the metropole.[37] And the use of the pejorative term *maltôtiers* (tax extorters) to denounce the Indies Company's agents in Saint-Domingue indicates familiarity with the tradition of fiscal protest in France. But the uprising in Saint-Domingue had become a movement to reinvent the colonial order based on principles of self-determination framed in direct (and clearly contradictory) relationship to the institutions of slavery and the slave trade. In a 1723 plea direct to the king, the insurgents explained that, faced with the threat of a company whose "sole object," like that of all companies, "has only ever been to establish new colonies," they had decided to refuse the fate of "becoming a land of conquest for the company and its harsh, mercenary armies that are the horror and abomination of this new world."[38] Its histrionic language notwithstanding, this statement of the insurgents' case accurately presaged that the long reign of corporate colonization, which went back to the earliest French forays into the New World, was about to come to an end. And the insurgents could claim much of the responsibility for that outcome—even if they could not yet anticipate the full range of its consequences.

The effort to frame the uprising in exclusively anticorporate terms—connected as it was to the hope of royal clemency for the "seditious" acts of late 1722—would not long survive the Cul de Sac Treaty, however. Signed on December 29 by Sorel and Montholon for the government and by the twelve deputies representing the insurgents of the Artibonite and Cul de Sac plains, the treaty itself became a powerful symbol of the deep rift the revolt had introduced between the colonists and royal sovereignty in Saint-Domingue. It not only posed a radical challenge to principles of absolutist government; it also marked a new militancy in the western planter movement. Over the course of 1723, this militancy led to armed confrontations that effectively suspended the government of Saint-Domingue.

Having breached the theory of absolutism in the treaty, the planters now moved against it in practice. They began with the king's representatives in Saint-Domingue. On January 5, agitated by reports that the company's directors in the west and south were planning to stay in place, the insurgents placed an ailing Governor Sorel under the functional equivalent of house arrest at the plantation of the Sieur de Vernon, the very first *habitant* to set down roots in the Cul de Sac area and a man highly respected by the local community. By January 8, somewhere between 1,200 and 1,400 armed rebels were descending upon Léogâne. Facing no other option, Lesgut and his clerks joined the Saint-Louis director, Grenon, and the rest of the Indies Company staff (minus a single, low-level representative) aboard *La Jolie*, which departed for Nantes just in time to avoid the wrath of the approaching army. The next day, the insurgents released Sorel from house arrest at Vernon's plantation, permitting the governor and intendant to return to their official residence at Léogâne.[39]

The planters then proceeded to implement their most important victory in the Cul de Sac Treaty: representation. From January 19 to 24, 1723, colonists from the Artibonite valley, the Cul de Sac plain, Léogâne, and Mirebalais nominated two delegates each to represent them at the Conseil Supérieur in the capital. In February, the districts of the southern coast—Jacmel, l'Isle à Vache, and Aquin—added their nominations, followed, lastly, by Petit Goâve (which, along with l'Isle à Vache, selected only one deputy). Of the fourteen individuals nominated, one name, previously disclosed on the December 16 flyers as an organizer of the insurgent Artibonite valley planters who assembled at the Bac de l'Artibonite, stands out: Champflour. Selected along with Meugnier to represent the Artibonite region, Maurice-César de Champflour was descended from an old family of the Auvergne province in south-central France. An infantry captain turned planter and a relative of the bishop of La Rochelle, he had only recently arrived in the colony (1719), and married soon thereafter.[40] Following Champmeslin's mission to restore order in Saint-Domingue, Champflour would become notorious as one of a handful of colonists singled out for punishment as the prime instigators and masterminds of the rebellion. For the moment, his appointment as deputy of the Artibonite community, pursuant to the Cul de Sac Treaty, gave his role in the resistance a veneer of legal authority.

Sixty years later, the creole jurist Moreau de Saint-Méry conspicuously declined to reproduce the text of the treaty in his compendium of colonial law. Instead, he noted, "we mention this Treaty here only to demonstrate our exactitude," referring readers to his later-published *Description de Saint-Domingue* for discussion of the document.[41] Moreau seized on a promise from Sorel and Montholon to have the treaty registered by the conseils supérieurs to justify his own effacement of the document from the colony's legal history.[42] The Léogâne court, Moreau explained, had only registered the agreement after a delay of more than two months, and then subject to the king's ruling on the validity of the treaty. In a closing allusion to the provocation for which the agreement would come to stand, Moreau added: "Stricken and expunged on December 7, 1723, by virtue of the King's Orders."[43] Consistent with his denial of the Cul de Sac treaty itself, Moreau de Saint-Méry recorded only the titles and dates of the January 1723 nominations before adding that they had been "stricken and expunged" pursuant to the same court orders of December 1723.[44] Direct representation of the colonists in the governing institutions of Saint-Domingue could have no place in this exhaustive archive of colonial legislation. The effacement of the Cul de Sac Treaty was part of a larger effort to turn back the clock on all of these developments.

Moreau published the final volumes of his series in the waning years of the Old Regime, just as the colonists were pushing for the right to send delegates to the Estates General (and then the National Assembly). Even he could have had little notion that the issue of colonial representation in the metropole was about to disrupt the legal order of Saint-Domingue in a manner no one could possibly have anticipated in the 1720s.[45]

———

The question of representation soon gave way to a second dispute that would echo just as loudly in the revolutionary North Atlantic decades later. The arrival of another company slave ship, the *Duc de Noailles*, on January 29, 1723, returned the northern region to a state of armed resistance. After a Middle Passage of 31 days, the ship, under Captain Sicard, anchored in the Cap Français harbor with only 296 West African captives out of a starting cargo of 346; twenty crew members had also been lost.[46] In these circumstances, an immediate unloading of his vessel was Captain Sicard's only priority, as it was for French ship captains generally upon approaching the ports of the greater Caribbean. As the historian Gwendolyn Midlo Hall has shown, Indies Company personnel worked with a sense of great urgency to bring arriving slave cargoes from La Balize, near the southernmost mouth of the Mississippi Delta, upriver to New Orleans. That part of the journey was often as perilous and deadly as the Middle Passage itself given the effects of scurvy and other ailments attendant to the Atlantic crossing. Enslaved persons were the most vulnerable to these sicknesses because of the poor quality of the nourishment they were given.[47]

So it was with the *Duc de Noailles*, as with the *Pontchartrain* before it. With his ship's occupants at or near starvation, Sicard attempted to make an immediate emergency unloading but was prevented from doing so. On February 5, more than a month after the *Duc de Noailles* had landed, its cargo still confined in miserable conditions to the ship's hold, the local assembly convened at Haut du Cap pursuant to the Cul de Sac Treaty. There, they demanded the expulsion of the *Duc de Noailles* from Saint-Domingue within ten days. Another month would pass before an end to the tug-of-war between the rebels and the administrators was in sight. Via d'Arquian and Duclos, Sicard presented a petition to the delegates on February 11, describing the state of his crew and cargo. On February 17, d'Arquian and Duclos unilaterally authorized the sale of two hundred of the enslaved to proceed, leading to talk of burning the plantations of those who purchased them. Finally, in early March, the Haut du Cap Assembly decided that colonists who had already purchased one of the enslaved should pay two hundred livres per head into the public fund for the colony.[48] And the

Léogâne high court, with Sorel and Montholon presiding, banned the wholesale purchase of any newly arriving slave cargoes with the intent to resell them later at retail, on pain of confiscation and a heavy fine. This ruling, which Moreau tells us was adopted with the deliberative input of the recently named district deputies, was among those "stricken and expunged" from the colonial legislative record in December 1723.[49]

No episode better illustrates the disjuncture between the insurgents' denunciations of corporate "enslavement" and their own role in an increasingly militant brand of slavery in Saint-Domingue. As enslaved persons were left to suffer in the holds of Indies Company ships, the white communities of Saint-Domingue argued, extorted, and otherwise forced their way to "a free trade in negroes."[50] Looking back at this travesty several decades later, the creole jurist Bourgeois, ever the contrarian, charged that the rebels who raised the greatest fuss over the *Duc de Noailles* were among the leading buyers of its slave cargo.[51] The comment foreshadowed the British essayist Samuel Johnson's more famous quip, in *Taxation No Tyranny* (1775), about the American "drivers of negroes" and their propensity to produce the "loudest yelps for liberty."[52] Indeed, this chapter of the uprising in Saint-Domingue prefigured the iconic tactics of the American Tea Crisis as well as the more general moral dissonance of the American revolutionary language of liberty and equality.

What made this demonstration an act of militant slavery was the colonists' apparent readiness to embargo the very institution on which their livelihood depended. The insurgents' appeal for a "free trade" in slaves was, in fact, an appeal for larger numbers of west African captives at Dutch and British contraband prices. They were willing to accept short-term costs to ensure this long-term goal.

Or at least some of them were. Bourgeois's behind-the-scenes portrait of planters jostling for the right to acquire the very slave labor they claimed was the product of an illegitimate monopoly suggests that some colonists had no compunctions about taking company slaves. That account was confirmed by the very need to prohibit wholesale purchases of slaves for resale at retail at a subsequent time. The decision to strike and expunge the Léogâne conseil's order on this point in December 1723 adds an additional wrinkle to the narrative. Exactly how the planters' deputies opined is unknown, but the erasure of the order cannot be explained by the mere fact of their participation in the court's deliberations. Another ruling on which the deputies also held forth, issued the same day by the same court, but more favorable to the administration in substance, was allowed to stand.[53] The erasure of the ban on wholesale purchase therefore targeted the effort by a colonial tribunal to alter the terms of the colony's slave trade contrary to royal decree. As Charlevoix indicated, colonists at Cap Français criticized the Léogâne court's ruling because wholesale purchases meant shorter, more efficient voyages for slaving vessels and cheaper prices for end buyers. But they also believed that the slave trade in Saint-Domingue was a matter for the governor and intendant to regulate, not the conseil.[54]

With such conflicts and contradictions as these at work, it is no surprise that the insurgency soon moved on, forcing what would turn out to be a final major confrontation with the administration. On March 3, citing distribution of a flyer in Léogâne the day before that proclaimed their removal from office and called upon the people of the Artibonite valley to rise up, the governor and intendant evacuated the capital and transferred the seat of government to Petit Goâve.[55] A decision to transfer the seat of government bore equally on the judicial and executive arms of the colonial administration, which meant that the members of the Léogâne conseil would soon face a difficult decision. Their initial response was to denounce the authors of the "seditious" flyers as

> malicious spirits, enthusiasts for disorder, and disruptors of public peace who, by means of anonymous letters, posters, bills, and defamatory libels, written under the name of *Colonies, Sans-Quartiers, the Angel Raphaël,* and other signatures of a similar nature, all tend to stir up (*émouvoir*) the people.

The elections of January–February notwithstanding, the rule of anonymity that had protected the architects of the uprising from the beginning was still in force. To judge from this document, the insurgency still aimed to speak in the unitary, collective voice of "the colony," which identified with no single region (hence the appellation "Sans-Quartier," which conveniently protected any one district from retaliation for the actions of its residents). The conseil ordered the militia officers of the western region to apprehend "masked men and other bearers of the anonymous bills."[56] Sorel and Montholon may well have believed these strictures to partake of bad faith, since it was now becoming an open secret that Champflour had authored the offending "Sans-Quartier" poster in tandem with another wealthy Artibonite landholder named Charpentier.[57] Awkwardly, Champflour was now deputized to the same conseil that purported to denounce the anonymous flyers.

Bad faith or not, the men behind the latest agitation probably also rallied around a shared experience of debt. Financial vulnerability was certainly not the only reason for their discontent. Charpentier, for example, a recent immigrant to Saint-Domingue, was the son of a Protestant refugee newspaper editor hostile to the French government. He was also a relative and correspondent of the Butler family, slave traders operating out of La Rochelle. Along with several other Artibonite colonists—the Baron de Courseul, Legrand, the chevalier de Bengalas, Fortier, Chauvet, and Roger—Charpentier and Champflour formed the core of an informal coordinating group that met in the home of Robiou, a large planter from Trou Bordet, on the western coast about halfway between Léogâne and what is now Port-au-Prince. There may have been other Protestants in this group.[58]

As Sorel and Montholon described them in a list of culpable parties drawn up at Petit Goâve on March 26, however, the coordinators also included several men "weighed down by debt"—a phrase used to describe Champflour himself. Champflour's fellow Artibonite planter Le Grandhomme was said to have "consumed a large amount of assets" through "bad conduct." At least two other members of this "seditious" group had gone bankrupt with the crash of John Law's System: Meunier of the Artibonite, a "dangerous spirit" and former secretary to Governor Choiseul, and Drouïllard of Léogâne. Another "dangerous spirit," Descopins of Aquin, was identified as someone "considerably in debt to the Company." The financial condition of the "cabalists" was not uniform. Robiou and several others, Drouïllard among them, were described as holding significant assets. Remarkably or not for a tavern keeper, La Sagona was identified as having accumulated fifty thousand livres of wealth. In at least some cases, these asset holdings may also have implied a vulnerability to foreclosure. The overall portrait is mixed, but suggestive enough of the pervasive influence of debt, whether actual or anticipated.[59]

For such men, promoting what Tramond describes as a state of "open war" with the governor and intendant may have seemed the only way forward.[60] The members of the Léogâne court not only refused to cooperate with the transfer of the capital to Petit Goâve. On March 6, they also called on Sorel and Montholon to return to their habitual seat of power in Léogâne, claiming the unrest in the Artibonite had been blown out of proportion. The administrators' April 11 ordinance formally transferring the Léogâne conseil to Petit Goâve deepened the deadlock. Although a few loyalist members of the conseil agreed to relocate, a dissenting majority of eight remained at Léogâne to create a kind of rump court. Ordering a cessation of all construction work on the colony's fortifications and replacing the sitting tax collector with one more sympathetic to the insurgents' goals, the Léogâne magistrates managed to bring effective governance in the colony to a standstill for several months.[61]

Cornered in Petit Goâve and with few options at their disposal, Sorel and Montholon responded with their own variations on the theme of militant slavery. These included some increasingly radical measures for the restoration of order. Military action of some kind seemed now inevitable. Already in mid-February, the colony's director of fortifications, Amédée-François Frézier, had drafted a plan to expand the fort at Petit-Goâve to accommodate a garrison as large as five hundred soldiers, instead of the one hundred approved by the monarchy in April 1720 (figure 18). In the lower-right corner of his proposed expansion, Frezier observed that "the recent seditions have made it known that

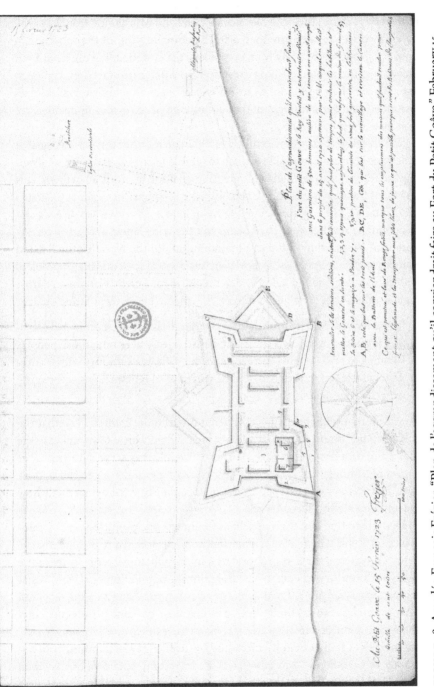

FIGURE 18. Amadée-François Frézier, "Plan de l'aggrandissement qu'il conviendrait faire au Fort du Petit Goâve," February 15, 1723. Courtesy of the Archives nationales d'outre-mer, Aix-en-Provence, France.

we must have more troops in order to contain the *habitants* and ensure the Governor's safety." The need to evacuate Sorel and Montholon from Léogâne barely two weeks later provided a stark demonstration of the rationale of Frézier's proposal. By early March, Nolivos, the commanding officer at Petit Goâve, was desperately rushing to reinforce the defenses of the new capital in anticipation of an imminent siege. And Sorel began to mobilize available detachments of troops throughout the colony in preparation for a more offensive response to the insurgents.[62]

The traditional answer to sedition in the French Caribbean was to dispatch a metropolitan armada sizable enough to remind local insurgents of the advantages of returning to the fold while granting a pardon to nearly all of them. This had been the strategy used to quell both the 1670 uprising against Colbert's West Indies Company (although the naval fleet in that case was already stationed in the southeastern Caribbean) and the 1717 Gaoulé in Martinique. As Sorel and Montholon noted in a memorandum to the Naval Council dated March 20, 1723, at Petit Goâve, however, there was at least one major problem with this strategy: it had failed to deter recidivism. Titled "Plan for an Armament for the Coast of Saint-Domingue," the memo began by pointing out that

> impunity of Martinique has authorized the most recent revolt in St. Domingue, and it is certain that if His Majesty does not punish peoples so quick to take up arms and throw off the yoke, his authority will be completely forfeited in this land, and he will have to renounce his sovereignty over the American islands.

Punishment was therefore necessary but ought to be calibrated so that the colony could "bounce back." The sword must fall only on "a few families of the island and on a few leaders (*chefs*), whose example may serve in the future as a form of intimidation so powerful that it can contain these peoples in their duty."[63] If this was easy enough to articulate in theory, it left open exactly how the implementation should work.

Demonstrating that their penchant for unorthodox solutions to the colonial crisis was still intact, Sorel and Montholon proceeded to outline what is, to my knowledge, the first proposal by a metropolitan Atlantic power in the eighteenth century to emancipate a significant population of slaves.[64] That this proposal was drafted with a mind toward suppressing a creole rebellion makes it no less radical for its time. The colonists of Saint-Domingue, Sorel and Montholon explained, were "jealous of their liberty to the point of risking their lives to maintain it," including by "arm[ing] a great number of negroes for their defense." Any conventional force sent to put down the rebellion would have to deal not only with this variable, but also with "the remoteness of the place and the diseases that reigned in the land [which] were more than sufficient means, without other arms, to kill off all the soldiers that the King might send."[65]

This discussion is one of the clearest indications we have that insurgent planters had moved well beyond using slaves for merely logistical purposes, e.g., to distribute anonymous posters in remote reaches of the colony. They were now actively arming their slaves. That policy was not itself unprecedented in the long history of slavery.[66] But no Atlantic colonial administration had before considered adopting the strategy on a large scale for the purpose of ensuring domestic tranquility. And that was exactly what Sorel and Montholon now proceeded to suggest. "As regards the arming of slaves," they argued, "nothing is easier than to prevent it, by promising freedom to those who will abandon their masters in order to side with the flags of the king, if it were necessary, which is the thing that the colonists fear the most."[67] Indeed it was, but what is remarkable about this passage is that the administrators would have feared the strategy any less. In proposing open-ended emancipation as a means of quashing a revolt, Sorel and Montholon were unquestionably far ahead of their time. Their memorandum pointed forward to the tactics of Lord Dunmore in Virginia during the American revolutionary war and the French civil commissioners Sonthonax and Polverel during the conflict between Governor Galbaud's supporters and free people of color in Cap Français in 1793.[68] Whether Sorel and Montholon would ever have followed through on this proposal is another matter. They regarded the insurgency as threatening enough to justify the concept, and that in turn suggests the administrators had joined the planters in embracing a form of militant slavery. Unlike the planters' variation, this form aimed at defending the colonial order from the slaveholders themselves. But the proposal shared the same precautionary approach of embracing short-term risks to achieve long-term goals that was reflected in the boycott of the *Duc de Noailles*.

This groundwork of their strategy established, Sorel and Montholon proceeded to outline the particulars of their proposal for a metropolitan expeditionary force that would, in fact, eventually come. The invasion would ideally begin at Cap Français where the uprising itself had first put down roots. From there, the squadron would proceed with the work of pacification in a more or less southerly direction. The Artibonite valley and Cul de Sac plain required special care: at least 150 troops (under a new *lieutenant du roi*) would need to be stationed in the former, and a minimum of 200 men (reporting to a new *major*) in the latter. In total, the colony required a minimum of 2,000 new soldiers in peacetime to contain the settlers' rebellious instincts.[69]

Such figures were ambitious even by the colony's recent wartime standards. If Sorel and Montholon were able, in the end, to dispense with the need for a broad emancipation of the Saint-Domingue slave population, the woeful state of the colony's garrisons did not help them do so. Instead, the administrators benefited from a relaxation of the pace and intensity of the revolt after March 1723. Meanwhile, the governor and intendant dispatched Nolivos to the metropole on April 1 with copies of their March 20 memorandum as well as the list of principal rebel suspects drawn up on March 26. By mid-August, those documents were in the hands of the secretary of state for the colonies, Maurepas (who had just succeeded to Morville). Rejecting the administrators' call for a military occupation of Saint-Domingue, Maurepas and his staff orchestrated a rather different kind of mission than the one Sorel and Montholon had envisioned. Still, a royal naval squadron from France would soon be on its way, and the administrators could avoid pushing at the boundaries of their local military capabilities, whether white or Afro-Haitian.[70]

———

The final steps in securing the future of the sugar revolution in Saint-Domingue were decided far from the scene of the rebellion. In the fall of 1723, the monarchy dispatched an expedition under the command of Desnos-Champmeslin (Champmeslin for short), the former head of the French navy, to restore royal sovereignty in Saint-Domingue in response to the petitions of Sorel and Montholon. The squadron departed Brest on October 1. Upon arriving in late November, Champmeslin spent several weeks systematically touring all of the cities associated with rebel encampments or marches during the prior year. At nearly all of these locations, he followed the same script: military reviews, loyalty oaths, and court sessions designed to symbolize the colonists' return to the metropolitan fold. Immediately following the loyalty oath in Léogâne, Charlevoix reported, the assembled crowd duly cried out "LONG LIVE THE KING." In the back rows of the crowd, others pointedly added "without the Company"—a bit of heckling that Champmeslin would, shortly after, attribute to "some mulattoes" whose words he did not personally hear but dismissed as "seditious speech" worthy only of his "scorn."[71]

Champmeslin was treated to a similarly ambiguous welcome involving nonwhite actors at his next destination, Saint Marc (a town on the western coast about forty to fifty miles north of Léogâne). There, Charlevoix observed, "some negroes or mulattoes" had yelled out "LONG LIVE THE KING WITHOUT THE COMPANY" following the administration of the loyalty oath. When Champflour failed to appear at the ceremony as head of the local militia, Champmeslin proceeded to strip him of his commission. In retaliation, Charlevoix wrote, a planter of the Artibonite area took advantage of a lull just before the military review to hand the general an anonymous note signed "freedom" (la liberté) and threatening repercussions unless Champflour was left at peace.[72]

As these anecdotes suggest, the ceremonial displays could not disguise the de facto redistribution of power from company to colony that had taken place over the course of 1722 and 1723. As a matter of formal law, Champmeslin retained the company's monopoly over the slave trade to Saint-Domingue. But he repealed most of the company's other privileges, notably the export tax exemption, as well as the royal ordinance impeding the local use of Spanish silver money.[73] The colony's special tax arrangement with the monarchy—effective immunity from the obligations of the Domaine d'Occident in exchange for the *octroi* levy on slaveholdings—was preserved, with the added reassurance that "in no event will [tax] farmers be established in the Colony."[74] These concessions to planter sovereignty coexisted uneasily alongside repeated signs that the upheaval of 1722–23 had opened the door to the political mobilization of free people of color and other Afro-Haitians. That Charlevoix felt the need to express "scorn" for their having veered from the script of the loyalty ceremonies suggests that he had not entirely invented their presence.

There remained the knotty problem of how to disincentivize the creole insurrectionary recidivism that Sorel and Montholon had identified in their 1723 "Plan for an Armament." Two of the most prominent rebel leaders, Champflour and his fellow Artibonite planter Fortier, were tried in absentia by the reconstituted (and chastised) Conseil Supérieur of Léogâne in December 1723. Both were identified on the list that Sorel and Montholon had submitted on March 26, and it was now believed that Champflour's principal collaborator on the "Sans-Quartier" flyers was Fortier rather than Charpentier.[75] In March 1724, the two defendants were sentenced to death as "drivers of the colony's troubles." Their location unknown, they were hung in effigy in the public square of Petit Goâve.[76] Champflour would die on the Spanish side of the island in 1731. For many years, his widow fought to obtain rehabilitation of her husband's name. Absolution for "Sans-Quartier" finally came in 1753.[77]

For the others, a mix of exile and softer measures was the order of the day. La Sagona and the Baron de Courseul were deported to the metropole. As a condition of her exile, La Sagona was prohibited from residing within thirty leagues of a maritime port city. Courseul would receive permission to return to the colony in July 1728. Two magistrates of the Léogâne conseil were stripped of their offices. Charpentier escaped punishment altogether. No other colonists were pursued for their roles in the uprising. This may not have amounted to "impunity" along the lines of Sorel and Montholon's March 20 warning about the dangers of following in the footsteps of Martinique after the Gaoulé. But it was an extremely broad amnesty that left the vast majority of the insurgent leaders free to pick up their pecuniary pursuits where they left off in the fall of 1722.[78]

Champmeslin returned to France in March 1724, leaving behind a colony in which the raw social antagonisms of Atlantic commerce persisted. On June 3, another Indies Company captive ship, the *Prince de Conti*, arrived in the Cap Français harbor carrying 350 captives.[79] Three days later, another anonymous actor nailed a poster to the doors of the city's cathedral that read in significant part: "On behalf of the Colony: to all burghers and inhabitants, under no conditions whatsoever may negroes be purchased from the [Indies] Company, on pain of being torched (*brûlé*) without mercy." The Conseil Supérieur of Cap Français promptly sentenced the unidentified author of the "seditious" poster to be hung in effigy. Anonymous agitation was still a favored modus operandi in Saint-Domingue. And the colony's "prior troubles"—as Moreau put it in his title for the court's ruling—were not so behind it after all.[80]

———

A rebellion that began as a struggle over silver ended with a showdown over the slave trade. And that showdown had a clear winner. A June 1725 edict announcing a further reorganization of the Indies Company contained no reference to a slave trading monopoly in describing the company's privileges. By August of that year, the French slave trade was once again officially opened to independent merchants, handing Nantes, Bordeaux, and the other Ponant ports—not to mention the French Caribbean planters—a definitive, long-sought victory.[81] Silver was still there to attend this victory, to be sure. A manuscript history of Saint-Domingue by de Beauval Ségur, probably written shortly after 1750, captured the impact of these changes on the colony's economy:

> Freedom of trade brought a great number of blacks (*noirs*) and an abundance of everything, money was commonplace, luxury and spending increased, sugar plantations were established in all of the principal regions (*quartiers*). The other areas were gradually populated and settled, though more slowly than they ought to have been.[82]

As de Beauval Ségur suggests, and as the data from the Slave Voyages project confirm (see figure 2), the takeoff was not immediate after 1725. The key changes were not only legal and economic, but also political, and they would take some time to register. But a fundamental shift from silver to sugar as the key organizing principle of mercantilist supremacy had taken place. And that shift coincided with the displacement of corporate authority by the planters' militant slavery.[83]

The company would continue for several more decades to bring west African captives to the New World on a nonmonopoly basis, and it retained a physical presence in both Cap Français and at Saint-Louis. A 1728 map of Cap Français still indicated the location of the company's plantation on the outskirts of Cap Français (see figure 19). After 1725, however, the company increasingly settled for selling permits to the independent traders.[84] Its operations along the west African coast were the work of one private company competing with others, and its slaving operations ended everywhere in 1744 except for the occasional Mascarene expedition.[85] The company also retained a notable role in the Canadian fur trade until the Seven Years' War. But the institution that had refused the label "east" or "west" was now becoming essentially a company of the east, its future dependent primarily on the cotton textiles of India and the tea of China.

Saint-Domingue was not the only driver of these changes. Although it came four years after the liberalization of the slave trade, another revolt against the Indies Company delivered a fatal blow to its remaining prospects in Louisiana. About one-tenth of the French population of Louisiana died in the uprising of the Natchez Indians at Fort Rosalie in 1729. Following a series of brutal retaliatory expeditions organized in conjunction with its Choctaw allies, the French colonial administration exiled the two surviving Natchez leaders to nowhere else than Saint-Domingue, where they were sold as slaves (and interviewed in 1733 by Bienville, the "founder" of New Orleans, en route from France to resume a final term as Louisiana governor). In his 1747 memoir, Dumont de Montigny, a French colonial officer serving in New Orleans at the time of the uprising, lamented only the deaths of French civilians at Natchez. But the principal object of his ire was the Indies Company, which, he said, had tried to blame its "losses" on the Natchez Indians even as the company itself was the prime cause of the uprising. By early 1731, the Indies Company had retroceded its rights in Louisiana to the French crown and fully withdrawn from the Mississippi Valley.[86]

The company's fate after 1725 was also tied to maritime logistics and conditions along the west African coast. A failure to control outfitting costs may have been part of its dilemma.[87] The company was also weighed down by inefficiencies associated with its larger shipping capacity, which yielded only 40 percent more captives than private ships with less than half the tonnage. Filling a ship with three hundred slaves meant requiring crews to wait for months until the vessel was fully loaded and ready to make the crossing.[88] Still, when all of these factors are accounted for, there remains the unmistakable impact of the upheaval of 1722–23 in Saint-Domingue. The shift to private trade after 1725 was definitive for the duration of the Old Regime.[89] And other changes set in motion during the early 1720s would prove to have a no less significant impact on the colony's future.

5

The Company of Jesus

WRITING OF the events of the early 1720s in Saint-Domingue more than two hundred years later, in 1929, the French naval historian Joannès Tramond described "a revolution and counter-revolution without a single cadaver that passed nearly unnoticed in Europe." He was not the first to believe that the best way to represent the significance of these years was to describe them as a "revolution." The Jesuit Le Pers did the same in the mid-1720s, though his account suggests that Tramond confused pacification with something much stronger: a "counter-revolution." According to Le Pers, something different was at stake: in the aftermath of the rebellion, he wrote, the general approach had been to "put it to sleep (*assoupir*) rather than delve into it (*approfondir*)." The unspoken implication was that the colonial authorities had discouraged deeper investigation of the revolt in favor of their overall strategy of letting bygones be bygones and avoiding additional conflict.[1]

More than any other group, the Jesuits would find a way to ensure that the uprising against the Indies Company did not disappear altogether from the colony's historical consciousness. They did so despite numerous indications that the revolt was especially sensitive territory for the Jesuits. Their involvement in both the rebellion itself and its transformation into history reveal a different version of the 1720s than those we have explored thus far. For there were, in fact, two monopoly companies, not just one, working on the ground in Saint-Domingue during the early 1720s, each striving to mold the colony in the image of a corporate vision, each holding a monopoly charter that sought to foreclose competition and created resentment in doing so.[2]

The Company (or Society) of Jesus did not provide much in the way of economic competition for the Indies Company, but not for lack of trying.[3] The Jesuits in Saint-Domingue, like their brothers elsewhere in the New World, themselves participated in the economy of slavery. Four dimensions of the Jesuit experience in Saint-Domingue during the 1720s impinged on the events of that decade. First, as the founders of Haitian historical writing, the Jesuits were the first to tell the story of the revolt against the Indies Company. Second, they were themselves key if mysterious participants in the rebellion against John Law's company. Third, they were invested in the sugar revolution as land and slave owners in the northern province. Matters of money, debt, and taxation affected them no less deeply than their lay neighbors. Fourth, the Jesuits were caretakers of the souls of the colony's white settlers.

In a departure from this last mission, the Jesuits would expand into the proselytization of slaves. There, they would discover what some of them would regard as their core vocation in Saint-Domingue. That vocation would draw the Jesuits into the work of mediating between the militant slavery of the planters and the responses of the enslaved. The rebellion within the rebellion that the Jesuits encountered in this intermediate space would define both the fate of the Company of Jesus and the destiny of Saint-Domingue.

The sensitive task of chronicling the history of the Indies Company in Saint-Domingue emerged organically from these overlapping Jesuit commitments. The time that several first-generation Jesuits spent in the colony coincided in whole or part with the revolt against the Indies Company, and so it is not surprising that this event figured prominently in the histories they told of the colony. Pierre-François-Xavier de Charlevoix is the most well-known, but not the first or even the most important, of these Jesuit missionary-historians. As compared to his colleagues, he spent the least amount of time in the colony and departed just as the movement to evict the company was gaining steam. This forced him to rely on secondhand sources (including, most notably, his fellow Jesuit Le Pers) for his understanding of what happened, but it did not prevent him from producing an accomplished history. Others, including Le Pers and Père Margat, dedicated most of their lives as Jesuits to the service of the Church in Saint-Domingue, in conditions that often tested their will and came close to exhausting their spirituality.

The history that these missionaries wrote was the story of the founding of Saint-Domingue and its rise to a position of economic prominence. The Jesuits documented the colony's development of a distinct, corporate identity within the French empire. And the writing of that history, in turn, reinforced the identity. We can glimpse this transition merely by reviewing the titles of the various surveys that different French missionaries in the West Indies produced between the 1660s and the time of Charlevoix. For the Dominican Jean-Baptiste du Tertre, the operative framework was the *General history of the Antilles inhabited by the French*, published between 1667 and 1671. Père Labat, another Dominican, produced the equally general *New travels to the American islands* in 1722, just before the revolt against John Law's company. As of 1726–27, the Jesuit Le

Pers was chronicling (in manuscript form) what he called the *History of St. Domingue*. That manuscript would, in turn, serve as a key resource for another Jesuit account, by Charlevoix, titled the *History of the Spanish Island or St. Domingue*, published in 1730–31. By the end of the 1720s, the history of the colony had come into its own as a distinct, coherent story. The revolt against the Indies Company not only helped to make that story possible but formed one of its key chapters as it came to be written down.

Le Pers and Charlevoix formed a unique intellectual and spiritual duo, born of a collaboration turned competition that pitted one against the other in a race to publish the first history of Saint-Domingue. After a long journey that took him from Québec all the way down the Mississippi River to the Gulf Coast, Charlevoix arrived in Saint-Domingue in September 1722 and stayed just long enough to witness the colonists' first grumblings in response to the arrival of the Indies Company directors. By late October, he had departed for France, leaving his longtime mentor, Le Pers, behind. Of Walloon origin—he hailed from the French-speaking region of the Low Countries that is now southern and eastern Belgium—Le Pers had advised Charlevoix during the latter's novitiate years in Paris. A founding member of the Jesuit community in Cap Français, Le Pers's long tenure in Saint-Domingue began in 1704—when Louis XIV authorized the Jesuits to replace the Capuchins in the West Indian colony—and ended nearly a quarter century later, in 1729.

The seeds of the eventual rupture between these two priests and friends were sown at the end of 1722, with Charlevoix's arrival in France. Having resolved to publish a narrative of his voyages in French America, Charlevoix worked on and off over the next few years, collecting the necessary materials. At some point between 1723 and 1729, Le Pers entrusted his Saint-Domingue papers to Charlevoix with the hope that his France-based colleague would eventually publish them. These memoirs, along with Charlevoix's own archival research at the Dépôt de la Marine, became the basis for the *Histoire de l'Isle espagnole ou de St. Domingue* that Charlevoix published in two volumes in 1730–31—including its day-by-day, almost hour-by-hour account of the Saint-Domingue revolt.[4]

In the book's opening pages, Charlevoix paid touching tribute to his primary informant:

> For twenty-five years, he has labored in the Lord's Vineyard with a zeal that the heavens favor with their most abundant blessings. Three thousand adult Negroes, and a larger number of infants baptized by his hand, and nine or ten churches constructed through his efforts in the outlying regions of Cap Français and Port-de-Paix are the proof.[5]

This testament to a life of exceptional missionary accomplishments was no doubt heartfelt, but it obscured the more secular ambitions that both Le Pers

THE COMPANY OF JESUS   131

and Charlevoix harbored as aspiring historians. In the years after La Sagona's uprising, Le Pers prepared or oversaw at least three undated manuscript versions of a "History of Saint-Domingue," now preserved in the Bibliothèque nationale de France in Paris. Two of these are in Le Pers's own hand. The third, and most complete, version was composed by a third person at some point after the first volume of Charlevoix's history came out, and it was clearly intended for imminent publication (the *avertissement* opens with Le Pers denouncing Charlevoix's text). But the earliest of the three manuscripts, which was composed no later than 1727 and possibly as early as 1723, is closest in time and spirit to the revolt against the Indies Company, and it reveals the most about how Le Pers approached his work as a historian.[6]

Even as he described the rebellion as an epochal event in the life of the colony, Le Pers hinted at a curiously withdrawn, almost fearful attitude toward the task of reconstructing it. The uprising initiated by La Sagona was nothing less than "a revolution that just missed setting everything upside down." Such a description implied an obligation on the part of the historian to leave no stone unturned, but Le Pers was in no position to feign an intimate understanding of his subject. It was not simply that his duties as priest had called him to the comparably tranquil settlement at Port-de-Paix, on Haiti's northern coast (opposite l'île de la Tortue), by the late fall of 1722. It was also that the internal dynamics of the rebellion itself, and particularly the manner of its pacification, placed serious obstacles in the way of historical investigation. The job of the historian, wrote Le Pers, was to "discover the principal authors [of the rebellion], their views, their designs." But this was precisely "what has not been done and what I will not do." The responsibility to discover the truth ran headlong into the government's desire to lay the revolt to rest (*assoupir*). "I will conform myself to that conduct," Le Pers announced, "even though nobody is persuaded that such a revolution could have occurred without a prime mover (*premier mobile*) who put the entire thing in motion." The narrative then trails off melodramatically, having recounted "a story beyond which there is only the future, impenetrable darkness that only time will dissipate."[7]

The mystery is only slightly clarified by Charlevoix's interpretation of the rebellion. He converged with Le Pers on key points, including the pivotal character of the insurgency of 1722–23. As Charlevoix put it, the uprising was "an incident that in less skillful hands could have led to the ruin of our most flourishing colony"—an echo of Le Pers's image of a "revolution" that stopped just short of overturning the colonial order. Charlevoix was similarly determined to maintain the veil of secrecy over the rebellion's inner workings, even while he suggested that there was more to the story than met the public's eye. In a delicately worded passage, he alluded to the "secret causes of the movements that had agitated the colony"—an apparent reference to the list of leading rebel suspects that Sorel and Montholon had drawn up at Petit Goâve on March 26, 1723. An observer not privy to these "secrets," explained Charlevoix, might well criticize Governor Sorel for having failed to clamp down on the uprising more forcefully. Assuming the truth of the "discovery" that Sorel made, however, one could only praise the governor's "great wisdom and moderation."[8]

These cryptic observations, as far as they went, overlooked that Sorel had, in fact, called for a more aggressive approach to the rebels than the French government had adopted in Martinique or would adopt in Saint-Domingue with the Champmeslin mission. At issue here, though, is not Charlevoix's accuracy, but rather his view of the government's response. And that understanding—not to mention the "truth" of the revolt more generally—would have to remain just beyond the reach of his readers:

> This is all that I can say about the matter. These are among the mysteries of evil, about which it is right to warn the public, in order to prevent it from rushing to judgment about events the springs [*ressorts*] of which are hidden from it, but which it would serve no purpose to reveal.[9]

The only clear point of this puzzling passage seems to be that the rebellion was a puzzle to be preserved as such. Charlevoix's caginess, like that of Le Pers, stands out as an advertisement for knowledge that only these Jesuit historians seem to possess, but Charlevoix frames the matter as an effort at preserving the colonists from themselves. The reference to the "mysteries of evil" is from St. Paul's warning to the Thessalonians not to be too eager to expect the second coming of Christ. "The mystery of lawlessness is already at work; only he who now restrains it will do so until he is out of the way." In other words, evil—the "man of lawlessness," also known as Satan or the Antichrist—will operate secretly until the final unmasking at the end of times. Those who refuse to believe in Christ, in the meantime, are afflicted by God with "a strong delusion, to make them believe what is false, so that all may be condemned who did not believe in truth but had pleasure in unrighteousness."[10]

Who was Satan in all of this? Which persons can be said to have fallen under the spell of lawlessness? These and other elements of Charlevoix's political theology are anyone's guess. There is a vague intimation that the crowd actions of 1722 and 1723 qualify as the work of the devil. At the same time, Charlevoix pulls away from any clear condemnations by describing the uprising as an "unfortunate" but "bloodless" affair in which—excepting only a "very small number of individuals (*particuliers*)"—"there were, properly speaking, no rebels," only "vagabonds and anonymous persons." In this way, the rebellion had confirmed a truth about the French people as a whole: though "capable of sometimes forgetting the respect due to Royal Majesty," at the end of the day they return to draw on that "inexhaustible fund of true attachment that they naturally have for their Sovereign."[11]

Was Charlevoix, in a roundabout way, trying to protect the Protestant community of Saint-Domingue from the repercussions of disclosing that Charpentier, a French Huguenot, was one of the rebellion's masterminds? Alternatively, was the real mystery in all of this the role of the Society of Jesus itself? Was Charlevoix, in other words, trying to shield the Jesuits of Cap Français from suspicions that they supported either the insurgents or a fellow company? If so, why?

At least part of the answer to these questions almost certainly involves Jansenism, the major controversy roiling French Catholic institutions and thinkers in the 1720s. Tramond highlighted the passage quoted above in 1929 to suggest that Charlevoix, as a Jesuit, had written with such "great discretion" for self-protective reasons. Without naming Jansenism, Tramond observed that it "must have seemed singularly dangerous for a Jesuit under the reign of Louis XV to show that there could have been a revolt against royal authority, and that this revolt could have gone unpunished."[12] A religious movement whose complex views on free will and divine grace were inspired by Saint Augustine, Jansenism was a dissident force within the Catholic Church generally. The Jansenist controversy overlapped with the question of Gallicanism: Were French Catholics subject to the "ultramontane" sovereignty of the Pope in Rome, or to the authority of the monarch and clergy of France? Gallican sympathizers in the *parlements* denounced the claims of papal power to be supreme over French institutions.[13]

As Jansenism spread in France in the late seventeenth and early eighteenth century, it placed the Jesuits, seen as foot soldiers of the Pope despite their professions of loyalty to the Bourbon throne in worldly matters, increasingly on the defensive. With Pope Clement XI's denunciation of Jansenism in the 1713 constitution *Unigenitus*, the Jesuits were put to a choice, and they rallied resoundingly around the papal position—leading to charges that they, too, were part of an ultramontane conspiracy operating within France.[14] Though the Jesuits had grown influential in the court of Louis XIV, Louis XV's relatively hands-off approach to government left them exposed to a rising tide of suspicion and animosity within France that would culminate with the suppression of the Society of Jesus in 1764.[15] These developments necessarily weighed on Charlevoix and Le Pers as they wrote their histories of Saint-Domingue. And the storm over Jansenism may, in an indirect way, explain why the Jesuit missionaries were determined to defer to royal administrators who sought to put a lid on the agitation surrounding the Indies Company.

The Jansenist controversy was a shared experience for Le Pers and Charlevoix, but the competition to produce the first full-scale history of France's most prosperous colony strained their relationship. Le Pers had originally given Charlevoix full powers to correct his manuscripts and use them as he saw fit. As Père Margat describes their relationship, Le Pers lacked confidence in his own stylistic powers and yearned to indulge his second passion of botany, so he may have entrusted his material to the more literary Charlevoix for these reasons. Upon returning to Paris, Charlevoix was drawn into other projects and put the Saint-Domingue history largely to one side, pessimistic, at first, that it could attract a meaningful readership in France. These delays exasperated Le Pers, who began to complain of a betrayal of trust. Charlevoix then set himself to the task with renewed hope and interest. He subjected the promising Le Pers materials to scrutiny in light of new research that Maurepas encouraged him to undertake in the original papers of the Archives de la Marine.[16]

Le Pers was later deeply aggrieved by what he saw as the alterations that Charlevoix had made to his manuscripts, including its truncated rendering of the colony's physical and natural topography. When Charlevoix finally published the *Histoire de l'Isle espagnole* in 1730–31, Le Pers lashed out and sought leave from the Society of Jesus to prepare his own manuscript. Charlevoix, Le Pers felt, was unqualified to produce a history of Saint-Domingue, and his effort to improve the Le Pers manuscripts had yielded "a little monster." The rancor between the two men rose to such a level that Neuville, the Paris-based *procureur* for the Jesuit missions in the West Indies, prohibited Le Pers from publishing his own manuscript history after learning of the content of his letters to Charlevoix. The manuscript is preserved in the Bibliothèque nationale in Paris, and its opening *avertissement* makes clear Le Pers's dismissive attitude toward his former mentee: "A few years ago, a History of St. Domingue appeared, on the basis of my memoirs, and with which I was not content. Here is another, truer, more ample, and entirely new history." Père Margat, another Jesuit who had arrived in Saint-Domingue several years before the rebellion and would end up serving more than twenty years there, withdrew his own proposal for a history of the colony upon the publication of Charlevoix's text.[17]

———

Such rivalries make clear that the Jesuits were not a unitary force in Saint-Domingue. Nor were they a monastic one. In addition to recording the history of the revolt, they were themselves participants in the intrigue and drama of the early 1720s.

The Jesuits found themselves at the center of the controversy from its earliest moments. Le Pers had placed the Indies Company director La Ferrière at the scene of the Jesuit compound immediately following the ransacking of the Africa House. This aspect of his account was confirmed by d'Arquian and

Duclos in their letter to the administrators in Léogâne on November 24, 1722. Without identifying any of these sources by name, Charlevoix rejected the suggestion as "absolutely false." If Charlevoix's motivation here was to discourage a perception of the Society of Jesus as sympathetic to the Indies Company, the effort was in vain. On the very next page of his history, he reported as an uncontested fact that La Ferrière "went to seek refuge in the Jesuit House" on November 23 (a full day after La Sagona's siege), following an unsuccessful appeal by d'Arquian and Duclos for the director to switch places with his counterpart at Saint-Louis.[18]

This fastidious defensiveness warrants a closer look at the circumstances of La Ferrière's flight from the Africa House. A detailed 1728 map of Cap Français (figure 19) provides a revealing, bird's-eye view of the city's rapidly increasing density about four years after the end of the revolt. The full extent of the Jesuit compound at the top center was already marked out in the earlier maps of 1723 (figures 9 and 10). And the general contours of the city as it was depicted in La Sagona's time are still recognizable in the horizontal view at the top of the 1728 map. As the city's largest enclosed property by far, the Jesuit compound (denoted by the letter "B" at top and the number "2" at bottom) was a good choice for someone who was on the run in Cap Français in 1722 and did not want to leave town altogether.[19]

La Ferrière may have sought refuge in the Jesuit compound out of some sense that a religious space would provide him sanctuary in a legal sense. Alternatively, he may have simply aimed to escape the immediate wrath of the crowd.[20] In any case, neither the sacred character of the Jesuit mission nor the scope of its property in Le Cap proved much of a deterrent to the insurgents. Having made his way to the Jesuit compound, La Ferrière almost immediately realized that he would soon have to find another hiding place. The risk was to the Jesuit missionaries no less than the company's representative. "The fathers were threatened with their residence being set aflame unless they put [La Ferrière] outside," wrote Le Pers. "There was no choice but to obey."[21]

The forced expulsion of La Ferrière from the Jesuit compound may not have been the last time the Society of Jesus was pressured to cooperate with the rebellion. In a fascinating collection of materials on the religious orders of Saint-Domingue published in 1951, Jean-Marie Jan, the Catholic bishop of Cap Haïtien from 1929 to 1953, relates that one of the local Jesuits, Père Michel, was compelled to chant a *Te Deum* in honor of the insurgents' early victories over the company in the main cathedral of Cap Français in January 1723. (The cathedral faced the town's main public square, called the Place d'Armes, a few minutes' walk from the Jesuit compound [indicated as "4" on the 1728 map].) According to Jan, the coercive ritual featured a woman—who could only have been La Sagona—taking a seat of honor at the altar of the church.[22]

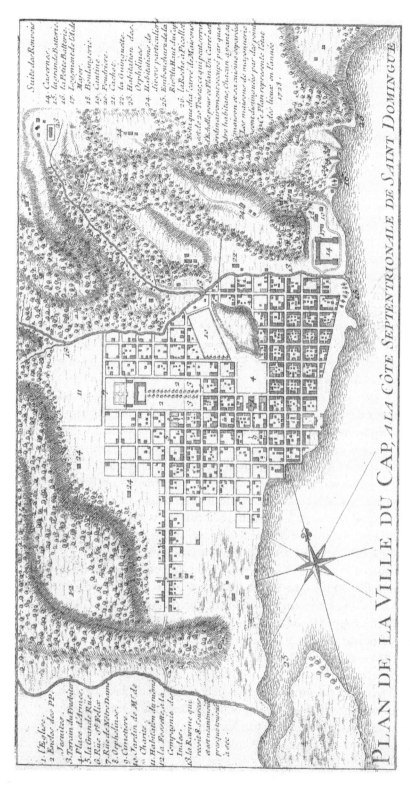

FIGURE 19. "Plan de la ville du Cap, à la côte septentrionale de Saint Domingue," 1728. Courtesy of the Musée d'Aquitaine, Bordeaux.

If true, the anecdote describes an almost sacrilegious, if not altogether pagan, act of heroine worship that would have deeply offended the pious sensibilities of the Jesuit order in Le Cap. But Jan's account, which cites no sources on this point, tells only this small piece of the story and may mislead in its portrayal of Michel's and the Jesuits' relationship to the insurgency. In the March 26, 1723, list of principal rebel suspects that Sorel and Montholon drew up at Petit Goâve, the administrators noted that "songs were composed in praise of La Sagona" to commemorate her pillaging of the Africa House.[23] One of these songs was written by none other than Michel, and it is one of the more remarkable documents in the rich archive of the revolt against the Indies Company.

Dated 1723, Michel's ode to La Sagona suggests that at least some Jesuits had imbibed the political-economic grievances of the insurgents. In lieu of an actual signature, the title lines indicate that the composition was "done by Père Michel." Though titled a "song," the lyrics seem to have been composed in the spirit of an opera, for the composition opens with a note stating that the "arias" are by an individual identified only as "Frère Andouillard."[24] Translated into English, the verses lose their rhythmic relation and satirical effect, but the overall message is unmistakable. This is a song suffused with resentment toward the August 1722 royal ordinance on money and with sympathy for the women who challenged it.

There lived once in France "a virgin, innocent and beautiful," it begins, whose battles against men earned her the title of greatest of warriors. In Saint-Domingue, a "great warrior even braver and prouder" than Joan of Arc has arisen to rid the colony of "a greater danger": a squadron of "hired tax-collecting extortionists (*maltôtiers à gages*), made for robbery . . . [and] resolved to make off with our crowns [*écus*]." In the margins, Michel (or someone writing on his behalf) has annotated some of the lines of the song. Here, he identifies the extortionists in question as clerks of the French Indies Company, "whose establishment in this island the inhabitants had no wish to endure." La Sagona, for her part, is identified as "the wife of a man who called himself a gentleman but was a merchant and owned a shop in Le Cap."[25]

In Michel's account, the company's henchmen came to Saint-Domingue for the express purpose of wreaking havoc with the local residents' currency, and only a band of hardy "Amazons" stood in the way of that plot. "Rascal," says La Sagona to the arriving henchmen, "you claim to weigh our quarter crowns, do you?" (Recall that the August 1722 royal ordinance effectively reduced the colonists' buying power by discounting their often clipped or otherwise underweight Spanish coins to reflect only the actual amount of silver they contained—an amount to be determined by weighing them in relation to the French mark, a unit of measurement equivalent to eight ounces. Instead of

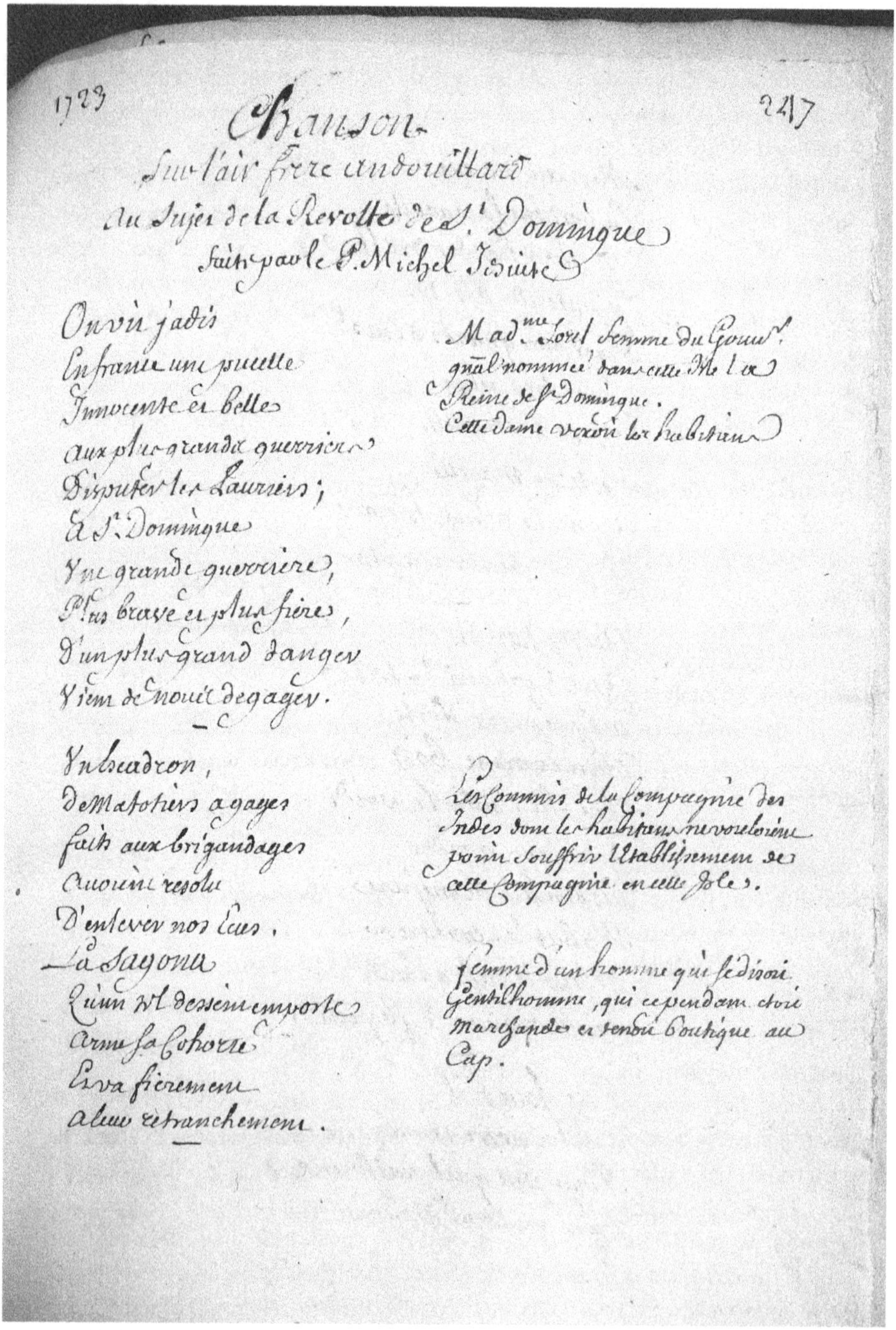

1723 247

Chanson
Sur l'air frere andouillart
Au sujet de la Revolte de St. Domingue
faite par le P. Michel Jesuite

On vit jadis
En france une pucelle
Innocente et belle
aux plus grands guerriers
Disputer les Lauriers;
A St. Domingue
Une grande guerriere,
Plus brave et plus fiere,
d'un plus grand danger
Vient de nous degager.

Un escadron,
de Matotiers a gages
faits aux brigandages
Avoient resolu
D'enlever nos Ecus.
La Sagona
Qu'un tel dessein emporte
Arme sa cohorte
Et va fierement
a leur retranchement.

Madme. Sorel femme du Gouvr. gnal nommee dans cette isle la Reine de St Domingue. Cette dame vexoit les habitans

Les Commis de la Compagnie des Indes dont les habitans ne vouloient point souffrir l'Etablissement de cette Compagnie en cette Isle.

femme d'un homme qui se disoit Gentilhomme, qui cependant etoit marchande et tenoit boutique au Cap.

FIGURE 20. Title and opening lyrics of Père Michel, "Au sujet de la révolte de S. Domingue" [1723]. Courtesy of the Bibliothèque nationale de France, Département des manuscrits, Ms. 13658.

tendering their piastres by tale, that is, by count, the colonists would have to tender them by weight.) Michel has his Caribbean Joan of Arc give the company's "scoundrel" of a director a sound box on the side of the head for this audacity.[26]

Somewhat strangely, Michel then compares the "poor idiot" director to Nicodemus, the Pharisee and member of the Sanhedrin council who (in the Gospel of John) first came to Jesus at night to discuss his teachings and later helped Joseph of Arimathea to take Jesus down from the cross and bury him.[27] Like Nicodemus, La Ferrière "runs, escapes, flees in the thick of night" to find refuge on a company ship moored in the Cap Français harbor. "He wanted to make off with our *pistoles* [Spanish gold coins] but, without even an *obole* [French silver halfpenny] in hand, is said to be going to Pluto to weigh them."[28] (The parody here involves the notion that the Indies Company would dilute the colonists' money even more than the August 1722 ordinance required, essentially treating their coins as weightless as they would be in outer space.) Michel closes with a final flourish: "Glory to the female troop" for confronting this "universally cursed race." Without La Sagona's heroism, "our colony would perish forever."[29]

Awkward, at times bizarre in his allegorical references, Michel did sustain one literary allusion that would have resonated with his audience. The figure of the Amazonian heroine was a widely recognized trope of European music, art, theater, and literature. The specifically French version of this story was popularized only a few years before Michel's song, in Marie-Jeanne L'Héritier de Villandon's story by the same title. Mademoiselle L'Héritier's version was in fact a reworking of an older French tale, one that she conspicuously situated in an indeterminate point in the past, "the time when France was shared between several kings—I am not told under whose reign, nor in which century, but it matters little." As Natalie Zemon Davis notes, the "French Amazon" was part of a subcategory of sexual inversion or substitution stories in which women served to defend rather than undermine the established order. In L'Héritier de Villandon's narrative, for example, the heroine takes the place of her dead brother to defend her father's honor and position at court. The women in these stories, writes Davis, "used their power to support a legitimate cause, not to unmask the truth about social relationships." As "embodiments of order," stories of the French Amazon were not about "moving masses of people to resistance."[30]

In this case, the French colonial authorities seem, unsurprisingly, to have felt otherwise. In a 1723 memorandum summarizing the events of the uprising, Antoine-Denis Raudot, a senior official in the naval ministry in Paris, observed that "the song in praise of [La Sagona] by the Jesuit Father Michel caught on greatly in the colony."[31] The lyrics certainly cast doubt on Jan's claim that

Michel was coerced by La Sagona and her "female troupe." He fully channeled settler anxiety about being undercut by the company's manipulation of weights and scales. Perhaps the song thereby highlights the extent of the Jesuits' own investment in the colonial economy: both the mundane economy of daily sustenance, and the more formal economy of trade and investment attached to the plantations, with all of their tax implications. On the other hand, Michel entirely obscured the theme of creole opposition to the company's slaving monopoly: the trade in west African captives is not mentioned at all. Although few if any critics in the 1720s were unmasking the truth about colonial social relationships by denouncing slavery or the slave trade, the omission is especially conspicuous, given the prominence of calls for a "free trade" in slaves during this period.

The upshot, thus far, is a complicated and conflicting mix of signals about the Society of Jesus's relationship to the rebellion. One other piece of evidence leaves less room for doubt on this score: an anonymous document titled "Sentiments and Resolutions of the Colony," addressed to a quartet of colonial notables in the northern region of Saint-Domingue in early February 1723. This coincided with the renewed storm caused by the recent arrival of the *Duc de Noailles* slave ship at Le Cap. The recipients included Philippe, the naval treasurer at Cap Français who was the likely subject of the death threat anonymously posted on the door of the church in Le Cap shortly after the arrival of the Indies Company directors in the fall of 1722. On the fold of the packet, the anonymous author(s) directed Philippe and his colleagues, on pain of death, to open the document only in the presence of the northern delegates preparing to meet at Haut du Cap.[32]

When the Haut du Cap assembly convened on February 5 to demand enforcement of the Cul de Sac Treaty provision barring Indies Company ships from staying more than four days in port, the text was opened and read aloud to the gathered deputies. The contents were deemed "so absurd and so appalling" as to trigger an immediate demand that the colonial executioner burn the papers at once. The executioner being unavailable, the members of the Haut du Cap assembly took it upon themselves to burn the document while swearing a solemn oath never to reveal its contents. As a result, neither the original nor any copy of this document has survived, and we are left to rely on the anonymous "Account of What Has Happened in St. Domingue" (dated 1723 and which Charlevoix himself then reproduced more or less verbatim in his history) for an understanding of its contents and reception.[33]

According to that account, religious and fiscal grievances figured prominently in the "Sentiments and Resolutions." One priority was the expulsion of the Jesuits and their replacement by the Capuchins, who had preceded the Jesuits in Saint-Domingue and were themselves recalled to the metropole by

Louis XIV in 1704. In addition, the government was expected to guarantee "full freedom of conscience" to all of the colony's inhabitants. The document further demanded that the proceeds of the *octroi* levy on slaveholdings in the Cap Français area were not to be diverted to other regions of Saint-Domingue. The remaining articles—apparently even "more violent" in tenor—"tended no less than to erect the land into a republic."[34]

Charles Frostin argues that these demands indicate a Protestant influence over the insurgency that likely emanated from the Léogâne area.[35] The appeal for "full freedom of conscience" in a region of the French empire where Huguenot immigrants had a long-established presence is difficult to dismiss, and the term "republic" had long-standing Protestant associations in the eyes of French Catholic defenders of the absolute monarchy. Insisting on an oath of silence may have been one more way of trying to protect the opposition to the Indies Company from the claim that it was designed to overthrow the king's sovereignty—and French Catholic sovereignty along with it. The demand that tax revenues not be diverted from the north, by contrast, suggests that the document was composed by insurgents from the Cap Français area.

As for the call to expel the Jesuits, their role in harboring La Ferrière did nothing to endear them to enemies of the Indies Company, Catholic or Protestant. It is certainly possible that the Jesuit mission in Cap Français adopted a more aggressive stance toward enforcement of the Code Noir articles affecting Protestants (and Jews, for that matter) than had the Capuchins before 1704. These rules included a prohibition on the public exercise of any non-Catholic religions and the threat of "exemplary punishment" for any Protestants who interfered with the Catholic observance of either whites or enslaved persons.[36] But, according to the "Account of What Has Happened at St. Domingue," the demand to expel the Jesuits was perceived as one of several "absurd" and "horrifying" aspects of the "Sentiments and Resolutions."[37] The thrust of the Haut du Cap assembly was to defend rather than criticize the Jesuits. And that description suggests the possibility that someone affiliated with the Society of Jesus authored the anonymous source on which our understanding of the entire episode is based.

———

Given the significance of money in the rebellion, following the trail of Jesuit money may be the only way to drill down beneath the ambiguity of such partial, highly opinionated voices. The Society of Jesus's corporate structure lent itself naturally to a concern with fiscal administration. Led by a superior general based in Rome, the French Jesuits were organized into an "Assistancy" that consisted of four provinces, each of which sent out its own mission. The Jesuits in Saint-Domingue answered to the *procureur* for the society's Caribbean missions, who in turn obeyed the Provincial for the Province of Paris. Some twenty thousand Jesuits spanned the globe by 1710, reflecting processes of corporate and imperial expansion that were nearly indistinguishable in many contexts.[38]

What did not come naturally was the Jesuits' reputation for exploiting secular legal loopholes and pushing boundaries. Other religious orders benefited from tax exemptions and immunities comparable to those that were granted to the society in 1651 and 1701. The Franciscans, for example, who were installed in the western province at Léogâne while the Jesuits held sway over the north, enjoyed some of the same privileges. And the tax exemption of the metropolitan clergy, of course, would eventually become one of the great grievances of the French prerevolutionary era. But the Jesuits seemingly defied the image of missionaries who were supposed to have as their "goal and object only the glory of God," in the words of the 1651 Letters Patent.[39]

By comparison to their peers in Canada and (especially) Asia, the Jesuits were rather late and unenthusiastic converts to the Caribbean. They began to percolate into Martinique as early as 1640. By the 1650s and 1660s, Jesuits could be found throughout the French West Indies, including Saint-Domingue, even though they would not be officially installed there until 1704. The Capuchin order staffed the priesthood of Saint-Domingue as of 1659, but by the turn of the century had declined significantly in numbers owing to sheer fatigue and sickness. When the Capuchin provincial of Normandy was unable to send new missionaries to replace those who left or passed away, Louis XIV turned to the Society of Jesus instead.[40]

The Saint-Domingue mission depended, at least at first, on a combination of state support and its own industriousness. The crown granted an annual stipend of five thousand livres to the *procureur* for the Jesuit missions in the New World beginning in 1651. That amount was increased to fifteen thousand livres by the early eighteenth century, some of which was funneled to the society's delegation in Saint-Domingue. Parish taxes covered other expenses, and Jesuit priests charged fees for some curial rites and ecclesiastical ceremonies. Finally, the Saint-Domingue mission was granted extensive land concessions—particularly in Port-de-Paix and Cap Français, where the principal Jesuit compounds were located—and the right to acquire domestic slaves to help maintain those concessions.[41]

This last privilege brought the Society of Jesus into contact with the colony's emerging sugar industry. The French crown was careful to specifically tie the permissible scope of Jesuit slaveholding to the extent of their landholdings (and vice versa). The October 1704 Letters Patent stated that the Jesuits had the right "to acquire residences (*maisons*) and lands, provided that these do not exceed what is necessary for the work (*emploi*) of one hundred negroes (*nègres*)."[42] Did this mean that any one Jesuit plantation could not have more than one hundred slaves working on it? Or was it a cap on the total number of slaves the Jesuits could own throughout the colony? Colonial administrators argued, very reasonably, for the latter interpretation. The Jesuits seem to have believed that their Letters Patent blessed them with the promise of significantly more abundance where land and slaves were concerned.

Jesuit slaveholding in the Americas raised eyebrows within the society itself, at least before 1600. "I don't know how appropriate it is to the piety of the Society of Jesus to bring slaves loaded in irons like the laity," a Mexican Jesuit confessed in 1582. The hierarchy in Rome voiced similar concerns. With the takeover of Saint-Domingue by Colbert's West Indies Company in 1664, George Breathett writes, local Jesuit missionaries "felt that the totally economic motivations of the company might clash with the policies they were attempting to implement." Those policies included securing adequate revenues for the company's (spiritual) works, however, so the line between secular and sacred was inevitably fluid. With the aid of another land grant from the colonial administration and funds at their disposal, the Jesuits acquired additional territories outside the perimeter of their missionary bases in Le Cap and Port-de-Paix.[43]

One such territory, at Terrier-Rouge, east of Cap Français about halfway toward Fort Liberté, became the site of a major Jesuit-operated sugar plantation and mill. Even at the height of its productivity, according to Moreau, the plantation generated only modest revenues owing to the arid, relatively infertile soil of the Terrier-Rouge area. With dry irony, Moreau confessed to surprise that the Jesuits, so skilled at obtaining profitable concessions elsewhere in the colony, might have chosen to invest in such an unpromising location.[44]

But invest they did, and with little apparent sense of shame at the contradiction between the teachings of Jesus and the practice of human bondage. At some point before their expulsion in 1763, the Jesuits began to brand their slaves with the letters "IHS"—a contraction of the Greek word for Jesus and the symbol of the Society of Jesus. The Franciscans, for their part, did likewise, stamping their slaves with the letters "FP" for "Frères Prêcheurs," the name of their order in French. By the standard of other Ignatian missions in the New World, such Jesuit participation in the slave economy of Saint-Domingue was unexceptional.[45]

Given that Saint-Domingue had a total slave population of about fifty thousand in 1720, the Jesuits were only one relatively small piece of the overall plantation economy in that colony. But they were a growing force and an especially enterprising community: in 1725, Jesuits would bring the first coffee plants to Saint-Domingue (from Martinique).[46] Their inability to abstain from the sugar business, moreover, had local political consequences disproportionate to the scale of the order's investment in slavery. The expansion of Jesuit landholding prompted the imposition of new parish taxes to support the construction of new churches and the activities of an increasingly large priesthood. Unsurprisingly, in a colony that had made a name for its ability to minimize its residents' fiscal liabilities, those levies generated resentment, especially in the period after 1712, when the administration consolidated several of the existing parishes. One indication of local resistance to Jesuit prerogatives in the colony is that the society's 1651 Letters Patent was not registered in Saint-Domingue until 1716.[47]

Controversy over the Jesuits' economic conquests in Saint-Domingue came to a head in the years just prior to the uprising against the Indies Company. In 1719, Governor Chateaumorant and Intendant Mithon chastised the Society of Jesus in a remarkable, elaborate response to a Jesuit memorandum that, unfortunately, does not seem to have survived:

> The reverend Jesuit fathers did not accept the American missions in order to amass worldly riches but with the sole object of the love and glory of God in attending, not to savages or barbarians (at least not in the southern American colonies), [but] to Catholic peoples and their slaves, of which they are the pastors.

With the pungent exception of the reference to amassing worldly riches, this was a close paraphrase, almost verbatim, of the 1651 Letters Patent—down to the archaically styled distinction between the indigenous peoples of Canada and the French settlers and their slaves of the Caribbean. That distinction was apparently intended to make the Jesuits feel more fortunate in having been consigned to the unrelenting heat and humidity of the West Indies.[48]

But what really should have made the Jesuits content with their lot, according to the administrators, was that they enjoyed a series of plum pensions, tax exemptions, and economic liberties. These included a pension of 1,500 livres per year for the support of the Jesuit residences at Le Cap and Port-de-Paix, and a pension of three hundred piastres per year for each of two *curé des nègres* ("priests of the blacks"). Such benefits notwithstanding, the Jesuits claimed in their own memorandum that they enjoyed a special status in Saint-Domingue stemming from their relationship with the former West Indies Company. After it dissolved the company in 1674, the Jesuits alleged, the crown assumed the company's responsibility for supporting the Jesuits, maintaining and repairing the churches of Saint-Domingue, and other services. In their response, Chateaumorant and Mithon simply pointed out that Saint-Domingue was not a part of France prior to 1674 (since it was a privately owned corporate territory at that time) and that the 1704 Letters Patent was the definitive and sole statement of Jesuit privileges.[49]

Such an effort to trade on the close connections between the Jesuits and a monopoly trading company would have sounded especially insensitive only a few years later. Indeed, the Jesuit memorandum gave the administrators no shortage of material to capitalize on parallels and connections between religious and commercial monopolies to the detriment of the Society of Jesus. These included the Jesuit assertion that the West Indies Company had issued the missionaries "a certificate or a kind of declaration of unlimited entitlements and exemptions"—prerogatives that, among their other issues, would have applied only to the French Leeward colonies, said Chateaumorant and Mithon. Another parallel involved tax exemptions. The Jesuits had gone so far as to claim immunity not only from corvée labor taxes on their slaves but also from the voluntary *octroi* levy of three livres per laboring slave that funded military expenditures and fortifications.[50]

Not even the metropolitan clergy had been so audacious as to assert such an immunity. Nor could they, for the notion that those who benefit from the fruits of the earth must support the upkeep of public roads and other common expenses was an expression of nothing less than natural law. A reference here to the situation of planters who owned a mere five or six slaves—and were therefore in far less of a position to divert part of their labor force to public projects— suggests that the Jesuits were already perceived (correctly) as relatively large sugar planters by Saint-Domingue standards at this time and that they were likely resented for that reason. To make matters worse, the Jesuits claimed the 1704 charter exempted even their domestic and indentured servants from the corvée labor tax that applied to watchmen and house guards. This last claim seemed especially parsimonious given that the society had already been granted an exemption for this very purpose, not to mention an immunity for up to thirty of the one hundred slaves allowed them by the charter.[51]

But nothing rankled more than the Jesuits' persistent violation of this overall slaveholding limit, which effectively made them tax evaders in addition to merely entrepreneurial planters. The administrators traced the origins and rationale of the policy to a 1703 British attack on Guadeloupe, but it was always an awkward way to limit religious landholding in the French colonies. Chateaumorant and Mithon observed that the Jesuits had been given a compound of 1500 by 1200 feet, not including savannah areas, in Cap Français—an expanse larger than needed to justify the hundred-slave limit. This was on top of their Terrier-Rouge plantation, which worked 150 slaves, and another at Port-de-Paix that the Jesuits could have been forced to sell in light of their slave cap.[52]

The Jesuits' only defense was that they interpreted the cap to mean one hundred slaves per plantation rather than one hundred in total. Dismissing this interpretation out of hand, the administrators again pointed to the hypocrisy of the society's claim to represent Jesus: "What use could there be for such an accumulation of superfluous wealth to members of religious orders who have no communities, and no other object than the love and glory of God in coming here, and whom the King moreover has generously pensioned?" The "avarice" and "spirit of interest" the Jesuits and their religious brethren elsewhere had consistently shown could only be checked by strictly enforcing the terms of the 1704 charter.[53]

Accordingly, in 1721 the monarchy issued new Letters Patent endorsing Chateaumorant and Mithon's analysis, prohibiting the Jesuits from acquiring new plantations or residences in Saint-Domingue without royal permission. The corvée exemption for thirty out of one hundred slaves, previously allowed at a local administrative level, was formalized as a matter of royal law. The following years witnessed repeated attempts to enforce these rules, most particularly the one hundred slave cap. And Champmeslin was specifically ordered to enforce the new 1721 Letters Patent during his 1723–24 pacification tour of Saint-Domingue. That order directly connects the cap on Jesuit slaveholding to the rebellion against the Indies Company.[54]

Denouncing the scofflaw tendencies and cupidity of the Jesuits took for granted the legitimacy of slavery and slave trade—just as Michel had done in praising La Sagona without mentioning either slavery or the slave trade. Yes, the Jesuits were greedy. Yes, they aspired to own as many slaves and as much land as they could. Yes, they sought to minimize their tax burdens. These sins described every other actual or aspiring sugar planter in Saint-Domingue as well.

Discussing the pensions paid to missionaries serving in Saint-Domingue in 1719, Chateaumorant and Mithon essentially conceded as much. They acknowledged that the three hundred piastre amount specified in the 1704 Letters Patent was now being paid in relation to the unit of account (the livre tournois) at a rate of one to three, or nine hundred livres per year. The Jesuits argued that this effectively reduced their pensions in view of the monarchy's decision to increase the value of the livre tournois in the trying economic circumstances that followed the War of the Spanish Succession. That increase devalued Spanish silver relative to the unit of account. The financial logic of the Jesuit case seemed inescapable, as the intrinsic value of the piece of eight remained constant throughout this period. The best the administrators could do was to say that silver and gold were a throwback to an earlier era, when buccaneers traded with their immediate Spanish neighbors in western Hispaniola rather than with France. In the years since, however, it had long been the practice to pay debts and contracts originally drawn up in piastres on the basis of a one-to-three exchange rate defined in terms of the unit of account (the livre tournois).[55]

This argument sounded like nothing so much as an effort to justify the August 1722 royal ordinance on money. In 1719, of course, Chateaumorant and Mithon could not have foreseen the extent of the disturbance that would ensue from attempting to apply that measure to the specie-deprived world of Saint-Domingue a few years later. But Spanish silver was already hard enough to come by in 1719, and had been for some time. Like everyone else in the colony—from white women and free people of color to vagabonds and sugar barons in the making—the Jesuits stood to lose big when the diminution in the value of Spanish coins was announced in August 1722. Priests who ministered to the parishes of northern Saint-Domingue suddenly had less reason to perform their duties as clergy with the same zeal as before. And those who ministered to the slaves as curé des nègres had similar occasion to wonder whether their loyalties were owed more to Caesar or to God.

———

The Jesuits' economic motives were therefore very real. But they coexisted alongside other motives that make it difficult to speak of a sharp distinction between amassing temporal riches and enacting the love and glory of God, as Chateaumorant and Mithon put it in 1719. The worldliness of the Jesuit project stemmed from the Ignatian spiritual ethos itself. As Joseph de Guibert has explained, the essence of Ignatius's worldview was to deny that the realm of the sacred had any boundaries. This "worldly asceticism" drove the Jesuits to embrace their fourth and perhaps most important mission in Saint-Domingue: ministering to the enslaved. Once commerce, colonization, and plantation agriculture were conceived of as necessary, if subordinate and morally troubling, aspects of the propagation of the faith, the project of converting (and thus saving) the souls of slaves acquired an unmistakably pragmatic, if not altogether utilitarian, character.[56]

Absolutist law undoubtedly shaped the Jesuit commitment to this mission. The 1685 Code Noir envisioned that all slaves in the French colonies would be "baptized and instructed" in the Catholic faith. And the 1704 Letters Patent specifically provided for the position of curé des nègres, which came with what Chateaumorant and Mithon, at least, felt was a generous pension.[57] Neither law nor economic reason alone defined the Jesuit approach to the enslaved. The spirituality of Ignatius involved "a union of surging enthusiasm and of reason." The basic message of the order's founder was one of

> service through love, apostolic service for the greatest possible conformity to the will of God, in the abnegation or sacrifice of all self-love and personal interest in order to follow Christ, the Leader who is ardently loved.

What distinguished this mission from the more monastic nature of religious orders that came before was Ignatius's emphasis on "service in the open fields, and even by journeys and far-flung expeditions for the sake of the Master's interests." In other words, the Ignatian conception of apostolic service could not be satisfied in the domestic space of a religious home, as it could be for the Benedictines, for example. This anti-monastic philosophy combined with an ethic of self-sacrifice that urged the Jesuits to acquire "a facility in finding God in all things, and in uniting themselves to Him even in the midst of the most absorbing labors."[58]

Christianity has long struggled with the distinction between ministering and showing compassion to the enslaved, on the one hand, and opposing the structural conditions of their oppression, on the other. Neither the Bible nor such frameworks of Ignatian spirituality as the *Spiritual Exercises* denounced human bondage. The early Christian Church accepted Roman slavery, and later Christians found proslavery support in some passages of the Old Testament. True, the Dominican friars who inspired Bartolomé de las Casas rejected Spanish enslavement of the Indians of Hispaniola. And the occasional Catholic commentator on the Atlantic slave trade, such as the Jesuit Alonso de Sandoval, connected theological justifications for slavery in Spanish America with the need for broader institutional reforms. During the seventeenth century, a handful of Christian voices, European and Afro-Atlantic, challenged the enslavement of baptized persons. But these were the exceptions.[59]

A fundamental grounding in the salvific effects of communion with Christ tended naturally towards an accommodation of slavery. As Père Margat put it in a letter to one of his fellow Jesuits in 1725, by bringing west African captives to Saint-Domingue, "it seems that providence ... wanted to compensate their earthly bondage, to which their unfortunate condition has subjected them, with the genuine freedom of children of God." But the work of tending to the souls of slaves changed both Christianity and, in some respects, the experience of slavery itself. In confronting the formidable problems of linguistic understanding that ministry to captives of west African origin entailed, the Society of Jesus invented new ways of ministering—a capacity that may have been distinctively Jesuit in nature—and helped to engender new forms of Catholic belief.[60]

The founding generation of Jesuits in Saint-Domingue preached first to white settlers before attempting to catechize the enslaved. Margat captured the impact this movement had on their self-conception and sense of their institutional role in Saint-Domingue when he wrote, in 1725, that "the black slaves are no less an object of our zeal" than white French colonists. "We can even consider them," he said, "as our crown and glory." The demographic aspect of this shift was clear: by 1725, the enslaved population under the society's spiritual jurisdiction in the north of Saint-Domingue had grown to fifty thousand, roughly half the colony's total slave population at that time. The Jesuits adjusted their numbers accordingly—increasing from six missionaries in 1706 to sixteen in 1721—but without any pretense that they would be able to give the enslaved the individuated ministerial attention that white colonists received. By 1725, another two priests were added, making for a ratio of one pastor for every 2,778 slaves.[61]

The growing Jesuit presence offered neither freedom nor even a softening of the brutal conditions of plantation labor. The Code Noir's injunction to convert slaves to Catholicism ensured that baptism would not automatically bring manumission in its wake. And the iconic Jesuit voice in seventeenth-century Spanish America, Pedro Claver (1580–1654), embodied the limits of the Jesuit vocation for ministering to the enslaved. Claver's example would inspire compassion for the suffering of the enslaved but not opposition to the institution per se. And Jesuit missionaries were well aware that, even if a more humane regimen of enslaved labor were possible, it would tend toward the preservation of slavery.[62]

The Christianization of west African captives nonetheless met with ingrained resistance from the planters of Saint-Domingue. Montholon wrote to Naval Minister Maurepas in 1724 to remind him of the traditional French Catholic justification for slavery in the Americas. "We are only permitted to have slaves because the Church expects that we will work toward instilling in them the sentiments of religion." This was a Bourbon delusion, but the planters opposed it all the same. Part of the concern was that religious instruction and ceremonies cut down on the time available for agricultural productivity and required travel from plantations to parish churches and back. But the political implications of spiritual empowerment and protection were unavoidable. No doubt part of the hostility the Jesuits encountered in Saint-Domingue during the eighteenth century stemmed from their status as the agents of Christianization in the colony. The improvisational development of the position of the curé des nègres was the lightning rod around which controversy pivoted. As Charles Frostin has shown, the Jesuits developed a very integrative conception of this role, giving it a triple function as spiritual guide, confidant, and arbiter that was perceived, at least, to translate into a powerful influence over the enslaved.[63]

No person exercised these functions with greater impact than Père Boutin, the most famous of the curé des nègres under the Old Regime.[64] His fellow Jesuits revered him. Margat writes that he singlehandedly undertook the construction of the church at Saint-Louis (the headquarters of the Saint-Domingue Company in the south) and, together with his Jesuit brother Larcher, helped to build the colony's major cathedral at Cap Français, which survives in rebuilt form to this day. The unspoken truth is that the physical labor of building this cathedral was almost certainly the work of the enslaved first and foremost. But Boutin does genuinely seem to have compiled an extraordinary record of apostolic service over the course of his long career in the colony from 1705–42. Margat observes that he "constantly gave examples of his heroic virtue" and that his reputation for "saintliness had spread all over France well before his death," to the point that he was universally known as the "Apostle of Saint-Domingue."[65]

The role of curé des nègres originated in 1684, when the Jesuits asked the administrators of the French West Indies to establish parish limits on the island of Guadeloupe. The Carmelites were assigned the role of ministering to the white community while the Jesuits inherited pastoral duties toward the black population. The curé des nègres in Saint-Domingue was part of a team of priests who operated according to a division of labor. The parish priest of Cap Français proper ministered to the white inhabitants of the town with the aid of a vicar who served under him. The separate position of "priest of the blacks" also ministered to (white) sailors.[66]

Boutin first came to assume his dual responsibilities toward slaves and sailors because of a conflict involving money that had been brewing in the colony for more than a decade. The business of expanding the Jesuit mission in Saint-Domingue from only a handful of priests in 1704 to nearly twenty by the end of the 1710s was funded through local taxes. Resentful colonists responded, first, by refusing to pay for the pensions specified in the 1704 Letters Patent, and then by successfully petitioning the Conseil Supérieur in Léogâne to temporarily evict the entire Jesuit delegation from the colony in 1716. Boutin inherited these rumblings against the fiscal tyranny of clerical rule and added to them his own penchant for assuming loans on behalf of the mission that he apparently had difficulty repaying. Parishioners accused him of self-dealing in addition to having a blunt and hardheaded personality, but Bishop Jan contends that Boutin's zeal for apostolic service led him to act firmly to repair the disarray in the Church's local finances. The churchwardens also disliked Boutin's proprietary attitude toward the cathedral in Le Cap (perhaps because he was instrumental in constructing it), his excessive commitment to using the Sunday offerings for the poor, and his role in the controversies over priestly salaries.[67]

All of this led Boutin's superior to reassign him from parish priest to the role of curé des nègres in the summer of 1719. Tenure as "priest of the blacks" brought with it its own share of political contestation, and Boutin took to the work of expanding the Jesuits' spiritual empire in Saint-Domingue with evident zest, as if this role had been foreordained. The position opened up a vast, and almost entirely unserved, new pastoral mission for which there were few models or precedents. The curé des nègres of Le Cap ministered to no less than four thousand members of the enslaved community. (The sources are conspicuously silent on where free people of color went for their spiritual needs, but it would be surprising if Boutin did not minister to them as well.) For the next twenty-three years, until 1742, Boutin would overshadow in this role even the man who had replaced him as parish priest of Cap Français, to such an extent that many parishioners continued to see him as one of the "city pastors" proper—which, of course, in a deeper sense he was, notwithstanding the element of racial segregation baked into his functions.[68]

Segregation required Boutin to develop an innovative vision for implementing the Code Noir mandate of Christianization. The central element of that vision involved Boutin's creation of a "mass of the blacks" (*messe des nègres*). In addition, he offered weekly catechisms every Sunday following the evening vespers prayer service, as well as weekday evening sessions with those not yet baptized designed to initiate them into the ways of prayer and incline them toward being received into the faith. Nearly all of the Catholic sacraments—baptism, confirmation, the eucharist, penance and reconciliation, anointing of the sick, holy orders, and matrimony—raised unprecedented issues of doctrine and protocol for the Caribbean church. And Boutin exercised a good deal of discretion in resolving most, if not all, of these matters.[69]

The racial politics of the sacrament of marriage were especially sensitive where masters were concerned. The Code Noir equivocated on the matter, effectively acknowledging that Christianization would encourage slaves to marry but prohibiting priests "from conducting weddings between slaves if it appears that they do not have their masters' permission." The master's property interests were further protected by a guarantee that the child of a marriage between slaves would inherit slave status. Even so, Le Pers reported, colonists resisted sacramental marriage for their slaves as "not in the master's best interest." The Jesuits seem to have pushed back, but with their hands legally tied there was only so much they could do. Margat described marriage in 1725 as a means whereby to "perfect" the conversion of the enslaved. Once married, they would make "excellent Christians" and even not infrequently form "holy families where the fear of God prevails." Between the moralistic language, on the one hand, and a legal arrangement that seemed ripe for generating political conflict between clergy and colonists, on the other, it is difficult to know how far the Jesuits pressed their sacramental hand.[70]

In practice, the pastoral repertoire of the curé des nègres entwined its practitioners in the social world of the enslaved in ways both mundane and profound. Ministry exposed the Jesuits to the cruelties and sins of servitude, awakening in them a sensitivity to the other's suffering and not just their own. Delivering last

152   CHAPTER 5

rites and hearing confessions are two cases in point. Margat left a graphic portrait of what anointing of the sick entailed: "We find them in their cabins stretched out on the ground lying on a stretch of rotted leather that serves as a bed, amidst blood and shit, often covered in ulcers from head to toe." Hearing confessions—even if they were at times tedious, by Margat's account—spilled over into the secular domain of settling disputes between one slave and another. And the information gleaned from the sacrament of penitence, even if subject to the seal of confession (which prohibited priests from disclosing anything they hear in the confessional), necessarily exposed priests to a subaltern perspective on the world of the masters. Margat writes that even if some planters were praiseworthy, many others indulged in "barely regulated conduct that is a source of concern and affliction for those to whom God has entrusted the care of their souls." This circumspect allusion to planter brutality implicitly connected the failure to enforce the protective provisions of the Code Noir to the abuses endured by slaves on the road to the sugar revolution. Indeed, for the planters the biggest danger of allowing Jesuits to hear slave confessions was that it indirectly authorized a kind of priestly surveillance of the interior life of the plantations.[71]

Above all, however, it was the work of transmitting the Gospel that created tension with the demands of the sugar revolution. The Jesuits brought a heavy dose of cultural and religious chauvinism to this task. Margat, for example, allowed himself all too easily to believe that the "natural simplicity" of west Africans "disposed them in a way to better receive the Christian truths" in place of the "superstitions of their land," to which they were in any case "hardly attached." The absence of "prejudices to overcome" made their "minds (*esprits*) more amenable to the impressions of Christianity." Margat rejoiced that the birth rate of the west African "nation" in Saint-Domingue, combined with the regular arrival of French slaving ships, promised a steady supply of converts capable of rewarding the "zeal of an evangelical worker." The ideal candidates for baptism were, of course, infants, who lacked the "crudeness" of their fathers and spoke French "more purely and with greater ease than most of the peasants and artisans of France." Young or old, however, black converts came to regard the Jesuits "as their fathers in Jesus Christ" and would "turn to them in all of their miseries."[72]

The Jesuits seem to have had mixed success in surmounting the massive linguistic hurdles that had to be overcome before something resembling conversion could occur. Le Pers lamented that oftentimes the catechumens simply "do not understand what they are doing." Père Boutin was, by all accounts, the most industrious of the society's members at working to bridge the linguistic gap. "He had acquired sufficient knowledge of the languages of all the peoples of the Guinea coast who are transported to our colonies," wrote Margat. This knowledge was "infinitely difficult to obtain" not only because the west African languages lacked "any affinity with the known languages, but also because they are so different between them."[73]

With the growth in the size of the slave population born in Saint-Domingue over the early decades of the eighteenth century, the relevant medium was quickly becoming Kreyòl rather than the languages of west Africa. Boutin's effort to mediate linguistically between Christianity and the enslaved produced one of the most remarkable documents in the entire archive of the colonial period: a Kreyòl version of "the Passion of Our Lord according to St. John in the language of the slaves (*en langage nègre*)" that probably dates back to the 1730s. This text was not a translation of the Gospel so much as an effort to paraphrase it, using what seem to be relatively simple sentences and phrases. The effort likely reflected the limits of Boutin's mastery of Kreyòl expression as well as a certain Jesuit racial conceit about the supposed "natural simplicity" of Africans, as Margat put it in 1725.[74]

Documents like the Kreyòl passion narrative are reminders to avoid treating all of the Jesuit missionaries as part of a single, monolithic bloc. They were certainly all under the spell of the racial prejudices of their time. But some did more than others to enforce those prejudices. Père Larcher, for example, who served in the society's Cap Français headquarters at the same time as Boutin in the late 1710s and early 1720s, seems to have zealously guarded the color line on behalf of the Jesuits. In 1724, while Champmeslin was still in Saint-Domingue attending to the business of pacification, Larcher asked the acting governor for funds to support a girls' boarding school in Le Cap. His rationale, as Gabriel Debien has documented, was that it was necessary to "sequester" young girls from the paternal home so as not to expose them to the conduct of slaves, "whose crudeness and corruption are known well enough." Racial-sexual anxiety about the "danger" of "libertinage" affected clerics no less than lay white colonists, unsurprisingly.[75]

Boutin was no integrationist, but his record of ministry to the enslaved reads very differently, particularly when seen in light of his prior quarrels with the white residents of Cap Français. Indeed, those quarrels did not dissipate after Boutin was reassigned in 1719 from parish priest of Le Cap to curé des nègres. To serve the indigent sick who were not being cared for by the city's *hôpital général*, Boutin concocted a characteristically aggressive and risky scheme in 1721 with a widow named Guimon to raise funds for an additional poorhouse. The Conseil Supérieur of Cap Français annulled the gift, reprimanded Boutin for involvement in this "temporal affair," and barred him from further attempts to veer outside the spiritual lane. But Boutin remained defiant and tried to circumvent the annulment. Upon learning of Boutin's insubordination, the superior general referred the feisty missionary for disciplinary consequences that went all the way up the chain of command to the Conseil de Marine in France. In April 1722, the Duke of Bourbon, as president of the council, ordered Boutin and Guimon expelled from Saint-Domingue "so that other missionaries would exercise more self-restraint and not follow the bad example afforded them by an excess of zeal." Somehow Boutin managed to remain in Saint-Domingue until, a few months later, the revolt against the Indies Company intervened. He was still there fifteen years later, when he was again reprimanded, this time for performing "solemn burial" rites for an enslaved woman who had been executed by hanging.[76]

In the years immediately following the storm over money and monopoly, conflict between militant slavery and the Jesuits would intensify—and it would be shaped increasingly by the enslaved to whom the Jesuits ministered.

6

Maroons and the Military-Planter State

JESUITS LIKE Boutin and Margat envisioned a more humane form of servitude, softened by the dignity owed to those baptized in the image and with the spirit of Christ. What they did not imagine was a world without or beyond slavery. Only one group in Saint-Domingue at this time dared to entertain such a radical vision. The Jesuits' meliorative, evangelical program, tinged with shades of white supremacy blended with an ardent belief in universalism, fell far short of the dreams of the maroons and of the plantation communities from which they hailed.

At their outer limits, however, the Jesuits' evangelical commitments and the maroon's determination to forge a different path for Saint-Domingue intersected. At least some Jesuits seem to have ministered to maroons in the mountains of the north. These missionaries experimented with an especially notorious form of pastoral care that would ultimately lead to the Society's expulsion from the colony in 1763.

Enslaved resistance to the sugar revolution intersected also with the revolt against the Indies Company. Indeed, the rebellion coincided with the first great period of active, sustained Afro-Haitian opposition to the plantation system. In one of the most influential interpretations of the Haitian Revolution, Michel-Rolph Trouillot analyzed what he called the "war within the war" of Haitian independence. As Trouillot sees it, the brutal violence of the familiar confrontation between Napoleon's soldiers and the Haitian revolutionary army in 1802–3 disguised an important conflict within the world of the insurgent forces. The domination of creole Afro-Haitians—those born in Saint-Domingue and represented by the figure of Toussaint Louverture—in the earlier phases of the Haitian Revolution gave way in 1802–3 to the primacy of insurgents born in Africa (*bossales*) and embodied in the person of Jean-Jacques Dessalines, Louverture's successor and the father of Haitian independence.[1]

The early 1720s witnessed an analogous layering of social conflicts, a rebellion within the rebellion, albeit within the parameters of a colonial world in which whites still held the upper hand. The uprising of maroons against the plantation order unfolded just as white creoles mounted their own challenge to the mercantile-imperial order. It would be wrong to assume, however, that the maroon rebellion was somehow "contained" within the revolt against the Indies Company, as the lesser of two social movements. The archives of Saint-Domingue, as well as the leading accounts of this period, encode this error by granting both the first and the last word during these years to various white colonial actors and their battles over money and monopoly. The sparse references to people of color in the uprising against John Law's System showed little to no curiosity about the world to which they belonged. The unspoken implication was that Afro-Haitians mattered only insofar as they were aligned with the movement against the Indies Company, only insofar as they had something to say about money or monopoly as white colonial actors conceived these issues. The appearance of people of color at key moments of the uprising, from its first moments until its final pacification by Champmeslin, were indeed signs of political mobilization. Administrators did worry that the uprising against the Indies Company made the task of apprehending maroons more difficult, and they even considered freeing the enslaved population of Saint-Domingue at one point in the service of suppressing the planter revolt. Their very willingness to do so indicates the limits of their political imaginary.

For all their apprehensions about the maroon threat, neither administrators nor planters could see the rebellion against the Indies Company as a kind of family squabble unfolding against the backdrop of a much larger conflict involving black resistance to planter supremacy. Instead, they responded to the maroon uprising as if it reflected primarily the discontent of a few isolated enslaved persons, and in particular a maroon leader named Colas Jambes Coupées ("Colas whose legs are cut"). Apprehended and brutally punished in June 1723, Colas Jambes Coupées was the most visible expression of a radically different kind of popular resistance in Saint-Domingue at this time. He became the leading target of a sadistic counter-revolt that produced the military-planter state. The centerpiece of this effort was the creation of the *maréchaussée* system of slave patrols, the product of a panicked collaboration between planters and the very administrators with whom they were at war over the Indies Company.

The revolt against the Indies Company and the maroon rebellion offered contradictory maps of the colony's political future. Underneath the surface of events, both visions made a great deal of headway during the 1720s and after. In a rereading of E. P. Thompson's work on popular culture and the moral economy, Simona Cerutti argues that "history from below" involves "rescuing that which might have come to pass." Rather than the history of a particular social stratum, or the story of subaltern resistance per se, it is a history "in other terms," an exploration of alternative if unrealized outcomes, an act of recuperating what we have forgotten and what might have been.[2] It is tempting to see the maroon revolt of the 1720s in terms of what it failed to accomplish: an immediate overthrow of the plantation system. In time, the mobilization of Afro-Haitian enslaved resistance would accomplish just that. But even in its own time, the maroon uprising exerted as great an influence upon the new colonial order as the insurgency against Law's System. For all the differences between these two movements, they yielded at least one legacy in common: a bubble colony mindset. The resistance to the Indies Company expanded access to the sugar revolution and made Saint-Domingue a colony worth investing in, despite the risks. One of those risks was, precisely, the threat of marronage. The failure of colonial elites to understand the significance and meaning of the maroon uprising, and their decision to suppress it with violence, amounted to a kind of blind bet on the future of Saint-Domingue. That blindness, too, would become an enduring part of the bubble colony.

———

The failure was rooted in the belief that Afro-Haitians were somehow less than fully human. For all their ardent belief in universalism, the Jesuits struggled to transcend the white supremacy to which their mission was attached. Père Margat embodied these limits in his effort to explain the phenomenon of marronage to his superior, Père de la Neuville, in 1729. Writing from a parish church on the outskirts of Cap Français, Margat observed that the word maroon derives "from the Spanish *cimarron*, which means a monkey: these animals are known to withdraw into the woods, and only emerge furtively to pounce on the fruits found in areas adjacent to their retreat." Having thus animalized the maroons, Margat proceeded to outline what he saw as the parallel condition of enslaved persons who fled the plantations of French Saint-Domingue. They would venture forth at night from their forested hideaways in the mountains to retrieve food and supplies. On occasion they would even obtain arms for use in daytime ambushes of passersby on the colony's roads, which prompted sending in detachments of men to put a stop to their "banditry."[3] These fugitive slave patrols—the *maréchaussée*—would become the fundamental response of white colonial society to the maroon challenge. By 1729, Saint-Domingue was nearly a decade into that experiment, and the limits of repression as an answer to the Afro-Haitian quest for freedom were already apparent.

In his letter to Neuville, however, Margat was primarily concerned with a different question: Were fugitive slaves within the circle of those capable and worthy of being evangelized, or not? Aware that suspicions of complicity with marronage placed the order at risk, the senior Jesuit in Saint-Domingue was clear that "these sort of people" could not be considered legitimate objects of pastoral care:

> Would we be well advised in France to furnish priests for highway robbers? For that would be the job of a missionary assigned to the fugitive negroes (*nègres marons*). We settle for urging our negroes to have nothing to do with this detestable business, and when some of them have had the misfortune of doing so, if they come seek us out, we try to secure forgiveness for them, and to restore them to a state of grace with their master.

Margat's basic answer to his own question seemed simple enough: no ministering to maroons. "As vigorous as our zeal has been hitherto," he observed, "it has not extended thus far."[4]

But his answer was not nearly so simple. To begin with, the very need to raise the question implies that not all Jesuits were of one mind on this issue. Evidently, the mission had engaged in a discussion of whether to "assign" a Jesuit to the maroon communities. Margat made this clear in the opening paragraph of his letter, where, with his usual discretion, he alluded to (without naming) a certain "good clergyman" about whom Neuville had just written, apparently seeking information. (The *Lettres edifiantes* does not include this incoming letter from the *procureur général*.) As Margat summarizes Neuville's inquiry, the "abandonment" of maroons in the French colonies had "moved" the unnamed priest to petition the monarch for permission to "provide them with the spiritual supports they lack." It is unclear whether the missionary in question was Boutin. On the one hand, Margat's portrait of the passion with which Boutin tackled every aspect of his ministry matches his diagnosis of the anonymous Jesuit's willingness to take on maroon ministry:

> If this virtuous clergyman, whose charity is praiseworthy, had had a fair idea of negro maroons, he would no doubt have sought out other objects for his zeal, and would have done more justice to our conduct.

On the other hand, Margat attributed a surplus of zeal to more than one of his colleagues, and it would be surprising if the colonial authorities would have allowed Boutin to remain as curé des nègres in this situation.[5]

In any case, Margat's concern to protect the identity of his colleague indicates that the explosive revelation had reached Saint-Domingue only in anonymized fashion. Unfortunately for the Jesuits, it was not so anonymous as to disguise the affiliation with the Society of Jesus. Thus, not only was there at least some discord over this sensitive issue within the Jesuit community, but that controversy had bubbled over far enough to damage the society's reputation in Saint-Domingue.

The controversy confirms that Catholic doctrine and practice constrained Jesuit choices and forced the missionaries to recognize the limits of their universalism. Even in Margat's own more conservative approach, the duty to administer the sacrament of penance and reconciliation would not permit simply leaving the maroon to his own devices. Seeking pardon for the maroon was not simply a matter of hearing a confession and absolving the penitent of his sins. The missionary had an obligation to mediate between the master and the slave. This role embroiled the priest in the prickly work of negotiating a truce between parties not easily reconciled to one another. If the truce were to break down, or the maroon somehow to return to his former ways, to whom could the planter turn in hopes of reclaiming his lost bondsman? And if the maroon then refused to return, who would be held responsible for that outcome?

In short, everything about the Jesuit willingness to minister around the margins of this conflict was highly fraught. Even if not all Jesuits were willing to participate as intermediaries in this way, it would be very easy for the planters to confuse one or two Jesuits with the society's as a whole (just as they had evidently identified the unnamed priest in Margat's letter with the attitude of the entire Jesuit order in Saint-Domingue). In the era of polarizing contestation over early-eighteenth-century Jansenism, no one knew better than the Jesuits how easy it was for an entire religious order to become stigmatized.

Paranoia, conspiracy theories, and panics pervaded early modern perceptions of the Jesuit order throughout Europe. The paranoia was never entirely without some factual basis. Jesuit military interventions in Ireland during the Elizabethan era, for example, produced "sheer panic" on the part of English authorities and triggered the brutal persecution of the Society's missionaries in England. Here and elsewhere in Europe, as James E. Kelly points, out, the fuzziness of the line between temporal and spiritual authority meant that "religion was politics and vice-versa." Suspicions of Jesuit complicity in plots to overthrow royal authority in France, Spain, Portugal, and other continental states would feed directly into the mid-eighteenth-century campaign to suppress the Society of Jesus.[6]

It is all too easy to read that later fate backward into the Jesuits' earlier experience. Doing so would not be entirely anachronistic. The charge of complicity with enslaved resistance was laid against the Jesuits as early as the 1720s, not only in Saint-Domingue—as Margat's letter ruefully confirms—but also in Guadeloupe, where the Society's situation was even more tenuous. Jesuit missionaries there intervened in several trials in the early 1720s to insist upon the innocence of slaves condemned to death on charges of poisoning. The last of these protests, in 1725, prompted a public outcry—which one historian describes as a "riot"—against the judges involved in the case. When the intendant for Guadeloupe appealed to the Jesuit Superior, Père Dubois, for help in calming the storm, Dubois stood with his priests. As the white community split over the charges and counterclaims, the controversy spilled over into 1726, culminating in an enslaved uprising (albeit on what appears to be a limited scale) that led Louis XV to recall one of the three Jesuit priests involved in the affair.[7]

The Jesuits were therefore entirely capable of taking strong stands against injustice, at least within the narrow, situational parameters of a legal regime that systematically devalued enslaved lives. The main difficulty with reading the Jesuit expulsion of 1763 back into the earlier history of Saint-Domingue is that it places too much emphasis on Jesuit influence over the maroons. After all, the enslaved had plenty of motivation, and much justification, to use marronage as a technique of power in the power struggle that was Atlantic slavery. That can be hard to perceive when virtually everything we know about the maroons in this period derives either from the defensive ruminations of Catholic missionaries or the retributive anxieties of colonial administrators and planters.

As Crystal Eddins has shown, the key to recovering maroon experience in these circumstances is to recognize that marronage was a border-crossing phenomenon—in several senses. Maroons transgressed the boundary between slavery and freedom, most obviously. In Saint-Domingue, they were able to do so in large part because of their ability to navigate the physical border between the French and Spanish sides of Hispaniola. The creative use of boundary spaces as a core element of maroon world-making figured through the greater Caribbean. In Saint-Domingue, it went back to the early-sixteenth-century collaborations between Taino Indians and Africans, who rose up against the Spanish conquistadors before retreating to the Bahoruco mountain range that straddles the border area east of Port-au-Prince. These early fugitive communities established a pattern of border-crossing freedom that would greatly intensify the political turmoil of Saint-Domingue in the 1720s and after.[8]

Maroon rebellions during the second half of the seventeenth century unfolded against the backdrop of the colonists' own uprisings against monopoly trading companies during this period. The most notable was led by the maroon Padrejean in 1679 at Saint-Louis du Nord, near Port-de-Paix. According to Charlevoix, Padrejean had killed his Spanish master and took refuge on nearby l'île de la Tortue, where he was then freed. Returning to Hispaniola, Padrejean recruited a maroon collaborative consisting of enslaved persons once owned by Spanish proprietors but now forming part of the small slave community of French Saint-Domingue. As Charlevoix portrays it, Padrejean led his forces eastward on a campaign of pillage and killing toward Cap Français. The governor then succeeded in assembling a band of twenty buccaneers who subdued Padrejean and six of his fellow rebels and put them to death. Charlevoix's villain narrative is rejected by Haitian scholars (such as Saint-Victor Jean-Baptiste) who see in Padrejean the forerunner to the heroes of Haitian independence.[9]

Padrejean's campaign highlights themes that would become central to marronage in the subsequent century, especially its intersection with French-Spanish competition for control over the movement of peoples across the border. Borrowing from Stephanie Camp, Eddins describes marronage in Saint-Domingue as an expression of the creative use of "rival geographies": "alternative way[s] of knowing and using space that conflicted with planters' ideals and demands." Some of the largest maroon communities in the early eighteenth century clustered along the indeterminate French-Spanish border dividing the western and eastern halves of Hispaniola.[10]

Maroons were the true authors of the map of Saint-Domingue because, more than anyone, they controlled the border region that defined the limits of French sovereignty. The boundary is often understood to have been fixed in the 1697 Treaty of Ryswick that ended the Nine Years' War between France and the League of Augsburg, which included Spain. In fact, the decisive line was not established until 1777, with the Treaty of Aranjuez. Until then, the border remained in flux, at times shifting to the benefit of the Spanish empire, at other times the French. The early eighteenth century was an especially unstable period, the pretensions of French cartographers notwithstanding. Maps of Hispaniola from this time showed clear boundary lines but differed starkly as to where exactly the line lay, underscoring their character as political claims rather than sovereign facts.[11]

The same map could be generous to French territorial ambitions in one respect and parsimonious in another. The 1722 map by the French royal cartographer Delisle, for example (figure 21), accords a large swath of the great savannah plains of Goâve, in the north-central border region, to France. By contrast, Delisle designates Spain as sovereign over much of the southern peninsula border region. (The northern area of this peninsula, in the Bahoruco mountain range, became home to a maroon community known as *le Maniel* by the end of the seventeenth century. It would become the most famous of the maroon settlements of the colonial period, surviving nearly a century of French attempts to destroy it.)[12] The Delisle map was based on documentation provided by the royal engineer Frèzier, who himself depicted a very different boundary in a map first sketched in 1721 but not published until 1724 (figure 7). The cartouche for Frèzier's map indicates that, over the course of those three years, Frèzier revisited his assessment of the limits of Spanish authority, which was

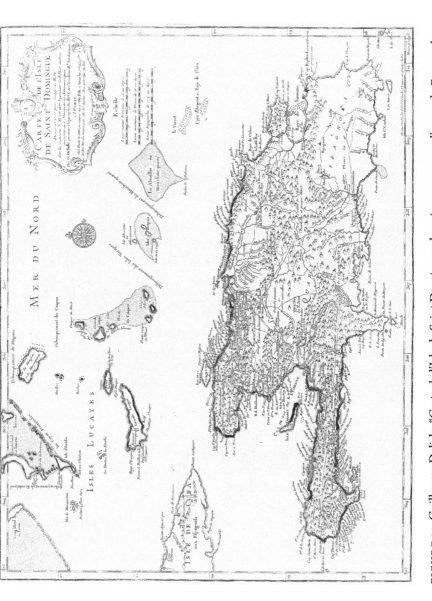

FIGURE 21. Guillaume Delisle, "Carte de l'Isle de Saint Domingue dressée en 1722 pour l'usage du Roy sur les mémoires de Mr. Frèzier Ingénieur de S.M. et autres" (Paris, 1725). Courtesy of the John Carter Brown Library, Providence, RI.

based on information provided by a French colonial military official named Buttet. In the end, Frézier writes, he was sufficiently confident in Buttet's information to leave the boundary essentially unchanged. The result was a map that gave France the entirety of the southern peninsula but showed Spanish sovereignty extending well into territory marked as French in Delisle's rendering, including the entirety of the great savannah plains of Goâve, nearly as far west as Petite Rivière in the Artibonite valley.

Empires attempted to establish on paper an authority they did not exercise on land.[13] They did not exercise this authority on land because the de facto sovereigns of this border region were the maroon communities that used it as a refuge from the brutality of the sugar revolution. Cartographic claims would either assert imperial power or deny it. In either case these assertions depended heavily on the politics of the campaign to vanquish maroon settlements. Asserting that a part of the border region was French implied the legitimacy of French efforts to apprehend fugitives in that area. Portraying another part of the border region as Spanish implied a duty on the part of the Spanish crown to play its part in the recovery of persons alleged to be held as slaves on French plantations—assuming the two empires could arrive at an agreement to this effect.

That was not necessarily a safe assumption. Maroon communities were well aware of imperial squabbling over the border because they were the key issue in the dispute. Bilateral negotiations between France and Spain stopped and started repeatedly under the Old Regime, consistently stumbling over the status of fugitives who sought refuge in each other's territory. The primary concern lay on the French side, where the sugar revolution was in full swing, rather than in Santo Domingo, where cattle herding was the primary industry and produced less pressure for flight. The single most prominent complaint of French colonial administrators during the 1710s and 1720s, Eddins explains, was the Spanish "refusal" to repatriate maroons who had traversed the border in search of a way of life that provided an alternative to the sugar revolution:

> [E]nslaved Africans had knowledge of and exploited the geopolitical conflicts between the French and Spanish crowns by traversing the border between Saint-Domingue and Santo Domingo and establishing liberated zones on their own terms. By committing marronage within and against the French colonial enterprise of Saint-Domingue, runaways forced authorities to reckon with questions of imperial reach and power.

As this analysis suggests, the intersecting conflicts over maroons and the border were so intractable because maroons were controlled neither by the French nor the Spanish authorities. They were not necessarily available to be given up by the king of Spain, though Spanish colonists in Santo Domingo do seem to have observed a kind of hands-off policy toward refugees from the French side.

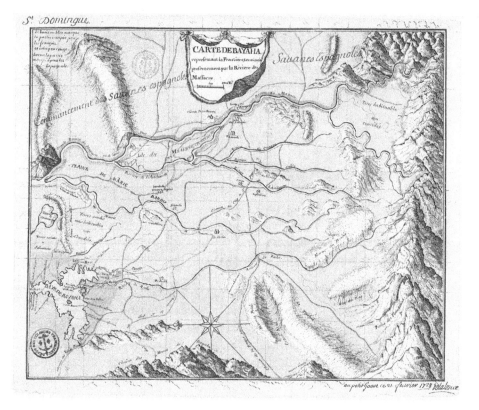

FIGURE 22. Joseph-Louis de la Lance, "Carte de Bayaha représentant la frontière terminée présentement par la rivière du Massacre," (1728). Courtesy of the Bibliothèque nationale de France.

That exercise of restraint may well have seemed indistinguishable from actual protection in the eyes of the Saint-Domingue planters.[14]

Where, exactly, the line demarcating French and Spanish jurisdiction was to be drawn mattered little to the maroons themselves. It helped that the border region was traversed by relatively forbidding mountain ranges, hard to penetrate by French forces. Some maroon communities evaded detection for long stretches of time. The maroons of the Maniel settlement in the Bahoruco region, the Saint-Domingue administrators observed in 1717, "had been there for seventeen or eighteen years without any white person even having known." Staking out territory in topography like the Bahoruco mountains of the southern border area, or the Bayaha mountains in the north, was inherently challenging. A 1728 map of the northern border region of Bayaha illustrates the French colonial predicament (figure 22). It is here that the Artibonite and Massacre (today known as the Dajabón) rivers merge and form part of the contemporary border between Haiti and the Dominican Republic. (In 1937, the Massacre River was the site of a mass slaughter of Haitians ordered by the Dominican dictator Rafael Trujillo.) To the west of the border (to the south on the map) lies the Bay of Bayaha and what is now the town of Fort Liberté. The 1728 map by Joseph-Louis de la Lance depicts the valley region as home to only a few French colonial settlements. Spanish and French guard stations lay on either side of the Massacre River. The Bayaha mountains at the bottom of the map form a border on the western side of the valley. To the south (at right in the map) lies the Cordillera Septentrional mountain range, which runs parallel to the north coast of Hispaniola. Regions such as this were isolated and made vulnerable by mountains from a white settler perspective. From a maroon vantage point, the mountains facilitated refuge and autonomy while also permitting access to the resources of the valley region. The nebulous French-Spanish border delivered such advantages to maroons from north to south. The result was that maroon communities, rather than empires, effectively "shaped the border itself as an ongoing political project," "leveraging" conflict over it to their benefit. Meanwhile, the French and Spanish authorities continued to blame each other for their inability to repress maroon activity, as if the problem was a failure to follow diplomatic protocols rather than the structural instabilities of plantation slavery itself.[15]

The many expressions of frustration over border insecurity that we find in the correspondence of imperial administrators read like a microcosm of the eighteenth-century tendency to double down on the repressive tactics of state violence. That approach foreclosed any opportunity for Saint-Domingue to retreat from the road of militant white supremacy. On May 27, 1722, for example, the Conseil de Marine wrote to the French minister of foreign affairs, Cardinal Dubois, to urge him to act quickly on "the frequent desertion of negroes" from Saint-Domingue across the border to Santo Domingo. The movement of peoples "was causing significant damage to the inhabitants of this colony, would ruin them in the long term, and would cause a rupture between the two nations on this island." The proposed solution—a bilateral agreement to repatriate any maroons or soldiers who crossed over from one side to the other—captured the self-defeating tactics of both French and Spanish maroon policy in this era.[16]

Agreements like that had already come and gone. In 1718, for example, the king of Spain ordered the return of all "French" maroons who had taken refuge in Santo Domingo. French colonial officials observed that such orders and agreements, drafted as they were at multiple removes from the lived experience of maroons, were not necessarily worth the paper on which they were written. In the meantime, the maroons had succeeded in demonstrating the futility of any military solution to the proliferation of fugitive slave communities. They had done so not only by their strategic use of the boundary rifts between France and Spain in Hispaniola, but also by making a home for themselves in another "rival geography": the mountainous interstices between plantations and towns in several different regions of Saint-Domingue.[17]

Unlike the border zone, these maroon settlements—the word should be used with a grain of salt, given the mobility that was essential to avoiding apprehension—could not be avoided by the planters of Saint-Domingue. They were simply too integrated with the existing institutions and practices of daily life in the colony. The paradoxical key to the success of maroon culture was that it systematically transgressed the very geographical isolation upon which it depended. Eddins writes of the "connections constructed by enslaved people and maroons in living quarters, ritual spaces, markets, mountains, caves, and other unmonitored areas"—all of these were part of a complex, integrated circuit that was just as difficult to police, in some ways, as the more distant border regions.[18]

When planters and administrators began to search in the late 1710s for new ways to counteract the threat they perceived in maroon activity, they had these dispersed yet integrated circuits foremost in mind. As Charlevoix's text suggested, the ability to assert their presence both on the plantations and on the roads that connected them gave the maroons authority over the anxious minds of their pursuers. The latter responded by ratcheting up the levels of violence to match the depth of the planter anxiety that maroon autonomy created. Colonial administrators were tasked with the responsibility for squaring this circle.

Little is known about the career of marronage over the two decades following Padrejean's uprising in 1679, but this is perhaps only an indication that maroons during this period did not undertake offensive campaigns against white settlers. Franklin Midy emphasizes the distinction between marronage per se and rebellious acts by maroons, arguing that colonial authorities and planters alike clearly distinguished between these two forms of conduct. Whether that is the case, the spontaneous flight of the enslaved from colonial plantations was almost certainly a continuous part of the life of western Hispaniola under colonization.[19]

The opening years of the eighteenth century were a turning point in the perception of marronage: after this point it became more difficult to compartmentalize between marronage as spontaneous release from bondage and marronage as subaltern resistance to power. One official account from 1700 estimated the number of maroons in Saint-Domingue at six hundred. In 1701–2, a settlement near Morne Noir, in the mountains of the southern province due south of Port-au-Prince, gave rise to the most visible signs of maroon mobilization since France formalized its claim to the western third of Hispaniola in the Ryswick treaty.[20]

The first efforts at patrolling maroons were undertaken by racially mixed militia companies charged with carrying out public works projects and serving the needs of colonial defense. Free blacks served alongside whites in these companies as early as the 1690s (participating in the siege of Cartagena in 1697), and some even commanded groups of free black recruits. The historian Baptiste Bonnefoy cites the case of Jacques Sambourg, a free black captain who was buried near Léogâne in 1699. Parish records memorialize the deaths of other free black captains and majors in the 1710s and 1720s. Such companies of free people of color, Bonnefoy writes, "did not imply a systematic separation of whites and people of color." Free black and free colored militiamen comprised 16 percent of the Léogâne militia in 1718, and detachments periodically assigned to pursue maroons remained mixed.[21]

Specialization (if not yet segregation) was becoming the order of the day. In 1705, the Superior Council of Léogâne responded to the increasing prominence of maroon activity by prohibiting enslaved persons from carrying arms or assembling outside their plantations. And the roots of what would become known as the maréchaussée were put down: thirty-six men from each of three districts—Petit Goâve, Léogâne, and Cul de Sac—whose sole function was to "hunt negro maroons (chasser les nègres marons)." Maroons, the high court wrote, had taken to stealing from passersby on the main colonial roads, pilfering cattle from plantations, and hiding out in the cabins of their "comrades." The failure to crack down on such a contagion of "libertinism" would only attract increasing numbers of enslaved to the cause, the judges explained.[22]

The financing of specialized slave patrols reflected the conflicts and corruptions associated with the broader political crisis of money during these years. Those who signed up for service had the authority to shoot any fugitive they pursued and were paid an annual salary of three hundred livres, plus a bounty for each maroon captured. The amount of that bounty increased according to whether the capture took place on the roads or in the sugar fields, in the mountains, or even further afield. A special fund covered the cost of reimbursing masters whose slaves were killed in the act of chase. Funding for the overall scheme came from a levy on planters, assessed according to the number of slaves each owned. This required that each planter provide a "faithful accounting" of the number of enslaved under his jurisdiction, whether baptized or not. Unreported slaves were to be confiscated and sold, with half of the proceeds going back into the fugitive slave patrol fund, the other half to the whistleblower.[23]

Taken as a whole, the new regime was a calculation that planters would see they stood to lose more from confiscation of unreported slaves than they would gain by not paying taxes on them. Colonial administrators would never fully solve the collective action dilemma at work here, despite widely shared concerns about the nature of the threat to white planter society. Nor could they, because marronage was a product of plantation slavery itself and would not subside so long as slavery persisted. A 1714 decision of the Superior Council of Cap Français testified to this reality, absolving an enslaved person named Songo, owned by the planter Le Febvre, who had been captured as a maroon. The court alluded obliquely to "special reasons" for its decision and made clear that its ruling did not establish a precedent. The creole jurist Moreau's annotations, compiled at the end of the eighteenth century, revealed the truth of the matter: "The unjust treatment of masters has sometimes necessitated similar rulings."[24]

———

Moreau's "sometimes" notwithstanding, the mercy that spared Songo was not the spirit of the emerging law. The 1705 decision of the high court judges of Léogâne to attack marronage as a contagion of "libertinism" placed Saint-Domingue on the road toward becoming a military-planter state. As John Law was blowing his Mississippi Bubble, the colonists of Saint-Domingue continued to invest in the scaffolding of this deeply conflicted, fiscally unstable, and increasingly harsh system. In 1718, a new set of bounties for the capture of maroons in different regions of the colony was established. The tariffs paid tribute to the basic importance of geography. The reward for capture in the northern plain surrounding Cap Français was set at twelve livres. In the "double mountain" areas farther away from the plantations, seventy-five livres was the prize.[25]

The border disputes with Spain, which had long inflated the stakes of neutralizing maroon resistance, assumed especially thorny dimensions when France declared war with Spain in 1719, marking the temporary return of conflict for the first time since the Utrecht peace in 1713. Though the two nations avoided actual conflict in Hispaniola, their mutual hostilities provided another opening for maroons from the French side. Reading the tea leaves of French-Spanish conflict this time was a man named Michel, the head of a community of fugitives based in the Bahoruco mountains at their southernmost point, in the border peninsula region known as la Béate. The maroons of la Béate were in flight from both the French and Spanish sides, leading French and Spanish forces to collaborate on a "hunt" in 1715 that was compensated at a rate of 25 piastres for each maroon captured, dead or alive. Although the mission made some inroads by 1717—such that it "might serve to make the desertion of slaves less frequent"—Michel continued to evade capture. His uprising even

MAROONS AND THE MILITARY-PLANTER STATE   169

led Governor Châteaumorant to enlist the support of metropolitan soldiers convicted to galley slavery for having deserted their posts, a practice the Conseil de Marine condemned as "contrary to all the laws of the kingdom." The existing mechanisms for policing slaves remained evidently insufficient.[26]

Michel was finally captured and executed by the French authorities in 1719. But other maroon leaders were not far behind in the race to succeed him. In 1720, maroon bands based in the Maribaroux parish of northeast Saint-Domingue (near what is now Fort Liberté) gathered force. Finally, and above all, Colas Jambes Coupées became an overriding target of whites throughout the colony's northeastern region from 1720 to 1724. The period of the rebellion against the Indies Company, in short, was one of maximum tensions over the issue of fugitive slaves in Saint-Domingue.[27]

There was a two-way relationship between the corporate political crisis and maroon resistance. Subaltern "[r]epertoires and mobilization," Eddins writes, "are particularly efficacious when regimes experience periods of economic or political crisis." More than once, wartime economic pressures and food shortages in Saint-Domingue "provided moments of opportunity for maroons to flee without fear of retribution from an already weakened state." The point clearly applies to the years of the rebellion against the Indies Company (though Eddins does not make the connection). Maroon resistance awakened the dormant forces of colonial state-building, which white supremacy then shaped in the direction of the military-planter state. This was a historically specific but particularly tenacious type of state, and its impact on Saint-Domingue and Haiti over the longer term would rival that of the sugar revolution.

The crackdown was fueled in part by a sense that the Spanish were now positively conspiring to undermine French plantation agriculture. The paranoia reflected local policies more than metropolitan ones. As of 1720, over one thousand maroons were scattered across the northern part of Saint-Domingue. Hundreds more had taken refuge on the Spanish side of Hispaniola. Far from dispelling anxieties that he was actively collaborating with maroons from the French side, the governor of the Spanish colony, Fernando Costanzo Ramirez, declared outright in 1721 that he would no longer return French runaways to Saint-Domingue. This was contrary to the instructions of the Spanish crown—which issued three royal *cédulas* on this topic in the space of a few years—but it came at a time when Costanzo was facing an uprising of his own. The year before, four militia captains rebelled against Costanzo's establishment of a frontier post on the Massacre (Dajabón) River that was designed to help clamp down on illegal cross-border trade with French colonists in Cap Français. Costanzo's policy on French maroons bought him some support at this sensitive time from his own subjects, who were desperate to bolster their ranks at a time of demographic decline in Santo Domingo. Equally significant,

Costanzo knew that repatriation would face stiff opposition from the maroons themselves.[28]

Mounting numbers of maroons coincided with the escalating Spanish colonial disregard for French claims during the early 1720s. Administrators in Saint-Domingue conveyed a sense of the scale and urgency of the crisis but in a way that guaranteed its perpetuation: the problem, they argued, was not simply rebellion or marronage per se, but an epidemic of slave insubordination and lawlessness more generally. And they held both blacks and whites responsible for the problem. In January 1720, Governor Sorel and Intendant Mithon reiterated the Code Noir's ban on enslaved assemblies in the face of a new and unfamiliar political challenge: the appointment of "captains" and "chiefs" by a group of slaves gathered from different estates at the Beaujeau plantation in the Maribaroux district near Cap Français. The ordinance implied that the offending slaves enacted their leadership rituals, ominous in themselves as expressions of Afro-Haitian sovereignty, by mounting on horseback and brandishing rifles, pistols, flaming torches, and other weapons. In other words, these were armed gatherings of the enslaved in public spaces: one of the cardinal sins in planters' eyes, punishable by the Code Noir in the form of whipping and branding with the symbol of the fleur de lis. To strengthen those deterrents, the ordinance imposed monetary penalties (thirty livres per offense) not on plantation owners, but on mid- and low-level plantation agents—managers and slave drivers—who tolerated these acts. Denis Colas, the manager of the Beaujeau estate, was the first to pay. Plantation owners themselves remained conspicuously immune from liability.[29]

The conduct described in the 1720 ordinance was something both more and less than marronage. Maribaroux was one of the leading centers of maroon mobilization in the north, but here was an attempt to reassert control over the plantations themselves. Documents like these give us a sense of the rich theater of Afro-Haitian empowerment colluding with planter anxiety that was so prominent a feature of the political culture of the early 1720s. This was the world within which the militarization of plantation society unfolded in Saint-Domingue.

———

The decisive step in that process came on March 27, 1721, with the establishment of a colonial maréchaussée by Sorel and Duclos. The term itself had roots deep in French military history. The maréchaussée was an institution born of the Hundred Years' War (1337–1453), when it served as a police force with court-martial jurisdiction over crimes committed by soldiers. By the early sixteenth century it had evolved into a rural policing mechanism that targeted vagabonds for banditry and other crimes committed on the major roads connecting the cities and towns of France. Saint-Domingue had no such institution at first because it did not have that vulnerable nexus of wealth, major public roads, and urban concentrations that drove the development of the Parisian maréchaussée, for example. The text creating the system of fugitive slave patrols in 1705 did not use this term. But there was no shortage of communities living on the margins of early colonial Saint-Domingue, including *gens sans aveu* and, above all, maroons. Once parallel institutions like public roads connecting the major towns and plantation areas of the north were in place, fear of maroon ambushes provided Saint-Domingue with the opportunity to invent its own version of the maréchaussée. In doing so, moreover, the colony's leaders could tap into the lessons learned from the general reorganization of the royal maréchaussée that took place in France in 1720, which occasioned the creation of the influential company that policed the Paris region.[30]

In adapting this metropolitan institution to Caribbean circumstances, Sorel and Duclos showed a systematic attention to organizational detail and a willingness to harness resources that went far beyond anything the colony had ever contemplated in the past. The new regime responded specifically to the raft of "very frequent and repeated" complaints from northern planters. Maroons "descend from all areas to the Spanish side where they are perfectly well received, and from which it is impossible to recall them":

> This reception has produced in their minds an impression tending toward a general revolt and, as a consequence, the total ruin of the inhabitants of Le Cap, and even the entire loss of the colony by way of bad example.

The understanding of marronage laid out in this opening paragraph of the ordinance reads like a road map for the dead ends and vicious circles of the colonial policies of the next seventy to eighty years in Saint-Domingue and revolutionary Haiti. The minds of Afro-Haitians, according to the 1721 ordinance, respond to the stimuli received from Europeans: reception triggers revolt, discipline stimulates obedience. The cardinal habit of the slave mind is habit itself, above all the "bad example" set for one slave by another. And the stakes of stamping out those bad habits—of erasing the mental impression that makes rebellion possible— were nothing less than the survival of white society as such. (The administrators were ambiguous as to whether they meant survival in a physical or economic sense: marronage was a threat both to the person of the planter and to his ability to rely on forced labor for profits.)[31]

Sorel and Duclos professed that they "had not found any other means" to address marronage than the one France had adopted almost two centuries earlier for purposes of controlling robbery on the high roads. But they went to great lengths to customize this military regime to counteract the rival geographies that maroons had mastered and to exploit the logics of racial hierarchy and division in Saint-Domingue. In all, 125 men would be called into service for the colony's domestic defense. Royal guards of twenty-five men each would police the areas around Massacre (at the northern end of the border region) and Grande-Rivière (in the mountains south of Cap Français, near what is now Milot)—two of the key points of transit used by maroon communities on the way to their havens. Because of the difficulty of scouting every maroon passageway, the colony would also form a mobile "maréchaussée company" of seventy-five men, the vast majority of whom—sixty-six—would be archers. These men were to be chosen by the governor or the commandant of Le Cap, paid monthly salaries according to their rank (thirty pounds a month for the archers), and divided into at least three brigades. The racial criteria used to determine eligibility for service laid the basis for an enduring civil war between free people of color, on the one hand, and enslaved Afro-Haitians and their descendants, on the other. Both whites and free people of color (*mulâtres*) qualified, whereas free blacks (*nègres libres*) could be called into duty only when whites were unavailable. The patrols' principal mission was to prevent anyone—whites, free people of color, free blacks, or slaves—from crossing the border to the Spanish side. But they could also search plantations, including slave quarters, for evidence of maroons being harbored or weapons concealed.[32]

In the already long history of Hispaniola, no power had proved itself capable of preventing the movement of peoples between the western and eastern halves of the island. No amount of money could change this reality. The new financing regime showed that the administrators recognized some, but not all, of the conflicts baked into the 1705 patrols. The new regime promised one hundred pounds for each maroon captured dead or alive on the Spanish side, thirty pounds for those taken on the northern plains outside the parish boundaries of their plantation, and twelve pounds for all other captures. These sums would flow not to the individual but to the company as a whole and would be shared based on a sliding scale according to rank. All funding would come from the colonial treasury—though the administrators left the judges of the Conseil Supérieur in Le Cap to decide whether to continue relying on taxing planters by heads of slaves (as had been the case since 1705). The upshot was a path that, depending on how it was to be funded, might skirt some of the corruption and unintended consequences of the earlier system. But by guaranteeing the same payment for capturing a maroon whether dead or alive, the administrators gave the militia company little reason to try to protect the property interests of planters.[33]

Indeed the 1721 ordinance expressly vested the fugitive slave patrols with judicial powers over the life and death of the maroon, a jurisdictional vestige of the maréchaussée's origins in the Hundred Years' War. The company's officers were made court-martial judges empowered to hang fugitives captured in the frontier regions without a trial, provided that three officers were present, including the provost marshal or his lieutenant. (Only black fugitives were subject to this power; whites and free people of color who deserted from military service were not.) The bodies of those captured were to be suspended from trees visible from the colony's main road so as to "serve as an example" to others. And to take care of the grisly work of death, the colonial executioner was assigned to accompany the maréchaussée on its patrols, at an annual salary of five hundred pounds.[34]

These policies officially made Saint-Domingue an irretrievably lawless and racially murderous society. By incorporating free people of color into the work of policing marronage, the new regime injected a structural dose of violence into their relationship with the enslaved. The growth of a community of free colored coffee planters, particularly in the southern province, had already begun to drive a hierarchical wedge between the two groups. The lawlessness and murderousness of the 1721 system, moreover, extended beyond the arbitrary powers of life and death exercised by the maréchaussée company itself. Under the new rules, each individual white inhabitant of Saint-Domingue was given a similar power: "We permit all inhabitants who encounter a negro (*nègre*) at night to shoot and kill him if he fails to stop at the first command." That provision effectively created a roving, nocturnal, white supremacist vigilante authority that made the maréchaussée, by comparison, seem like a model of restraint.[35]

Indeed, whether the militia system would have any capacity to displace private violence through collective action depended very much on the major question left open by Sorel and Duclos: financing. In a July 1721 memorandum to the Conseil Supérieur in Cap Français, Sorel and Duclos boasted that the mere announcement of the militia system in March had put a sudden lid on planter talk of a maroon crisis. But it had also sounded the alarm that a new effort to tax northern planters was afoot, under the guise of instituting the new fugitive slave militia. Sorel and Duclos danced gingerly around the issue, sensitive to the colony's historic status as a tax-free domain that obeyed only a voluntary tradition of granting revenues as a gift to the monarch to cover the cost of public works. In the months since March, a new strand of resistance had emerged: the reluctance of planters of the Cap Français region to shoulder what they feared would be a larger share of the maréchaussée burden than all other areas of the colony combined. These concerns impeded raising the funds envisioned in the March 1721 ordinance. And without money, there was little chance of assembling a fully staffed militia ready and willing to do the violent work of policing maroons.[36]

Two specific aspects of the financing scheme loomed largest. First, the thirty-pound salary specified for archers, Sorel and Duclos wrote in July 1721, was simply too miserly to support the costs of keeping them adequately outfitted. Second, the company was being shortchanged on the bounties it was owed for the capture of maroons. Without a consensus on how to raise the necessary public funds, Sorel and Duclos did not see a road forward—other than possibly reducing the number of archers, thereby inflating the amount that each individual militia member would take home.[37]

And so the administrators did what one might expect of officials charged with solving a collective action dilemma that had no real solution: they appealed to a mix of incentives and fears. Had the people of Saint-Domingue already forgotten their all too recent fears of "going to bed with one hundred and two hundred negroes while not being sure of waking in the morning with a single one"? As Sorel and Duclos saw it, this was a realistic worry, not a scare tactic—even if they conceived of ruin in economic rather than physical terms. Surely the rational planter would be willing to look beyond the presence or absence of immediate dangers and act in the best long-term interests of the colony by shouldering his fair share of the collective costs—if for no other reason than that the new regime dispensed with the need to divert oneself from plantation work to participate in maroon patrols.[38]

In short, as with every other issue involved in the creation of a prosperous slave economy, fugitive surveillance depended on money and taxes. The militia system was part and parcel of a political economy that required subordinating a narrow conception of self-interest to a white supremacist definition of the public good. Sorel and Duclos made clear that the monarchy was not coming to save the colonists from their self-inflicted dilemmas: first, because repeated entreaties to the Conseil de Marine had been met with indifference; and second, because royal troops sent from France would not survive the Caribbean climate long enough to make an impact on the maroon crisis. In short, there was no alternative but to accept the maréchaussée as an inevitable public resource to be funded by the colony as a whole.[39]

When read between its lines, the administrators' lengthy, meandering, and at times confusing letter appeared to be an appeal to the Conseil Supérieur to take the heat for imposing another tax on planters based on the number of slaves each owned: in other words, the old wine of 1705 served in a new bottle of rational self-interest and strategic realism. The judges of the high court wasted little time in calling the administrators' bluff, ordering a levy of fifty sous, or two and half pounds, on the head of each slave serving on a plantation in the northern province (excepting only Port-de-Paix), beginning on the first of July.[40]

The new militia system was another microcosm of the political-economic conflicts that fueled the agitation against the Indies Company. In a society where silver money was scarce, the task of persuading colonists to part with it, even for the sake of preserving their own status as slaveholders, was a distinctly uphill battle. And it would not get any easier in the coming months, notwithstanding the quickening pace of the commerce between maroon mobilization and planter anxiety during the months and years that followed the institutionalization of the fugitive slave company. The problem remained, at one level, a matter of the paucity of local specie. In October, a few months after collection of the new fugitive slave levy was supposed to have begun, Sorel and Duclos ordered the planters of the northern province to surrender to their parish churchwardens the necessary monies—which had now been reduced by half, to twenty-five sous (or a little more than a livre), but included back payment for the first six months of 1721. The measures prescribed to force planters to comply give a good sense of the depth of the resistance to the new regime and the administrative willingness to overcome it: confiscation of chattel property and domestic slaves, and, in the most refractory situations, arrest.[41]

The other aspect of the stalemate involved dysfunctions in the actual execution of the maréchaussée patrols, stemming from the corruptions to which the system was still prone. Because some plantations were located directly on the path of the colony's main roads, the company's archers resorted to an array of illicit tactics in pursuit of their indemnities. These included: (1) arresting enslaved persons who had never left their master's estate, claiming that these "maroons" lacked the requisite passports for travel; (2) responding to the display of a valid passport by tearing it up; and (3) confiscating as maroon accessories horses used with permission by enslaved persons for overnight visits to neighboring properties. Most of these abuses were attributed to vagabonds (*gens sans aveu*) falsely claiming to be members of the company. (This was about nine months before Louis XV's declaration in July 1722 that France would no longer deport vagabonds to the French colonies.) In response, the administrators concocted another series of stopgap measures—requiring archers to wear blue shoulder straps featuring the fleur de lis symbol of the Bourbon monarchy, and prohibiting archers from arresting slaves within the confines of their masters' plantations.[42]

The circle of abuses and the efforts to reform them permitted the administrators to claim that the maréchaussée system could, if fully implemented, deter fugitivity in Saint-Domingue. Whether it ever actually did is a much different question. The evidence suggests that it did not, though we have no models or data sufficiently developed or granular to test the hypothesis. What remains, instead, are the records of legal proceedings involving punishment of some of the colony's most wanted maroon rebels. These indicate that the fugitive slave system succeeded only in inflicting great violence upon maroons, who continued to defy colonial law notwithstanding the grave bodily risks that flight from the plantation incurred.

The vicious circle of resistance and repression that had come to characterize militant slavery in Saint-Domingue is captured by two judgments spanning the years of the rebellion against the Indies Company. The first, from 1721, involves a group of twenty-one slaves accused of seeking refuge on the Spanish side, five of them while armed, the others carrying their belongings. Their case, the court explained, was to be considered in light of the "frequent disorders that arise from the desertion and rebellion of negroes." That is, they were to be judged not so much for what they actually did, but to "prevent the consequences" of the example they might give to others. The only semblance of due process they were accorded in an otherwise summary proceeding was the opportunity to answer the charges against them. "They responded that although they had some weapons, their plan was to return." The two alleged leaders of the "revolt," Alexandre and César, were sentenced to be hung forthwith at the Place d'Armes in Le Cap by the colony's high executioner, their heads cut off and displayed on pikes at their master's plantation "to serve as an example." After being forced to witness this punishment, six of the nineteen coconspirators were carried off to prison for whipping and branding with the fleur de lis by a hot iron before being released on pain of death in case of recidivism.[43]

The second judgment, dated June 4, 1723, condemned a maroon whose life demonstrates, more than any other, the interlocking nature of the rebellions of the 1720s. His very name—Colas Jambes Coupées (Colas whose legs are cut)—tells us that this was his third offense under Article 38 of the Code Noir, which required cutting the hamstrings of two-time maroons. For four to five years, from his base near the mountains south of Cap Français, Colas was said to have repeatedly fled to the Spanish side, "seduced" others to join him, served as the "head of an armed cabal" consisting of four other maroons (Cézar, Jupiter, Louis, and Chéri), and committed robbery on the high roads by day and night alike. The indictment against him further alleged that he had attacked white colonists and plotted through "secret correspondence" to abolish the colonies altogether. In a trope that would be applied to the colony's most famous maroons, including Makandal in the 1750s, Colas was said to have repeatedly evaded punishment through the aid of "sorcery and magic," escaping from prison repeatedly despite being held in irons. As a result, Colas had been convicted in absentia multiple times by the very same high court in Le Cap. This time, the court declared, he would be hung by the colony's high executioner on a scaffold erected in the vicinity of the conduct for which he was being punished, his body there to remain on view "for the public example of the negroes with whom he is in correspondence."[44]

The quest to subdue Colas became an all-consuming priority for the planters of Saint-Domingue, leading them to propose private remedies to supplement the limitations of the maréchaussée system. The fugitive slave patrol regime was supposed to serve as a monopoly on the use of violence against maroons, but the perception of escalating maroon activity opened the door to other forms of violence. On May 20, 1723, about two weeks before Colas was apprehended and punished, a group of the leading planters of the Léogâne and Cul de Sac regions petitioned Intendant Montholon for an allocation of funds to support a special search into Spanish territory for maroons who had fled from their properties. With Governor Sorel's approval, Montholon directed the Saint-Domingue tax receiver to disburse a loan of three thousand livres against the colonial treasury to the military commander of Cul de Sac, Dubois. The need to rely on credit indicated that, two years after the administrators' frantic efforts to compel planters to fund the maréchaussée, they remained unwilling (or unable) to do so. Given its timing, the Dubois mission—the word captures something of the religious fervor with which fugitives were pursued and punished at this time—was almost certainly the one that led to the arrest of Colas.[45]

Making an example out of Colas did little to solve the colonists' problems, real or perceived—including an inability to master the topography and border region of Hispaniola. On July 24, 1723, Sorel and Montholon entered into another private contract for maroon recovery operations, this time with the planter Jean Lejeune of Nippes, in the southern province. Lejeune's chief qualification was that he owned an armed vessel, the *Trancardine*, large enough to travel to Santo Domingo city and return with at least 160 maroons. By this time, Philip V, the monarch of Spain, had issued the third of three *cédulas* (or royal decrees) requiring Governor Costanzo to resume cooperating with the French by repatriating their fugitives—the practice Costanzo had suspended in 1721 under local pressure. Two agents for the French colonists, Lestrade and Lagrange, were dispatched in advance of the operation to secure custody of as many maroons as they could assemble with the aid of their Spanish counterparts.[46]

The provisions of Lejeune's contract give a clinical sense of the extraordinary lengths to which French colonists were willing to go to recover maroons across the border, provided, of course, that they did not have to foot the bill. "For the good and benefit of the colony," as Lejeune put it in petitioning several months later for his payment, the contract stipulated as follows:

- One hundred and thirty-five pounds for each maroon embarked on Lejeune's vessel, with a guaranteed minimum payment for no less than 160 maroons, or a total of 21,600 livres;
- Lejeune's expenses would be covered for twenty days spent at port on the Spanish side, at a rate of twenty pounds per day;

- Twenty-five pounds for each day that Lejeune spent in Santo Domingo;
- For the cost of feeding crew and maroons, Lejeune would receive six thousand pounds;
- To "reinforce" his crew, arrangements would be made for thirty free people of color or free blacks (or whites if neither of the former could be procured) to join the mission at a rate of thirty livres per month each.

As it happens, Lejeune had to resort to recruiting fifteen soldiers from the colonial regiments to round out his crew, along with a surgeon required at the insistence of the captain of the regiment.[47]

Lejeune finally set sail for Santo Domingo on August 23. On August 29, he moored in the Bay of Ocoa, about thirty miles west of the capital city, and from there dispatched a letter to Lestrade and Costanzo in Santo Domingo informing them of his arrival. On September 3, with no news from Lestrade or sign of the maroons, Lejeune left to go investigate matters in Santo Domingo for himself. He arrived two days later to discover that only "a portion" of the maroons had been arrested and detained in the city prisons, even though Lestrade and Lagrange had done everything necessary on their part to assemble a larger contingent.[48]

The difficulty, Lejeune learned, was that although the Spanish king might be able to compel obedience from Costanzo, the local Spanish colonists were far less enthusiastic about the recent *cédula*. Lestrade and Lagrange were unable to obtain custody of more fugitives "because of the revolt undertaken by the people of the city of Santo Domingo." Exactly what that rebellion looked like, Lejeune's petition for payment of the contract does not tell us, except to note that Lestrade and Lagrange were lucky to escape from it with their lives. Not one to be detained by the details of this remarkable display of Spanish creole treason, Lejeune explained that he then had no other choice but to leave Santo Domingo on October 6, dragging along with him only as many maroons as he and his forces could make off given the Santo Domingo popular revolt. By the time Lejeune's mission reached the Bay of Ocoa, the ship had been forced to remain at port ten days longer than contemplated by the contract. The 128 maroons who remained behind went on to found, near Santo Domingo, the village of Saint-Laurent-des-Mines, named after the African nation from which they came.[49]

Lejeune returned to Saint-Domingue with much less than his sponsors had wanted. Even so, the unanticipated drama of his mission had put him in no mood to show flexibility when it came to claiming payment. Lejeune asked for everything specified in writing and more:

MAROONS AND THE MILITARY-PLANTER STATE   179

- All 16,850 livres of his guaranteed minimum amount for the delivery of 160 maroons (most of whom never came near his ship);
- One hundred fifty pounds for the additional ten days at port;
- Eight hundred and fifteen pounds for the costs associated with transporting the maroons from Santo Domingo to the Bay of Ocoa;
- Discharge of all debts associated with the fifteen soldiers, whose wages were normally paid (he noted) "by the colony, which this matter concerns";
- And discharge of his debt for four hundred pounds for the cost of the surgeon.

Sorel and Montholon saw things differently. On October 29, they ordered that, contract or no contract, Lejeune be paid only five thousand livres—enough to make good on his obligations to the sailors and crew and cover his most pressing additional expenses. In addition, Lejeune seems to have been discharged of most, if not all, of the debts he incurred in connection with the colonial troops.[50]

———

French authorities claimed that the enslaved were especially susceptible to the rebellious influence of their maroon brethren and sisters. The confluence of settler uprisings on either side of the French-Spanish border in the early 1720s suggests that European colonists were no less susceptible to the contagion of "libertinism" (as the administrators of Saint-Domingue put it in 1705). The revolt against the Indies Company, the captains' rebellion of 1720–24 on the Spanish side, and the insurgency to shield the maroons from Lejeune's repatriation mission in 1723 were all connected as different expressions of the political economy of Hispaniola.[51] Whether the influences were direct and mutual does not really matter in the final analysis, however. Even as Lejeune was on his way to the office of the Saint-Domingue tax receiver to collect his five thousand livres, Champmeslin was in the process of undertaking his own mission to appease planter anxieties in the guise of punishing the colony's ambush of John Law's company.

For its part, the maroon rebellion of the 1720s would never really end in Saint-Domingue.[52] The story of Colas Jambes Coupées and of maroon resistance more broadly shows that the colony's political-economic crisis during these years was embedded within a much larger transformation of slave society. This transformation would ultimately overshadow the uprising against the Indies Company and the other creole rebellions of this period.

The turn toward the military-planter state in Saint-Domingue set the tone and agenda for other French Caribbean colonies. In 1723, the governor of

Martinique took steps to establish a permanent maréchaussée to address the surge in maroon activity there. The Martinique companies, unlike those in Saint-Domingue, excluded free blacks and other people of color from officer roles. But in both colonies, the burden of containing the maroon insurgency fell increasingly upon persons of African descent. And it was in Saint-Domingue, more than anywhere else in the French American colonies, that the militia companies and the fugitive slave patrols exerted the greatest influence on the course of events.[53]

In April 1724, the governor of Cap Français, citing the "libertinage, insubordination, and disorder of free blacks," ordered renewed adherence to the regulations governing the company of free blacks charged with tracking down maroons. Outsourcing the problems of white society to people of color, some of whom owned slaves themselves, did nothing to reduce the levels of violence entailed in the planters' counter-revolt. Metropolitan authorities moved to draw the attention of local administrators to the brutality of the methods used under their watch. In September 1727, the naval minister wrote to Governor Rochalard and Intendant Duclos, the former *commissaire-ordonnateur* who was integral to the design of the maréchaussée in 1721, to condemn planters who enacted extreme forms of violence upon the bodies of blacks accused of sorcery—including by burning them alive and breaking their bones with a hammer. White colonists remained perfectly willing to inflict such sadism even after 1733, when the maréchaussée began to recruit its members exclusively from the Afro-Haitian population, predominantly free people of color. The occasional taking of maroons by fugitive slave patrols persuaded the colonists that they stood to gain by digging their heels deeper and deeper into the path of violence. Forty-six fugitives from the maroon settlement near what is now Cabo Beata, the southernmost point of the Dominican Republic, were captured in 1728; another thirty-two in 1733, and fourteen in 1749.[54]

In a way, the French colonial administrators of 1705 had it right: liberty was indeed contagious. There was no way out of the vicious cycle formed by planter brutality and state-sponsored persecution of maroons so long as this contagion was seen as something peculiar to the condition of the enslaved in Saint-Domingue. Maroon resistance persisted to the end of slavery because it expressed a yearning shared by enslaved persons throughout the Caribbean. The experience of neighboring Jamaica was especially close in this respect. Administrators in Saint-Domingue were attuned to the affiliations between maroon movements in the two colonies, and even engaged in cynical machinations to exploit them in service of Franco-British imperial rivalry. In 1706, one year after fugitive slave patrols were initiated in Saint-Domingue, the French colonial minister wrote to Governor Deslandes urging him to support what he described as an enslaved uprising in Jamaica by providing arms and munitions.[55]

The contradictions between France's domestic maroon policy and its interimperial military strategy are striking. But they seem finally to belong to the same mindset that, in 1723, contemplated freeing the enslaved of Saint-Domingue in order to bring the planter rebellion against the Indies Company to its knees. Indeed, this transactional approach to freedom itself pervaded the revolt against Law's System, allowing planters to describe as "free trade" their quest for unimpeded access to the forced labor of west African captives.

The maroon uprising envisioned a fundamentally different form of liberty and, as a result, preserved for Haiti a radically different future than the one institutionalized in the military-planter state during the 1720s. In Jamaica, this alternative version of liberty would manifest most dramatically in the maroon war of the 1730s and in Tacky's revolt during the Seven Years' War.[56] In Haiti, it would culminate in the Haitian Revolution. The Haitian variation on this theme was just that: a variation on an Afro-Atlantic narrative rather than a singular destiny. But Haiti's experience during the revolutionary era was also an expression of resistance to the particular version of the sugar revolution it had endured during the preceding decades.

Conclusion

IN THE years after the Mississippi Bubble, Saint-Domingue became a bubble colony, internalizing and privatizing the financial and economic logic of the System against which the planters had rebelled. The total control of economic life to which John Law's scheme for the reconstruction of French finance aspired became the modus operandi of the sugar revolution. In place of the giant monopoly of the Indies Company, hundreds of individual monopolies prospered: large-scale sugar plantations governed by masters who had succeeded in establishing their effective sovereignty over the colony by dominating its factors of production and trade.

The planters remained subject to the vagaries of debt and the profit-maximizing pursuits of merchants, to be sure. The lure of great wealth made debt a constitutive feature of the colonial economy. And the problem of silver was never really solved, at least not in the empire.[1] The colony's specie shortage remained an object of concern even toward the very end of the Old Regime.[2] These same dynamics were, in fact, key elements of the bubble mentality that kept so many knocking on the doors of the Saint-Domingue sugar industry. Sugar became the new silver, even as silver continued to control access to the gates of sugar. The many aspiring planters of the Old Regime were like the investors of 1719–20, tempted by the bull market that was Saint-Domingue after the 1720s. Like the subscribers to the Indies Company during the Mississippi Bubble, many of those who bet on the sugar revolution would strike it rich.

These expectations were not irrational. By every available measure, the Saint-Domingue economy grew massively over the course of the late 1720s and the 1730s. The colony's enslaved population expanded from 42,760 in 1720 to 85,272 in 1732. By 1739 it stood at over 100,000, which represented a roughly 10,000 percent increase from the 1700 figure of 9,082. The number of sugar plantations also exploded over this same period: 181 in 1720 to 502 in 1732. Indigo plantations increased from 1,766 to 2,755. These surges were the most significant that Saint-Domingue would experience over the course of the eighteenth century: in 1789, there were 793 sugar plantations and 3,151 indigo plantations. Exports followed the growth in plantations: sugar exports rose over 200 percent between 1720 and 1753 (they would grow even more dramatically between mid-century and the revolutionary era).[3]

Not every sector of the Saint-Domingue economy took off at the same time. The vertiginous ascent of coffee and cotton is a story that belongs primarily to the second half of the eighteenth century. And, as we have seen, other factors were at play in the unfolding of the sugar revolution, such as the merger of smaller parcels of land into large plantations capable of exploiting the labor of hundreds of slaves at a time—a development that unfolded largely between 1713 and 1750. These caveats notwithstanding, the period after 1725 in Saint-Domingue was assuredly one of both singular expansion and pronounced *tassement* (to borrow the evocative term of Alphonse Cabon): the settling down of foundations, the compacting of hierarchies, the crystallization of long-term patterns.[4]

As was also true of the investors of 1719–20, however, the planters—all of them—would eventually be ruined when the sugar bubble burst in 1791–1804. In addition to debt and silver, one other constraint always loomed large on the planters' horizon: the resistance of enslaved persons. No institution better expressed the planters' aspiration to total control over the economic life of Saint-Domingue than the brutal maréchaussée. The fugitive slave patrol was not quite a monopoly on the use of racial violence in Saint-Domingue, but it came close, and not for lack of trying on the planters' part. So far as we can tell, no one within the white population was there to protest the basic legitimacy of this system, the Jesuits not excepted. Issues of funding aside, the maréchaussée was the one company in Haiti's long colonial history that seemed to speak for the many conflicting passions and interests of white society. Saint-Domingue would not recover from the ruthless violence and hatred written into the work of policing fugitive slaves.

Through the plantation, the maréchaussée, and other supporting institutions, the sugar revolution established foundations, hierarchies, and patterns that have yet to fade from the scene of Haitian life. As our story began with money and debt, let us end with them by way of example.

All of us must use money in our daily lives if we are to survive, even though we know (or should) that it is inherently connected to some very troubling practices and institutions in the contemporary world. Like the actors in this early-eighteenth-century story, we, too, are subject to money's vagaries: inflation makes life more costly; our currencies (and therefore our buying power) can go up or down in value; and our societies are riven with conflicts, both old and new, over access to forms of money and credit. Debt weaves racial inequality into the fabric of our financial system, making short-term opportunities possible at the cost of viability over the long run. Financial crisis periodically caps these dynamics, which are so tenacious that, even when suspended for emergency purposes, they manage to reconstitute themselves in ordinary time.[5]

That said, Euro-Atlantic financial practices have had an especially devastating impact on the people of Haiti. The 2022 *New York Times* series on the 1825 indemnity that Haiti paid as a condition of France recognizing its independence drew attention to the scandalous injustice of Haiti's financial relationships to the outside world.[6] That injustice reaches into the contemporary era. But it also reaches much further back in time than the current emphasis on the 1825 indemnity suggests. When France imposed its 1825 indemnity, it was acting again in the spirit of 1720: subordinating Haiti to the debt-financing needs and demands of the metropolitan economy. The 1825 indemnity was not part of a scheme to reconstitute French public finances as a whole. Rather, it funneled money away from the Haitian people and toward the former planters as private parties, now ruined and in debt. But private parties also invested in and profited from the 1720 bonanza, and the French state oversaw the 1825 arrangement and guaranteed it through the threat of military force.

These considerations suggest a larger, early modern context for the 1825 indemnity that purported to resolve French-Haitian differences following Haiti's successful war of independence in 1802–3. France's refusal to recognize Haitian independence after it was proclaimed on January 1, 1804, traveled with the threat of reconquest and the return of racial slavery. Such a threat could not be taken lightly after Napoleon's reinstatement of the reign of the Code Noir in Guadeloupe in 1802, an act that added much fuel to the fire of the Haitian war of independence. The perception of Haiti's independence as an unthinkable injury to prevailing norms of white supremacy and economic security was not limited to France. Atlantic slaveholding powers were united in this perception, even if President Alexandre Pétion (1807–18) managed to win several diplomatic victories with Latin American and Afro-Caribbean communities and some trade with Haiti's closest neighbors was possible.[7] But France harbored an especially virulent and toxic sense that Haiti deserved punishment for its refusal to play by the rules of racialized plantation slavery.[8]

At the same time, the historical context for the 1825 ransom makes it seem at least somewhat less "exceptional" than the *New York Times* account suggests. The revanchist imperial political culture of the post-1815 Restoration monarchy was aggravated by the recent reparations bill charged to France in 1815 for Napoleon's devastation of Europe.[9] That political culture nurtured the former planters' claims that they deserved to be made whole for the "losses" they had suffered in the course of the revolutionary war. Such a context does not lessen the injustice that France did to Haiti in 1825. But it does remind us that demands to repair wartime violations and injuries—real and perceived, legitimate and outlandish—were part of the post-Napoleonic international settlement, which necessarily influenced the winning and losing parties alike. Moreover, from a broader nineteenth-century vantage point, the 1825 ransom was not the only occasion when wartime aggressors successfully claimed a right to be rewarded by the victims of their imperious conduct. As Ekaterina Pravilova has shown in her recent history of the ruble, the Russian empire paid neither in 1856 nor in 1905 for its role in the Crimean and Russo-Japanese wars. To the contrary—and not unlike France in 1825—the czarist state managed to collect a war indemnity from its opponents after both conflicts.[10] The political and military dimensions of nineteenth-century wartime justice did not always track each other.

Haiti, for its part, had compelling diplomatic and economic interests in having its independence broadly recognized, and continued hostilities with France stood in the way of that goal. Some historians, such as Alex Dupuy, have also argued that President Jean-Pierre Boyer (1818–43) had an incentive to resolve the former planters' property claims, since Haiti's wealthiest landowners had appropriated the largest land parcels after independence. By settling with France, Dupuy has argued, Boyer in effect saddled the country with a massive debt so that Haiti's ruling elite could enjoy secure title to the land it now claimed—land on which Haiti's recently emancipated peasantry was compelled to work under Boyer's draconian labor policies.[11] Other accounts, including the New York Times's "Ransom" series, emphasize the thinly veiled threat of the French naval armada stationed off the coast of Port-au-Prince pending Boyer's signature of the 1825 accord.

The issue of Boyer's leeway seems less important than the actual effect of the 1825 accord on Haitian finances, which was debilitating in the extreme. The initial demand of 150 million francs, to be paid in installments of 30 million francs over five years, required the Haitian state to take out loans serviced by none other than the Parisian international banking establishment. In other words, Haiti went into long-term debt in order to liquidate the debts of the former planters, measured in terms of land, enslaved persons, and other commercial goods. The onerous financing terms turned Haiti's new debt into a "double debt," one that required the country to pay, in total, the equivalent of about $560 million over a period of more than a hundred years.[12] Economists consulted by the New York Times determined that, had this money not been transferred to French (and later American) financial interests, it would have added some $21 billion to the Haitian economy over time—which happens to correspond rather closely to the amount demanded from France as restitution by Haiti's former president Jean-Bertrand Aristide at the time of the bicentennial of Haitian independence in 2004.[13]

This vast extortion—a term that need not depend on the scope of President Boyer's leeway in 1825—is best understood as an early-nineteenth-century reassertion of the Old Regime. That reassertion took both legal and political-economic forms. The legal form, which I will address only in passing here, involves the property rules of the 1685 Code Noir. Article 44 of the code declared slaves to be *meubles*, or movable property, and as such subject to the regime of "community" property acquired by husband and wife after marriage. Elsewhere the code imposed strict disciplinary rules on the enslaved, including the death penalty for three-time fugitives from the plantations. The notion that planters ought to be indemnified for the loss of their slave property was already part of a commonplace (and horrific) practice under the Old Regime. Colonial law authorized the reimbursement of planters when their enslaved persons were executed for engaging in conduct deemed a capital crime under the Code Noir—except when the planter was himself complicit in the crime. These and other rules made clear that, even if slaves were granted certain limited protections under the code (protections that applied more in theory than practice), they were definitively property for purposes of civil law.[14] And no less an authority than the 1789 Declaration of the Rights of Man and the Citizen established in Article 17 that the "sacred and inviolable" rights of property could not be extinguished by the state without just compensation—notwithstanding the declaration's guarantees of liberty and equality in articles 1 and 2.[15]

Slavery had been abolished by the National Convention in February 1794, but Napoleon's restoration of the Code Noir in French law in 1802, combined with the property guarantee of the 1789 declaration, provided a legal underpinning for the former planters' demands in 1825. That reassertion of Old Regime property rights was very much part of the logic of "debt" and money baked into the 1825 indemnity. But the Old Regime was alive and at work in 1825 in an additional sense. The indemnity held the Haitian state of 1825 liable as the party responsible in law for the "injury" of revolution and emancipation. And that liability ran from the Haitian state, acting as the representative of Haiti's emancipated people, to the French state, acting as the representative of the former planters.

In this way, Haiti as a polity remained subordinated to the debt-financing edicts of the French state. France under Charles X in 1825 confronted a debt crisis not altogether different from the one it faced in 1719–20, except that the debtors in this context included private citizens, acting in the (arrogant and racist) guise of Haiti's "creditors." The mediation of the Banque de France and of private French banks in financing Haiti's repayment of the 1825 indemnity only accentuated the shared ethos of the two situations. This was a reassertion of the imperial financial logic of 1719–20 that aimed to convert public debt into private equity. In 1825, that logic was extended so as to serve as a model for France's relationship to its former territory going forward, even in the seemingly (one might say fundamentally) different circumstances of the postcolonial world.

The parallels between 1720 and 1825 apply beyond the realm of analogy and metaphor. The Haitian indemnity coincided with the rise of a sovereign debt market in the 1820s that was focused primarily on Latin America. The 1825 indemnity was not a sovereign debt-funding scheme, but it shared some of the same assumptions and financing mechanisms, including the quasi-imperial role of metropolitan establishment banks. As Trevor Jackson, Marc Flandreau, and Juan Flores have shown, the market power and prestige of Europe's leading private banks subsidized the 1820s sovereign debt market. That market included a bubble, as exemplified in Gregor MacGregor's ability to successfully market the shares of a fictitious Latin American state known as "Poyais"—a fantastical scheme that resembles nothing so much as some of the more inventive (and fraudulent) flotations of the South Sea and Mississippi bubble era.[16] But fiction was no match for the reality of Latin America's subordination of its state debts to the metropolitan banking industry, and that turned out to be persistent. Haiti did not have the benefit of access to a sovereign debt market—the debt with which it was saddled was, in a sense, the very opposite of an arrangement purporting to support public finance—but it was vulnerable to the same monetary power imbalances that enabled the Latin American market.

Those imbalances condemned the 1825 indemnity to become another of the persistent colonial legacies that have shaped modern Latin American history generally.[17] As the *New York Times* series so compellingly demonstrates, the Haitian indemnity became a (if not necessarily the) key factor in the immiseration of Haiti's people over the long term. It did this by systematically compromising Haitian monetary sovereignty from the outset. For roughly the first eight decades of its history as a formally sovereign nation, Haiti did not have a central bank of its own. And the reason is not hard to discover. A state that disposed of very little in the way of tax revenues did not have the resources to sustain a central bank. The indemnity effectively led the Haitian government to outsource a core state function—central banking—to the French banks that funded the double debt. Default in these circumstances was almost immediate.[18]

When a Bank nationale de la République d'Haiti was finally created in 1880, it was little more than a front for French financial interests, notably Credit Industriel et Commercial (CIC), the bank that had taken over financing of the debt in the 1870s. Later, in 1910, management of Haiti's central bank passed to a multinational board of French, German, and American directors. This transfer of power coincided with a period when US banks were quite systematically canvassing the Caribbean for overseas opportunities. Haiti and Cuba became the central foci of that search, but it was a broad, even greater Caribbean movement.[19] A combination of financial weakness stemming from the 1825 indemnity and domestic political strife enabled National Citi (the predecessor of today's Citibank) to take over the Bank of Haiti from CIC. Haiti's immiseration thenceforth passed into American hands—the United States militarily occupied Haiti from 1915 to 1934—and to some extent the country's fate has remained there ever since.[20]

Meanwhile, the international monetary system has continued to evolve in dramatic ways that have further compounded Haiti's loss of monetary sovereignty. The postwar displacement of the pound sterling by the dollar as the dominant global currency under the Bretton Woods system meant that Haiti could not evade US influence even after American boots left the ground in 1935. The dollar's influence only expanded when it was unhinged from the gold standard in the 1970s. Nixon's decision to abandon the gold standard ushered in our contemporary era of floating exchange rates and sophisticated foreign exchange trading.[21]

In this political-economic context, Haiti's monetary sovereignty remains a distant mirage. In a broad sense, the nation's financial disempowerment at the hands of more powerful and wealthier nations is entirely unremarkable. Even if we were to limit the analysis strictly to nations falling within France's post-colonial orbit, we can see how readily imperial monetary power has cast a long and wide shadow over the decolonizing world. Lebanon, which gained independence from France in 1943, only succeeded in establishing a central bank in 1964, and then only in the form of an institution that served local and international financial oligarchies.[22] Fanny Pigeaud and Ndongo Samba Sylla have shown that the CFA franc (originally created by French President Charles de Gaulle in 1945 as the Franc of the French African Colonies), still in use across much of French West Africa, has enabled France to exert an ongoing monetary imperialism decades after decolonization.[23] This is to say nothing of Europe's other shadow banking empires and their legacies across the globe.

When all of that international and comparative context is taken into consideration, however, the Haitian case seems especially urgent, now two hundred years after the 1825 ransom. It has been and continues to be the canary in the coal mine of the international financial order. The thoroughgoing dollarization of the country's economy, which began in the early twentieth century and is still unfolding, has rendered the gourde a national currency in name only. International transactions are denominated almost exclusively in dollars.[24] And the Federal Reserve's recent inflation-targeting regimen has intensified the gourde's downward spiral: higher interest rates mean that the dollar appreciates relative to the gourde. The dollar's value relative to the Haitian gourde grew from 100 to 150 from 2022 to 2023 alone. At the same time, for all their relative value, dollars remain scarce in Haiti, particularly for those who most need them to satisfy the demands of daily life. The power of the dollar in Haiti, as in so many other countries around the world today, represents a kind of financial sanction.[25]

If the international configuration of this monetary crisis is quite different from the eighteenth-century version, the underlying problem is similar.[26] Haiti remains in the grips of a kind of mercantilist competition for scarce supplies of a highly valuable, de facto transnational currency—with the American dollar currently occupying the monetary space that Spanish silver once did.[27]

Haiti is still in rebellion against this world. It is not alone in that rebellion. But it has endured a version of it that seems very much like a long loneliness.

ACKNOWLEDGMENTS

THANK YOU to Lynn Hunt, Kate Desbarats, and Lige Gould for their wise restraint of an earlier, more nomadic version of this project. Jean Casimir, Chris Desan, and François Velde have been equal parts generous and inspiring. I owe a very big debt of gratitude to Emma Rothschild for her role in helping this book to see the light of day. To Jeff Ravel and Craig Wilder, for kindnesses too numerous to repay over a long period, thank you. Chris Capozzola also eased my burdens during the writing of this book. Thank you to Margo Collett, Meghan Pepin, Patty Alves, Abbie Katz, and Kathleen Lopes for many acts of support large and small over the last ten years. Mabel Chin Sorett did so much to facilitate my research that I hardly know where to start in thanking her. Deans Melissa Nobles and Agustín Rayo made sure that I had the resources needed to complete this work. The Massachusetts Institute of Technology and its history faculty have provided a wonderful base of operations.

Thank you to Priya Nelson for bringing this book to Princeton University Press and accommodating more than a few hiccups. The three (mostly) anonymous readers for the press raised hard and important questions about an earlier version of this book. The final product is better for the mix of insight and generosity they brought to the task. Emma Wagh has done more to get me to the finish line than I suspect she realizes. Thank you, Emma, for the patient kindness that you showed me. Thank you also to Jaden Young for her excellent work as production editor and to Leah Caldwell for meticulous copyediting.

I presented research in progress to the French Politics, Culture, and Society Workshop of Harvard's Center for European Studies, the Mahindra Eighteenth-Century Studies Seminar at Harvard, the Fourteenth International Congress for Eighteenth-Century Studies in Rotterdam, the Boston Area French History Workshop, the joint meeting of the Omohundro Institute for Early American History and Culture and the Society of Early Americanists in Chicago, the University of Minnesota Legal History Workshop, the Society for French Historical Studies, the Eighteenth World Economic History Congress in Boston (where a conversation about money with François Velde was particularly helpful), the Newhouse Humanities Center, the Radcliffe Institute for Advanced Study, the American Historical Association, the Yale University Early Modern Empires Workshop, the Johns Hopkins History Department Seminar, Janet Polasky's graduate colloquium on comparative history at the University of New Hampshire, the Charles Warren Center Faculty Fellows Seminar at Harvard University, the Haiti Seminar on Money, Finance, and Empire, 1825–2025 (where Arnaud Orain and François Velde were my interlocutors), and the Currency and Empire Workshop. Thank you to the organizers and hosts of these events, and to everyone who chipped in to help me think more clearly about Haiti's early history.

Six conferences were critical to the development of my ideas: "Legal Bodies: Corpus, Persona, Communitas," held at Leiden University in May 2014; "Boom, Bust, and Beyond: New Perspectives on the 1719–20 Stock Euphoria," at the University of Tübingen in April 2018; the "Voices of the Legal Archives in the French Atlantic" conference in North Hatley, Québec, in May 2018; "Exodus and Exile: Migrants, Refugees, and Asylum Seekers, 1750–1850," at UCLA's William Andrews Clark Memorial Library in February 2019; "Far from the Truth: Distance and the Problem of Credibility in the Early Modern World," at Leiden University in January 2020; and "Financing Reconstruction," a conference organized by the European Association for Banking and Financial History at Frankfurt, Germany, in June 2023. Thank you to Frans-Willem Korsten, Yasco Horsman, Nanne Timmer, Daniel Menning, Stefano Condorelli, Clare Crowston, Nancy Christie, Michael Gauvreau, Josephine McDonaugh, Jonathan Sachs, Sarah Tindel Kareem, Michiel van Groesen, Johannes Müller, Arthur Weststeijn, Esther Baakman, Tiffany Bousard, Carmen Hofmann, and Gabriella Massaglia for these memorable gatherings.

Two special institutions offered me sabbatical research homes to pursue this study: the Newhouse Humanities Center at Wellesley College (2015–16) and the Radcliffe Institute for Advanced Study (2018–19). Anjali Prabhu, Corey McMullen, and Tanekwah Hinds made my time at Wellesley rewarding. Thank you to Tomiko Brown-Nagin, Meredith Moss Quinn, Rebecca Haley, Sharon Bromberg-Lin, and Alison Ney for making every day at the Radcliffe Institute a joy. Props and gratitude to the amazing Radcliffe fellows class of 2019, particularly my partners in the "Second Book Writing Group" (one of Meredith's many gifts to us as director of the fellowship program): Cori Field, Robin Bernstein, Dana Sajdi, Tanisha Ford, and Katie Turk. None of this would have been possible without the generous support of a Frederick Burkhardt Residential Fellowship for Recently Tenured Scholars from the American Council of Learned Societies.

Archivists and librarians at the following institutions were indispensable to the success of my work: in France, the Archives nationales d'outre-mer and Bibliothèque Méjanes in Aix-en-Provence; the Archives nationales and

Bibliothèque nationale in Paris; the Centre des Archives diplomatiques de La Courneuve in Paris; the Archives françaises de la Compagnie de Jésus in Vanves; the Service historique de la Défense in Lorient; and the Archives départmentales de la Charente-Maritime in La Rochelle. In the United Kingdom: the British Library in London and the National Archives in Kew. In the United States: the Historical New Orleans Collection and the Louisiana Historical Center in New Orleans; and Houghton Library at Harvard University. In Canada: the Bibliothèque et Archives nationales du Québec in Québec City. And in Haiti: the Bibliothèque des Frères de l'Instruction Chrétienne. Thank you to Erin Greenwald for help navigating the New Orleans material.

In their different ways, Mikey Sweet and Tim Davis prodded me gently to get this book to the finish line: Chapo ba. Thank you also to Rocky for keeping me company during the loneliest phases of this work.

My wife Erica James not only accommodated the many research trips that this book required as our two children were growing up. She also traveled with me across Haiti to see all of the places that I write about in this book. Joining me on a rickety dinghy across the Bay of Saint-Louis to l'Île des Anglais to climb through the ruins of the abandoned fort there was an especially selfless act of spousal sacrifice. But there have been too many others where that came from. Thank you for the inspiration of your own work, for sharing with me a love of Haiti that has journeyed with us from the start, and for finding us a place on earth where I could find peace away from the stresses and strains of the recent past. June Cargile has been a rock for our family in good and bad times alike. Leila Govi has been a loving sister through the challenges of the last few years. Finally, thank you to Faisal and Ayanna for coming along with their parents on a different trip to Haiti and seeing for themselves why we do this work.

The rest of my debts I hold in the silence of my heart.

Prudence Island, Rhode Island
November 15, 2024

APPENDIX

The August 1722 Royal Ordinance on Money

Royal ordinance concerning the diminution of foreign specie, and their discounting to weight, August 3, 1722.

His Majesty, upon being shown the orders that he has given concerning the exchange rate and value of specie in the French American islands, and the ordinances issued on the subject of the prices of said specie, by the Chevalier de Feuquière, Governor and Lieutenant-General of the Windward Islands, and Besnard, Intendant; the Marquis de Sorel, Governor and Lieutenant-General of the Island of S. Domingue, and Duclos, Commissaire-Ordonnateur; He has resolved, on the advice of the Duke of Orléans, Regent, to lower the price of foreign specie on the islands, and to set, by the present ordinance, the exchange rate and value of said foreign specie on the said islands, as follows:

Art. I. The full-weight piastre will trade for seven pounds ten sous.

Art. II. The full-weight pistole will trade for thirty pounds.

Art. III. The piastre will be deemed full weight when only nine are needed to the mark.

Art. IV. The pistole will be deemed full weight when only thirty-six and a quarter pistoles are needed to the mark.

Art. V. Piastres that are not full weight will also trade, but only for the value of the (metal) material that they contain, in light of the price set by Art. 1 for the full-weight piastre.

Art. VI. Pistoles that are not full weight will also trade, but only for the value of the (metal) material they contain, in light of the price set by Art. 2 for the full-weight pistole.

Art. VII. Other foreign silver moneys, such as the half piastre, the quarter piastre, the eighth, or Réal, the sixteenth, or half Réal, will also trade, but only for the value of (metal) material that each piece of money contains, in light of the price set for the full-weight piastre, art. 1.

195

196 APPENDIX

Art. VIII. The other foreign gold monies, such as quadruples, double
pistoles, and half pistoles, will also trade, but only for the value of the
(metal) material that each piece of money contains, in light of the price
set for the full-weight pistole, art. 2.

Art. IV. His Majesty wishes that, effective on the publication date of
the present ordinance, all the different coins therein mentioned will
be accepted in the Windward Colonies and the Island of S. Domingue,
according to the price set for each of the said specie. His Majesty
mandates and orders his Governors and Lieutenant-Governors and
Intendants in Southern America, and all others to whom it pertains,
to hold to the enforcement of the present ordinance, which will be
read, published, and posted everywhere necessary, and entered into
the registries of the Superior Councils of the Windward Islands and
the Island of S. Domingue. Done at Versailles, etc.

Registered at the Léogâne Conseil, November 20, 1722.
And at the Cap Conseil, the 29th of the same month.
See the Ordinance of November 19, 1722.

NOTES

Introduction

1. Malick W. Ghachem, *The Old Regime and the Haitian Revolution* (Cambridge: Cambridge University Press, 2012).

2. The indigenous Taino name "Haiti" (*Ayiti*) long predates the advent of colonialism in Hispaniola. See David Geggus, *Haitian Revolutionary Studies* (Bloomington: Indiana University Press, 2002), 207, 211. Contemporaneous sources in this book use the term "Saint-Domingue" to describe the French colony established on the western half of Hispaniola in the later seventeenth and eighteenth centuries. Where the terms "Saint-Domingue" or "Dominguans" seem to marginalize Afro-Haitian influences on Haiti's long-term trajectory, I will sometimes use the term "Afro-Haitians" to describe part or all of the nonwhite population of Saint-Domingue in the early eighteenth century.

3. As Vincent Brown puts it, reading against the archival grain means "to investigate the things the sources never meant to illustrate." Reading along the archival grain is "to note how [the sources] constrain and shape our knowledge." See Vincent Brown, *Tacky's Revolt: The Story of an Atlantic Slave War* (Cambridge, MA: Harvard University Press, 2020), 13; Ann Stoler, *Along the Archival Grain: Epistemic Anxieties and Colonial Common Sense* (Princeton, NJ: Princeton University Press, 2010); Brett Rushforth, "The Gauolet Uprising of 1710: Maroons, Rebels, and the Informal Exchange Economy of a Caribbean Sugar Island," *William and Mary Quarterly* 76, no. 1 (2019): 75–110; Marisa J. Fuentes, *Dispossessed Lives: Enslaved Women, Violence, and the Archive* (Philadelphia: University of Pennsylvania Press, 2016); and Natalie Zemon Davis, "Judges, Masters, Diviners: Slaves' Experience of Criminal Justice in Colonial Suriname," *Law and History Review* 29, no. 4 (November 2011): 925–84.

4. "Relation de ce qui est arrivé à l'égard de la Compagnie des indes," [undated but probably 1723], Archives nationales d'outre-mer, Aix-en-Provence [hereafter ANOM], F/3/169, fol. 136 left.

5. See, e.g., Eric Toussaint, *Le système dette: Histoire des dettes souveraines et de leur répudiation* (Paris: Les liens qui libèrent, 2017); and David Graeber, *Debt: The First 5,000 Years* (New York: Melville House, 2012), 346–51. As Graeber emphasizes, some of the most deeply indebted actors in Europe's credit economy included the agents and overseers of empire in the New World.

6. See the four-part series by Catherine Porter, Constant Méheut, Matt Apuzzo, and Selam Gebrekidan: "The Root of Haiti's Misery: Reparations to Enslavers"; "How a French Bank Captured Haiti"; "Invade Haiti, Wall Street Urged. The US Obliged."; "Demanding Reparations, and Ending up in Exile"; *New York Times*, May 20, 2022, https://www.nytimes.com/spotlight/haiti.

7. For my understanding of how an "on the ground" history of political economy can be written, against the grain of the abstractive dynamics of financial and economic history, I am indebted to William H. Sewell, "The Capitalist Epoch," *Social Science History* 38, no. 1–2

198 NOTES TO INTRODUCTION

(January 2014): 1–11; and Jeremy Adelman and Jonathan Levy, "The Rise and Fall of Economic History," *The Chronicle of Higher Education*, December 1, 2014.

8. For my understanding of capitalism, I am indebted to Sewell, "The Capitalist Epoch," 7 (observing that capitalist growth is "constitutively sporadic and crisis-ridden"); Christine Desan, *Making Money: Coin, Currency, and the Coming of Capitalism* (New York: Oxford University Press, 2014) (connecting capitalism to the circulation of public debt and the monetary revolution associated with the Bank of England at the end of the seventeenth century); and John J. Clegg, "Capitalism and Slavery," *Critical Historical Studies* 2, no. 2 (2015): 281–304 (arguing that market dependence is the central characteristic of capitalism).

9. For examples of the textbook and popular historiography, see Thomas B. Costain, *The Mississippi Bubble* (New York: Random House, 1955); John Kenneth Galbraith, *A Short History of Financial Euphoria* (New York: Penguin Books, 1994); and Niall Ferguson, *The Ascent of Money: A Financial History of the World* (New York: Penguin, 2008), chap. 3. More scholarly accounts include Edgar Faure, *La banqueroute de Law, 17 juillet 1720* (Paris: Gallimard, 1977); James MacDonald, *A Free Nation Deep in Debt: The Financial Roots of Democracy* (New York: Farrar, Straus, and Giroux, 2003), 179–205; Larry Neal, *The Rise of Financial Capitalism: International Capital Markets in the Age of Reason* (New York: Cambridge University Press, 1990), chap. 4; François R. Velde, "Was John Law's System a Bubble? The Mississippi Bubble Revisited," in *The Origins and Development of Financial Markets and Institutions: From the Seventeenth Century to the Present*, eds. Larry Neal and Jeremy Atack (New York: Cambridge University Press, 2009), 99–120; François R. Velde, "French Public Finance between 1683 and 1726," in *Government Debts and Financial Markets in Europe*, ed. Fausto Piola Caselli (London: Pickering & Chatto, 2008), 135–65; and Antoin E. Murphy, *John Law: Economic Theorist and Policy-Maker* (Oxford: Oxford University Press, 1997). The place of the System in eighteenth-century French political culture is Arnaud Orain's subject in *La politique du merveilleux: Une autre histoire du Système de Law (1695–1795)* (Paris: Fayard, 2018). The European and especially Franco-British dimensions of John Law's revolution are discussed in John Shovlin, *Trading with the Enemy: Britain, France, and the 18th-Century Quest for a Peaceful World Order* (New Haven, CT: Yale University Press, 2021), chap. 3. For the Louisiana theater of the bubble, see Marcel Giraud, *Histoire de la Louisiane française*, vol. 3, *L'époque de John Law (1717–1720)* (Paris: Presses universitaires de France, 1966); Marcel Giraud, *Histoire de la Louisiane française*, vol. 4, *La Louisiane après le Système de Law (1721–1723)* (Paris: Presses universitaires de France, 1974); Lawrence N. Powell, *The Accidental City: Improvising New Orleans* (Cambridge, MA: Harvard University Press, 2012), chap. 2; and Erin Greenwald, *Marc-Antoine Caillot and the Company of the Indies in Louisiana: Trade in the French Atlantic World* (Baton Rouge: Louisiana State University Press, 2016), which follows the travels of an Indies Company clerk through Saint-Domingue on the way to New Orleans. Joan DeJean expands the traditional geographical and intellectual parameters of Mississippi Bubble scholarship in her *Mutinous Women: How French Convicts Became Founding Mothers of the Gulf Coast* (New York: Basic Books, 2022). On the South Sea Bubble, see especially John Carswell, *The South Sea Bubble* (London: Sutton, 1993); and, most recently, Thomas Levenson, *Money for Nothing: The Scientists, Fraudsters, and Corrupt Politicians Who Reinvented Money, Panicked a Nation, and Made the World Rich* (New York: Random House, 2020).

10. Under the 1494 Treaty of Tordesillas, sponsored by the papacy, the Spanish and Portuguese crowns effectively divided the world beyond Europe into two largely exclusive spheres. Spain would have control of nearly all of the Americas, while Portugal would control the African slave trade and the East Indies. This left the Spanish monarchy in the position of having to grant licenses (*asientos*) to foreign powers for the exclusive right to supply the Spanish territories in the New World with slaves. Robin Blackburn, *The Making of New World Slavery: From the Baroque to the Modern, 1492–1800* (London: Verso, 1997), 8, 141–42.

NOTES TO INTRODUCTION 199

11. To give a sense of the scale of this enterprise: "No joint-stock company anywhere has ever been priced in the market at more than twice the annual product of France." James Buchan, *John Law: A Scottish Adventurer of the Eighteenth Century* (London: MacLehose Press, 2018), 226.

12. On these themes, see esp. Orain, *La politique du merveilleux.* Orain argues that the System was conceived in the Hobbesian absolutist terms of a Leviathan state. Orain, *La politique du merveilleux,* 21, 124, 128. For the British version of the company-state, see Philip Stern, *The Company State: Corporate Sovereignty and the Early Modern Foundations of the British Empire in India* (New York: Oxford University Press, 2011). See Carl Wennerlind, *Casualties of Credit: The English Financial Revolution, 1620–1720* (Cambridge, MA: Harvard University Press, 2011), chap. 6, for a discussion of the role of slavery in the coming of the South Sea Bubble.

13. Indeed, the Mississippi Company itself remained mostly inactive after its flotation in 1717. Macdonald, *A Free Nation Deep in Debt,* 194.

14. On this see especially Dejean, *Mutinous Women.*

15. Ulbe Bosma, *The World of Sugar: How the Sweet Stuff Transformed Our Politics, Health, and Environment over 2,000 Years* (Cambridge, MA: Harvard University Press, 2023), 14.

16. The phenomenon of planter debt and the efforts of colonists to escape the ties of politics, economics, and culture that bound them to the metropole is a major theme of Atlantic economic history in general and the American Revolution in particular. See, e.g., Woody Holton, *Forced Founders: Indians, Debtors, Slaves, & the Making of the American Revolution in Virginia* (Chapel Hill: University of North Carolina Press, 1999); John M. Murrin, "1776: The Countercyclical Revolution," in *Revolutionary Currents: Nation Building in the Transatlantic World,* eds. Michael A. Morrison et al. (Lanham, MD: Rowman & Littlefield, 2004), 65–90; and Gerald Horne, *The Counter-Revolution of 1776: Slave Resistance and the Origins of the United States of America* (New York: New York University Press, 2014). The crisis of the 1720s in Saint-Domingue almost singlehandedly reversed the debtor-creditor relationship between Saint-Domingue planters and metropolitan merchants, making the former beholden to the latter for the duration of the eighteenth century. See Marcel Delafosse, "Planteurs de Saint-Domingue et négociants rochelais au temps de Law," *Revue d'histoire des colonies* 41, no. 142 (1954): 14–21. Despite the importance of this phenomenon, it is only one aspect of a larger, transracial story about debt that has enveloped virtually the entire span of Haitian history.

17. See the essays by Thierry Claeys and Philippe Haudrère in *Les Compagnes des Indes,* ed. René Estienne (Paris: Gallimard, 2013), 56–63, 186–91. The leading history of the Indies Company is Philippe Haudrère, *La Compagnie française des Indes au XVIIIe siècle,* 2nd ed., 2 vols. (Paris: Les Indes savantes, 2005).

18. Blackburn, *The Making of New World Slavery,* 283–85; James S. Pritchard, *In Search of Empire: The French in the Americas, 1670–1730* (New York: Cambridge University Press, 2004), 254–55. The immediate predecessor of the Indies Company was the Saint-Domingue Company, on which see Karsten Voss, *Sklaven als Ware und Kapital: Die Plantagenökonomie von Saint-Domingue als Entwicklungsprojekt* (Munich: C. H. Beck, 2016). Many thanks to the late Joseph Miller for drawing this study to my attention. Although not directed against a trading company per se, the powerful 1717 creole revolt in Martinique, known as the Gaoulé, reflected the same sense of anger at perceived metropolitan restraints on the growth of the sugar business. See Jacques Petitjean Roget, *Le Gaoulé: La révolte de la Martinique en 1717* (Fort de France: Société d'histoire de la Martinique, 1966).

19. The Mississippi crash began in early 1720, when the Prince de Conti insisted on converting his Indies Company shares into cash—which is to say, silver money. At one level, the company's September 1720 privilege for Saint-Domingue was part of a plan to stave off a declining stock market that Law had begun to put in place in the fall 1719. MacDonald, *A Free Nation Deep in Debt,* 202; Buchan, *John Law,* 256.

200 NOTES TO INTRODUCTION

20. See, inter alia, Stanley J. Stein and Barbara H. Stein, *Silver, Trade, and War: Spain and America in the Making of Early Modern Europe* (Baltimore, MD: Johns Hopkins University Press, 2000).

21. Along the west African coast, the means of payment included not just cowrie shells and gum but a wide assortment of European manufactured wares such as gunpowder, weapons, cotton cloth, liquor, and hats. See Anne Ruderman's "Intra-European Trade in Atlantic Africa and the African Atlantic," *William and Mary Quarterly* 77, no. 2 (2020): 211–44; as well as her forthcoming book *Supplying the Slave Trade* (New Haven, CT: Yale University Press, in press).

22. Arnaud Clairand and Michel Prieur, *Les monnaies royales françaises, 987–1793* (Paris: Chevau-légers, 2008), 231; Ernest Zay, *Histoire monétaire des colonies françaises d'après les documents officiels* (Paris: J. Montorier, 1892), 52–56.

23. Cf. Thomas J. Sargent and François R. Velde, *The Big Problem of Small Change* (Princeton, NJ: Princeton University Press, 2002). In situating this problem in the context of early colonial Haiti, I build on the pioneering work of Robert Richard, "À propos de Saint-Domingue: La monnaie dans l'économie coloniale (1674–1803)," *Revue d'histoire des colonies* 41, no. 142 (1954): 22–46; and Robert Lacombe, "Histoire monétaire de Saint-Domingue et de la République d'Haïti, des origines à 1874," *Revue d'histoire des colonies* 43, no. 152 (1956): 273–337. Adolphe Cabon raises the question of whether the monetary reforms of 1722 were against the colonists' "true interests" in his *Histoire d'Haïti: Cours professé au Petit séminaire-collège Saint-Martial*, 4 vols. (Port-au-Prince: Éditions de la Petite Revue, 1920s), 1:118.

24. For an insightful analysis of the sugar revolution in the eastern Caribbean (or "lesser Antilles") as a contest between French planters and the indigenous Kalinago people that yielded a diverse, inter-island society, see Tessa Murphy, *The Creole Archipelago: Race and Borders in the Colonial Caribbean* (Philadelphia: University of Pennsylvania Press, 2021), chap. 1. The basic outlines of the sugar revolution in the lesser Antilles can be found in Laurent Dubois and Richard Turits, *Freedom Roots: Histories from the Caribbean* (Chapel Hill: University of North Carolina Press, 2021), 69–73; Stephan Palmié, "Toward Sugar and Slavery," in *The Caribbean: A History of the Region and Its Peoples*, eds. Stephan Palmié and Francisco A. Scarano (Chicago: University of Chicago Press, 2011), 139–57; Hilary McD. Beckles, "Servants and Slaves during the 17th-Century Sugar Revolution," in *The Caribbean: A History of the Region and Its Peoples*, 205–15; Sidney W. Mintz, *Sweetness and Power: The Place of Sugar in Modern History* (New York: Penguin, 1985), 37–46; Richard S. Dunn, *Sugar and Slaves: The Rise of the Planter Class in the English West Indies, 1624–1713* (Chapel Hill: University of North Carolina Press, for the Institute of Early American History and Culture, 1972); Bosma, *The World of Sugar*, 52–56. Christian Schnakenbourg discusses the sugar revolution in Guadeloupe in *L'économie de plantation aux Antilles françaises: XVIIIè siècle* (Paris: L'Harmattan, 2020), 101–3.

25. A more empirical, economic history of the expansion of plantation slavery in Saint-Domingue during the first half of the eighteenth century would need to consider west African developments in detail, which, though crucial, are beyond the scope of this book. In particular, Toby Green's account of the monetization of enslaved persons and the rise of the "fiscal-military state" in west African politics, and their relationship to the massive expansion of the west African slave trade from the late seventeenth century onward, is relevant here. See Toby Green, *A Fistful of Shells: From the Rise of the Slave Trade to the Age of Revolution* (London: Penguin, 2020), chaps. 6–7.

26. On the concept of the "sugar revolution," see B. W. Higman, "The Sugar Revolution," *Economic History Review* 53, no. 2 (2000): 213–36. While I share some of Nuala Zahedieh's important criticisms of the concept, it remains useful for characterizing a large and very real transformation that was common to the entire Caribbean but unfolded at different times and in different ways depending upon the locale. See Nuala Zahedieh, "The Rise of 'King Sugar' and Enslaved Labor in Early English Jamaica," *Early American Studies: An Interdisciplinary Journal* 20, no. 4 (September 2022): 576–96.

27. On the sugar revolution as tragedy, cf. Vincent Brown, *The Reaper's Garden: Death and Power in the World of Atlantic Slavery* (Cambridge, MA: Harvard University Press, 2008)

28. Robin Blackburn considers the possibility that the shift from white indentured servitude to Afro-Atlantic slavery was not a necessary condition for the rise of plantation slavery in *The Making of New World Slavery*, 353–60. Necessary or sufficient, it was one of multiple overlapping factors that came together to fuel the sugar revolution.

29. Schnakenbourg, *L'économie de plantation aux Antilles françaises*, 104–5.

30. Caribbean piracy, rampant in the 1710s and resourceful enough to survive the peace of 1713, was only really domesticated in Saint-Domingue after the 1720s and persisted thereafter in parts of the British empire. Charles Frostin, "La piraterie américaine des années 1720, vue de Saint-Domingue," *Cahiers d'histoire* 25, no. 2 (1980): 177–210; Guy Chet, *The Ocean Is a Wilderness: Atlantic Piracy and the Limits of State Authority, 1688–1856* (Amherst: University of Massachusetts Press, 2014); Mark G. Hanna, *Pirate Nests and the Rise of the British Empire, 1570–1740* (Chapel Hill: University of North Carolina Press, for the Omohundro Institute of Early American History and Culture, 2015); Peggy K. Liss, *Atlantic Empires: The Network of Trade and Revolution, 1713–1826* (Baltimore, MD: Johns Hopkins University Press, 1983), 1.

31. The "mature" era of the Saint-Domingue plantation complex is well described in Trevor G. Burnard and John D. Garrigus, *The Plantation Machine: Atlantic Capitalism in French Saint-Domingue and British Jamaica* (Philadelphia: University of Pennsylvania Press, 2016). Like most of the existing literature on the topic, this work emphasizes the period after the Seven Years' War in Haiti. See also Paul Cheney, *Cul de Sac: Patrimony, Capitalism, and Slavery in French Saint-Domingue* (Chicago: University of Chicago Press, 2017). For an argument that slavery in Saint-Domingue became part of an "economic machine" as early as the 1720s, with the rise of large sugar plantations and absentee ownership of slaves, see Gabriel Debien, "Aux origines de quelques plantations des quartiers de Léogâne et du Cul-de-Sac (1680–1715)," *Revue de la Société d'Histoire et de Géographie d'Haïti* 18, no. 64 (January 1947): 68–69.

32. For a model of how to write Atlantic history as an entangled synthesis of the stories of different groups, see Brown, *Tacky's Revolt*. As Brown writes, "[W]hat we know as Tacky's Revolt combined the itineraries of many people: merchants, planters, imperial functionaries, soldiers and sailors from Europe, Africa, and the Caribbean, and enslaved men, women, and children" (2).

33. On the theme of domestic sovereignty, see Yvan Debbasch, "Au cœur du 'gouvernement des esclaves': La souveraineté domestique aux Antilles françaises (XVIIe-XVIIIe siècles)," *Revue française d'histoire d'outre-mer* 72, no. 266 (1985): 31–53. By the late seventeenth century, the enslaved had already come to be understood precisely as "domestic enemies" by the emerging planter class and their administrative overlords. Ghachem, *The Old Regime and the Haitian Revolution*, chap. 1.

34. Militant slavery is thus a variation on the theme of militant democracy, a concept coined by the political scientist Karl Loewenstein in 1937. Karl Loewenstein, "Militant Democracy and Fundamental Rights, I," *American Political Science Review* 31, no. 3 (1937): 417–32; Karl Loewenstein, "Militant Democracy and Fundamental Rights, II," *American Political Science Review* 31, no. 4 (1937): 638–58.

35. The military-planter state was as important to the viability of French colonial administration in Saint-Domingue as the fiscal-military state was to the development of the eighteenth-century British empire or the rise of powerful west African kingdoms from the late seventeenth century onward. See the brilliant analysis of John Brewer in *Sinews of Power: War, Power, and the English State, 1688–1783* (Cambridge, MA: Harvard University Press, 1988); and Green, *A Fistful of Shells*, chap. 7. For a critical historiographical review of Brewer's concept, see Aaron Graham, *Corruption, Party, and Government in Britain, 1702–1713* (Oxford University Press, 2015), chap. 1.

36. The comments in this and the prior paragraph should make clear how my interpretation differs from one of the most important works to bear on my subject: Charles Frostin, *Les révoltes*

blanches à Saint-Domingue aux XVIIe et XVIIIe siècles (Haïti avant 1789) (Paris: l'École, 1975; reprint, Rennes: Presses universitaires de Rennes, 2008). Citations refer to the 2008 Rennes edition. Chapters 4 and 5 of this book remain an outstanding treatment of the rebellion against the Indies Company, and I am highly indebted to it.

37. Historians have devised various terms and concepts to describe the rise to self-consciousness of the sugar planters of Saint-Domingue: the emergence of a movement for creole "autonomy," the creation of whiteness as a racial construct, and the rise of an ideology of "domestic sovereignty," among other approaches. See, e.g., Vertus Saint-Louis, *Mer et liberté (1492–1794)* (Port-au-Prince, Haïti: Imprimeur II, 2009), 49–51; Gabriel Debien, *Esprit colon et esprit d'autonomie à Saint-Domingue au xviiie siècle* (Paris: Larose, 1954); Yvonne Fabella, "Redeeming the 'Character of the Creoles': Whiteness, Gender and Creolization in Pre-Revolutionary Saint Domingue," *Journal of Historical Sociology* 23, no. 1 (March 2010): 40–72; Burnard and Garrigus, *The Plantation Machine*, 164, 197–98; and Debbasch, "Au coeur du 'gouvernement des esclaves.'" Most of these interpretations emphasize the late eighteenth century. Surveys of the early French Caribbean, meanwhile, often end with the dramas of the frontier era, including piracy and indentured servitude, leaving a chronological gap that coincides roughly with the first three or four decades after 1700. See Philip P. Boucher, *France and the American Tropics to 1700: Tropics of Discontent?* (Baltimore, MD: Johns Hopkins University Press, 2008); Philip P. Boucher, "The 'Frontier Era' of the French Caribbean, 1620–1690s," in *Negotiated Empires: Centers and Peripheries in the Americas, 1500–1820*, eds. Christine Daniels and Michael V. Kennedy (New York: Routledge, 2002), 207–34. Gabriel Debien's many articles, several of which I draw on below, are important for understanding the intermediate period between the frontier era and the sugar revolution. See, for example, his "Aux origines de quelques plantations des quartiers de Léogâne et du Cul-de-Sac." See also James S. Pritchard, *In Search of Empire: The French in the Americas, 1670–1730* (New York: Cambridge University Press, 2004). Georges Pollet's doctoral thesis, *Saint-Domingue et l'autonomie, 1629–1730* (Saint-Amand, Cher [France]: Imprimerie Leclerc, 1934), strikes a note of imperial nostalgia but has some useful material on the early eighteenth century and the rebellion. The gap between the frontier era and the late eighteenth century has been filled in large part with stories of a triumphant breakthrough toward a sudden and dramatic era of capitalist prosperity, apotheosized in the ambiguous and still prevalent image of Saint-Domingue as the "Pearl of the Antilles." See, for example, Philippe R. Girard, *Haiti: The Tumultuous History: From Pearl of the Caribbean to Broken Nation* (New York: Palgrave Macmillan, 2010); and Schnakenbourg, *L'économie de plantation aux Antilles françaises*, chap. 1 (titled "Saint-Domingue, 'Perle des Antilles'").

38. Cf. Pritchard, *In Search of Empire* (suggesting that "empire" came to Saint-Domingue only in the 1730s).

39. John D. Garrigus carries the story of enslaved resistance back into the 1740s in his new study: *A Secret among the Blacks: Slave Resistance before the Haitian Revolution* (Cambridge, MA: Harvard University Press, 2023). Methods of resistance other than marronage—including the use of poisoning, a major concern for white colonists beginning around mid-century—were often perceived in terms of their relationship to maroon autonomy.

40. See Geggus, *Haitian Revolutionary Studies*, chaps. 4–5; and Carolyn Fick, *The Making of Haiti: The Saint-Domingue Revolution from Below* (Knoxville: University of Tennessee Press, 1990), 4–9, 59–73.

41. David Geggus, "The Caribbean in the Age of Revolution," in *The Age of Revolutions in Global Context, c. 1760–1840*, eds. David Armitage and Sanjay Subrahmanyam (New York: Palgrave Macmillan, 2010), 95–100. See also Robert Fatton Jr., *The Roots of Haitian Despotism* (Boulder, CO: Lynne Riener, 2007), 60.

42. David Scott, *Conscripts of Modernity: The Tragedy of Colonial Enlightenment* (Durham, NC: Duke University Press, 2004).

43. See Jean Casimir, *Une lecture décoloniale de l'histoire des Haïtiens: Du Traité de Ryswick à l'Occupation américaine* (1697–1915) (Port-au-Prince: L'Imprimeur S. A., 2018); and Johnhenry Gonzalez, *Maroon Nation: A History of Revolutionary Haiti* (New Haven, CT: Yale University Press, 2019).

44. Cf. Bernard Ethéart, "La filière canne (2)," *Haïti en Marche* 30, no. 27 (July 20, 2016): 13. As Ethéart points out, twenty years after Haitian independence, the country was producing very little sugar. The Haitian sugar industry would resume in the last quarter of the nineteenth century. B. W. Higman addresses the tension between the contingency of the Caribbean sugar revolution and its seemingly permanent legacies in "The Sugar Revolution," 229; Higman, *A Concise History of the Caribbean* (New York: Cambridge University Press, 2011), 99–100.

45. Georges Corvington, *Port-au-Prince au cours des ans*, vol. 1: *La ville coloniale et les convulsions révolutionnaires, 1743–1804* (Montréal: CIDIHCA, 2007), 18–19.

46. For the Anglo-American variation on this theme, see David McNally, *Blood and Money: War, Slavery, Finance, and Empire* (Chicago: Haymarket, 2020), esp. chap. 4. McNally argues (at pp. 123–24) that the full strength of Britain's imperial power and slave economy in the Atlantic world were not unleashed until the 1690s, with the financial revolution wrought by the Bank of England, the South Sea Company, the Royal African Company, and other institutions. The situation in France seems to have been closer to the obverse: it was the failure of, and the opposition to, John Law's financial revolution during the interregnum between Louis XIV and Louis XV that allowed the dam to burst in Saint-Domingue.

1. Company Colony

1. Under the 1494 Treaty of Tordesillas, sponsored by the papacy, the Spanish and Portuguese crowns effectively divided the world beyond Europe into two largely exclusive spheres. Spain would have control of nearly all of the Americas, while Portugal would control the African slave trade and the East Indies. This left the Spanish monarchy in the position of having to grant licenses (*asientos*) to foreign powers for the exclusive right to supply the Spanish territories in the New World with slaves. Blackburn, *The Making of New World Slavery*, 8, 141–42.

2. Malick W. Ghachem, "'No Body to Be Kicked?' Monopoly, Financial Crisis, and Popular Revolt in 18th-Century Haiti and America," *Law & Literature* 28, no. 3 (2016): 403–31.

3. Code Noir, art. 48.

4. Green, *A Fistful of Shells*, chap. 6.

5. On the romantic invention of an autonomous, freebooter past by some Saint-Domingue colonists as of the 1720s, see Joannès Martial Marie Hippolyte Tramond, *Les troubles de Saint-Domingue en 1722–1724* (Paris: E. Leroux, 1929), 494.

6. Ghachem, *The Old Regime and the Haitian Revolution*, 33. The authoritative treatment of these "frontier-era" settlements is Boucher, *France and the American Tropics*.

7. See, e.g., Boucher's discussion of Governor d'Ogeron's commissioning of buccaneers to carry out raids on Spanish ships in 1674–75, in *France and the American Tropics*, 193.

8. Blackburn, *The Making of New World Slavery*, 281.

9. For Colbert's attitude toward Saint-Domingue, see Boucher, *France and the American Tropics*, 193.

10. A good summary of this traditional "consensus" position can be found in Cathy Matson, "Imperial Political Economy: An Ideological Debate and Shifting Practices," *William and Mary Quarterly* 69, no. 1 (2012): 35–40. See also Steven Pincus, "Rethinking Mercantilism: Political Economy, the British Empire, and the Atlantic World in the Seventeenth and Eighteenth Centuries," *William and Mary Quarterly* 69, no. 1 (2012): 3–34.

11. Pincus, "Rethinking Mercantilism"; Shovlin, *Trading with the Enemy*. Cf. Orain, *La politique du merveilleux*, 147–8.

204   NOTES TO CHAPTER 1

12. See Wim Klooster, "Inter-Imperial Smuggling in the Americas, 1600–1800," in *Soundings in Atlantic History: Latent Structures and Intellectual Currents, 1500–1830*, eds. Bernard Bailyn and Patricia L. Denault (Cambridge, MA: Harvard University Press, 2009), 141–80; and Saint-Louis, *Mer et liberté*, 22–25. For an annotated bibliography of the literature on smuggling in the early modern Atlantic, see Mark G. Hanna, "Smuggling," *Oxford Bibliographies Online*, 2013, http://www.oxfordbibliographies.com/view/document/obo-9780199730414/obo-9780199730414-0197.xml.

13. Boucher, *France and the American Tropics*, 180–81, 191; Nellis M. Crouse, *The French Struggle for the West Indies, 1665–1713* (New York: Columbia University Press, 1943), 129–30.

14. Crouse, *The French Struggle for the West Indies, 1665–1713*, 142–45; Boucher, *France and the American Tropics*, 191–93. Frostin, *Les révoltes blanches à Saint-Domingue*, 53–60 (quote at 58). The text of the October 1671 amnesty appears in Médéric Louis-Élie Moreau de Saint-Méry, *Loix et constitutions des colonies françoises de l'Amérique sous le vent*, 6 vols. (Paris and Cap Français: chez l'auteur, 1784–90), 1:249–51 [hereafter Moreau de Saint-Méry, *Loix et constitutions*].

15. Frostin, *Les révoltes blanches à Saint-Domingue*, 60.

16. On the experience of the West Indies Company in Saint-Domingue, see especially Boucher, *France and the American Tropics*, 180–93. See also Blackburn, *The Making of New World Slavery*, 282–83.

17. Crouse, *The French Struggle for the West Indies, 1665–1713*, 145; Frostin, *Les révoltes blanches à Saint-Domingue*, 65. Hence the commonplace designation of d'Ogeron as the "father" of Saint-Domingue. See, e.g., Renaud Hyppolite, "Si Le Cap m'était conté," in *Cap Haïtien: Excursions dans le temps: Au fils de nos souvenirs (1920–1995)*, ed. Max Manigat (Delmas, Haïti: Éditions Sanba, 2014), 124.

18. Crouse, *The French Struggle for the West Indies, 1665–1713*, 129–33.

19. Boucher, *France and the American Tropics*, 193; Debien, "Aux origines de quelques plantations des quartiers de Léogâne et du Cul-de-Sac," 18–19. See also Médéric Louis-Élie Moreau de Saint-Méry, *Description topographique, physique, civile, politique et historique de la partie française de l'isle Saint-Domingue*, 2 vols. (Philadelphia, 1797–98), 2:266–267 [hereafter *Description de la partie française de l'isle Saint-Domingue*].

20. Boucher, *France and the American Tropics*, 193; Moreau de Saint-Méry, *Description de la partie française de l'isle Saint-Domingue*, 1:297–98; Marcus Rainsford, *An Historical Account of the Black Empire of Hayti*, eds. Paul Youngquist and Grégory Pierrot (Durham, NC: Duke University Press, 2013), 46; Frostin, *Les révoltes blanches à Saint-Domingue*, 60, 73.

21. On the *Cinq grosses fermes* and the general farms, see Alfred Cobban, *A History of Modern France*, vol. 1, *1715–1799* (New York: Penguin, 1957), 46, 57–60; and Michael Kwass, *Privilege and the Politics of Taxation in Eighteenth-Century France* (New York: Cambridge University Press, 2000), 80–81, 106. On Colbert, the Domaine d'Occident, and the response to the tobacco farm in Saint-Domingue, see Frostin, *Les révoltes blanches à Saint-Domingue*, 67.

22. "Arrêt du Conseil d'État," June 4, 1671, in Moreau de Saint-Méry, *Loix et constitutions*, 1:226–27; "Arrêt du Conseil d'État," August 12, 1671, in Moreau de Saint-Méry, *Loix et constitutions*, 1:228–29; "Ordonnance du Roi," October 1671, in Moreau de Saint-Méry, *Loix et constitutions*, 1:250; Tramond, *Les troubles de Saint-Domingue*, 496; Philippe Hrodĕj, "L'État et ses principaux représentants à Saint-Domingue au XVIIIe siècle: Contradictions et manquements," *Outre-mers* 94, no. 354 (2007): 176n6.

23. Boucher, *France and the American Tropics*, 289. Boucher notes that free people of color and people of mixed race in the French Leeward islands did not have to pay the capitation prior to 1700.

24. Tramond, *Les troubles de Saint-Domingue*, 496–98; Hrodĕj, "L'État et ses principaux représentants à Saint-Domingue au XVIIIe siècle," 176. The *octroi* was levied at six livres per laboring slave, later reduced to three livres. Revenues raised to support the colonial administration

NOTES TO CHAPTER 1   205

thus went by the designation *octroi* in Saint-Domingue, and by the name of the Domaine d'Occident elsewhere in the French Antilles. Formalized in 1715, this fiscal reform followed on a larger administrative reorganization of the French Caribbean. In 1713, Saint-Domingue had been separated from the rest of the Antilles and placed under its own governorship and intendancy. François-Joseph-Ferdinand de Mauny, *Essai sur l'administration des colonies* (Paris: E. Duverger, 1837), 103; Ghachem, *The Old Regime and the Haitian Revolution*, 35.

25. Hrodĕj, "L'État et ses principaux représentants à Saint-Domingue," 176.

26. Boucher, *France and the American Tropics*, 208–9; Blackburn, *The Making of New World Slavery*, 284–85; Abdoulaye Ly, *La Compagnie du Sénégal* (Paris: Présence africaine, 1958), 151–68. Ly's book is the leading study of the Senegal Company for the period up to about 1695. On the Royal African Company, see, most recently, William A. Pettigrew, *Freedom's Debt: The Royal African Company and the Politics of the Atlantic Slave Trade, 1672–1752* (Chapel Hill: University of North Carolina Press, for the Omohundro Institute of Early American History and Culture, 2013).

27. Blackburn, *The Making of New World Slavery*, 284.

28. For the details in this and the preceding paragraph, see Pierre-François-Xavier de Charlevoix, *Histoire de l'Isle espagnole ou de St. Domingue*, 2 vols. (Paris: Jacques Guérin, 1730–1731), 1:125–27. Charlevoix's account is quoted at length in J. du Fresne de Francheville, *Histoire de la Compagnie des Indes* (Paris: De Bure, 1746), 127–29. Secondary accounts of the 1680 revolt can be found in Frostin, *Les révoltes blanches à Saint-Domingue*, 68–69; and Philippe Hrodĕj, "Les esclaves à Saint-Domingue aux temps pionniers (1630–1700)," in *L'esclave et les plantations: De l'établissement de la servitude à son abolition* (Rennes: Presses universitaires de Rennes, 2008), 67.

29. On the Senegal Company's fleet, see Boucher, *France and the American Tropics*, 208–9.

30. On the events of 1710 in Antigua, see Stephen Saunders Webb, *Marlborough's America* (New Haven, CT: Yale University Press, 2013), 267–90; and Natalie Zacek, "A Death in the Morning: The Murder of Daniel Parke," in *Cultures and Identities in Colonial British America*, eds. Robert Olwell and Alan Tully (Baltimore, MD: Johns Hopkins University Press, 2006), 223–43. As Zacek points out, the settler uprising against Parke was framed as a matter of vindicating the natural rights of Englishmen. The authoritative account of the Gaoulé is Petitjean Roget, *Le Gaoulé*.

31. Webb, *Marlborough's America*, 272.

32. Charles-André Julien, *Les Français en Amérique de 1713 à 1784* (Paris: Centre de documentation universitaire et Société d'édition d'enseignement supérieur réunis, 1977), 72–73; Blackburn, *The Making of New World Slavery*, 296.

33. Shovlin, *Trading with the Enemy*, 22–23. See also Nuala Zahedieh, "Monopoly and Free Trade: Changes in the Organization of the British Slave Trade, 1660–1720," in *Shiavitù e servaggio nell'economia Europea secc. XI-XVIII/Serfdom and Slavery in the European Economy 11th–18th centuries*, ed. Simonetta Cavaciocchi, 2 vols. (Florence, Italy: Firenze University Press, 2014), 2:651 (arguing that the "binary opposition between monopoly and free trade is misleading" and that the English/British slave trade involved elements of both throughout the period from 1660–1720).

34. Istvan Hont, *Jealousy of Trade: International Competition and the Nation-State in Historical Perspective* (Cambridge, MA: Harvard University Press, 2005), 192 (discussing Quesnay's and Mirabeau's understanding of trade as "free by its very nature").

35. Andrea Finkelstein, *Harmony and the Balance: An Intellectual History of Seventeenth-Century English Economic Thought* (Ann Arbor: University of Michigan Press, 2000), 54–65 (quote at 65, emphasis in the original).

36. Malick W. Ghachem, "Royal Liberties," in *The Princeton Companion to Atlantic History*, ed. Joseph C. Miller (Princeton, NJ: Princeton University Press, 2015), 294. See also Finkelstein, *Harmony and the Balance*, 65 (noting the interdependence of privilege and liberty).

206   NOTES TO CHAPTER 1

37. Finkelstein, *Harmony and the Balance*, 65, 67.

38. Stern, *The Company-State*, 46–47.

39. Sir Edward Coke, *The Third Part of the Institutes of the Laws of England: Concerning High Treason, and other Pleas of the Crown, and Criminal Causes*, 4th ed. (London, 1669), 181. The forty-first clause of the "Great Charter" stated that "all merchants may enter or leave England unharmed and without fear, and may stay or travel within it, by land or water, for purposes of trade, free from all illegal exactions, in accordance with ancient and lawful customs." Thank you to Ryan Greenwood for sharing with me materials used in the University of Minnesota Law School Library's exhibition marking the 800th anniversary of Magna Carta.

40. Magna Carta, cl. 40, in *Magna Carta: Law, Liberty, and Legacy*, eds. Claire Breay and Julian Harrison (London: British Library, 2015), 267 (noting the imprint of Magna Carta on the EIC's 1683 constitution for St. Helena). "Exactions" here refers to a customs duty or other tax on trade.

41. Stern, *The Company-State*, 53.

42. Hont, *Jealousy of Trade*, 15. Seventeenth-century Dutch visions of free trade as a strategy for commercial domination are discussed in Saint-Louis, *Mer et liberté*, 17–22.

43. Stern, *The Company-State*, 57–58.

44. "A Scheme for a New East India Company" (1690), in *Magna Carta*, eds. Breay and Harrison, 196. See also Stern, *The Company-State*, 142–63.

45. "A Scheme for a New East India Company," in *Magna Carta*, eds. Breay and Harrison, 196.

46. Charles Woolsey Cole, *French Mercantilism, 1683–1700* (New York: Columbia University Press, 1943), 254–65 (quotes at 264, 265). See also Saint-Louis, *Mer et liberté*, 28.

47. Lionel Rothkrug, *Opposition to Louis XIV: The Political and Social Origins of the French Enlightenment* (Princeton, NJ: Princeton University Press, 1965), 86, 117.

48. Shovlin, *Trading with the Enemy*, 80–84.

49. Josep M. Fradera, "The Caribbean between Empires: Colonists, Pirates, and Slaves," in *The Caribbean: A History of the Region and Its Peoples*, eds. Stephan Palmié and Francisco A. Scarano (Chicago: University of Chicago Press, 2011), 175; and Kenneth Gordon Davies, *The Royal African Company* (London: Longmans, Green, 1957), 100–1. For the RAC story, see also Pettigrew, *Freedom's Debt*; and Matthew D. Mitchell, "Joint-Stock Capitalism & the Atlantic Commercial Network: The Royal African Company, 1672–1752," PhD dissertation, University of Pennsylvania (2012).

50. Zahedieh, "Monopoly and Free Trade," 659. As Shovlin points out, the special privileges for the South Sea Company also undermined the European balance of power that the Utrecht Treaty was designed to restore. Beginning in the mid-1720s, French and Spanish officials moved to recalibrate the new imbalance introduced by the transfer of the *asiento* to Britain. Shovlin, *Trading with the Enemy*, 84.

51. Zahedieh, "Monopoly and Free Trade," 650, 655; Brown, *Tacky's Revolt*, 22; Abigail L. Swingen, *Competing Visions of Empire: Labor, Slavery, and the Origins of the British Atlantic Empire* (New Haven, CT: Yale University Press, 2015), 194–95.

52. Robert Louis Stein, *The French Slave Trade in the Eighteenth Century: An Old Regime Business* (Madison: University of Wisconsin Press, 1979), 13–14; Robert Harms, *The Diligent: The Worlds of The Slave Trade* (New York: Basic Books, 2002), 37–39. For the origins of these claims in lobbying before the Council of Commerce by the merchants of Nantes and Rouen between 1695 and 1701, see Rothkrug, *The Opposition to Louis XIV*, 409–19; and Cole, *French Mercantilism, 1683–1700*, 254–69.

53. Stein, *The French Slave Trade*, 13–15.

54. Harms, *The Diligent*, 40; Stein, *The French Slave Trade*, 14. See also Pritchard, *In Search of Empire*, 221.

NOTES TO CHAPTER 1   207

55. In 1696, a group of "merchants and traders of Virginia and Maryland" argued along these lines in a petition to the House of Commons calling for an end to the RAC monopoly. Horne, *The Counter-Revolution of 1776*, 5.

56. See generally Pettigrew, *Freedom's Debt* (21 for the claim about pioneering British deregulation).

57. Cf. Cathy Matson's critique of Steven Pincus in "Imperial Political Economy," 35–40.

58. John Garrigus, *Before Haiti: Race and Citizenship in French Saint-Domingue* (New York: Palgrave Macmillan, 2006), 36; Pritchard, *In Search of Empire*, 217–18.

59. Kenneth J. Banks, "Official Duplicity: The Illicit Slave Trade of Martinique, 1713–1763," in *The Atlantic Economy during the Seventeenth and Eighteenth Centuries: Organization, Operation, Practice, and Personnel*, ed. Peter A. Coclanis (Columbia: University of South Carolina Press, 2005), 230 (noting the "strangely acquiescent role of colonial officials regarding illicit trade in general and slave smuggling in particular").

60. Shovlin, *Trading with the Enemy*, 22–23.

61. Clarence J. Munford, *The Black Ordeal of Slavery and Slave Trading in the French West Indies, 1625–1715*, vol. 2, *The Middle Passage and the Plantation Economy* (Lewiston, NY: Mellen Press, 1991), 387.

62. Richard Pares, *Yankees and Creoles: The Trade between North America and the West Indies before the American Revolution* (Cambridge, MA: Harvard University Press, 1956).

63. Klooster, "Inter-Imperial Smuggling in the Americas, 1600–1800," 165.

64. Wim Klooster, *Illicit Riches: Dutch Trade in the Caribbean, 1648–1795* (Leiden: KITLV Press, 1998), 109.

65. P. C. Emmer, *The Dutch in the Atlantic Economy, 1580–1880: Trade, Slavery and Emancipation* (Brookfield, VT: Ashgate, 1998), 105.

66. Klooster, *Illicit Riches*, 119.

67. Pritchard, *In Search of Empire*, 219; Klooster, "Inter-Imperial Smuggling in the Americas," 163. Gregory O'Malley supplies some context for this trade with his discussion of the 1694 arrival in Saint-Domingue of a vessel of one hundred west Africans coming from St. Thomas. See O'Malley, *Final Passages: The Intercolonial Slave Trade of British America* (Chapel Hill: University of North Carolina Press, for the Omohundro Institute of Early American History and Culture, 2014), 158.

68. Emmer, *The Dutch in the Atlantic Economy*, 105. For more details on the Dutch contraband slave trade during this period, see Johannes Postma, *The Dutch in the Atlantic Slave Trade, 1600–1815* (Cambridge: Cambridge University Press, 1990), 199–200, which breaks down the interlope trade to Statia by year; and the doctoral thesis of Rudolf Paesie, "Lorrendrayen op Africa: de illegale goederen- en slavenhandel op West-Afrika tijdens het achttiende-eeuwse handelsmonopolie van de West-Indische Compagnie, 1700–1734," PhD dissertation, Leiden University (April 17, 2008), https://openaccess.leidenuniv.nl/handle/1887/12702. An English summary of Paesie's findings, which are based on the Postma database, appears on pp. 411–15 of his thesis. Thanks to Karwan Fatah-Black for guidance on recent Dutch work in this area.

69. Klooster, *Illicit Riches*, 120; Klooster, "Inter-Imperial Smuggling in the Americas," 164.

70. O'Malley, *Final Passages*, 158. See also Pritchard, *In Search of Empire*, 219.

71. O'Malley, *Final Passages*, 159.

72. O'Malley, *Final Passages*, 159.

73. David Geggus, "The French Slave Trade: An Overview," *William and Mary Quarterly* 58, no. 1 (January 2001): 126.

74. Garrigus, *Before Haiti*, 37. On this topic, see especially Frostin, "La piraterie américaine des années 1720."

75. Garrigus, *Before Haiti*, 37 (citing Frostin, *Les révoltes blanches à Saint-Domingue*, 167).

76. Carswell, *The South Sea Bubble*, 40.

208 NOTES TO CHAPTER 1

77. "Edit en forme de Lettres Patentes," September 1698, in Moreau, *Loix et constitutions*, 2:611.

78. The territory was defined as a space, running the length of the southern peninsula from Cap Tiberon in the west to the Neybe River at the eastern border with Spanish Santo Domingo, of three leagues between the southern coastline and the mountainous interior. "Édit en forme de Lettres-Patentes pour l'Établissement de la Compagnie Royale de Saint-Domingue," September 1698, in Moreau, *Loix et constitutions*, 1:611.

79. Pritchard, *In Search of Empire*, 326–33.

80. On the role of the Guinea Company in the *asiento* from 1703–13, see Gregory E. O'Malley and Alex Borucki, "Patterns in the Intercolonial Slave Trade across the Americas before the Nineteenth Century," *Tempo* 23, no. 2 (August 2017): 314–38, at 326.

81. Klooster, "Inter-Imperial Smuggling in the Americas," 162–64. See also Shovlin, *Trading with the Enemy*, 89.

82. Garrigus, *Before Haiti*, 34–36; Pritchard, *In Search of Empire*, 128–29.

83. "Règlement de la Compagnie de Saint-Domingue," September 22, 1716, in Moreau, *Loix et constitutions*, 2:513. Another attempt to reassert the liabilities of the Domaine d'Occident in Saint-Domingue in 1720 raised heckles sufficient to persuade the Conseil de Marine to formally "prohibit" collection of the Domaine in that territory. This ban settled the fiscal question for the time being. Sorel and Mithon (Montholon's predecessor as intendant) conveyed the ban in a letter registered at the Conseil Supérieur in Léogâne in September 1720. "Extrait de la Lettre du Conseil de Marine a MM. de Sorel et Mithon, qui préscrit le droit du Domaine d'Occident à Saint-Domingue," June 25, 1720, in Moreau, *Loix et constitutions*, 2:670.

84. Clarence J. Munford, *The Black Ordeal of Slavery and Slave Trading in the French West Indies, 1625–1715*, vol. 1, *Slave Trading in Africa* (Lewiston, NY: Mellen Press, 1991), 204.

85. "Lettres-Patentes, portent révocation de la Compagnie royale de Saint-Domingue," April 1720, in Moreau, *Loix et constitutions*, 2:666.

86. See generally Lacombe, "Histoire monétaire de Saint-Domingue et de la République d'Haïti," 292; and Richard, "A propos de Saint-Domingue: 22–46. On the contemporary situation, see Jean-Éric Paul, *La décote de la gourde face au dollar: Quelques pistes pour sortir du marasme économique actuel* (Port-au-Prince: C3 Editions, 2016).

87. See Stein and Stein, *Silver, Trade, and War*.

88. Sargent and Velde, *The Big Problem of Small Change*, 8–14. See also Desan, *Making Money*, 117–20.

89. Michel Foucault, *The Order of Things: An Archaeology of the Human Sciences*, trans. Alan Sheridan (New York: Vintage Books, 1994), 180. See also Guy Rowlands, *The Financial Decline of a Great Power: War, Influence, and Money in Louis XIV's France* (Oxford: Oxford University Press, 2012), 92, 96–97; and Guy Rowlands, *Dangerous and Dishonest Men: The International Bankers of Louis XIV's France* (London: Palgrave Macmillan UK, 2015), 3.

90. John J. McCusker, *Money and Exchange in Europe and North America, 1600–1775: A — Handbook* (Chapel Hill: University of North Carolina Press, for the Omohundro Institute of Early American History and Culture, 1978), 119; Catherine Desbarats, "On Being Surprised: By New France's Card Money, for Example," *Canadian Historical Review* 102, 1 (March 2021): 125–51.

91. François R. Velde, "Was John Law's System a Bubble? The Mississippi Bubble Revisited," in *The Origins and Development of Financial Markets and Institutions: From the Seventeenth Century to the Present*, eds. Larry Neal and Jeremy Atack (New York: Cambridge University Press, 2009), 100, 114.

92. "Arrêt du Conseil d'État, portant augmentation des Espèces d'or et d'argent," in Moreau, *Loix et constitutions*, 2:676.

NOTES TO CHAPTER 1   209

93. For the details in this paragraph, see Paul Guilhiermoz, "Remarques diverses sur les poids et mesures du Moyen Âge," *Bibliothèque de l'École des chartes*, 80, no. 1 (1919): 5; and McCusker, *Money and Exchange in Europe and America*, 282–83.

94. Lacombe, "Histoire monétaire de Saint-Domingue," 282–300; Richard, "À propos de Saint-Domingue," 23–46; McCusker, *Money and Exchange in Europe and America*, 285.

95. Lacombe, "Histoire monétaire de Saint-Domingue," 290; Richard, "À propos de Saint-Domingue," 22–24.

96. In Saint-Domingue, as in Louisiana during the early decades of the eighteenth century, administration was shared between a governor charged with military duties and a *commissaire ordonnateur* who was commissioned with specific powers in the areas of royal finances and commerce. The two officers shared responsibility for general administration. The post of *commissaire ordonnateur*, to which Duclos was appointed in 1717, was distinct from that of intendant, who had formal jurisdiction over finance and justice, though Duclos also served as interim acting intendant of Saint-Domingue from May 1720 to March 1722, when François de Montholon took over as the colony's first fully vested intendant. See Donald J. Lemieux, "The Office of 'Commissaire Ordonnateur' in French Louisiana, 1731–1763: A Study in French Colonial Administration," PhD dissertation, Louisiana State University (1972), vi–vii.

97. Lacombe, "Histoire monétaire de Saint-Domingue," 290, 293; Richard, "À propos de Saint-Domingue," 22–25, 41; "Ordonnance des Administrateurs pour le paiement des marchandises d'Europe en denrées coloniales," October 6, 1720, in Moreau, *Loix et constitutions*, 2:701–6; "Ordonnance des administrators, touchant les Monnaies," Nov. 20, 1721, in Moreau, *Loix et constitutions*, 2:792–94.

98. McCusker, *Money and Exchange in Europe and North America*, 118–19, 281; Lacombe, "Histoire monétaire de Saint-Domingue," 284–85.

99. Lacombe, "Histoire monétaire de Saint-Domingue," 285.

100. On this transition, see the lucid synthesis by Michel Hector and Claude Moïse, *Colonisation et esclavage en Haïti: le régime colonial français à Saint-Domingue (1625–1789)* (Montréal: CIDIHCA, 1990), 61–66; Boucher, *France and the American Tropics*, chaps. 8–10; and Frostin, *Les révoltes blanches à Saint-Domingue*, 29.

101. Hector and Moïse, *Colonisation et esclavage en Haïti*, 61–62; and see generally Gabriel Debien, *Les engagés pour les Antilles (1634–1715)* (Abbeville, France: F. Paillart, 1951).

102. Debien, *Les engagés pour les Antilles* 83–89; Hector and Moïse, *Colonisation et esclavage en Haïti*, 61–62; and Philippe Hrodèj, "Les premiers colons de l'ancienne Haïti et leurs attaches en métropole, à l'aube des premiers établissements (1650–1700)," *Les Cahiers de Framespa: Nouveaux champs de l'histoire sociale* 9 (March 2012): 14–17.

103. Jean Meyer, "Des origines à 1763," in *Histoire de la France coloniale*, vol. 1, *La conquête*, eds. Jean Meyer, Jean Tarrade, and Annie Rey-Goldzeiguer (Paris: Pocket, 1996), 136; Frostin, *Les révoltes blanches à Saint-Domingue*, 261; Ghachem, *The Old Regime and the Haitian Revolution*, 82–84.

104. Debien, *Les engagés pour les Antilles*, 247; Hector and Moïse, *Colonisation et esclavage en Haïti*, 62, 66.

105. Garrigus, *Before Haiti*, 32, 36; Jean Meyer, "Des origines à 1763," 136; Frostin, *Les révoltes blanches à Saint-Domingue*, 261; Hector and Moïse, *Colonisation et esclavage en Haïti*, 62–63, 80.

106. Blackburn, *The Making of New World Slavery*, 433; Garrigus, *Before Haiti*, 36; Hector and Moïse, *Colonisation et esclavage en Haïti*, 77–79.

107. Garrigus, *Before Haiti*, 34–36; Hector and Moïse, *Colonisation et esclavage en Haïti*, 77.

108. For discussions that relate the 1722–24 revolt in Saint-Domingue to the earlier West Indian challenges to metropolitan authority, see Frostin, *Les révoltes blanches à Saint-Domingue*, 97–98; and Julien, *Les Français en Amérique*, 72–73.

210 NOTES TO CHAPTER 2

109. Nicolas Ponce, René Phelipeau, and Médéric Louis-Elie Moreau de Saint-Méry, *Recueil de vues des lieux principaux de la colonie française de Saint-Domingue* (Paris, 1791).

110. Nicolas Louis François de Neufchâteau, *Mémoire en forme de discours sur la disette du numéraire a Saint-Domingue, et sur les moyens d'y remédier* (Metz, 1788).

2. Colonial System

1. Karl Marx, *The Karl Marx Library*, vol. 1, ed. Saul K. Padover (New York: McGraw Hill, 1972), 245–46.

2. This remains true even of recent work. See, e.g., the essays of François Velde; Shovlin, *Trading with the Enemy*; and Orain, *La politique du merveilleux*. For an early example of the metropolitan staging of the "Mississippi Scheme," see Charles Mackay, *Extraordinary Popular Delusions and the Madness of Crowds* (London, 1841; reprint, Petersfield, UK: Harriman House Ltd., 2003). On the marketing of the lower Mississippi Valley and South America as untapped repositories of wealth, see Rik Frehen, William N. Goetzmann, and K. Geert Rouwenhorst, "Finance in the Great Mirror of Folly," in *The Great Mirror of Folly: Finance, Culture, and the Crash of 1720*, eds. William N. Goetzmann et al. (New Haven, CT: Yale University Press, 2013), 72–79; and Wennerlind, *Casualties of Credit*, 197–234.

3. See, e.g., MacDonald, *A Free Nation Deep in Debt*, 220; and Christian Chavagneux, *Une brève histoire des crises financières: Des tulipes aux subprimes* (Paris: Découverte, 2011), 55. François Velde emphasizes the innovative contributions of the Paris brothers to French public finance both immediately before and after the System in "French Public Finance between 1683 and 1726," 135–65.

4. Jonathan Sheehan and Dror Wahrman, *Invisible Hands: Self-Organization and the Eighteenth Century* (Chicago: University of Chicago Press, 2015), 118–20.

5. Quoted in Sheehan and Wahrman, *Invisible Hands*, 119. The authors, at 334n55, mistakenly describe the Visa of 1721, discussed in further detail below, as part of Law's plan for dealing with the public debt.

6. Cf. Shovlin, *Trading with the Enemy*, esp. chaps. 1–3 (arguing that the eighteenth-century Franco-British relationship involved a substitution of trade for war).

7. Antoin E. Murphy, "John Law: Innovating Theorist and Policymaker," in *The Origins of Value: The Financial Innovations That Created Modern Capital Markets*, eds. William N. Goetzmann and K. Geert Rouwenhorst (New York: Oxford University Press, 2005), 226–29.

8. John Law, *Money and Trade Considered, with a Proposal for Supplying the Nation with Money* (Edinburgh, 1705). For a more detailed account of Law's early career and writings, see Murphy, *John Law: Economic Theorist and Policy-Maker*, 20–34, 76–104.

9. Murphy, *John Law*, 105; Velde, "Was John Law's System a Bubble?," 100–3.

10. Orain, *La politique du merveilleux*, 93–94. An iconic example of the fantastical representations of the Americas as a vehicle for encouraging investment is the copperplate engraving with watercolor titled *Le Commerce que les Indiens du Mexique font avec les Français au Port de Mississipi* (Paris: François-Gérard Jollain, 1717). A black-and-white version of the image can be found at http://visualiseur.bnf.fr/Visualiseur?O=06700374.

11. Arlette Farge and Jacques Revel, *Logiques de la foule: L'affaire des enlèvements d'enfants à Paris en 1750* (Paris: Hachette, 1988), 36–37. The galley system was adapted in 1719 for purposes of transferring women and other prisoners from Paris to Rochefort, where they were deported to Louisiana. Dejean, *Mutinous Women*, 61.

12. Glenn Conrad, "Emigration Forcée: A French Attempt to Populate Louisiana, 1716–1720," in *Proceedings of the Fourth Meeting of the French Colonial Historical Society* (Washington, DC: University Press of America, 1979), 57–66. DeJean emphasizes the unjust nature of the

NOTES TO CHAPTER 2   211

accusations leveled against "prostitutes" deported to Louisiana in *Mutinous Women*, 5, 9–33; Frostin, *Les révoltes blanches à Saint-Domingue*, 107–8.

13. "Déclaration du Roi, pour ne plus envoyer de Vagabonds & gens sans aveu aux Colonies," in Moreau, *Loix et constitutions*, 3:14.

14. Frostin, *Les révoltes blanches à Saint-Domingue*, 101–9.

15. On Law's merger of all French trading companies as part of a Leviathan behemoth, see Orain, *La politique du merveilleux*, 132–141.

16. Lynn Hunt discusses the relationship between the Atlantic slave economy and the East Indies trade in "The Global Financial Origins of 1789," in *The French Revolution in Global Perspective*, eds. Suzanne Desan, Lynn Hunt, and William Max Nelson (Ithaca, NY: Cornell University Press, 2013), 36–38.

17. Macdonald, *A Free Nation Deep in Debt*, 194.

18. Orain, *La politique du merveilleux*, 132–161; Faure, *La banqueroute de Law*, 188; Velde, "Was John Law's System a Bubble?," 103–5. The Company of China had been created in 1660 by an influential and prosperous Catholic confraternity in France known as the Company of the Blessed Sacrament. Carlos M. N. Eire, *Reformations: The Early Modern World, 1450–1650* (New Haven, CT: Yale University Press, 2016), 514–15.

19. Albert Girard, "La réorganisation de la Compagnie des Indes (1719–1723), I: L'œuvre de John Law (1719–1721)," *Revue d'histoire moderne et contemporaine* 11, no. 1 (1908–9): 20; Harms, *The Diligent*, 51; Faure, *La banqueroute de Law*, 195. Orain argues that the Guinea privilege was designed to operate in the spirit of a cartel with Britain and Holland, in *La politique du merveilleux*, 145–6.

20. Macdonald, *A Free Nation Deep in Debt*, 199–201.

21. Thomas Crawford to James Craggs, September 30, 1719, UK National Archives, SP 78/165/84, fols. 224r-225r. Crawford's letter is referenced in Buchan, *John Law*, 256. Crawford seems to have been confused about the details of the September 13 and 28 issuances. He appears to have written at first that the fund of fifty million livres was priced at ten thousand livres per share, for an issuance of five thousand livres, before writing over the last zero in the price to indicate a share price of one thousand livres, for an issuance of fifty thousand shares. Compared to the data set forth in Antoine Murphy's account, both versions are incorrect. Murphy, *John Law*, 202.

22. Crawford to Craggs, September 30, 1719, fols. 224r-226r; Murphy, *John Law*, 208; Buchan, *John Law*, 107.

23. Velde, "Was John Law's System a Bubble?," 104–8; Macdonald, *A Free Nation Deep in Debt*, 201.

24. "Arrêt du Conseil d'État, qui subroge la Compagnie des indes aux droits et pretensions appartenants à la Compagnie de Saint-Domingue," Sept. 10, 1720, in Moreau, *Loix et constitutions*, 2:692–696.

25. The exact terms of the distribution are set forth in the "Arrêt du Conseil qui fixe l'indemnité crée par la Compagnie des indes," September 12, 1720, ANOM, F/2A/11, folder titled "Compagnie de Saint-Domingue, 1706–1720," no. 84.

26. "Arret du Conseil d'État, qui subroge la Compagnie des indes," September 10, 1720, in Moreau, *Loix et constitutions*, 2:695–96.

27. Cf. Harms, *The Diligent*, 48 (contrasting the Indies Company with its bankruptcy predecessors on the grounds that it had a "worldwide reach").

28. "Arrêt du Conseil d'État, qui subroge la Compagnie des indes," September 10, 1720, in Moreau, *Loix et constitutions*, 2:695.

29. Arrêt du Conseil d'État, qui subroge la Compagnie des indes," September 10, 1720, in Moreau, *Loix et constitutions*, 2:694. The Saint-Domingue Company had been granted what seems like a more limited tax exemption: viz., immunity from the *droits d'octrois*, as well as all import and export duties, for purposes of any materials associated with the construction, equipping, and supplying of its trading vessels. It also enjoyed an exemption from metropolitan entry

and exit duties for goods brought back to France for reexport to other countries. "Édit en forme de Lettres-Patentes," September 1698, in Moreau, *Loix et constitutions*, 1:616–17 (arts. 32–34).

30. Moreau de Saint-Méry, *Description de la partie française de l'isle Saint-Domingue*, 1:627. Contrary to Moreau's suggestion, however, it was not simply these "new ideas of hindrance and constraint," or even the arrival of the company's officers in October 1722, that triggered the revolt. Moreau de Saint-Méry, *Description de la partie française de l'isle Saint-Domingue*, 1:628. The Saint-Domingue Company's exclusive commercial jurisdiction over its southern territory was enshrined in Article 2 of the "Édit en forme de Lettres-Patentes," September 1698, in Moreau, *Loix et constitutions*, 1:611.

31. Haudrère, *La Compagnie française des Indes au XVIIIe siècle*, 1:102; Conseil de Marine to the Commissaires du Conseil de la Compagnie des indes, August 20, 1721, ANOM, B/44, fols. 77v-78r.

32. Conseil de Marine to d'Arquian, April 30, 1721, ANOM, C/2/196, no. 41. Gaultier is possibly the Indies Company ship captain, decommissioned in 1725 for incapacity, that Haudrère identifies in *La Compagnie française des Indes au XVIIIe siècle*, 1:388n98.

33. "Arrêt du Conseil d'État, qui accorde et réunit à perpetuité à la Compagnie des indes, le Privilège exclusif pour le Commerce de la Côte de Guinée," September 27, 1720, in Moreau, *Loix et constitutions*, 2:698–701.

34. See Charles Woolsey Cole, *Colbert and a Century of French Mercantilism*, 2 vols. (New York: Columbia University Press, 1939); Charles Woolsey Cole, *French Mercantilism*; and Girard, "La réorganisation de la Compagnie des Indes (I)," 8.

35. "Arrêt du Conseil d'État, qui subroge la Compagnie des indes," September 10, 1720, in Moreau, *Loix et constitutions*, 2:694 (clause 13).

36. Arrêt du Conseil d'État, qui subroge la Compagnie des indes," September 10, 1720, in Moreau, *Loix et constitutions*, 2:694 (clauses 8 and 10).

37. Joseph Lambert, "Décision théologique sur les actions de la Compagnie des indes," July 1720, Historic New Orleans Collection [HNOC], Mss. 735. For the dating of this manuscript and Lambert's background, see the curator's entry on Lambert in the online HNOC catalog, http://hnoc.minisisinc.com/thnoc/catalog/3/13693. A printed version of the document can be found in the Bibliothèque nationale in Paris.

38. Lambert, "Décision théologique," fol. 2.

39. Lambert, "Décision théologïque, fols. 7–8. According to Edgar Faure, this preamble was apparently written by John Law himself. Faure, *La banqueroute de Law*, 195.

40. Lambert, "Décision théologique," fol. 7. On Lambert's treatise and its theological context, see also Orain, *La politique du merveilleux*, 238–48.

41. David Brion Davis, *Inhuman Bondage: The Rise and Fall of Slavery in the New World* (New York: Oxford University Press, 2006), 38–39.

42. Lynn A. Hunt, Margaret C. Jacob, and W. W. Mijnhardt, *The Book That Changed Europe: Picart & Bernard's Religious Ceremonies of the World* (Cambridge, MA: Harvard University Press, 2010), 108–9; Charles Louis de Secondat, baron de Montesquieu, *Persian Letters*, trans. C. J. Betts (New York: Penguin Books, 1973), 245, 256–58. The Beinecke Library at Yale University has produced an online version of *Het Groote* that can be accessed at http://beinecke.library .yale.edu/collections/highlights/great-mirror-folly-or-het-groote-tafereel-der-dwaasheid. On the *Het Groote*, see Goetzmann et al., *The Great Mirror of Folly*.

43. Charles Louis de Secondat, baron de Montesquieu, *Persian Letters*, trans. C. J. Betts (New York: Penguin Books, 1973), 245.

44. Thomas Gordon, "The Fatal Effects of the South-Sea Scheme, and the Necessity of Punishing the Directors," no. 2, November 12, 1720; Thomas Gordon, "Against False Methods of Restoring Public Credit," no. 4, November 26, 1720; John Trenchard and Thomas Gordon, "The Iniquity of Late and New Projects about the South-Sea Considered. How Fatally They Affect the Publick," no. 10, January 3, 1721; Trenchard, "Monopolies and Exclusive Companies,

How Pernicious to Trade," no. 90, August 17, 1722; Trenchard, "How Exclusive Companies Influence and Hurt Our Government," no. 91, August 25, 1722, in *Cato's Letters, or Essays on Liberty, Civil and Religious, and Other Important Subjects*, ed. Ronald Hamowy, 4 vols., in vol. 2, Online Library of Liberty (Indianapolis, IN: Liberty Fund, 1995), 1:30, 35–37, 55–62; 3:107–10, 111–14.

45. For the French context, see Thomas E. Kaiser, "Money, Despotism, and Public Opinion in Early Eighteenth-Century France: John Law and the Debate on Royal Credit," *Journal of Modern History* 63, no. 1 (1991): 1–28. On the colonial American reception of Trenchard and Gordon, see Bernard Bailyn, *The Origins of American Politics* (New York: Vintage Books, 1970), 40–45, 54–56; James Kloppenberg, *Toward Democracy: The Struggle for Self-Rule in European and American Thought* (New York: Oxford University Press, 2016), 266; and, especially, Heather E. Barry, *A Dress Rehearsal for Revolution: John Trenchard and Thomas Gordon's Works in Eighteenth-Century British America* (Lanham, MD: University Press of America, 2007). Barry's careful study shows that between the 1720s and 1770s colonial American newspapers reprinted only 50 of the total 144 essays. Those reprinted included Essay 10 (on the South Sea Company's government connections) but not Essay 90 (on the evils of monopoly)—both discussed above. But Trenchard and Gordon also circulated in book form, particularly in the southern colonies. See Barry, *Dress Rehearsal for Revolution*, 31, 43, 44n19–20. For a skeptical reading of the influence of *Cato's Letters* in late colonial America, at least as concerns England's commercial system, see T. H. Breen, *The Marketplace of Revolution: How Consumer Politics Shaped American Independence* (New York: Oxford University Press, 2004), 87.

46. Carswell, *The South Sea Bubble*, 129; Edward Chancellor, *Devil Take the Hindmost: A History of Financial Speculation* (New York: Farrar, Straus, and Giroux, 1999), 88–89. The Bubble Act would remain on the books until 1825.

47. Murphy, *John Law*, 308–22 (quote at 308).

48. Albert Girard, "La réorganisation de la Compagnie des Indes (1719–1723), II: L'œuvre de Paris-Duverney (1721–1723) (Suite et Fin)," *Revue d'histoire moderne et contemporaine* 11, no. 3 (1908–9): 177–97; Haudrère, *La Compagnie française des Indes au XVIIIe siècle*, 1:80–88; Velde, "French Public Finance between 1683 and 1726," 154. The company's receivership period was known as the "régie royale." The company's administration in Louisiana during this period is covered in Giraud, *Histoire de la Louisiane française*, vol. 4.

49. Velde, "French Public Finance between 1683 and 1726," 154–56; François Velde, introduction to François-Michel-Chrétien Deschamps, *Lettres sur le Visa des dettes de l'État ordonné en 1721*, ed. François R. Velde (Paris: Classiques Garnier, 2015), xxii–xxiv. The commissioners implicated in the fraud case, known as the Talhouët affair, were sentenced to capital punishment. See Velde's appendix to Deschamp, *Lettres sur le Visa*, 215–28.

50. "French Public Finance between 1683 and 1726," 154. See also Velde, introduction to Deschamps, *Lettres sur le Visa*, xli–xliv.

51. Charlevoix's account was based on the eyewitness narrative of Jean-Baptiste Le Pers, a fellow Jesuit priest who had lived through the revolt, as well as official correspondence of the period. This secondhand recounting of the events of the early 1720s is problematic. Le Pers arrived in Saint-Domingue in 1704 and remained through the 1720s. Charlevoix had himself passed through Saint-Domingue in September–October 1722, but departed for France just prior to the outbreak of the rebellion. On Charlevoix's connection to Le Pers, whom Charlevoix met during his novitiate years in Paris, see J.-Edmond Roy, "Essai sur Charlevoix," in *Proceedings and Transactions of the Royal Society of Canada*, 3rd series, vol. 1 (1907): 55.

52. Pierre-François-Xavier de Charlevoix, *Histoire de l'Isle espagnole ou de St. Domingue*, 2 vols. (Paris: Jacques Guérin, 1731), 2:394. The South Sea crash in Britain similarly caused some who lost money on the stock market to seek a new start in the New World, far from the reach of their creditors. Daniel Horsmanden, the future chief justice of New York's high court, who presided over the 1741 slave conspiracy trial, was one of the casualties of the 1720 crisis. Serena R.

Zabin, *Dangerous Economies: Status and Commerce in Imperial New York* (Philadelphia: University of Pennsylvania Press, 2009), 150.

53. Marcel Delafosse, "Planteurs de Saint-Domingue et négociants rochelais au temps de Law," *Revue d'histoire des colonies* 41, no. 142 (1954): 14–15, 17; Lacombe, "Histoire monétaire de Saint-Domingue," 292. Cf. Haudrère, *La Compagnie française des Indes au XVIIIe siècle,* 1:78, cautioning against overestimating the extent to which Banque Royale notes and shares of the French Indies Company were diffused beyond a narrow circle of the financially active public.

54. Delafosse, "Planteurs de Saint-Domingue et négociants Rochelais," 1–18. See also Lacombe, "Histoire monétaire de Saint-Domingue," 292–293. The notarial records at issue were created by the notaries Rivière and Soullard and can be consulted in the Archives départmentales de la Charente-Maritime in La Rochelle under the call numbers 3E/1803 and 3E/1816, inter alia.

55. Delafosse, "Planteurs de Saint-Domingue et négociants Rochelais," 20; Charlevoix, *Histoire de l'Isle espagnole,* 2:394; Lacombe, "Histoire monétaire de Saint-Domingue," 293.

56. Charlevoix, *Histoire de l'Isle espagnole,* 2:394.

57. Haudrère, *La Compagnie française des Indes au XVIIIe siècle,* 1:102; Stein, *The French Slave Trade,* 18.

58. The bonus would be paid upon the company's presentation of a certificate issued by the intendant of the receiving colony. "Arrêt du Conseil d'État," September 27, 1720, in Moreau, *Loix et constitutions,* 2:699–700 (arts. 6 and 8). See also Harms, *The Diligent,* 52.

59. Stein, *The French Slave Trade,* 18.

60. Haudrère, *La Compagnie française des Indes au XVIIIe siècle,* 1:85. See also Stein, *The French Slave Trade,* 17.

61. Harms, *The Diligent,* 52.

62. Stein, *The French Slave Trade,* 19; Harms, *The Diligent,* 52.

63. See Gwendolyn Midlo Hall, *Africans in Colonial Louisiana: The Development of Afro-Creole Culture in the Eighteenth Century* (Baton Rouge: Louisiana State University Press, 1992), chaps. 2–3.

64. Stein, *The French Slave Trade,* 19; Harms, *The Diligent,* 59.

65. "Ordonnance du Roi, concernant la diminution des Espèces étrangères, et leur réduction au poids," in Moreau, *Loix et constitutions,* 3:16–17.

66. Rowlands, *The Financial Decline of a Great Power,* 92, 96–97. See also Velde, "French Public Finance between 1683 and 1726," 145–47; and Foucault, *The Order of Things,* 180–81.

67. Gail Bossenga, "Society," in *Old Regime France, 1648–1788,* ed. William Doyle (New York: Oxford University Press, 2001), 74.

68. Jacob M. Price, "Credit in the Slave Trade and Plantation Economies," in *Slavery and the Rise of the Atlantic System,* ed. Barbara L. Solow (New York: Cambridge University Press, 1991), 294–332. As Price notes, British slave traders also had difficulties with bills drawn by planters and took to using bills drawn by merchants and factors instead. I am indebted to Vertus Saint-Louis for drawing my attention to Price's important essay. On the use of letters of exchange in Saint-Domingue, see Saint-Louis, *Mer et liberté,* 48. For an example of continued experimentation with bills of exchange in the mid-eighteenth-century French Caribbean, involving a Jesuit bank and commodity exchange in Martinique, see W. J. Eccles, *The French in North America, 1500–1783,* rev. ed. (East Lansing: Michigan State University Press, 1998), 175.

69. Price, "Credit in the Slave Trade and Plantation Economies," 332; Code Noir (1685), arts. 44 and 46–48.

70. Price, "Credit in the Slave Trade and Plantation Economies," 333–35; Richard Pares, *Merchants and Planters, "Economic History Review* Supplements," no. 4 (New York: Cambridge University Press, 1960), 33.

NOTES TO CHAPTER 3   215

3. "Women, Negroes, and Unknown, Unimportant People"

1. Elias Canetti, *Crowds and Power*, trans. Carol Stewart (New York: Farrar, Straus, and Giroux, 1984), 48, 90, 183. On the 1923 hyperinflation and the targeting of Jews, see Volker Ullrich, *Germany 1923: Hyperinflation, Hitler's Putsch, and Democracy in Crisis*, trans. Jefferson Chase (New York: Liveright, 2023), 83, 198–99, 236–37.

2. William H. Sewell, *Logics of History: Social Theory and Social Transformation* (Chicago: University of Chicago Press, 2005), 248.

3. See the anonymous 1723 account titled "Révolte de St. Domingue," probably by Antoine-Denis Raudot, a naval ministry official, in ANOM, F/3/169, fol. 142 left. (Several of the documents in this volume are foliated as left-right rather than recto-verso pages; where this is the case, I will use the full terms left and right to avoid confusion with the abbreviation for recto, "r.") See also "Provisions de Lieutenant-Général du Roi," September 7, 1723, in Moreau, *Loix et constitutions*, 3:59.

4. [Anonymous], "Relation de ce qui s'est passé en l'isle de St. Domingue au sujet de l'Établissement de la Compagnie des Indes," [undated but probably 1723], ANOM, F/3/169, fol. 130r. See also "Arrêt du Conseil de Léogâne, qui défend les Actes et Discours séditieux," March 1, 1723, in Moreau, *Loix et constitutions*, 3:40.

5. Alain Rey, *Dictionnaire historique de la langue française*, 3 vols. (Paris: Dictionnaires le Robert, 1998), 1:1221; "Copie des demandes des habitants du Cap," [undated but referencing events of Jan.–Feb. 1723], ANOM, F/3/169, fol. 177r. For a mid-eighteenth-century example of "émeute" as "émotion populaire," see Farge and Revel, *Logiques de la foule*, 24.

6. William Beik, *A Social and Cultural History of Early Modern France* (New York: Cambridge University Press, 2009), 243. See also Natalie Zemon Davis, *Society and Culture in Early Modern France: Eight Essays* (Stanford, CA: Stanford University Press, 1975), chap. 5; Cynthia A. Bouton, *The Flour War: Gender, Class, and Community in Late Ancien Régime French Society* (University Park: Pennsylvania State University Press, 1993), 17; and Peter Sahlins, *Forest Rites: The War of the Demoiselles in Nineteenth-Century France* (Cambridge, MA: Harvard University Press, 1994), 24–28.

7. [Père] Michel, "Au sujet de la révolte de St. Domingue" [1723], BnF, Département des manuscrits, Ms. 10475.

8. Cf. Robert M. Isherwood, *Farce and Fantasy: Popular Entertainment in Eighteenth-Century Paris* (New York: Oxford University Press, 1986), 37.

9. "Relation de ce qui est arrivé à l'égard de la Compagnie des indes," [undated but probably 1723], ANOM, F/3/169, fol. 136 left. Adrien Dessalles summarizes the events of La Sagona's life in his *Histoire générale des Antilles*, 4 vols. (Paris: France Librairie, 1847), 4:125.

10. See, e.g., Bernard Bailyn, *The Ideological Origins of the American Revolution*, (Cambridge, MA: Harvard University Press, 1992), 232 ff.; Peter A. Dorsey, *Common Bondage: Slavery as Metaphor in Revolutionary America* (Knoxville: University of Tennessee Press, 2009); Rushforth, "The Gaulet Uprising of 1710," 108.

11. On the dual function of free trade as both metaphor and social practice, see Emma Rothschild's discussion of the theoretical writings of Adam Smith in Britain and the physiocrats in France, in *Economic Sentiments: Adam Smith, Condorcet, and the Enlightenment* (Cambridge, MA: Harvard University Press, 2001). See also Shovlin's analysis of free trade as a pragmatic accommodation by imperial administrators within the ambit of protectionism, in *Trading with the Enemy*, 22–23.

12. Cf. Alexis de Tocqueville, *The Ancien Régime and the French Revolution*, ed. Jon Elster, trans. Arthur Goldhammer (New York: Cambridge University Press, 2011), 225–27.

13. The mantra is cited, inter alia, in Charlevoix, *Histoire de l'Isle espagnole ou de St. Domingue*, 2:402–3. Sewell defines a historical event as a process of reinforcing ruptures that transform the meaning of key cultural markers in *Logics of History*, 219, 227–29. Charles Frostin describes

216 NOTES TO CHAPTER 3

the November 1722 insurgency as a *petit blanc* movement in *Les révoltes blanches à Saint-Domingue*, chap. 3.

14. Roberto Cassá, *Rebelión de los Capitanes* (Santo Domingo: Archivo General de la Nación, 2011), 264.

15. On the importance of the Caribbean Sea as a "powerful agent, continuously shaping human affairs" in the West Indies, see Philip D. Morgan, "The Caribbean Environment to 1850," in *Sea and Land: An Environmental History of the Caribbean*, eds. Philip D. Morgan et al. (New York: Oxford University Press, 2022), 19.

16. Haudrère, *La Compagnie française des Indes au XVIIIe siècle*, 1:102. Grenon's departure for Saint-Domingue is noted in the July 1722 *arrêt* naming his replacement as inspector. See Germain Dernis, *Recueil ou collection des titres, édits, déclarations, arrêts, règlemens et autres pièces concernant la Compagnie des indes orientales* (Paris, 1755), 3:495–496.

17. The voyage records of the *Philippe* and other Indies Company ships are available on the database "Mémoire des hommes" of the Ministère de la défense, at http://www.memoire deshommes.sga.defense.gouv.fr/fr/arkotheque/client/mdh/compagnie_des_indes/armement_navires.php.

18. For the voyage records of the *Pontchartrain*, including the outfitting report, see the "Mémoire des hommes" website referenced in the preceding footnote, and "Voyages: The Transatlantic Slave Trade Database," http://slavevoyages.org/voyage/32476/variables.

19. Sorel to d'Armenonville, March 3, 1721, ANOM, F/3/169, fols. 11r-11v.

20. Seventeen crew members had also perished on the Middle Crossing. *Pontchartrain* Voyage Data, 1722–23, "Voyages: The Trans-Atlantic Slave Trade Database," http://slavevoyages.org/tast/database/search.faces?yearFrom=1722&yearTo=1723&shipname=Pontchartrain. The average figures cited here are from Geggus, "The French Slave Trade," 122, 136.

21. Charlevoix, *Histoire de l'Isle espagnole ou de St. Domingue*, 2:396; "Relation de ce qui c'est passé en l'isle de St. Domingue au sujet de l'Établissement de la Compagnie des Indes" [undated but probably 1723], fol. 128 left. The "Relation" gives the date of the *Philippe*'s arrival as October 12, which is inconsistent with all other sources.

22. William A. Pettigrew, *Freedom's Debt*, 46.

23. "Relation de ce qui s'est passé en l'isle de St. Domingue au sujet de l'Établissement de la Compagnie des Indes," [undated but probably 1723], fol. 128 left; Charlevoix, *Histoire de l'Isle espagnole ou de St. Domingue*, 2:395–96.

24. "Copie d'un placard trouvé à la porte de l'Église de la ville du Cap," [undated but probably around October 17–19, 1722], ANOM, F/3/169, fol. 47r. Châtenoye declined to transcribe one word that he recorded only as "f . . . ," noting that it was "hardly left blank in the poster"—from which I deduce that the word may have been "foutu" (damned). For Charlevoix's reference to Philippe as *Trésorier de la Marine*, see his *Histoire de l'Isle espagnole ou de St. Domingue*, 2:425. On the functions of the naval cashier in the colonies, see John Keyes, "Un commis des trésoriers généraux de la marine à Québec: Nicolas Lanoullier de Boisclerc," *Revue d'histoire de l'Amérique française* 32, no. 2 (1978): 181–202. For the February–March 1723 sale overseen by Philippe, see "Relation de M. Duclos," March 25, 1723, ANOM, F/3/169, fol. 150 left.

25. "Relation de ce qui s'est passé en l'isle de St. Domingue au sujet de l'Établissement de la Compagnie des Indes," [undated but probably 1723], fol. 128 right.

26. Charlevoix, *Histoire de l'Isle espagnole ou de St. Domingue*, 2:395–96.

27. Farge and Revel, *Logiques de la foule*, 98–119. See also Wim Klooster, "Slave Revolts, Royal Justice, and a Ubiquitous Rumor in the Age of Revolutions," *William and Mary Quarterly* 71, no. 3 (2014): 401–24.

28. Montholon replaced Duclos as intendant in March 1722. Morville replaced his father d'Armenonville as secretary of state for the colonies and served from February 1722 to August 1723.

NOTES TO CHAPTER 3 217

29. Sorel and Montholon to Charles-Jean-Baptiste Fleuriau de Morville, secretary of state for the colonies, and the Conseil de la Marine, November 18, 1722, ANOM, F/3/169, fols. 66r-67v. In a later letter, the administrators noted that the money ordinance had arrived "at the same time" as the initial outpouring of grievances against the company's monopoly in the weeks following October 16. Sorel and Montholon to Arquian and Duclos, December 5, 1722, ANOM, C9A/20, fol. 167r.

30. D'Arquian and Duclos to Sorel and Montholon, November 24, 1722, ANOM, F/3/169, fol. 77r.

31. "Relation de ce qui s'est passé en l'isle de St. Domingue au sujet de l'Établissement de la Compagnie des Indes," [undated but probably 1723], fols. 128 right - 129 right.

32. "Relation de ce qui s'est passé en l'isle de St. Domingue au sujet de l'Établissement de la Compagnie des Indes," [undated but probably 1723], fols. 129 left - 129 right.

33. Lesgut to the Commissaires of the Indies Company, November 23, 1722, ANOM, F/3/169, fols. 67r-69v. Moreau de Saint-Méry appears to have misidentified this document as a letter from Lesgut to the magistrates of the Léogâne Conseil Supérieur.

34. Lesgut to the Commissaires of the Indies Company, November 23, 1722, ANOM, F/3/169, fols. 69v-70v.

35. The records in the "Memoire des hommes" online database give August 31, 1723 as the departure date and provide inventory of the cargo of returning colonial goods.

36. For the earlier dating, see the "Relation de ce qui s'est passé en l'isle de St. Domingue au sujet de l'Établissement de la Compagnie des Indes," [undated but probably 1723], fol. 130 left.

37. "Arrêt du Conseil de Léogâne, sur la présentation de plusieurs Arrêts du Conseil d'État, par le Directeur de la Compagnie des Indes," November 7, 1722, in Moreau, *Loix et constitutions*, 3:29–31.

38. "Arrêt du Conseil de Léogâne, sur la présentation de plusieurs Arrêts du Conseil d'État, par le Directeur de la Compagnie des Indes," November 7, 1722, in Moreau, *Loix et constitutions*, 3:30. Boismorand's title was "Commissaire-Ordonnateur de la Marine au Quartier de St. Louis."

39. See "Relation de ce qui s'est passé en l'isle de St. Domingue au sujet de l'Établissement de la Compagnie des Indes," [undated but probably 1723], fol. 129 right (noting that Grenon's petition to the Léogâne Conseil included rulings of the Conseil of State that "went against the Company's debtors just as much as they favored the Company's establishment and the trade in negroes").

40. Sorel and Montholon to Morville and the Conseil de Marine, November 18, 1722, ANOM, F/3/169, fol. 67v.

41. "Ordonnance des administrateurs, qui surseoit à l'exécution des Articles VI, VII, VIII, de l'Ordonnance du Roi du 3 avril précédent, sur les monnaies," November 19, 1722, in Moreau, *Loix et constitutions*, 3:32. Moreau's compilation contained numerous typographical errors, and his title for this ordinance both omits one of the key provisions of the August 1722 ordinance—Article 5—and mistakes its month.

42. As the naval minister had made clear in 1709, when he wrote to then Governor Choiseul instructing him not to intervene in monetary policy because it was the exclusive domain of the king. "Extrait de la Lettre du Ministre à Choiseul, sur l'augmentation des espèces," January 2, 1709, in Moreau, *Loix et constitutions*, 2 :137.

43. D'Arquian and Duclos to Sorel and Montholon (copy), November 24, 1722, ANOM, F/3/169, fol. 76r.

44. Cf. Stoler, *Along the Archival Grain*, 1–2. Stoler's interpretation of the "fragile security of the Dutch police state" (18) suggests that fluid state authority was, at some level, a common condition of colonial governance rather than a characteristic of a particular stage in the development of the colonial state.

218   NOTES TO CHAPTER 3

45. Nicolas-Louis Bourgeois and Pierre-Jean-Baptiste Nougaret, *Voyages intéressants dans différentes colonies françaises, espagnoles, anglaises* (London: J.-F. Bastien, 1788), 185–200 [hereafter Bourgeois, *Voyages intéressants*].

46. A brief reference to La Sagona's life before 1722, lacking many of the details found in Bourgeois, can be found in the anonymous "Révolte de St. Domingue," 1723, ANOM, F/3/169, fol. 142 left.

47. Bourgeois, *Voyages intéressants*, 190.

48. Bourgeois, *Voyages intéressants*, 190–91.

49. On the old regime theater as a space of open, politicized debate, see, most recently, Lauren Clay, *Stagestruck: The Business of Theater in Eighteenth-Century France and Its Colonies* (Ithaca, NY: Cornell University Press, 2013), 6.

50. See, e.g., "Arrêt du Conseil de Léogâne, concernant les Habitans et Cabaretiers qui reçoivent et logent des gens sans aveu," July 10, 1721, in Moreau, *Loix et constitutions*, 2:760.

51. "Arrêt du Conseil du Cap, portant Tarif du prix au Pain et du Vin, rendu en conséquence d'une Ordonnance du Juge de Police de la même Ville, October 6, 1721," in Moreau, *Loix et constitutions*, 2:783–84.

52. Bourgeois, *Voyages intéressants*, 191.

53. See Robert Darnton's interpretation of early modern popular riots as a back-and-forth between action and interpretation in "Reading a Riot," *New York Review of Books* (October 22, 1992).

54. Cabon, *Histoire d'Haïti*, 1:101–3.

55. D'Arquian to Sorel and Montholon, November 23, 1722, ANOM, F/3/169, fols. 73r-73v.

56. D'Arquian to Sorel and Montholon, November 23, 1722, ANOM, F/3/169, fols. 73v-74v.

57. D'Arquian to Sorel and Montholon, November 23, 1722, ANOM, F/3/169, fols. 74v-76r.

58. D'Arquian and Duclos to Sorel and Montholon, November 24, 1722, ANOM, F/3/169, fols. 77r-77v, 78v.

59. Ibid., fols. 78v-79v. La Ferrière vehemently denied making any such statements when d'Arquian finally reached the Africa House after dinner, having been alerted to the unfolding drama by a sailboat bearing his distraught valet. Langot is identified as La Ferrière's host and the *octroi* receiver in the "Relation de ce qui s'est passé à St. Domingue," 1723, fol. 146 right; and "Extrait de ce qui s'est passé au Cap Français," 1723, ANOM, F/3/169, fols. 152 left-152 right. See also Charlevoix, *Histoire de l'Isle espagnole ou de St. Domingue*, 2:399–400; and Tramond, *Les troubles de Saint-Domingue*, 512. On the Boston Port Act of March 1774 requiring indemnification of East India Company tea, see Mary Beth Norton, *1774: The Long Year of Revolution* (New York: Knopf, 2020), 81–82.

60. D'Arquian and Duclos to Sorel and Montholon, November 24, 1722, fols. 79r-79v. The nineteenth-century historian Adrien Dessalles would emphasize this suspicion in his 1847 history of the French Caribbean, discussed below.

61. The June 1721 royal edict authorizing the minting of the coins and other documents recounting their fate are reprinted in Zay, *Histoire monétaire des colonies françaises*, 52–56. See also Clairand and Prieur, *Les monnaies royales françaises*, 231; Victor Gadoury and Georges Cousinié, *Monnaies coloniales françaises, 1670–1980* (Monte Carlo: V. Gadoury, 1980), 16; and Jean Mazard, *Histoire monétaire et numismatique des colonies et de l'Union française, 1670–1952* (Paris: Émile Bourgey, 1953), 19. In December 1719, the monarchy had authorized a large minting of silver coins for the account of the Indies Company in exchange for an advance of fifty million livres. These one-quarter crown (*écu*) coins became known as "livres of the Indies Company." Unlike the 1721 copper coinage, these 1720 silver coins were never destined for the colonies, probably never made their way there, and in any case were soon overtaken by the failure of the System. They were demonetized in December 1720 at a rate of twenty *sous tournois* (the equivalent of

one livre), having been worth as much as thirty *sous* in April. Clairand and Prieur, *Les monnaies royales françaises*, 228. An example of the Indies Company pound can be found at https://fr.numista.com/catalogue/pieces27846.html.

62. D'Arquian and Duclos to Sorel and Montholon, November 24, 1722, fols. 79r-80r.

63. D'Arquian and Duclos to Sorel and Montholon, November 24, 1722, fols. 80v-82r.

64. D'Arquian and Duclos to Sorel and Montholon, November 24, 1722, fols. 82r-82v, 84r.

65. "Relation de ce qui s'est passé à St. Domingue," 1723, fol. 143 right. Exceptionally, in this account, La Sagona's name is spelled with a double "n." On the role of cross-dressing and the carnivalesque in early modern France, see Davis, *Society and Culture in Early Modern France*, chap. 5; and Sahlins, *Forest Rites*, 24–28. John Wood Sweet discusses the racial cross-dressing of the Boston Tea Party in *Bodies Politic: Negotiating Race in the American North, 1730–1830* (Baltimore: Johns Hopkins University Press, 2003), 193–94.

66. "Relation de ce qui s'est passé à St. Domingue," 1723, fol. 144 left.

67. I thank Sue Lanser for this comparison.

68. "Relation de ce qui s'est passé à St. Domingue," 1723, fol. 144 left.

69. "Relation de ce qui est arrivé à l'égard de la Compagnie des indes," fols. 136 left - 136 right. The context and language of this manuscript suggest that it may have been written by Châtenoye, the commander of the Cap Français harbor. For the translation of *menu peuple* as "unimportant people," see Rey, ed., *Dictionnaire historique de la langue française*, 2:2197; and François Furet, "Pour une définition des classes inférieures à l'époque moderne," *Annales* 18, no. 3 (1963): 459.

70. "Relation de ce qui est arrivé à l'égard de la Compagnie des indes," fol. 136 right.

71. "Relation de ce qui est arrivé à l'égard de la Compagnie des indes," fols. 136 right-137 left.

72. Jean-Baptiste Le Pers, "Mémoires pour l'histoire de l'isle de St. Domingue," [1726–27], BnF, Département des manuscrits, Fr. 8990, fol. 346v.

73. Roy, "Essai sur Charlevoix," 32–43; Tramond, *Les troubles de Saint-Domingue*, 507; Adrien Dessalles, *Histoire générale des Antilles* (Paris: Libraire-éditeur, 1847), 4:124n3.

74. Charlevoix, *Histoire de l'Isle espagnole ou de St. Domingue*, 2:399–400, 402.

75. The Amazon allegory is perhaps best understood as a reflection of the larger association in Renaissance and early modern culture between female heroism and popular resistance. By the early eighteenth century, writes Natalie Zemon Davis, the tale of the virtuous Amazon "could be used not only to praise the wise rule of contemporary lawful queens (as it had been already in Elizabeth I's day), but also to hint at the possibility of a wider role of citizenship for women." Davis, *Society and Culture in Early Modern France*, 133, 144. Such hints seem few and far between in contemporaneous readings of the November 1722 uprising in Saint-Domingue. See also Celeste Turner Wright, "The Amazons in Elizabethan Literature," *Studies in Philology* 37, no. 3 (1940): 433–56; and Marina Warner, *Joan of Arc: The Image of Female Heroism* (New York: Knopf, 1981), 198–217. In 1718, Marie-Jeanne L'Héritier de Villandon reworked the Amazon tale in her "L'Amazone française," part of *Les caprices du destin, ou Recueil d'histoires singulières et amusantes arrivées de nos jours* (Paris: Pierre Michel Huart, 1718), 230–96. I discuss this motif at further length in chapter 5.

76. Bourgeois and Nougaret, *Voyages intéressants*, 186–87.

77. Bourgeois and Nougaret, *Voyages intéressants*, 188.]

78. *Lettres édifiantes et curieuses, écrites des missions étrangères*, nouv. ed. (Paris: J. G. Merigot, 1780), 7:188–89; Marcel Châtillon et al., "Papiers privés sur l'histoire des Antilles," *Revue française d'histoire d'outre-mer* 59, no. 216 (1972): 439–40.

79. Châtillon et al., "Papiers privés sur l'histoire des Antilles," 440–442.

80. Châtillon et al., "Papiers privés sur l'histoire des Antilles," 442.

81. Bourgeois and Nougaret, *Voyages intéressants*, 190.

82. Bourgeois and Nougaret, *Voyages intéressants*, 191.

220 NOTES TO CHAPTER 4

83. On Dessalles' grandfather, Pierre Régis Dessalles, see the biographical notice in Dessalles, *Histoire générale des Antilles*, 3:3–21.

84. Dessalles, *Histoire générale des Antilles*, 4:125–26. Dessalles observed that the new details revealed in his account had eluded Charlevoix and were the product of Dessalles's own research. Dessalles, *Histoire générale des Antilles*, 4:124n3.

85. Catherine Benoît, *Corps, jardins, mémoires: Anthropologie du corps et de l'espace à la Guadeloupe* (Paris: CNRS Éditions, 2000), 106.

86. "Relation de ce qui est arrivé à l'égard de la Compagnie des indes," [undated but probably 1723], fol. 136 right.

87. Cf. Edmund S. Morgan, *American Slavery, American Freedom: The Ordeal of Colonial Virginia* (New York: W. W. Norton, 1975).

4. Militant Slavery

1. Karl Loewenstein, "Militant Democracy and Fundamental Rights, I," *American Political Science Review* 31, no. 3 (1937): 417–32 (quotations at 424 and 430); Karl Loewenstein, "Militant Democracy and Fundamental Rights, II," *American Political Science Review* 31, no. 4 (1937): 638–58. See also András Sajó, ed., *Militant Democracy* (Utrecht, the Netherlands: Eleven International Publishing, 2004).

2. Cf. Malick W. Ghachem, "Empire, War, and Racial Hierarchy in the Making of the Atlantic Revolutionary Nations," in *The Cambridge History of Nationhood and Nationalism*, vol. 1, *Patterns and Trajectories over the Longue Durée*, eds. Cathie Carmichael, Matthew d'Auria, and Aviel Roshwald (New York: Cambridge University Press, 2023), 210.

3. Moreau de Saint-Méry, *Description de la partie française de l'isle Saint-Domingue*, 1:493, 705. In 1750, Léogâne would give way to Port-au-Prince as the new and permanent capital of Saint-Domingue/Haiti.

4. Marquis de Roux, *Louis XIV et les provinces conquises* (Paris: Les Éditions de France, 1938), 179; Ghachem, *The Old Regime and the Haitian Revolution*, 41.

5. Quoted in Garrigus, *Before Haiti*, 30.

6. See the brilliant discussion of the *conseils* as legal entrepôts in Laurie M. Wood, *Archipelago of Justice: Law in France's Early Modern Empire* (New Haven, CT: Yale University Press, 2020), esp. 3–8.

7. Lesgut to the commissaires of the French Indies Company in Paris, November 23, 1722, ANOM, F/3/169, fols. 69r-69v. This letter is mislabeled by Moreau de Saint-Méry (who assembled the F/3/169 volume) as addressed to the magistrates of the Conseil Supérieur of Léogâne.

8. "Ordonnance des administrateurs, touchant le payment du droit d'Octroi par tête de Negre travaillant," November 18, 1719, in Moreau, *Loix et constitutions*, 2:656–57.

9. Sorel and Montholon to the Conseil and Ministre de Marine, November 18, 1722, ANOM, F/3/169, fol. 66r.

10. Lesgut to the commissaires of the French Indies Company in Paris, November 23, 1722, fol. 70r.

11. Lesgut to the commissaires of the French Indies Company in Paris, November 23, 1722, fols. 71r-72r.

12. Sorel and Montholon to d'Arquian and Duclos, December 4, 1722, ANOM, C9A/20, fols. 176r - 176(b)r. The folio following 176 is not numbered; I designate it here as 176(b).

13. Sorel and Montholon to d'Arquian and Duclos, December 4, 1722, ANOM, C9A/20, fols. 176v-176(b)v.

14. Sorel and Montholon to d'Arquian and Duclos, December 4, 1722, ANOM, C9A/20, fol. 176(b)v. For the original rumor, see d'Arquian and Duclos to Sorel and Montholon, November 24, 1722, ANOM, F/3/169, fol. 84r.

NOTES TO CHAPTER 4   221

15. Sorel and Montholon to d'Arquian and Duclos, December 4, 1722, fols. 176(b)v-177r.

16. Sorel and Montholon to d'Arquian and Duclos, December 4, 1722, fols. 178r-178v.

17. Sorel and Montholon to d'Arquian and Duclos, December 4, 1722, fols. 177v-178r.

18. Sorel and Montholon to d'Arquian and Duclos, December 4, 1722, fols. 177r-177v, 179r; D'Arquian and Duclos to Sorel and Montholon, November 24, 1722, ANOM, F/3/169, fol. 83v. It is unclear whether La Ferrière had threatened to seize the sugar because he held dame Robineau and Castaing personally responsible for the damage to the African House. If Bourgeois's account of dame Robineau's collaboration with La Sagona is accurate, that collaboration might well account for some of La Ferrière's motivation here.

19. Sorel and Montholon to d'Arquian and Duclos, December 5, 1722, ANOM, C9A/20, fol. 166r.

20. Rey, ed., *Dictionnaire historique de la langue française*, 1:278-79. See also Marc Bloch, *La société féodale*, 2 vols. (Paris: Michel, 1939), 1:365.

21. Charlevoix, *Histoire de l'Isle espagnole ou de St. Domingue*, 2:407.

22. Charlevoix, *Histoire de l'Isle espagnole ou de St. Domingue*, fols. 167v-168v.

23. Charlevoix, *Histoire de l'Isle espagnole ou de St. Domingue*, 2:406.

24. For Boismorant's appointment to the Léogâne Conseil, see Moreau, *Loix et constitutions*, 2:778.

25. D'Arquian and Duclos to the Conseil de Marine, December 18, 1722, fols. 92r-93v.

26. D'Arquian and Duclos to the Conseil de Marine, December 18, 1722, fol. 94r.

27. Charlevoix, *Histoire de l'Isle espagnole ou de St. Domingue*, 2:406.

28. D'Arquian and Duclos to the Conseil de Marine, December 18, 1722, fols. 95v-96v.

29. Charlevoix, *Histoire de l'Isle espagnole ou de St. Domingue*, 2:415. On the Bac de l'Artibonite, see Jacques de Cauna, "Patrimoine et mémoire de l'esclavage en Haïti: Les vestiges de la société d'habitation coloniale," *In Situ: Revue des patrimoines*, no. 20 (2013): 43.

30. Order of Sorel and Montholon, December 27, 1722, ANOM, C9A/20, fols. 169r-169v.

31. "Demandes que fait la Colonie à MM. Sorel et de Montholon," Dec. 28, 1722, ANOM, C9A/20, fol. 173v.

32. "Ordonnance qui nomme quatre habitans pour calmer les troubles de St. Domingue, suivie des demandes du peuple et des réponses des chefs," December 27-29, 1722, ANOM, F/3/169, fols. 99r-100v.

33. "Ordonnance qui nomme quatre habitants pour calmer les troubles de St. Domingue, suivie des demandes du peuple et des réponses des chefs," December 27-29, 1722, ANOM, F/3/169, fols. 101r-102r. Boismorant's appointment to the conseil in 1720 was one such clear indication. Another warning sign appeared in the "innovations" of an "equally suspect" member of the Léogâne tribunal named Bizoton, the subject of Article 8. On a recent trip to France, Bizoton had obtained the supplementary title of Keeper of the Seals (*garde des sceaux*), a position that he quickly began using to require the payment of stamp taxes on legal documents submitted by the colonists. He attracted further attention in the "Très humble supplication du peuple de St. Domingue au Roi, touchant le renvoi des directeurs et préposés de la Compagnie des indes," [January or February] 1723, ANOM, F/3/169, fols. 118v-119r.

34. "Ordonnance qui nomme quatre habitants," December 27-29, 1722, fols. 101v-102r.

35. "Ordonnance qui nomme quatre habitants," December 27-29, 1722, fols. 102v-103r.

36. On the basis of a kingdom-wide survey of documented rebellions between 1661 and the French Revolution, Jean Nicolas has found that approximately 40 percent (3,336 instances) were driven by tax-related grievances. Jean Nicolas, *La rébellion française: Mouvements populaires et conscience sociale (1661–1789)* (Paris: Éditions du Seuil, 2002; reprint Paris: Gallimard, 2008), Annex 2. Citations are to the 2008 Gallimard edition. On the prominence of tax riots relative to other forms of political protest in early modern France, see William Beik, "Protest and Rebellion in Seventeenth-Century France," in *Crowd Actions in Britain and France from the Middle Ages*

222   NOTES TO CHAPTER 4

to the Modern World, ed. Michael T. Davis (New York: Palgrave Macmillan, 2015), 45–48; William Beik, *A Social and Cultural History of Early Modern France*, 237–41; William Beik, *Urban Protest in Seventeenth-Century France: The Culture of Retribution* (New York: Cambridge University Press, 1997), 5–6, 52; Yves-Marie Bercé, *Révoltes et révolutions dans l'Europe moderne: XVIe-XVIIIe siècles* (Paris: CNRS, 2013); François Hincker, *Les Français devant l'impôt sous l'Ancien Régime* (Paris: Flammarion, 1971), 12, 65–65, 82, 95; Michael Kwass, *Contraband: Louis Mandrin and the Making of a Global Underground* (Cambridge, MA: Harvard University Press, 2014); Michael Kwass, "The Global Underground: Smuggling, Rebellion, and the Origins of the French Revolution," in *The French Revolution in Global Perspective*, eds. Suzanne Desan, Lynn Hunt, and William Max Nelson (Ithaca, NY: Cornell University Press, 2013), 20–21.

37. Hincker, *Les Français devant l'impôt sous l'Ancien Régime*, 12.

38. "Très humble supplication du peuple de St. Domingue au roi," [January or February] 1723, fols. 121v-122r.

39. Cabon, *Histoire d'Haïti*, 1:120; Charlevoix, *Histoire de l'Isle espagnole ou de St. Domingue*, 2:419–421; Tramond, *Les troubles de Saint-Domingue*, 524–526.

40. Charlevoix, *Histoire de l'Isle espagnole ou de St. Domingue*, 415; Tramond, *Les troubles de Saint-Domingue en 1722–1724*, 515.

41. "Traité entre les Administrateurs et les Habitans, sur le mécontement de ces derniers, relativement à la Compagnie des indes," December 28–29, 1722, in Moreau, *Loix et constitutions*, 3:36. Moreau seems not to have carried through on this promise: his brief account of the revolt in the *Description* contains no mention of the Cul de Sac Treaty. Moreau de Saint-Méry, *Description de la partie française de l'isle Saint-Domingue*, 2:627–28.

42. "Ordonnance qui nomme quatre habitans," December 27–29, fol. 103r.

43. "Traité entre les Administrateurs et les Habitans," December 28–29, 1722, in Moreau, *Loix et constitutions*, 3:36. For the order expunging the treaty, see "Arrêt du Conseil du Petit Goâve, touchant la Radiation du Traité d'entre les Habitans et les Administrateurs," December 7, 1723, in Moreau, *Loix et constitutions*, 3:74.

44. Moreau, *Loix et constitutions*, 3:37–39.

45. See Gabriel Debien, *Les colons de Saint-Domingue et la Révolution; essai sur le club Massiac (août 1789-août 1792)* (Paris: Armand Colin, 1953); and Malick W. Ghachem, "The 'Trap' of Representation: Sovereignty, Slavery, and the Road to the Haitian Revolution," *Historical Reflections/Réflexions historiques* 29, no. 1 (2003): 123–44.

46. *Duc de Noailles* Voyage Data, 1722–23, "Voyages: The Trans-Atlantic Slave Trade Database," http://slavevoyages.org/tast/database/search.faces?yearFrom=1722&yearTo=1723&shipname=Duc+de+Noailles.

47. Hall, *Africans in Colonial Louisiana*, 76.

48. Charlevoix, *Histoire de l'Isle espagnole ou de St. Domingue*, 2:423–36.

49. "Arrêt du Conseil de Léogâne, qui défend à toutes Personnes d'acheter en gros les cargaisons des Nègres pour les revendre," March 1, 1723, in Moreau, *Loix et constitutions*, 3:40. As Père Cabon explains, by adopting this policy the Léogâne Conseil was conforming to the position of the Haut du Cap assembly. Cabon, *Histoire d'Haïti*, 1:122. See also Charlevoix, *Histoire de l'Isle espagnole ou de St. Domingue*, 438–39.

50. "Ordonnance qui nomme quatre habitans pour calmer les troubles de St. Domingue," December 27–29, 1722, fol. 99r.

51. Bourgeois, *Voyages intéressants*, 196.

52. See Dorsey, *Common Bondage*, 85. The full quip reads: "If slavery be thus fatally contagious, how is it that we hear the loudest yelps for liberty among the drivers of negroes?"

53. "Arrêt du Conseil de Léogâne, qui défend à toutes Personnes d'acheter en gros les cargaisons des Nègres pour les revendre," March 1, 1723, and "Arrêt du Conseil de Léogâne, qui défend les Actes et Discours séditieux," March 1, 1723, in Moreau, *Loix et constitutions*, 3:39–40.

54. Charlevoix, *Histoire de l'Isle espagnole ou de St. Domingue*, 439.

NOTES TO CHAPTER 4   223

55. Frostin, *Les révoltes blanches à Saint-Domingue*, 150. No copy of this flyer has survived.

56. "Arrêt du Conseil de Léogâne, qui défend les Actes et Discours séditieux," March 1, 1723, in Moreau, *Loix et constitutions*, 3:39–40 (emphases in the original). On the meaning of "Sans-Quartier," see Tramond, *Les Troubles de Saint-Domingue en 1722–1724*, 552n1.

57. As we have seen, Champflour's name had already been mentioned on the flyer from December 16, 1722, calling for the assembly of the western habitants at the Bac de l'Artibonite, a flyer that was also signed "Sans-Quartier." Tramond, *Les troubles de Saint-Domingue en 1722–1724*, 551–52; Charlevoix, *Histoire de l'Isle espagnole ou de St. Domingue*, 415. One historian posits that Fortier was the man behind the "Sans-Quartier" signature. Pollet, *Saint-Domingue et l'autonomie*, 264n1.

58. See Tramond, *Les troubles de Saint-Domingue en 1722–1724*, 534; and Frostin, *Les révoltes blanches à Saint-Domingue*, 100, 157. Robiou served, in effect, as secretary for the insurgent coordinating group, drafting such critical documents as the "Very humble supplication of the people of Saint-Domingue to the King" (January–February 1723).

59. "Liste des habitants de St. Domingue qui ont paru avoir le plus de part aux mouvements séditieux contre la Compagnie des indes," March 26, 1723, ANOM, C9A/21, fols. 65–69. Along with Champflour, Meunier and Robiou had been elected as deputies to the Léogâne Conseil in January. "Élection de deux députés par quartier, au Conseil Souverain de Léogâne," February 22, 1723, ANOM, Col. A 28, fol. 108; "Nomination, faite par les Habitants du Quartier du Cul-de-Sac, des Sieurs Duvivier et Robiou," January 19, 1723, in Moreau, *Loix et constitutions*, 3:37. For one piece of evidence that Champflour and Charpentier may have been coordinating their efforts with La Sagona as of March 1723, see "Sans-Quartier" to "Madame Sagonna," [March 1723], ANOM, F/3/169, fols. 140 right–141 left.

60. Tramond, *Les troubles de Saint-Domingue en 1722–1724*, 537.

61. "Ordonnance des Administrateurs, qui transfère le Conseil Superieur de Léogâne au Petit Goâve," April 11, 1723, in Moreau, *Loix et constitutions*, 3:42; Tramond, *Les troubles de Saint-Domingue*, 537–39; Frostin, *Les révoltes blanches à Saint-Domingue*, 157. The March 6 document does not appear in Moreau but Charlevoix reproduces it in his *Histoire de l'Isle espagnole ou de St. Domingue*, 2:440–42.

62. Tramond, *Les troubles de Saint-Domingue en 1722–1724*, 535.

63. Sorel and Montholon, "Projet pour un armament pour la Côte S. Domingue," March 20, 1723, ANOM, C9A/20, fol. 56r.

64. In 1706, the French colonial minister wrote to the governor of Saint-Domingue urging him to support an enslaved uprising in Jamaica by providing arms and munitions. "Extrait de la lettre du Ministre à M. Deslandes, touchant la révolte des nègres de la Jamaïque," April 21, 1706, ANOM, COL B/28, fol. 142.

65. Sorel and Montholon, "Projet pour un armament pour la Côte S. Domingue," March 20, 1723, fols. 56r–56v.

66. On this theme, see Christopher Leslie Brown and Philip D. Morgan, eds., *Arming Slaves from Classical Times to the Modern Age* (New Haven, CT: Yale University Press, 2006).

67. Sorel and Montholon, "Projet pour un armament," March 20, 1723, fols. 56v–57r. See also Frostin, *Les révoltes blanches à Saint-Domingue*, 121.

68. On which see Benjamin Quarles, *The Negro in the American Revolution* (Chapel Hill: University of North Carolina Press, for the Institute of Early American History and Culture, 1961); Simon Schama, *Rough Crossings: Britain, the Slaves, and the American Revolution* (New York: Ecco, 2006); and Jeremy D. Popkin, *You Are All Free: The Haitian Revolution and the Abolition of Slavery* (New York: Cambridge University Press, 2010), 1–2, 20, 189–216.

69. Sorel and Montholon, "Projet pour un armament," March 20, 1723, fols. 57r–57v, 61r, 62r.

70. Frostin, *Les révoltes blanches à Saint-Domingue*, 122, 151, 153n70, 154. As Frostin points out, one of the key officials in the colonial ministry at this time was Antoine-Denis Raudot, son of a former intendant of Canada, and a director of the Indies Company.

224 NOTES TO CHAPTER 4

71. Charlevoix, *Histoire de l'Isle espagnole ou de St. Domingue*, 2:458; Frostin, *Lés revoltes blanches à Saint-Domingue*, 154.

72. Charlevoix, *Histoire de l'Isle espagnole ou de St. Domingue*, 2:460.

73. "Ordonnance de M. le Comte d'Esnos-Champmeslin, au sujet des droits que doit payer la Compagnie des Indes pour l'introduction des Nègres, Vaisseaux, Marchandises, etc. et de la monnaie d'Espagne," February 14, 1724, in Moreau, *Loix et constitutions*, 3:83–84.

74. "Declaration du Roi, sur l'Octroi, les Receveurs publics, leurs comptes, et les pouvoirs donnés par Sa Majesté, à M. le Comte de Champmeslin, par rapport aux exemptions accordées à la Compagnie des Indes," in Moreau, *Loix et constitutions*, 3:65–67. Tramond argues that these concessions constituted a near-complete capitulation to the rebel demands dressed up in a language of formal adherence to royal authority. Tramond, *Les troubles de Saint-Domingue en 1722–1724*, 559–61.

75. Tramond, *Les troubles de Saint-Domingue en 1722–1724*, 550.

76. "Arret du Conseil du Petit Goâve, qui nomme le Sénéchal de Léogâne, Commissaire à l'effet d'instruire le Procès d'un des Moteurs des troubles de la Colonie," December 9, 1723; "Ordonnance du M. de Champmeslin, qui attribue au Conseiller du Petit Goâve, Commissaire nommé pour l'instruction du Procès d'un des Moteurs de Troubles de la colonie, tout pouvoir et autorité," December 10, 1723; "Arrêt du Conseil du Petit-Goâve, qui condamne les nommés [Champflour] et [Fortin] à être pendus, comme moteurs de troubles de la colonie, & confisque leurs biens au profit de Sa Majesté," March 10, 1724, all in Moreau, *Loix et constitutions*, 3:75–77, 88. See also *Frostin, Les révoltes blanches à Saint-Domingue*, 155.

77. "Lettres patentes qui purgent la mémoire de feu César Maurice de Champflour, capitaine de cavalerie à Saint-Domingue," August 20, 1753, ANOM, Col. A 6, fol. 32; "Arrêt qui ordonne l'exécution des lettres obtenues en la Grande Chancellerie par César Maurice de Champflour," July 27, 1754, ANOM, Col. A 6, fol. 70.

78. Tramond, *Les troubles de Saint-Domingue en 1722–1724*, 550, 555; Frostin, *Les révoltes blanches à Saint-Domingue*, 158.

79. *Prince de Conti* Voyage Data, 1724–25, "Slave Voyages: The Trans-Atlantic Slave Trade Database," http://slavevoyages.org/tast/database/search.faces?yearFrom=1723&yearTo =1725&shipname=Prince+de+Conti.

80. "Arrêt du Conseil du Cap, contre les Auteurs, Complices, etc. d'un Placard mis à la porte de l'Église du Cap, ayant trait aux troubles antérieurs de la Colonie," June 17, 1724, in Moreau, *Loix et constitutions*, 3:101–2.

81. See Haudrère, *Les Français dans l'océan Indien (XVIIe-XIXe siècle)* (Rennes: Presses Universitaires de Rennes, 2014), 232; and Stein, *The French Slave Trade*, 19.

82. De Beauval Ségur, "Histoire de Saint-Domingue," *Boletín del Archivo General de la Nación (República Dominicana)* 44–45, no. 2 (1946): 25. The author was here describing the good fortune of Governor Rochelard's timing as successor to Sorel. The original of this document is in the Bibliothèque nationale, Paris. For the dating of the manuscript, see Stewart L. Mims, *Colbert's West India Policy* (New Haven, CT: Yale University Press, 1912), 356.

83. Cf. Tramond, *Les troubles de Saint-Domingue en 1722–1724*, 561.

84. Stein, *The French Slave Trade*, 19; Haudrère, *Les Français dans l'océan Indien*, 232–35.

85. Stein, *The French Slave Trade*, 21. By comparison, the South Sea and Royal African companies retained a much larger influence in the organization of the British slave trade, supplying 64,399 enslaved persons to Spanish America over the period from 1712 (when the RAC monopoly was formally revoked) to 1739. Zahedieh, "Monopoly and Free Trade," 660.

86. Dumont de Montigny, *Regards sur le monde atlantique, 1715–1747* (Sillery, Québec: Septentrion, 2008), 257; Hall, *Africans in Colonial Louisiana*, 86; John A. Green, "Governor Perier's Expedition against the Natchez Indians," *Louisiana Historical Quarterly* 19, no. 3 (July 1936): 559; Bienville to the Ministre de la marine, Jan. 28, 1733, ANOM, C13A/16, fols. 223–24. See also Arnaud Balvay, *La révolte des Natchez* (Paris: Félin, 2008); and Greenwald, *Marc-Antoine Caillot*

and the Company of the Indies, 139–52. One early-twentieth-century source contends that the Natchez chiefs were not in fact held as slaves in Saint-Domingue. Instead, says Maurice Besson, they were returned to Louisiana after three months and sold into slavery there when the French government refused to reimburse the Indies Company for the costs of the Indians' maintenance in Saint-Domingue. That account is inconsistent with the sources cited above. See Maurice Besson, *Vieux papiers du temps des Isles* (Paris: Société d'éditions géographiques, maritimes et coloniales, 1925), 24.

87. Stein, *The French Slave Trade*, 19.

88. Harms, *The Diligent*, 60.

89. Stein, *The French Slave Trade*, 19; Harms, *The Diligent*, 61.

5. The Company of Jesus

1. Tramond, *Les troubles de Saint-Domingue en 1722–1724*, 557; Le Pers, "Mémoires pour l'histoire de l'île de St-Domingue," fol. 356r.

2. The key surveys of Jesuit missionaries in Haiti are George Breathett, "The Jesuits in Colonial Haiti," *Historian* 24, no. 2 (February 1, 1962): 153–71; and François Kawas, *Sources documentaires de l'histoire des jésuites en Haïti aux XVIIIe et XXe siècles: 1704–1763, 1953–1964* (Paris: L'Harmattan, 2006). See also Benjamin E. Heidgerken, "The Jesuits' Complicated Past in Haiti: From Owning Plantations to Serving the Black Community," *America: The Jesuit Review*, June 17, 2022.

3. The original Italian phrase was "una compagnia di Jesu," which was then latinized as the *Societas jesu* in 1540, with the papal bull of Pope Paul III that created the society. John W. O'Malley, *The Jesuits: A History from Ignatius to the Present* (Lanham, MD: Rowman & Little-field, 2014), 2.

4. For the details in this and the preceding paragraph, see Roy, "Essai sur Charlevoix," 32–43, 47, 54–55. Charlevoix's sources are acknowledged in the book's extended title: *Histoire de l'Isle espagnole, écrite particulièrement sur des Mémoires Manuscrits du P. Jean-Baptiste le Pers, Jésuite, Missionnaire à Saint Domingue, & sur les Pièces Originales, qui se conservent au Dépôt de la Marine.*

5. Charlevoix, *Histoire de l'Isle espagnole ou de St. Domingue*, 2:vii.

6. Jean-Baptiste Le Pers, "Memoires pour l'histoire de l'isle de St. Domingue," [1726–1727], BnF, Département des manuscrits, Fr. 8990–8992. For a careful comparison of the three manuscripts, see Jacques Dampierre, *Essai sur les sources de l'histoire des Antilles françaises (1492–1664)* (Paris: A. Picard, 1904), 159–65. The French Jesuit Archives in Vanves conserve another, more ethnographic manuscript by Le Pers entitled "Le Portrait ou Miroir de Saint-Domingue" that is discussed in Jacques de Cauna, "En Haïti il y a trois siècles : les observations morales et prédictions d'un Jésuite (un manuscrit inédit du père Le Pers)," in *Actes du Congrès national des sociétés historiques et scientifiques* 130, no. 13 (2011): 204–220.

7. Le Pers, "Mémoires pour l'histoire de l'isle de St. Domingue," Fr. 8990, fols. 346, 349r.

8. Le Pers, "Mémoires pour l'histoire de l'isle de St. Domingue," Fr. 8990, fol. 451.

9. Charlevoix, *Histoire de l'Isle espagnole ou de St. Domingue*, 2:451–52.

10. 2 Thessalonians 7–12 (RSV-CE2).

11. Charlevoix, *Histoire de l'Isle espagnole ou de St. Domingue*, 2:467.

12. Tramond, *Les troubles de Saint-Domingue en 1722–1724*, 557–58.

13. William V. Bangert, S. J., *A History of the Society of Jesus*, rev. ed. (St. Louis, MO: Institute of Jesuit Sources, 1972), 204–8, 301–3; Keith Michael Baker, *Inventing the French Revolution: Essays on French Political Culture in the Eighteenth Century* (Cambridge: Cambridge University Press, 1990), 59–60.

14. A constitution is a binding papal ordinance, here issued in the form of a bull or official proclamation of the pope.

15. Mita Choudhury, *The Wanton Jesuit and the Wayward Saint: A Tale of Sex, Religion, and Politics in Eighteenth-Century France* (University Park: Pennsylvania State University Press,

226   NOTES TO CHAPTER 5

2015), 113–14; Dale Van Kley, *The Jansenists and the Expulsion of the Jesuits from France, 1757–1765* (New Haven, CT: Yale University Press, 1975), 22–23. See also Van Kley's work on the international campaign to suppress the Jesuits: *Reform Catholicism and the International Suppression of the Jesuits in Enlightenment Europe* (New Haven, CT: Yale University Press, 2018). Ulrich L. Lehner compares Jansenist and Jesuit theologies in *The Catholic Enlightenment: The Forgotten History of a Global Movement* (New York: Oxford University Press, 2016), 20.

16. Charlevoix, *Histoire de l'Isle espagnole ou de St. Domingue*, 468; "Lettre du Père Margat, Missionnaire de la Compagnie de Jésus, au Procureur Général des Missions de la même Compagnie aux Îles de l'Amérique," [July 20, 1743], in *Lettres édifiantes*, 7:221; Dampierre, *Essai sur les sources de l'histoire des Antilles françaises*, 166–67.

17. Dampierre, *Essai sur les sources de l'histoire des Antilles françaises*, 166–67; Le Pers, "Mémoires pour l'histoire de l'isle de St. Domingue," Fr. 8992, fol. 1v; J. M. Jan, *Les congrégations religieuses à Saint-Domingue, 1681–1793* (Port-au-Prince: H. Deschamps, 1951), 97–100. See also Kawas, *Sources documentaires de l'histoire des jésuites en Haïti*, 41. The *Journal de Trevoux* published a prospectus of Margat's forthcoming work in June 1730, but the actual book never appeared. Margat's remarkable ministry in Saint-Domingue is described in Breathett, "The Jesuits In Colonial Haiti," 161–64.

18. Charlevoix, *Histoire de l'Isle espagnole ou de St. Domingue*, 400–1.

19. For comparison's sake, the next largest parcel was the garden of the Brothers of Charity (denoted by the number "10"), another Catholic religious order, closer to the northern end of town.

20. On the sanctuary tradition, see Karl Shoemaker, *Sanctuary and Crime in the Middle Ages, 400–1500* (New York: Fordham University Press, 2011). Sanctuary's importance had begun to fade in metropolitan Europe by the early modern period, but it remained influential in Catholic colonies overseas under the influence of the powerful baroque church in the seventeenth century. Cf. Michelle McKinley, "Standing on Shaky Ground: Criminal Jurisdiction and Ecclesiastical Immunity in Seventeenth-Century Lima, 1600–1700," *UC Irvine Law Review* 4 (2014): 145–46.

21. Le Pers, "Mémoires pour l'histoire de l'isle de St. Domingue," Fr. 8990, fol. 346v.

22. Jan, *Les congrégations religieuses à Saint-Domingue*, 66. As Jan explains in the preface to his book, this volume brings together materials discovered by Père Cabon in the course of his archival searches in France.

23. "Liste des habitants de St. Domingue qui ont paru avoir le plus de part aux mouvements séditieux contre la Compagnie des indes," March 26, 1723, ANOM, C9A/21, fol. 65r.

24. Michel, "Au sujet de la révolte de St. Domingue." The BnF houses another, identical version of the poem as Ms. 13658. See also the online version of the song in a collection of "Satirical Poems of the Eighteenth Century" put together by the Institut Claude Longeon at the Université Jean Monnet in Saint-Etienne, France, https://satires18.univ-st-etienne.fr/texte/r%C3%A9volte-de -saint-domingue/au-sujet-de-la-r%C3%A9volte-de-saint-domingue#footnote3_nhpiasa. Andouillard may have been a Carmelite friar serving in Saint-Domingue. See the possible reference to him in a later collection of eighteenth-century songs: *La Lyre gaillarde, ou, Nouveau recueil d'amusemens* ([N.p.]: [n.p.], 1776), 8.

25. Michel, "Au sujet de la révolte de St. Domingue," fol. 242. Michel also provides a gloss that appears next to the opening lines about Jean of Arc, but his reference appears to bear no direct connection to the text: "Madame Sorel, wife of the governor general, called in this island the Queen of Saint-Domingue. This lady vexed the inhabitants."

26. Michel, "Au sujet de la révolte de St. Domingue," fol. 242v.

27. John 3:1–21, 19:39–40.

28. Michel, "Au sujet de la révolte de St. Domingue," fols. 242v-243r.

29. Michel, "Au sujet de la révolte de St. Domingue," fol. 243v. Michel would himself perish sometime before 1725 of an illness incurred during the rainy season while traversing the colony's

NOTES TO CHAPTER 5   227

rivers, mountains, and forests en route to the parishes surrounding Le Cap. "Lettre du Père Margat, Missionnaire de la Compagnie de Jesus, au Père *** de la même Compagnie," February 27, 1725, in *Lettres édifiantes*, 7:124. Margat's letter is addressed from a parish church in the *quartier* of Petite Anse.

30. L'Héritier de Villandon, "L'Amazone française: Histoire ancienne," in *Les caprices du destin*, 230; Davis, *Society and Culture in Early Modern France*, 133. The gender "substitution" motif is discussed in Nicole Dufournaud, "Femmes en armes au XVI siècle," in *Penser la violence des femmes*, eds. Coline Cardi and Geneviève Pruvost (Paris: La Découverte, 2012), 83. For the casting of Joan of Arc's life as an Amazon story after her death, see Warner, *Joan of Arc*, 198–217. See also Wright, "The Amazons in Elizabethan Literature," 433–56.

31. [Antoine-Denis] Raudot, "Révolte de St. Domingue," 1723, ANOM, F/3/169, fol. 143 left.

32. "Relation de ce qui c'est passé à Saint-Domingue," 1723, ANOM, F/3/169, fol. 148 left.

33. "Relation de ce qui c'est passé à Saint-Domingue," 1723, ANOM, F/3/169, fol. 148 left; Charlevoix, *Histoire de l'Isle espagnole ou de St. Domingue*, 45–426.

34. "Relation de ce qui c'est passé à Saint-Domingue," 1723, fol. 148 left.

35. Frostin, *Les révoltes blanches à Saint-Domingue*, 157. Frostin also points to the prominent role of Charpentier in the Artibonite valley.

36. Code Noir (1685), arts. 3 and 5.

37. "Relation de ce qui c'est passé à Saint-Domingue," 1723, fol. 148 left.

38. Bangert, *A History of the Society of Jesus*, 21–22; O'Malley, *The Jesuits*, 3; Diarmaid MacCulloch, *The Reformation* (New York: Viking, 2004), 222–24; Luke Clossey, *Salvation and Globalization in the Early Jesuit Missions* (New York: Cambridge University Press, 2008), 22–23.

39. "Lettres-Patentes contenant les Privilèges accordés aux Pères de la Compagnie de Jésus," July 1651, in Moreau, *Loix et constitutions*, 2:71.

40. Markus Friedrich, *The Jesuits: A History*, trans. John Noël Dillon (Princeton, NJ: Princeton University Press, 2022), 468; Kawas, *Sources documentaires de l'histoire des jésuites en Haïti*, 28n13, 29; Breathett, "The Jesuits in Colonial Haiti," 155–56; "Lettres-Patentes contenant les Privilèges accordés aux Pères de la Compagnie de Jésus, dans l'une et l'autre Amérique Septentrionale et Méridionale," July 1651 and March 11, 1658, in Moreau, *Loix et constitutions*, 2:71; "Lettres-Patentes, portante Établissement des Religieux de la Compagnie de Jésus dans l'Ile Saint-Domingue," October 1704, in Moreau, *Loix et constitutions*, 2:18–20.

41. Jonathan Spence, *The Memory Palace of Matteo Ricci* (New York: Viking, 1984), 176; Breathett, "The Jesuits in Colonial Haiti," 153, 157, 165. Breathett's somewhat dated article likens the Jesuits' treatment of their domestic slaves to the status of a "free Negro" in Saint-Domingue at this time (165).

42. "Lettres-Patentes," October 1704, in Moreau, *Loix et constitutions*, 2:19.

43. Friedrich, *The Jesuits*, 484; Breathett, "The Jesuits in Colonial Haiti," 154, 156–57, 166.

44. Moreau de Saint-Méry, *Description de la partie française de l'isle Saint-Domingue*, 2:157, cited in Breathett, "The Jesuits of Colonial Haiti," 167. Breathett misreads Moreau to mean that the Jesuits owned five (rather than one of five) plantations in the Terrier-Rouge region.

45. Jean Fouchard, *Les marrons de la liberté* (Port-au-Prince: H. Deschamps, 1988), 229, 237. The evidence here is drawn from fugitive slave ads published in Saint-Domingue newspapers during the second half of the eighteenth century. Since no Jesuits could have been legally present as members of the society in Saint-Domingue after 1763, this practice almost certainly began at some point during the first half of the eighteenth century. On Jesuit slaveholding elsewhere in the Americas, see Thomas Murphy, *Jesuit Slaveholding in Maryland, 1717–1838* (New York: Routledge, 2001); Craig Steven Wilder, "War and Priests: Catholic Colleges and Slavery in the Age of Revolution," in *Slavery's Capitalism: A New History of American Economic Development*, eds. Sven Beckert and Seth Rockman (Philadelphia: University of Pennsylvania Press, 2016), 232–33; John Tutino, "Capitalism, Christianity, and Slavery: Jesuits in New Spain,

1572–1767," *Journal of Jesuit Studies* 8, no. 1 (2020): 20–25; Jean-Pierre Tardieu, "Los esclavos de los jesuitas del Perú en la época de la expulsión (1767)," *C.M.H.L.B. Caravelle*, no. 81 (2003): 68; C. R. Boxer, *Race Relations in the Portuguese Colonial Empire, 1415–1825* (Oxford: Clarendon Press, 1963), 9; Carlos Alberto de Moura Ribero, *Ligne de foi: la Compagnie de Jésus et l'esclavage dans le processus de formation de la société coloniale en Amérique portugaise, XVIe-XVIIe siècles* (Paris: Honoré Champion, 2009).

46. Cauna, "Patrimoine et mémoire de l'esclavage en Haïti," 38.

47. Breathett, "The Jesuits in Colonial Haiti," 166; "Lettres-Patentes contenant les Privilèges accordés aux Pères de la Compagnie de Jésus," July 1651, in Moreau, *Loix et constitutions*, 2:73.

48. "Réponse [de Chateaumorant et Mithon] au mémoire presenté au Conseil de Marine par les R. P. Jésuites pour le maintien de leurs privileges par eux pretendus dans la colonie de St. Domingue en vertu de leurs lettres patentes et autres titres par eux produits," February 29, 1719, ANOM, C9B/7 [without folio or page numbers]; "Lettres-Patentes contenant les Privilèges accordés aux Pères de la Compagnie de Jésus," July 1651, in Moreau, *Loix et constitutions*, 2:71.

49. "Réponse [de Chateaumorant et Mithon]," February 29, 1719.

50. "Réponse [de Chateaumorant et Mithon]," February 29, 1719.

51. "Réponse [de Chateaumorant et Mithon]," February 29, 1719.

52. "Réponse [de Chateaumorant et Mithon]," February 29, 1719. Catholic missionaries occupied prime real estate in Basse Terre, the capital of Guadeloupe and a site of great military importance. They also took advantage of residential and tax exemptions that minimized their fiscal contributions to the common defense (while of course being unable, as men of the cloth, to contribute to the military effort itself). The result, according to Chateaumorant and Mithon, was that the British were able to capture Basse Terre and lay siege to the French castle and fort there for nearly a month. How, exactly, the limit on religious slaveholding was supposed to prevent the same from happening in Saint-Domingue or elsewhere was unclear.

53. "Réponse [de Chateaumorant et Mithon]," February 29, 1719.

54. "Lettres patentes en forme d'Édit concernant les privileges des ordres religieux établis dans l'île de St. Domingue," August 1721, ANOM, B/44/2, fol. 448r-449r; Instructions to Governor-General Blondel de Jouvancourt, January 4, 1723, AN, Marine G/46, fol. 98; Instructions to Champmeslin, September 7, 1723, AN, Marine G/51, fol. 83.

55. "Réponse [de Chateaumorant et Mithon]," February 29, 1719. On the stable intrinsic value of Spanish silver as compared to its fluctuating value in France during these years, see McCusker, *Money and Exchange in Europe and America*, 283.

56. On the difficulty of capturing Jesuit motives in economic or secular terms, cf. Clossey, *Salvation and Globalization in the Early Jesuit Missions*, 7. Joseph de Guibert, S. J., historicizes the Jesuit spirituality of finding God in all things in *The Jesuits: Their Spiritual Doctrine and Practice: A Historical Study*, trans. William J. Young, S.J. (Chicago: Institute of Jesuit Sources, 1964), 170. On the Jesuits' "worldly asceticism," see Eire, *Reformations*, 447.

57. Code Noir (1685), art. 2; "Lettres-Patentes," October 1704, in Moreau, *Loix et constitutions*, 2:19.

58. De Guibert, *The Jesuits*, 170, 175, 180–81.

59. Ibram Kendi, *Stamped from the Beginning: The Definitive History of Racist Ideas in America* (New York: Nation Books, 2016), 26; Friedrich, *The Jesuits*, 481; Sue Peabody, "'A Dangerous Zeal': Catholic Missions to Slaves in the French Antilles, 1635–1800," *French Historical Studies* 25, no. 1 (2002): 69; Richard Gray, "The Papacy and the Atlantic Slave Trade: Lourenço da Silva, the Capuchins and the Decisions of the Holy Office," *Past & Present* 115, no. 1 (1987): 52, 58–61; Roberto Hofmeister Pich, "Alonso de Sandoval S.J. (1576/1577–1652) and the Ideology of Black Slavery: Some Theological and Philosophical Arguments," *Patristica et Mediaevalia* 36 (2015): 51–74. The *Spiritual Exercises* is the basic text of Jesuit spirituality, first published with

NOTES TO CHAPTER 5   229

papal approval in 1548, and which Ignatius began as a collection of notes in the context of conducting retreats for his earliest followers in Paris in the early 1530s. O'Malley, *The Jesuits*, 8–10.

60. Philippians 2:6–7 (RSV-CE2, which indicates either "servant" or "slave" can be used in this passage); "Lettre du Père Margat, Missionnaire de la Compagnie de Jésus, au Père *** de la même Compagnie," February 27, 1725, in *Lettres édifiantes*, 7:109. For the Jesuit facility at inventing new forms of ministry, see Eire, *Reformations*, 442.

61. Kawas, *Sources documentaires de l'histoire des jésuites en Haïti*, 36–37.

62. Code Noir (1685), art. 2; Friedrich, *The Jesuits*, 482–83, 487.

63. Charles Frostin, "Méthodologie missionnaire et sentiment religieux en Amérique françaises aux XVIIe et XVIIIe siècles: Le cas de Saint-Domingue," *Cahiers d'histoire* 24, no. 1 (1979): 20–23; Joseph Janin, *La religion aux colonies françaises sous l'Ancien régime: de 1626 à la Révolution* (Paris: Auteuil, 1942), 133–34; Friedrich, *The Jesuits*, 477–78.

64. The evidence for this discussion of Boutin comes primarily in the form of four letters that Père Margat wrote between 1725 and 1743. All four were published in 1781 in the seventh volume of an epistolary collection titled *Lettres édifiantes et curieuses, écrites des missions étrangères*—the eighteenth-century Caribbean version of the seventeenth-century Jesuit *Relations* from North America. The first of Margat's letters (1725) was a sobering account of the rigors of the Saint-Domingue mission for one of his fellow Jesuits who had been assigned to join it. The second and third, 1730 and 1729, respectively, were written as reports to the *Procureur Général* of the Jesuit missions in the Americas. A fourth letter, also to the *Procureur Général*, is undated in the edition I have consulted but has been attributed to July 20, 1743. See Marie-Christine Hazaël-Massieux, *Textes anciens en créole français de la Caraïbe: Histoire et analyse* (Paris: Publibook, 2008), 55. All four letters are first-person narratives based on Margat's service in Saint-Domingue from 1718 or 1719 until 1747. The retrospective nature of the later letters can be corroborated by the manuscripts of Le Pers, which date entirely from the period of the early 1720s or before.

65. "Lettre du Père Margat, Missionnaire de la Compagnie de Jésus, au Procureur Général des Missions de la même Compagnie aux Îles de l'Amérique," [July 20, 1743], in *Lettres édifiantes*, 7:195, 234.

66. "Lettre du Père Margat" [1743], 205–6; Gabriel Debien, *Les esclaves aux Antilles françaises, XVIIe–XVIIIe siècles* (Basse-Terre: Société d'histoire de la Guadeloupe, 1974), 283.

67. "Lettre du Père Margat" [1743], 239; Kawas, *Sources documentaires de l'histoire des jésuites en Haïti*, 47; Breathett, "The Jesuits in Colonial Haiti," 166–67; Jan, *Les congrégations religieuses à Saint-Domingue*, 60–63, 65.

68. "Lettre du Père Margat" [1743], 239–40; Jan, *Les congrégations religieuses à Saint-Domingue*, 62.

69. Janin, *La Réligion aux colonies françaises sous l'Ancien régime*, 81; Debien, *Les esclaves aux Antilles françaises*, 284.

70. Code Noir, arts. 11–12 (1685); Breathett, "The Jesuits in Colonial Haiti," 163; "Lettre du Père Margat," February 27, 1725, 111–112.

71. "Lettre du Père Margat," February 27, 1725, 124, 127–129; Janin, *La Réligion aux colonies françaises sous l'Ancien régime*, 134. In describing the penuries of priestly service in Saint-Domingue, Margat (at 124) evokes the names of his predecessors who died in the job: Père de Baste, Père Lexi, Père Allain, and Père Michel.

72. "Lettre du Père Margat," February 27, 1725, 110–13.

73. Le Pers quoted in Breathett, "The Jesuits in Colonial Haiti," 162–63; "Lettre du Margat" [1743], in *Lettres édifiantes*, 7:240. French Dominican missionaries attempted to learn the rudiments of west African languages in the seventeenth century. See Peabody, "'A Dangerous Zeal,'" 61.

74. [Pierre-Louis Boutin], "La Passion de Notre Seigneur selon St. Jean en langage nègre," [1730s], manuscript in the private collection of François Moureau (Paris); Hazaël-Massieux,

Textes anciens en créole français, 55–59. French Catholic missionaries in the eastern Caribbean began using a form of creolized French for instructional purposes in the 1650s and 1660s. Peabody, "'A Dangerous Zeal,'" 60–61. Without a sustained example of what that language looked or sounded like, it is difficult to know to what extent Boutin's Kreyòl was an advance over the earlier forms. The brief examples quoted by Peabody suggest Boutin had moved beyond, even if he did not completely break with, the creolized French of the seventeenth century.

75. Gabriel Debien, "Une maison d'éducation à Saint-Domingue: 'Les religieuses du Cap,'" 1731–1802 (1er article)," *Revue d'histoire de l'Amérique française* 2, no. 4 (1949): 559. Jacques de Cauna argues for Le Pers's relative emphasis on the humanity of the enslaved in "En Haïti il y a trois siècles," 214.

76. Boutin's role in the scheme with the widow Gimon is described in Jan, *Les congrégations religieuses à Saint-Domingue*, 64–65; and Debien, "Une maison d'éducation à Saint-Domingue," 560–64. For the conseil rulings against Boutin in 1721, see "Arrêt du Conseil du Cap, qui déclare nulles les donations faites," September 1, 1721; and "Arrêt du Conseil du Cap, portant que le Supérieur des Missions n'est pas responsable des faits de ses Religieux," September 2, 1721; in Moreau, *Loix et constitutions*, 2: 772–73 (cited in Peabody, "'A Dangerous Zeal,'" 79n71). For the 1737 burial controversy, see "Extrait de la Lettre du Ministre aux Administrateurs, sur l'inhumation solomnelle d'une Négresse pendue," in Moreau, *Loix et constitutions*, 3:485 (cited in Peabody, "'A Dangerous Zeal,'" 78–79).

6. Maroons and the Military-Planter State

1. Michel-Rolph Trouillot, *Silencing the Past: Power and the Production of History* (Boston: Beacon Press, 1995), 37–40.

2. Simona Cerutti, "Who Is Below? E. P. Thompson, historien des sociétés modernes: une relecture," *Annales: Histoire, Sciences Sociales* 70, no. 4 (February 2016): 943, 950, 952. In thinking about marronage in Saint-Domingue in relationship to the violence of colonial planter society, I am also indebted to two remarkable recent studies: Brown, *Tacky's Revolt*; and Rushforth, "The Gaulet Uprising of 1710."

3. "Lettre du Père Margat, Missionnaire de la Compagnie de Jésus, au Père de la Neuville, de la même Compagnie, Procureur des Missions de l'Amérique," February 2, 1729, in *Lettres édifiantes et curieuses*, 7:150–51. For a discussion of the zoological prism through which maroons (and the enslaved) were viewed, see Dénétam Touam Bona, "Les métamorphoses du marronnage," *Lignes* 1, no. 16 (2015): 37–38.

4. "Lettre du Père Margat," February 2, 1729, in *Lettres édifiantes et curieuses*, 7:150–51.

5. "Lettre du Père Margat," February 2, 1729, in *Lettres édifiantes et curieuses*, 7:149–50. With some justice, George Breathett concludes that "a further objective of the Jesuits was conversion of the *Marons*." But the evidence he cites for this assertion is drawn from the wrong source: Margat's 1743 letter, which provides no support for any such claim. Breathett, "The Jesuits in Colonial Haiti," 164.

6. James E. Kelly, "Panic, Plots, and Polemic: The Jesuits and the Early Modern English Mission," *Journal of Jesuit Studies* 1, no. 4 (2014): 515, 517; Dale Van Kley, "Plots and Rumors of Plots: The Role of Conspiracy in the International Campaign against the Society of Jesus, 1758–1768," in *The Jesuit Suppression in Global Context: Causes, Events, and Consequences*, eds. Jeffrey D. Burson and Jonathan Wright (New York: Cambridge University Press, 2015), 13–39.

7. Janin, *La religion aux colonies françaises sous l'Ancien régime*, 128, which relies on Jules Ballet, *La Guadeloupe: Renseignements sur l'histoire, la flore, la faune, la géologie, la minéralogie, l'agriculture, le commerce, l'industrie, la législation, l'administration*, 3 vols. (Basse-Terre, Guadeloupe: Imprimerie du gouvernement, 1896), 2:115; Peabody, "'A Dangerous Zeal,'" 78.

8. Crystal Eddins, *Rituals, Runaways, and the Haitian Revolution: Collective Action in the African Diaspora* (New York: Cambridge University Press, 2022), 211; Saint-Louis, *Mer et liberté*, 52–53.

NOTES TO CHAPTER 6   231

9. Charlevoix, *Histoire de l'Isle espagnole ou de St. Domingue*, 1:122–24; Saint-Victor Jean-Baptiste, *Haïti: Sa lutte pour l'émancipation: Deux concepts d'indépendance à Saint-Domingue* (Paris: La Nef de Paris, 1957), 42–44.

10. Eddins, *Rituals, Runaways, and the Haitian Revolution*, 210-11.

11. Eddins, *Rituals, Runaways, and the Haitian Revolution*, 210–12; François Blancpain, *Haïti et la République dominicaine: une question de frontières* (Matory, Guyane: Ibis rouge, 2008); Yvan Debbasch, "Le Marronage: Essai sur la désertion de l'esclave antillais," *L'Année sociologique* 12 (1961): 72–73.

12. Debbasch, "Le Marronage," *L'Année sociologique* 12 (1961): 73–75; Saint-Louis, *Mer et liberté*, 53.

13. Cf. S. Max Edelson, *The New Map of Empire: How Britain Imagined America before Independence* (Cambridge, MA: Harvard University Press, 2017), 4–7.

14. Debbasch, "Le Marronage," *L'Année sociologique* 12 (1961): 53–54, 75; Eddins, *Rituals, Runaways, and the Haitian Revolution*, 208; Hector and Moïse, *Colonisation et esclavage en Haïti*, 87.

15. Debbasch, "Le Marronage," *L'Année sociologique* 12 (1961): 74n2 (quoting the 1717 statement); Eddins, *Rituals, Runaways, and the Haitian Revolution*, 211–12.

16. Eddins, *Rituals, Runaways, and the Haitian Revolution*, 211–12; Conseil de Marine to Minister of Foreign Affairs Cardinal Dubois, May 27, 1722, AN, G/46, fol. 94. The revolutionary-era legacies of these border conflicts are brilliantly captured in Graham Nessler, *An Islandwide Struggle for Freedom: Revolution, Emancipation, and Reenslavement in Hispaniola, 1789–1809* (Chapel Hill: University of North Carolina Press, 2016).

17. Eddins, *Rituals, Runaways, and the Haitian Revolution*, 210, 232.

18. Eddins, *Rituals, Runaways, and the Haitian Revolution*, 210.

19. Franklin Midy, "Marrons de la liberté, révoltés de la libération: Le Marron inconnu revisité," in *Genèse de l'État haïtien (1804–1859)*, eds. Michel Hector and Laënnec Hurbon (Paris: Éditions de la Maison des sciences de l'homme, 2018), 127–8.

20. Midy, "Marrons de la liberté," 127-30, 132; Hector and Moïse, *Colonisation et esclavage en Haïti*, 87.

21. Baptiste Bonnefoy, *Au-delà de la couleur: Miliciens noirs et mulâtres de la Caraïbe (XVIIe-XVIII- siècles)* (Rennes, France: Presses Universitaires de Rennes, 2022), 56–58. The era of strict segregation of militia companies in Saint-Domingue would arrive in the 1760s. See Garrigus, *Before Haiti*.

22. "Arrêt de Réglement du Conseil de Léogâne qui établit 36 hommes dans chacun des Quartiers désignés pour chasser les Nègres Marrons," March 16, 1705, in Moreau, *Loix et constitutions*, 2:25.

23. "Arrêt de Réglement du Conseil de Léogâne," March 16, 1705, in Moreau, *Loix et constitutions*, 2:26–27. See also Moreau's account in the *Description de la partie française de l'isle Saint-Domingue*, 1:448–49.

24. "Arrêt du Conseil du Cap, qui, sans tirer à consequence, renvoie absous un Nègre pris en marronage," May 8, 1714, in Moreau, *Loix et constitutions*, 2:422. On the incentive that per capita slave taxes gave planters to undercount their slave populations for purposes of the colonial census later in the eighteenth century, see Ghachem, *The Old Regime and the Haitian Revolution*, 36n14.

25. "Tarif par M. le Général, et Réglement du Conseil du Cap, touchant les droits du Prévôt de Maréchaussée," April 13 and December 5, 1718, in Moreau, *Loix et constitutions*, 2:611.

26. "Ordonnance des Administrateurs touchant une Chasse des Nègres Marons étant à la Béate," October 25, 1715, in Moreau, *Loix et constitutions*, 2:474; "Extrait de la lettre du Conseil de Marine à Chateaumorant, touchant une chasse des nègres à la Béate," October 20, 1717, in Moreau, *Loix et constitutions*, 2:601.

27. Cabon, *Histoire d'Haïti*, 1:111; Midy, "Marrons de la liberté," 132; Hector and Moïse, *Colonisation et esclavage en Haïti*, 87; Jean Fouchard, *Les marrons du syllabaire: Quelques aspects du*

232 NOTES TO CHAPTER 6

problème de l'instruction et de l'éducation des esclaves et affranchis de Saint-Domingue (Port-au-Prince: Henri Deschamps, 1988), 32–33.

28. Cassá, *Rebelión de los capitanes*, 266–68; Margarita Gascón, "The Military of Santo Domingo, 1720–1764," *Hispanic American Historical Review* 73, no. 3 (1993): 437.

29. "Ordonnance des Administrateurs, qui defend les assemblées d'esclaves," January 11, 1720, in Moreau, *Loix et constitutions*, 2:660–61. The surging numbers (and perceived menace) of maroons are described in Hector et Moise, *Colonisation et esclavage en Haïti*, 87; Frostin, *Les révoltes blanches*, 156; and Eddins, *Rituals, Runaways, and the Haitian Revolution*, 252.

30. Julien Gomez Pardo, *La Maréchaussée et le crime en Île de France sous Louis XIV et Louis XV* (Paris: Les Indes Savantes, 2012), 17, 21, 47. See also Stewart R. King, "The Maréchaussée of Saint-Domingue: Balancing the Ancien Regime and Modernity," *Journal of Colonialism and Colonial History* 5, no. 2 (Fall 2004).

31. "Ordonnance des Administrateurs, pour l'établissement d'une Maréchaussée," March 27, 1721, in Moreau, *Loix et constitutions*, 2:726.

32. "Ordonnance des Administrateurs, pour l'établissement d'une Maréchaussée," March 27, 1721, in Moreau, *Loix et constitutions*, 2:726–27.

33. "Ordonnance des Administrateurs, pour l'établissement d'une Maréchaussée," March 27, 1721, in Moreau, *Loix et constitutions*, 2:728.

34. "Ordonnance des Administrateurs, pour l'établissement d'une Maréchaussée," March 27, 1721, in Moreau, *Loix et constitutions*, 2:728–29, 732; Cabon, *Histoire d'Haïti*, 1:111–12.

35. "Ordonnance des Administrateurs," March 27, 1721, in Moreau, *Loix et constitutions*, 2:730.

36. "Mémoire des Administrateurs au Conseil Supérieur du Cap . . . touchant la Maréchaussée," July 7, 1721, in Moreau, *Loix et constitutions*, 2:750–58.

37. "Mémoire des Administrateurs au Conseil Supérieur du Cap . . . touchant la Maréchaussée," July 7, 1721, in Moreau, *Loix et constitutions*, 2:752–53.

38. "Mémoire des Administrateurs au Conseil Supérieur du Cap . . . touchant la Maréchaussée," July 7, 1721, in Moreau, *Loix et constitutions*, 2:753–54.

39. "Mémoire des Administrateurs au Conseil Supérieur du Cap . . . touchant la Maréchaussée," July 7, 1721, in Moreau, *Loix et constitutions*, 2:755–56.

40. "Mémoire des Administrateurs au Conseil Supérieur du Cap . . . touchant la Maréchaussée," July 7, 1721, in Moreau, *Loix et constitutions*, 2:758.

41. "Ordonnance des Administrateurs, touchant le paiement de droits de Maréchaussée," October 10, 1721, in Moreau, *Loix et constitutions*, 2:788.

42. "Ordonnance des Administrateurs, concernant la maréchaussée, et qui lui enjoint notamment de porter des bandoulières," October 10, 1721, in Moreau, *Loix et constitutions*, 2:785–87.

43. "Arrêt du Conseil du Cap, . . . condamne deux Nègres à être pendus, comme chefs d'une révolte," September 22, 1721, in Moreau, *Loix et constitutions*, 2:781–82. See also Eddins, *Rituals, Runaways, and the Haitian Revolution*, 251.

44. "Arrêt du Conseil du Cap, qui condamne, sans autre Prodédure, un Nègre, Chef de Bande, au dernier supplice," June 4, 1723, Moreau, *Loix et constitutions*, 3:48–49; Code Noir (1685), art. 38. See also Hector and Moïse, *Colonisation et esclavage en Haïti*, 87. John Garrigus analyzes the colonial refrain that enslaved resistance was animated by sorcery and magic in *A Secret among the Blacks*.

45. Petition of Léogâne and Cul-de-Sac planters to Montholon, May 20, 1723, F/3/169, fols. 219 right-220 left.

46. Médéric-Louis-Élie Moreau de Saint-Méry, *Description topographique et politique de la partie espagnole de l'isle Saint*-Domingue, 2 vols. (Paris: l'auteur, 1796), 2:175; Cabon, *Histoire d'Haïti*, 1:112; Eddins, *Rituals, Runaways, and the Haitian Revolution*, 232.

47. Petition of Jean Lejeune to Sorel and Montholon, October 29, 1723, in ANOM, F/3/169, fols. 272 right-273 right.

48. Petition of Jean Lejeune to Sorel and Montholon, October 29, 1723, in ANOM, F/3/169, fols. 273 right-274 left.

49. Petition of Jean Lejeune to Sorel and Montholon, October 29, 1723, in ANOM, F/3/169, fol. 274 left; Moreau de Saint-Méry, *Description de la partie espagnole de Saint-Domingue*, 2:175; Cabon, *Histoire d'Haïti*, 1:112; Eddins, *Rituals, Runaways, and the Haitian Revolution*, 232.

50. Petition of Jean Lejeune to Sorel and Montholon, October 29, 1723, in ANOM, F/3/169, fols. 274 left-274 right.

51. On the relationship between the captains' rebellion in Santo Domingo and illicit trade between the French and Spanish colonists of Hispaniola, see Cassá, *Rebelión de los capitanes*.

52. For an analysis of the impact of marronage on the Haitian Revolution and postrevolutionary Haitian society, see Gonzalez, *Maroon Nation*.

53. Bonnefoy, *Au-delà de la couleur*, 56. Bonnefoy ascribes the limitation of militia leadership roles to whites in Martinique to local anxieties over the availability of land and a hardening of social and legal restrictions against free people of color.

54. "Règlement fait par le Gouverneur du Cap pour la Compagnie des Nègres-Libres," April 29, 1724, in Moreau, *Loix et constitutions*, 3:96; "Lettre du Ministre à MM. de la Rochalard et Duclos, sur plusieurs objets d'humanité et de religion," September 30, 1727, in Moreau, *Loix et constitutions*, 3:221–22; King, "The Maréchaussée of Saint-Domingue," par. 3; Midy, "Marrons de la liberté," 132.

55. "Extrait de la lettre du Ministre à M. Deslandes, touchant la révolte des nègres de la Jamaïque," April 21, 1706, ANOM, COL B/28, fol. 142.

56. See Brown, *Tacky's Revolt*.

Conclusion

1. Europe's economies benefited from an influx of Brazilian gold and Spanish silver around the middle of the eighteenth century owing to technological changes in the mining industry. Eugene Weber, *Europe since 1715: A Modern History* (New York: W. W. Norton, 1972), 52.

2. Neufchâteau, *Mémoire en forme de discours sur la disette du numéraire a Saint-Domingue*.

3. Schnakenbourg, *L'économie de plantation aux Antilles françaises*, 43.

4. Schnakenbourg, *L'économie de plantation aux Antilles françaises*, 105; Cabon, *Histoire d'Haïti*, 1:125, 138–39.

5. See William H. Sewell, Jr., "Economic Crises and the Shape of Modern History," *Public Culture* 24, no. 2 (2012): 325 (observing that financial crises are occasions "to grasp the intertwined economic and political histories in which we are enmeshed"); Barbara Ehrenreich and Dedrick Muhammad, "The Recession's Racial Divide," *New York Times*, September 12, 2009; Gillian B. White, "The Recession's Racial Slant," *The Atlantic*, June 24, 2015; Keeanga-Yahmatta Taylor, *Race for Profit: How Banks and the Real Estate Industry Undermined Black Homeownership* (Chapel Hill: University of North Carolina Press, 2019); and Dirk Willem te Velde, "Africa 10 Years after the Global Financial Crisis: What We've Learned," ODI Insights, September 2018, https://odi.org/en/insights/africa-10-years-after-the-global-financial-crisis-what-weve-learned/.

6. Catherine Porter, Constant Méheut, Matt Apuzzo, and Selam Gebrekidan: "The Root of Haiti's Misery: Reparations to Enslavers"; "How a French Bank Captured Haiti"; "Invade Haiti, Wall Street Urged. The US Obliged."; "Demanding Reparations, and Ending up in Exile"; *New York Times*, May 20, 2022.

7. See Ada Ferrer, *Freedom's Mirror: Cuba and Haiti in the Age of Revolution* (New York: Cambridge University Press, 2014); and Julia Gaffield, *Haitian Connections in the Atlantic World: Recognition after Revolution* (Chapel Hill: University of North Carolina Press, 2015).

8. For more on this context, and on the 1825 indemnity generally, see the essays in *Haïti-France: Les chaînes de la dette: Le rapport Mackau (1825)*, eds. Marcel Dorigny et al. (Paris: Maisonneuve & Larose; Hémisphères, 2021). This volume includes an essay by Gusti-Klara Gaillard, one of the leading contemporary Haitian historians of the indemnity and its legacies.

9. Eugene White, "Making the French Pay: The Costs and Consequences of the Napoleonic Reparations," *European Review of Economic History* 5, no. 3 (2001): 337–65.

10. Ekaterina Pravilova, "Ruble's Wars" (paper presented at the European Association for Banking History "Financing Reconstruction" conference, Frankfurt, Germany, June 30, 2023). See also her recent book *The Ruble: A Political History* (New York: Oxford University Press, 2023), chaps. 3 and 9.

11. Alex Dupuy, presentation to the "Haiti: Reparations and Restitution" Symposium of the *Inter-American Law Review*, University of Miami School of Law, March 24, 2023.

12. The initial demand of 150 million francs was later renegotiated to 90 million francs, but Haiti ended up paying 112 million francs overall, or $560 million in today's terms.

13. Lazaro Gamio et al., "Haiti's Lost Billions," *New York Times*, May 20, 2022.

14. Code Noir (1685), arts. 38, 40, 44.

15. Declaration of the Rights of Man and the Citizen (1789), art. 17.

16. Trevor Jackson, *Impunity and Capitalism: The Afterlives of European Financial Crises, 1690–1830* (New York: Cambridge University Press, 2022), chap. 6; Marc Flandreau and Juan Flores, "Bonds and Brands: Foundations of Sovereign Debt Markets, 1820–1830," *Journal of Economic History* 69, no. 3 (2009): 646–84.

17. Cf. Jeremy Adelman, *Colonial Legacies: The Problem of Persistence in Latin American History* (New York: Routledge, 1999).

18. Gamio et al., "Haiti's Lost Billions."

19. See Peter Hudson, *Bankers and Empire: How Wall Street Colonized the Caribbean* (Chicago: University of Chicago Press, 2017).

20. See Catherine Porter, Constant Méheut, Matt Apuzzo, and Selam Gebrekidan, "How a French Bank Captured Haiti"; "Invade Haiti, Wall Street Urged. The US Obliged," *New York Times*, May 20, 2022.

21. See David McNally, *Blood and Money: War, Slavery, Finance, and Empire* (Chicago: Haymarket Books, 2020), chap. 5; and the excellent *Finance and History* podcast on "Exchange Rate History" with Alain Naef and Carmen Hoffmann, March 3, 2023, https://podcasts.apple.com/vn/podcast/exchange-rate-history/id1558032792?i=1000602631032.

22. Hicham Safieddine, *Banking on the State: The Financial Foundations of Lebanon* (Stanford, CA: Stanford University Press, 2019).

23. Fanny Pigeaud and Ndongo Samba Sylla, *Africa's Last Colonial Currency: The CFA Franc Story*, trans. Thomas Fazi (London: Pluto Press, 2021).

24. Paul, *La décote de la gourde face au dollar.*

25. Frantz Duval, "Le dollar, denrée rare," *Le Nouvelliste*, December 7, 2022, https://lenouvelliste.com/article/239376/le-dollar-denree-rare.

26. See McNally, *Blood and Money*, chap. 5. For accounts of the effect of dollarization on the contemporary developing world, see Asdrúbal Oliveros, "Dollarization Can't Save the Venezuelan Economy," *Americas Quarterly*, October 5, 2021; Russell W. Cooper and Hubert Kempf, "Dollarization and the Conquest of Hyperinflation in Divided Societies," *Federal Reserve Bank of Minneapolis Quarterly Review* 25, no. 3 (2001): 3–12; and Karl Russell, Joe Rennison, and Jason Karaian, "The Dollar Is Extremely Strong, Pushing Down the World," *New York Times*, July 16, 2022.

27. The shift from an early modern, Atlantic-wide dependence on Spanish silver and gold to the territorial and national currencies of the modern era is discussed in Eric Helleiner, *The Making of National Money: Territorial Currencies in Historical Perspective* (Ithaca, NY: Cornell University Press, 2003).

BIBLIOGRAPHY

Archival and Manuscript Sources

Archives départementales de la Charente-Maritime, Archives notariales, La Rochelle, France
3E/1803
3E/1816

Bibliotheque Nationale, Département des manuscrits, Anciens "Supplément Français," Paris, France
Fr. 8990–8992 (Jean-Baptiste Le Pers, "Mémoires pour l'histoire de l'isle de St-Domingue," [1726–27]).
Fr. 10475 ([Père] Michel, "Au sujet de la révolte de St. Domingue," [1723]).
Archives nationales d'outre-mer, Collection Moreau de Saint-Méry, Aix-en-Provence, France
COL A 6 and A 28. Secrétariat d'État à la Marine. Actes du pouvoir souverain (1628–1779).
COL B 28 and B 44. Secrétariat d'Etat à la Marine. Correspondance au départ avec les colonies.
C/2/196. Secrétariat d'Etat à la Marine. Correspondance à l'arrivée des colonies. Compagnies des Indes et Inde française.
C/9A/20-21, C/13A/16, and C9B/7. Secrétariat d'Etat à la Marine. Correspondance à l'arrivée des colonies. Saint-Domingue et Iles Sous-le-Vent.
F/2A/11. Documents divers. Compagnies de commerce (1626-1821). Folder titled "Compagnie de Saint- Domingue."
F/3/169. Historique de Saint-Domingue: lettres, mémoires, notes, originaux et copies. 1721–25.
Historic New Orleans Collection, New Orleans
Mss. 735 (Joseph Lambert, "Décision théologique sur les actions de la Compagnie des indes," July 1720).
National Archives, Kew, United Kingdom
SP 78/165/84. State Papers Foreign. France. 1577–1780.

Printed Primary Sources

Bourgeois, Nicolas-Louis, and Pierre-Jean-Baptiste Nougaret. *Voyages intéressants dans différentes colonies françaises, espagnoles, anglaises, etc.* London: J.-F. Bastien (Londres), 1788.
Charlevoix, Pierre-François-Xavier de. *Histoire de l'Isle espagnole ou de S. Domingue.* 2 vols. Paris: Jacques Guérin, 1730–31.
Code Noir. 1685.
Coke, Edward. *The Third Part of the Institutes of the Laws of England: Concerning High Treason, and other Pleas of the Crown, and Criminal Causes.* 4th ed. London, 1669.

236 BIBLIOGRAPHY

De Beauval Ségur. "Histoire de Saint-Domingue." *Boletín del Archivo General de la Nación (República Dominicana)* 44–45, no. 2 (1946): 4–52.

Declaration of the Rights of Man and the Citizen (1789).

Dernis, Germain. *Recueil ou collection des titres, édits, déclarations, arrêts, règlemens et autres pièces concernant la Compagnie des indes orientales.* Paris, 1755.

Du Fresne de Francheville, J. *Histoire de la Compagnie des Indes.* Paris: De Bure, 1746.

Dumont de Montigny. *Regards sur le monde atlantique, 1715–1747.* Sillery, Québec: Septentrion, 2008.

François de Neufchâteau, Nicolas Louis. *Mémoire en forme de discours sur la disette du numéraire à Saint-Domingue, et sur les moyens d'y remédier.* Metz: Claude Lamort, 1788.

Het groote tafereel der dwaasheid. [Amsterdam]: n.p., [1720]. Yale University, Beinecke Library.

Jollain, Francois-Gerard. "Le Commerce que les Indiens du Mexique font avec les François au Port de Mississipi." Bibliothèque nationale de France, Cabinet des estampes. Paris: F. Gérard Jollain, 1717.

La Lyre gaillarde, ou, Nouveau recueil d'amusemens. N.p.: n.p., 1776.

Law, John. *Money and Trade Considered, with a Proposal for Supplying the Nation with Money.* Edinburgh, 1705.

Lettres édifiantes et curieuses, écrites des missions étrangères, nouv. ed., *Mémoires d'Amérique.* Vol. 7. Paris: J.G. Merigot, 1781.

L'Héritier de Villandon, Marie-Jeanne. *Les caprices du destin, ou Recueil d'histoires singulières et amusantes arrivées de nos jours.* Paris: Pierre-Michel Huart, 1718.

Magna Carta. 1215.

Montesquieu, Charles Louis de Secondat, baron de. *Persian Letters.* Translated by C. J. Betts. New York: Penguin Books, 1973.

Moreau de Saint-Méry, Médéric-Louis-Élie. *Description topographique et politique de la partie espagnole de l'isle Saint-Domingue.* 2 vols. Paris: l'auteur, 1796.

———. *Description topographique, physique, civile, politique et historique de la partie française de l'isle Saint-Domingue.* 2 vols. Philadelphia: chez l'auteur, 1797–98.

———. *Loix et constitutions des colonies françaises de l'Amérique sous le vent.* 6 vols. Paris and Cap Français: chez l'auteur, 1784–90.

Moreau de Saint-Méry, Médéric Louis-Élie, Nicolas Ponce, and René Phelipeau. *Recueil de vues des lieux principaux de la colonie française de Saint-Domingue, gravées par les soins de M. Ponce.* Paris: chez l'auteur, 1791.

Neufchâteau, Nicolas Louis François de. *Mémoire en forme de discours sur la disette du numéraire à Saint-Domingue, et sur les moyens d'y remédier.* Metz, 1788.

Rainsford, Marcus. *An Historical Account of the Black Empire of Hayti.* Edited by Paul Youngquist and Grégory Pierrot. Durham: Duke University Press, 2013.

"A Scheme for a New East India Company." 1690.

Trenchard, John, and Thomas Gordon. *Cato's Letters, or Essays on Liberty, Civil and Religious, and Other Important Subjects.* Edited by Ronald Hamowy, 4 vols., in vol. 2. Online Library of Liberty. Indianapolis, IN: Liberty Fund, 1995.

Secondary Sources

Adelman, Jeremy. *Colonial Legacies: The Problem of Persistence in Latin American History.* New York: Routledge, 1999.

Adelman, Jeremy, and Jonathan Levy. "The Rise and Fall of Economic History." *The Chronicle of Higher Education,* December 1, 2014.

Armitage, David, and Sanjay Subrahmanyam, eds. *The Age of Revolutions in Global Context, c. 1760–1840.* New York: Palgrave Macmillan, 2010.

BIBLIOGRAPHY   237

Bailyn, Bernard. *The Ideological Origins of the American Revolution*. Cambridge, MA: Harvard University Press, 1992.

———. *The Origins of American Politics*. New York: Vintage Books, 1970.

Baker, Keith Michael. *Inventing the French Revolution: Essays on French Political Culture in the Eighteenth Century*. New York: Cambridge University Press, 1990.

Ballet, Jules. *La Guadeloupe: Renseignements sur l'histoire, la flore, la faune, la géologie, la minéralogie, l'agriculture, le commerce, l'industrie, la législation, l'administration*. Vol. 2 (1715–74). Basse-Terre, Guadeloupe: Imprimerie du gouvernement, 1896.

Balvay, Arnaud. *La révolte des Natchez*. Paris: Félin, 2008.

Bangert, William V., S. J. *A History of the Society of Jesus*. St. Louis: Institute of Jesuit Sources, 1972.

Banks, Kenneth J. "Official Duplicity: The Illicit Slave Trade of Martinique, 1713–1763." In *The Atlantic Economy during the Seventeenth and Eighteenth Centuries: Organization, Operation, Practice, and Personnel*, edited by Peter A. Coclanis, 229–51. Columbia: University of South Carolina Press, 2005.

Barry, Heather E. *A Dress Rehearsal for Revolution: John Trenchard and Thomas Gordon's Works in Eighteenth-Century British America*. Lanham, MD: University Press of America, 2007.

Barry, William J., S. J., and Robert G. Doherty, S. J.. *Contemplatives in Action: The Jesuit Way*. New York: Paulist Press, 2002.

Beckles, Hilary McD. "Servants and Slaves during the 17th-Century Sugar Revolution." In *The Caribbean: A History of the Region and Its Peoples*, edited by Stephan Palmié and Francisco A. Scarano, 205–15. Chicago: University of Chicago Press, 2011.

Beik, William. "Protest and Rebellion in Seventeenth-Century France." In *Crowd Actions in Britain and France from the Middle Ages to the Modern World*, edited by Michael T. Davis, 43–57. New York: Palgrave Macmillan, 2015.

———. *A Social and Cultural History of Early Modern France*. New York: Cambridge University Press, 2009.

———. *Urban Protest in Seventeenth-Century France: The Culture of Retribution*. New York: Cambridge University Press, 1997.

Benoît, Catherine. *Corps, jardins, mémoires: Anthropologie du corps et de l'espace à la Guadeloupe*. Paris: CNRS Editions, 2000.

Bercé, Yves-Marie. *Révoltes et révolutions dans l'Europe moderne: XVIe-XVIIIe siècles*. Paris: CNRS, 2013.

Besson, Maurice. *Vieux papiers du temps des Isles*. Paris: Société d'éditions géographiques, maritimes et coloniales, 1925.

Blackburn, Robin. *The Making of New World Slavery: From the Baroque to the Modern, 1492–1800*. 2nd ed. London: Verso, 2010.

Blancpain, François. *Haïti et la République dominicaine: une question de frontières*. Matoury, Guyane: Ibis Rouge Editions, 2008.

Bloch, Marc. *La société féodale*. 2 vols. Paris: Michel, 1939.

Bona, Dénétam Touam. "Les métamorphoses du marronnage." *Lignes* 1, no. 16 (2015): 36–48.

Bonnefoy, Baptiste. *Au-delà de la couleur: Miliciens noirs et mulâtres de la Caraïbe (XVIIe-XVIIIe siècles)*. Rennes: Presses Universitaires de Rennes, 2022.

Bosma, Ulbe. *The World of Sugar: How the Sweet Stuff Transformed Our Politics, Health, and Environment over 2,000 Years*. Cambridge, MA: Harvard University Press, 2023.

Bossenga, Gail. "Society." In *Old Regime France, 1648–1788*, edited by William Doyle. Oxford: Oxford University Press, 2001.

Boucher, Philip P. *France and the American Tropics to 1700: Tropics of Discontent?* Baltimore, MD: Johns Hopkins University Press, 2008.

238 BIBLIOGRAPHY

———. "The 'Frontier Era' of the French Caribbean, 1620–1690s." In *Negotiated Empires: Centers and Peripheries in the Americas, 1500–1820*, edited by Christine Daniels and Michael V. Kennedy, 207–34. New York: Routledge, 2002.

Bouton, Cynthia A. *The Flour War: Gender, Class, and Community in Late Ancien Régime French Society*. University Park: Pennsylvania State University Press, 1993.

Boxer, Charles Ralph. *Race Relations in the Portuguese Colonial Empire, 1415–1825*. Clarendon Press, 1963.

Breathett, George. "The Jesuits in Colonial Haiti." *Historian* 24, no. 2 (1962): 153–71.

Breay, Claire, and Julian Harrison, eds. *Magna Carta: Law, Liberty, and Legacy*. London: British Library, 2015.

Breen, T. H. *The Marketplace of Revolution: How Consumer Politics Shaped American Independence*. New York: Oxford University Press, 2004.

Brewer, John. *Sinews of Power: War, Power, and the English State, 1688–1783*. Cambridge, MA: Harvard University Press, 1988.

Brown, Christopher Leslie, and Philip D. Morgan, eds. *Arming Slaves from Classical Times to the Modern Age*. New Haven, CT: Yale University Press, 2006.

Brown, Vincent. *The Reaper's Garden: Death and Power in the World of Atlantic Slavery*. Cambridge, MA: Harvard University Press, 2008.

———. *Tacky's Revolt: The Story of an Atlantic Slave War*. Cambridge, MA: Harvard University Press, 2020.

Buchan, James. *John Law: A Scottish Adventurer of the Eighteenth Century*. London: MacLehose Press, 2018.

Burnard, Trevor G., and John D. Garrigus. *The Plantation Machine: Atlantic Capitalism in French Saint-Domingue and British Jamaica*. Philadelphia: University of Pennsylvania Press, 2016.

Cabon, Adolphe. *Histoire d'Haïti; cours professé au Petit séminaire-collège Saint-Martial*. Vol. 1. 4 vols. Port-au-Prince: Édition de La Petite revue, 1920s.

Canetti, Elias. *Crowds and Power*. Translated by Carol Stewart. New York: Farrar, Straus, and Giroux, 1984.

Carswell, John. *The South Sea Bubble*. London: Cresset Press, 1960.

Casimir, Jean. *Une lecture décoloniale de l'histoire des Haïtiens: Du Traité de Ryswick à l'Occupation américaine (1697–1915)*. Port-au-Prince: L'Imprimeur S.A., 2018.

Cassá, Roberto. *Rebelión de los Capitanes*. Santo Domingo: Archivo General de la Nación, 2011.

Cauna, Jacques de. "En Haïti il y a trois siècles: les observations morales et prédictions d'un Jésuite (un manuscrit inédit du père Le Pers)." In *Actes du Congrès national des sociétés historiques et scientifiques* 130, no. 13 (2011): 204–220.

———. "Patrimoine et mémoire de l'esclavage en Haïti: les vestiges de la société d'habitation coloniale." *In Situ* 20 (2013): 2–15.

Cerutti, Simona. "Who is Below?" *Annales. Histoire, Sciences Sociales* 70, no. 4 (2016): 931–56.

Chancellor, Edward. *Devil Take the Hindmost: A History of Financial Speculation*. New York: Farrar, Straus, and Giroux, 1999.

Charlevoix, Pierre-François-Xavier de. *Histoire de l'Isle Espagnole ou de St. Domingue*. 2 vols. Vol. 2, 1731.

Chatillon, Marcel, Gabriel Debien, Xavier du Boisrouvray, and Gilles de Maupeou. "Papiers privés sur l'histoire des Antilles." *Revue française d'histoire d'outre-mer* 59, no. 216 (1972): 432–90.

Chavagneux, Christian. *Une brève histoire des crises financières: des tulipes aux subprimes*. Paris: Découverte, 2011.

Cheney, Paul. *Revolutionary Commerce: Globalization and the French Monarchy*. Cambridge, MA: Harvard University Press, 2010.

———. *Cul de Sac: Patrimony, Capitalism, and Slavery in French Saint-Domingue*. Chicago: University of Chicago Press, 2017.

Chet, Guy. *The Ocean Is a Wilderness: Atlantic Piracy and the Limits of State Authority, 1688–1856.* Amherst: University of Massachusetts Press, 2014.

Choudhury, Mita. *The Wanton Jesuit and the Wayward Saint: A Tale of Sex, Religion, and Politics in Eighteenth-Century France.* University Park, PA: Penn State University Press, 2015.

Clairand, Arnaud, and Michel Prieur. *Les monnaies royales françaises, 987–1793.* Paris: Chevau-légers, 2008.

Clay, Lauren. *Stagestruck: The Business of Theater in Eighteenth-Century France and Its Colonies.* Ithaca, NY: Cornell University Press, 2013.

Clegg, John J. "Capitalism and Slavery." *Critical Historical Studies* 2, no. 2 (2015): 281–304.

Clossey, Luke. *Salvation and Globalization in the Early Jesuit Missions.* New York: Cambridge University Press, 2008.

Cobban, Alfred. *A History of Modern France, 1715–1799.* Vol. 1. New York: Penguin, 1957.

Cole, Charles Woolsey. *Colbert and a Century of French Mercantilism.* 2 vols. New York: Columbia University Press, 1939.

———. *French Mercantilism, 1683–1700.* New York: Columbia University Press, 1943.

Conrad, Glenn. "Emigration Forcée: A French Attempt to Populate Louisiana, 1716–1720." In *Proceedings of the Fourth Meeting of the French Colonial Historical Society,* 57–66. Washington, DC: University Press of America, 1979.

Cooper, Russell W., and Hubert Kempf. "Dollarization and the Conquest of Hyperinflation in Divided Societies." *Federal Reserve Bank of Minneapolis Quarterly Review* 25, no. 3 (2001): 3–12.

Corvington, Georges. *Port-au-Prince au cours des ans: La ville coloniale et les convulsions révolutionnaires, 1743–1804.* 7 vols. Vol. 1. Montreal: CIDIHCA, 2007.

Costain, Thomas B. *The Mississippi Bubble.* New York: Random House, 1955.

Crouse, Nellis M. *The French Struggle for the West Indies, 1665–1713.* New York: Columbia University Press, 1943.

Dampierre, Jacques. *Essai sur les sources de l'histoire des Antilles françaises (1492–1664).* Paris: A. Picard, 1904.

Darnton, Robert. "Reading a Riot." *New York Review of Books.* March 29, 2016.

Davies, Kenneth Gordon. *The Royal African Company.* London: Longmans, Green, 1957.

Davis, David Brion. *Inhuman Bondage: The Rise and Fall of Slavery in the New World.* Oxford: Oxford University Press, 2006.

Davis, Natalie Zemon. "Judges, Masters, Diviners: Slaves' Experience of Criminal Justice in Colonial Suriname." *Law and History Review* 29, no. 4 (November 2011): 925–84.

———. *Society and Culture in Early Modern France: Eight Essays.* Stanford, CA: Stanford University Press, 1975.

Debbasch, Yvan. "Au cœur du 'gouvernement des esclaves': la souveraineté domestique aux Antilles françaises (XVIIe-XVIIIe siècles)." *Revue française d'histoire d'outre-mer* 72, no. 266 (1985): 31–53.

———. "Le marronage: Essai sur la désertion de l'esclave antillais." *L'Année sociologique* 12 (1961): 1–112.

Debien, Gabriel. "Aux origines de quelques plantations des quartiers de Léogâne et du Cul-de-Sac (1680–1715)." *Revue de La Société d'histoire et de Géographie d'Haiti* 18, no. 64 (January 1947): 11–78.

———. *Les engagés pour les Antilles (1634–1715).* Abbéville: F. Paillart, 1951.

———. *Les esclaves aux Antilles françaises, XVIIe-XVIIIe siècles.* Basse-Terre: Société d'histoire de la Guadeloupe, 1974.

———. *Esprit colon et esprit d'autonomie à Saint-Domingue au xviiie siècle.* Paris: Larose, 1954.

———. "Une maison d'éducation à Saint-Domingue: 'Les Religieuses du Cap,' 1731–1802." *Revue d'histoire de l'Amérique Francaise* 2, no. 4 (1949): 557–75.

DeJean, Joan. *Mutinous Women: How French Convicts Became Founding Mothers of the Gulf Coast.* New York: Basic Books, 2022.

Delafosse, Marcel. "Planteurs de Saint-Domingue et négociants rochelais au temps de Law." *Revue d'histoire des Colonies* 41, no. 142 (1954): 14–21.

Dernis, Germain, ed. *Recueil ou collection des titres, édits, déclarations, arrêts, règlemens et autres pièces concernant la Compagnie des indes orientales établie au mois d'août 1664.* 4 vols. Vol. 4 Paris: Boudet, 1755–56.

Desan, Christine. *Making Money: Coin, Currency, and the Coming of Capitalism.* New York: Oxford University Press, 2014.

Desan, Suzanne, Lynn Hunt, and William Max Nelson, eds. *The French Revolution in Global Perspective.* Ithaca, NY: Cornell University Press, 2013.

Desbarats, Catherine. "On Being Surprised: By New France's Card Money, for Example." *Canadian Historical Review* 102, no. 1 (2021): 125–51.

Dessalles, Adrien. *Histoire Générale des Antilles.* 4 vols. Vol. 4 (1st of the 2nd series). Paris: Librarie-Éditeur, 1847.

Dorigny, Marcel, Gusti-Klara Gaillard, Jean-Marie Théodat, and Jean-Claude Bruffaerts, eds. *Haïti-France: Les chaînes de la dette: Le rapport Mackau (1825).* Paris: Maisonneuve & Larose; Hémisphères, 2021.

Dorsey, Peter A. *Common Bondage: Slavery as Metaphor in Revolutionary America.* Knoxville: University of Tennessee Press, 2009.

Dubois, Laurent, and Richard Turits. *Freedom Roots: Histories from the Caribbean.* Chapel Hill: University of North Carolina Press, 2021.

Dufournaud, Nicole. "Femmes en armes au XVI siècle." In *Penser la violence des femmes*, edited by Coline Cardi and Genevieve Pruvost, 75–84. Paris: La Découverte, 2012.

Dunn, Richard S. *Sugar and Slaves: The Rise of the Planter Class in the English West Indies, 1624–1713.* Chapel Hill: University of North Carolina Press, for the Institute of Early American History and Culture, 1972.

Dupuy, Alex. Presentation to the "Haiti: Reparations and Restitution" Symposium of the *Inter-American Law Review*, University of Miami School of Law, March 24, 2023.

Duval, Frantz. "Le dollar, denrée rare." *Le Nouvelliste*, December 7, 2022.

Eccles, W. J. *The French in North America, 1500–1783.* Rev. ed. East Lansing: Michigan State University Press, 1998.

Edelson, S. Max. *The New Map of Empire: How Britain Imagined America before Independence.* Cambridge, MA: Harvard University Press, 2017.

Eddins, Crystal. *Rituals, Runaways, and the Haitian Revolution: Collective Action in the African Diaspora.* New York: Cambridge University Press, 2022.

Ehrenreich, Barbara, and Dedrick Muhammad. "The Recession's Racial Divide." *New York Times*, September 12, 2009.

Eire, Carlos M. N. *Reformations: The Early Modern World, 1450–1650.* New Haven, CT: Yale University Press, 2016.

Emmer, P. C. *The Dutch in the Atlantic Economy, 1580–1880: Trade, Slavery and Emancipation.* Brookfield, VT: Ashgate, 1998.

Estienne, René, ed. *Les Compagnes des Indes.* Paris: Gallimard, 2013.

Ethéart, Bernard. "La filière canne (2)." *Haïti en Marche* 30, no. 27 (July 2016): 13.

Fabella, Yvonne. "Redeeming the 'Character of the Creoles': Whiteness, Gender and Creolization in Pre-Revolutionary Saint Domingue." *Journal of Historical Sociology* 23, no. 1 (March 2010): 40–72.

Farge, Arlette, and Jacques Revel. *Logiques de la foule: L'affaire des enlèvements d'enfants Paris 1750.* [Paris]: Hachette, 1988.

Fatton, Robert. *The Roots of Haitian Despotism.* Boulder, CO: Lynne Riener, 2007.

Faure, Edgar. *La banqueroute de Law, 17 juillet 1720.* Paris: Gallimard, 1977.

Ferguson, Niall. *The Ascent of Money: A Financial History of the World*. New York: Penguin, 2008.

Ferrer, Ada. *Freedom's Mirror: Cuba and Haiti in the Age of Revolution*. New York: Cambridge University Press, 2014.

Fick, Carolyn. *The Making of Haiti: The Saint-Domingue Revolution from Below*. Knoxville: University of Tennessee Press, 1990.

Finkelstein, Andrea. *Harmony and the Balance: An Intellectual History of Seventeenth-Century English Economic Thought*. Ann Arbor: University of Michigan Press, 2000.

Flandreau, Marc, and Juan Flores. "Bonds and Brands: Foundations of Sovereign Debt Markets, 1820–1830." *Journal of Economic History* 69, no. 3 (2009): 646–84.

Foucault, Michel. *The Order of Things: An Archaeology of the Human Sciences*. New York: Vintage Books, 1994.

Fouchard, Jean. *Les marrons de la liberté*. Port-au-Prince: H. Deschamps, 1988.

———. *Les marrons du syllabaire: Quelques aspects du problème de l'instruction et de l'éducation des esclaves et affranchis de Saint-Domingue*. Port-au-Prince: H. Deschamps, 1988.

Fradera, Josep M. "The Caribbean between Empires: Colonists, Pirates, and Slaves." In *The Caribbean: A History of the Region and Its Peoples*, edited by Stephan Palmié and Francisco A. Scarano, 165–76. Chicago: University of Chicago Press, 2011.

Frehen, Rik, William N. Goetzmann, and K. Geert Rouwenhorst. "Finance in the Great Mirror of Folly." In *The Great Mirror of Folly: Finance, Culture, and the Crash of 1720*, edited by William N. Goetzmann et al., 72–79. New Haven, CT: Yale University Press, 2013.

Friedrich, Markus. *The Jesuits: A History*. Translated by John Noël Dillon. Princeton, NJ: Princeton University Press, 2022.

Frostin, Charles. "Méthodologie missionnaire et sentiment religieux en Amérique française aux XVIIe et XVIIIe siècles: Le cas de Saint-Domingue." *Cahiers d'histoire* 24, no. 1 (1979): 19–43.

———. "La piraterie américaine des années 1720, vue de Saint-Domingue." *Cahiers d'histoire* 25, no. 2 (1980): 177–210.

———. *Les révoltes blanches à Saint-Domingue aux XVIIe et XVIIIe siècles (Haïti avant 1789)*. Paris: l'École, 1975; reprint, Rennes: Presses universitaires de Rennes, 2008.

Fuentes, Marisa J. *Dispossessed Lives: Enslaved Women, Violence, and the Archive*. Philadelphia: University of Pennsylvania Press, 2016.

Gadoury, Victor, and Georges Cousinié. *Monnaies coloniales françaises, 1670–1980*. Monte Carlo: V. Gadoury, 1980.

Gaffield, Julia. *Haitian Connections in the Atlantic World: Recognition after Revolution*. Chapel Hill: University of North Carolina Press, 2015.

Galbraith, John Kenneth. *A Short History of Financial Euphoria*. Reprint edition. New York: Penguin Books, 1994.

Gamio, Lazaro, Constant Méheut, Catherine Porter, Selam Gebrekidan, Allison McCann, and Matt Apuzzo. "Haiti's Lost Billions." *New York Times*, May 20, 2022.

Garrigus, John. *Before Haiti: Race and Citizenship in French Saint-Domingue*. New York: Palgrave Macmillan, 2006.

———. *A Secret among the Blacks: Slave Resistance before the Haitian Revolution*. Cambridge, MA: Harvard University Press, 2023.

Gascón, Margarita. "The Military of Santo Domingo, 1720–1764." *Hispanic American Historical Review* 73, no. 3 (1993): 431–52.

Geggus, David. "The French Slave Trade: An Overview." *William and Mary Quarterly* 58, no. 1 (2001): 119–38.

———. *Haitian Revolutionary Studies*. Bloomington: Indiana University Press, 2002.

———. "The Caribbean in the Age of Revolution." In *The Age of Revolutions in Global Context, c. 1760–1840*, edited by David Armitage and Sanjay Subrahmanyam, 95–100. New York: Palgrave Macmillan, 2010.

Ghachem, Malick W. "The 'Trap' of Representation: Sovereignty, Slavery, and the Road to the Haitian Revolution." *Historical Reflections/Réflexions historiques* 29, no. 1 (2003): 123–44.

———. *The Old Regime and the Haitian Revolution.* Cambridge: Cambridge University Press, 2012.

———. "Royal Liberties." In *The Princeton Companion to Atlantic History*, edited by Joseph C Miller, 294–98. Princeton, NJ: Princeton University Press, 2015.

———. "'No Body to Be Kicked?' Monopoly, Financial Crisis, and Popular Revolt in 18th-Century Haiti and America." *Law & Literature* 28, no. 3 (2016): 403–31.

———. "Empire, War, and Racial Hierarchy in the Making of the Atlantic Revolutionary Nations." In *The Cambridge History of Nationhood and Nationalism: Patterns and Trajectories over the Longue Durée.* Vol. 1. Edited by Cathie Carmichael, Matthew d'Auria, and Aviel Roshwald, 208–30. New York: Cambridge University Press, 2023.

Girard, Albert. "La réorganisation de la Compagnie des indes (1719–1723), I, L'œuvre de Law (1719–1721)." *Revue d'histoire moderne et contemporaine (1899–1914)* 11, no. 1 (1908–9): 5–34.

———. "La réorganisation de la Compagnie des indes (1719–1723), II, L'œeuvre de Paris-Duverney (1721–1723) (Suite et Fin)." *Revue d'histoire moderne et contemporaine (1899–1914)* 11, no. 3 (1908–9): 177–97.

Girard, Philippe R. *Haiti: The Tumultuous History—from Pearl of the Caribbean to Broken Nation.* New York: Palgrave Macmillan, 2010.

Giraud, Marcel. *Histoire de la Louisiane française: L'époque de John Law (1717–1720).* 5 vols. Vol. 3. Paris: Presses universitaires de France, 1966.

———. *Histoire de la Louisiane française: La Louisiane après le Système de Law (1721–1723).* 5 vols. Vol. 4. Paris: Presses Universitaires de France, 1974.

Goetzmann, William N., Catherine Labio, K. Geert Rouwenhorst, and Timothy Young, eds. *The Great Mirror of Folly: Finance, Culture, and the Crash of 1720.* New Haven, CT: Yale University Press, 2013.

Goetzmann, William N., and K. Geert Rouwenhorst. *The Origins of Value: The Financial Innovations That Created Modern Capital Markets.* Oxford: Oxford University Press, 2005.

Gomez Pardo, Julian. *La Maréchaussée et le crime en Île de France sous Louis XIV et Louis XV.* Paris: Les Indes Savantes, 2012.

Gonzalez, Johnhenry. *Maroon Nation: A History of Revolutionary Haiti.* New Haven, CT: Yale University Press, 2019.

Graeber, David. *Debt: The First 5,000 Years.* New York: Melville House, 2012.

Graham, Aaron. *Corruption, Party, and Government in Britain, 1702–1713.* Oxford: Oxford University Press, 2015.

Gray, Richard. "The Papacy and the Atlantic Slave Trade: Lourenco da Silva, the Capuchins and the Decisions of the Holy Office." *Past & Present* 115, no. 1 (1987): 52–68.

Green, John A. "Governor Périer's Expedition against the Natchez Indians." *Louisiana Historical Quarterly* 19, no. 3 (1936): 547–77.

Green, Toby. *A Fistful of Shells: From the Rise of the Slave Trade to the Age of Revolution.* London: Penguin, 2020.

Greenwald, Erin. *Marc-Antoine Caillot and the Company of the Indies in Louisiana: Trade in the French Atlantic World.* Baton Rouge: Louisiana State University Press, 2016.

Grimes, Katie Walker. *Fugitive Saints: Catholicism and the Politics of Slavery.* Minneapolis, MI: Fortress Press, 2017.

Guibert, Joseph de, S. J.. *The Jesuits: Their Spiritual Doctrine and Practice: A Historical Study.* Translated by William J. Young, S. J.. Chicago: Institute of Jesuit Sources, 1964.

Guilhiermoz, Paul. "Remarques diverses sur les poids et mesures du Moyen Âge." *Bibliothèque de l'École des chartes,* 80, no. 1 (1919): 5–100.

Hall, Gwendolyn Midlo. *Africans in Colonial Louisiana: The Development of Afro-Creole Culture in the Eighteenth Century.* Baton Rouge: Louisiana State University Press, 1992.

Hanna, Mark G. *Pirate Nests and the Rise of the British Empire, 1570–1740*. Chapel Hill: University of North Carolina Press, for the Omohundro Institute of Early American History and Culture, 2015.

Harms, Robert. *The Diligent: The Worlds of the Slave Trade*. New York: Basic Books, 2002.

Haudrère, Philippe. *La Compagnie française des Indes au XVIIIe siècle*. 2 vols. Vol. 1. Paris: Les Indes savantes, 2005.

———. *Les Français dans l'océan Indien (XVIIe-XIXe siècle)*. Rennes: Presses Universitaires de Rennes, 2014.

Hazaël-Massieux, Marie-Christine. *Textes anciens en créole français de la Caraïbe: Histoire et analyse*. Paris: Publibook, 2008.

Hector, Michel, and Claude Moïse. *Colonisation et esclavage en Haïti: le régime colonial français à Saint-Domingue (1625–1789)*. Port-au-Prince: H. Deschamps; CIDIHCA, 1990.

Heidgerken, Benjamin E. "The Jesuits' Complicated Past in Haiti: From Owning Plantations to Serving the Black Community." *America: The Jesuit Review*, June 17, 2022.

Helleiner, Eric. *The Making of National Money: Territorial Currencies in Historical Perspective*. Ithaca, NY: Cornell University Press, 2003.

Higman, B. W. *A Concise History of the Caribbean*. New York: Cambridge University Press, 2011.

———. "The Sugar Revolution." *Economic History Review* 53, no. 2 (2000): 213–36.

Hincker, François. *Les Français devant l'impôt sous l'Ancien Régime*. [Paris]: Flammarion, 1971.

Hirschman, Albert O. *The Passions and the Interests: Political Arguments for Capitalism before Its Triumph*. Princeton, NJ: Princeton University Press, 1977.

Holton, Woody. *Forced Founders: Indians, Debtors, Slaves, & the Making of the American Revolution in Virginia*. Chapel Hill: University of North Carolina Press, 1999.

Hont, Istvan. *Jealousy of Trade: International Competition and the Nation-State in Historical Perspective*. Cambridge, MA: Harvard University Press, 2005.

Horne, Gerald. *The Counter-Revolution of 1776: Slave Resistance and the Origins of the United States of America*. New York: New York University Press, 2014.

Hrodĕj, Philippe. "Les esclaves à Saint-Domingue aux temps pionniers (1630–1700)." In *L'esclave et les plantations: De l'établissement de la servitude à son abolition*, 59–84. Rennes: Presses universitaires de Rennes, 2008.

———. "Les premiers colons de l'ancienne Haïti et leurs attaches en métropole, à l'aube des premiers établissements (1650–1700)." *Les Cahiers de Framespa: Nouveaux champs de l'histoire sociale*, no. 9 (2012).

———. "L'État et ses principaux représentants à Saint-Domingue au XVIIIe siècle: contradictions et manquements." *Outre-mers* 94, no. 354 (2007): 173–95.

Hudson, Peter. *Bankers and Empire: How Wall Street Colonized the Caribbean*. Chicago: University of Chicago Press, 2017.

Hunt, Lynn. "The Global Financial Origins of 1789." In *The French Revolution in Global Perspective*, edited by Suzanne Desan, Lynn Hunt, and William Max Nelson, 32–43. Ithaca, NY: Cornell University Press, 2013.

Hunt, Lynn Avery, Margaret C. Jacob, and W. W. Mijnhardt. *The Book That Changed Europe: Picart & Bernard's Religious Ceremonies of the World*. Cambridge, MA: Harvard University Press, 2010.

Hyppolite, Renaud. "Si Le Cap m'était conté." In *Cap Haïtien: Excursions dans le temps: Au fils de nos souvenirs (1920–1995)*, edited by Max Manigat, 121–54. Delmas, Haïti: Éditions Sanba, 2014.

Isherwood, Robert M. *Farce and Fantasy: Popular Entertainment in Eighteenth-Century Paris*. New York: Oxford University Press, 1986.

Jackson, Trevor. *Impunity and Capitalism: The Afterlives of European Financial Crises, 1690–1830*. New York: Cambridge University Press, 2022.

Jan, J. M. *Les congrégations religieuses à Saint-Domingue, 1681–1793*. Port-au-Prince: H. Deschamps, 1951.

Janin, Joseph. *La religion aux colonies françaises sous l'Ancien régime: De 1626 à la Révolution*. Paris: Auteuil, 1942.

Jean-Baptiste, Saint-Victor. *Haïti: Sa lutte pour l'émancipation: Deux concepts d'indépendance à Saint-Domingue*. Paris: La Nef de Paris, 1957.

Jesuits of Canada. "Jesuits Provide Hope for the Future in Haiti." June 8, 2015. https://jesuits.ca /press-release/jesuits-provide-hope-for-the-future-in-haiti/.

Julien, Charles-André. *Les Français en Amérique de 1713 à 1784*. Paris: Centre de documentation universitaire et Société d'édition d'enseignement supérieur réunis, 1977.

Kaiser, Thomas E. "Money, Despotism, and Public Opinion in Early Eighteenth-Century France: John Law and the Debate on Royal Credit." *Journal of Modern History* 63, no. 1 (1991): 1–28.

Kawas, François. *Sources documentaires de l'histoire des jésuites en Haïti aux XVIIIe et XXe siècles: 1704–1763, 1953–1964*. Paris: L'Harmattan, 2006.

Kelly, James E. "Panic, Plots, and Polemic: The Jesuits and the Early Modern English Mission." *Journal of Jesuit Studies* 1, no. 4 (2014): 511–19.

Keyes, John. "Un commis des trésoriers généraux de la marine à Québec: Nicolas Lanoullier de Boisclerc." *Revue d'histoire de l'Amérique française* 32, no. 2 (1978): 181–202.

Kendi, Ibram. *Stamped from the Beginning: The Definitive History of Racist Ideas in America*. New York: Nation Books, 2016.

King, Stewart. "The Maréchaussée of Saint-Domingue: Balancing the Ancien Régime and Modernity." *Journal of Colonialism and Colonial History* 5, no. 2 (2004).

Klooster, Wim. *Illicit Riches: Dutch Trade in the Caribbean, 1648–1795*. Leiden: KITLV Press, 1998.

———. "Inter-Imperial Smuggling in the Americas, 1600–1800." In *Soundings in Atlantic History: Latent Structures and Intellectual Currents, 1500–1830*, edited by Bernard Bailyn and Patricia L. Denault, 141–80. Cambridge, MA: Harvard University Press, 2009.

———. "Slave Revolts, Royal Justice, and a Ubiquitous Rumor in the Age of Revolutions." *William and Mary Quarterly* 71, no. 3 (2014): 401–24.

Kloppenberg, James. *Toward Democracy: The Struggle for Self-Rule in European and American Thought*. New York: Oxford University Press, 2016.

Kwass, Michael. *Contraband: Louis Mandrin and the Making of a Global Underground*. Cambridge, MA: Harvard University Press, 2014.

———. *Privilege and the Politics of Taxation in Eighteenth-Century France: Liberté, Egalité, Fiscalité*. Cambridge; New York: Cambridge University Press, 2000.

———. "The Global Underground: Smuggling, Rebellion, and the Origins of the French Revolution." In *The French Revolution in Global Perspective*, edited by Suzanne Desan, Lynn Hunt, and William Max Nelson, 15–31. Ithaca, NY: Cornell University Press, 2013.

Lacombe, Robert. "Histoire monétaire de Saint-Domingue et de la République d'Haïti, des origines à 1874." *Revue d'histoire des colonies* 43, no. 152 (1956): 273–337.

Laidlaw, Zoë. "Empire and After." In *Magna Carta: Law, Liberty, Legacy*, edited by Claire Breay and Julian Harrison, 191–207. London: British Library, 2015.

Lehner, Ulrich L. *The Catholic Enlightenment: The Forgotten History of a Global Movement*. New York: Oxford University Press, 2016.

Lemieux, Donald J. "The Office of 'Commissaire Ordonnateur' in French Louisiana, 1731–1763: A Study in French Colonial Administration." PhD dissertation, Louisiana State University, 1972.

Levenson, Thomas. *Money for Nothing: The Scientists, Fraudsters, and Corrupt Politicians Who Reinvented Money, Panicked a Nation, and Made the World Rich*. New York: Random House, 2020.

Liss, Peggy K. *Atlantic Empires: The Network of Trade and Revolution, 1713–1826*. Baltimore, MD: Johns Hopkins University Press, 1983.

Loewenstein, Karl. "Militant Democracy and Fundamental Rights, I." *American Political Science Review* 31, no. 3 (1937): 417–32.

———. "Militant Democracy and Fundamental Rights, II." *American Political Science Review* 31, no. 4 (1937): 638–58.

Lunn, Arnold. *A Saint in the Slave Trade: Peter Claver (1581–1654)*. Manchester, NH: Sophia Institute Press, 2021.

Ly, Abdoulaye. *La Compagnie du Sénégal*. Paris: Présence africaine, 1958; nouvel ed., Paris: Karthala, 1993.

MacCulloch, Diarmaid. *The Reformation*. New York: Viking, 2004.

MacDonald, James. *A Free Nation Deep in Debt: The Financial Roots of Democracy*. New York: Farrar, Straus, and Giroux, 2003.

Mackay, Charles. *Extraordinary Popular Delusions and the Madness of Crowds*. London, 1841; reprint, Petersfield, UK: Harriman House Ltd., 2003.

Marx, Karl. *The Karl Marx Library*. Vol. 1. Edited by Saul K. Padover. New York: McGraw Hill, 1972.

Matson, Cathy. "Imperial Political Economy: An Ideological Debate and Shifting Practices." *William and Mary Quarterly* 69, no. 1 (2012): 35–40.

Mauny, François-Joseph-Ferdinand de. *Essai sur l'administration des colonies*. Paris: E. Duverger, 1837.

Mazard, Jean. *Histoire monétaire et numismatique des colonies et de l'Union française, 1670–1952*. Paris: Émile Bourgey, 1953.

McCusker, John J. *Money and Exchange in Europe and North America, 1600–1775: A Handbook*. Chapel Hill: University of North Carolina Press, for the Omohundro Institute of Early American History and Culture, 1978.

McKinley, Michelle. "Standing on Shaky Ground: Criminal Jurisdiction and Ecclesiastical Immunity in Seventeenth-Century Lima, 1600–1700." *UC Irvine Law Review* 4 (2014): 141–74.

McNally, David. *Blood and Money: War, Slavery, Finance, and Empire*. Chicago: Haymarket, 2020.

Meyer, Jean, Jean Tarrade, and Annie Rey-Goldzeiguer. *Histoire de la France coloniale, La conquête*. Vol. 1. Paris: Pocket, 1996.

Midy, Franklin. "Marrons de la liberté, révoltés de la libération: Le Marron inconnu revisité." In *Genèse de l'État Haïtien (1804–1859)*, edited by Michel Hector and Laënnec Hurbon, 119–47. Paris: Éditions de la Maison des sciences de l'homme, 2018.

Mims, Stewart L. *Colbert's West India Policy*. New Haven, CT: Yale University Press, 1912.

Mintz, Sidney W. *Sweetness and Power: The Place of Sugar in Modern History*. New York: Penguin, 1985.

Mitchell, Matthew D. "Joint-Stock Capitalism & the Atlantic Commercial Network: The Royal African Company, 1672–1752." PhD dissertation, University of Pennsylvania, 2012.

Morgan, Edmund S. *American Slavery, American Freedom: The Ordeal of Colonial Virginia*. New York: W. W. Norton, 1975.

Morgan, Philip D. "The Caribbean Environment to 1850." In *Sea and Land: An Environmental History of the Caribbean*, edited by Philip D. Morgan et al., 19–129. New York: Oxford University Press, 2022.

Morrison, Michael A., and Melinda S. Zook, eds. *Revolutionary Currents: Nation Building in the Transatlantic World*. Lanham, MD: Rowman & Littlefield, 2004.

Munford, Clarence J. *The Black Ordeal of Slavery and Slave Trading in the French West Indies, 1625–1715, Slave Trading in Africa*. Vols. 1 and 2. Lewiston, NY: Mellen, 1991.

Murphy, Antoin E. *John Law: Economic Theorist and Policy-Maker*. Oxford: Oxford University Press, 1997.

———. "John Law: Innovating Theorist and Policymaker." In *The Origins of Value: The Financial Innovations That Created Modern Capital Markets*, edited by William N. Goetzmann and K. Geert Rouwenhorst, 226–38. New York: Oxford University Press, 2005.

Murphy, Tessa. *The Creole Archipelago: Race and Borders in the Colonial Caribbean*. Philadelphia: University of Pennsylvania Press, 2021.

Murphy, Thomas. *Jesuit Slaveholding in Maryland, 1717–1838*. New York: Routledge, 2001.

Murrin, John M. "1776: The Countercyclical Revolution." In *Revolutionary Currents: Nation Building in the Transatlantic World*, edited by Michael A. Morrison et al., 65–90. Lanham, MD: Rowman & Littlefield, 2004.

Naef, Alain, and Carmen Hoffmann. "Exchange Rate History." *Finance and History Podcast*, March 3, 2023. https://podcasts.apple.com/vn/podcast/exchange-rate-history/id1558032792?i=1000602631032.

Neal, Larry. *The Rise of Financial Capitalism: International Capital Markets in the Age of Reason*. Cambridge: Cambridge University Press, 1990.

Nessler, Graham. *An Islandwide Struggle for Freedom: Revolution, Emancipation, and Reenslavement in Hispaniola, 1789–1809*. Chapel Hill: University of North Carolina Press, 2016.

Nicolas, Jean. *La rébellion française: Mouvements populaires et conscience sociale (1661–1789)*. Paris: Éditions du Seuil, 2002; reprint, Paris: Gallimard, 2008.

Norton, Mary Beth. *1774: The Long Year of Revolution*. New York: Knopf, 2020.

Oliveros, Asdrúbal. "Dollarization Can't Save the Venezuelan Economy." *Americas Quarterly* (October 5, 2021).

O'Malley, Gregory E. *Final Passages: The Intercolonial Slave Trade of British America*. Chapel Hill: University of North Carolina Press, 2014.

O'Malley, Gregory E., and Alex Borucki. "Patterns in the Intercolonial Slave Trade across the Americas before the Nineteenth Century." *Tempo* 23, no. 2 (2017): 314–38.

O'Malley, John W. *The Jesuits: A History from Ignatius to the Present*. New York: Rowman & Littlefield, 2014.

Orain, Arnaud. *La politique du merveilleux: Une autre histoire du Système de Law (1695–1795)*. Paris: Fayard, 2018.

Paesie, Rudolf. "Lorrendrayen op Africa: de illegale goederen- en slavenhandel op West-Afrika tijdens het achttiende-eeuwse handelsmonopolie van de West-Indische Compagnie, 1700–1734." PhD dissertation, Leiden University, 2008.

Palmié, Stephan. "Toward Sugar and Slavery." In *The Caribbean: A History of the Region and Its Peoples*, edited by Stephan Palmié and Francisco A. Scarano, 139–57. Chicago: University of Chicago Press, 2011.

Palmié, Stephan, and Francisco A. Scarano, eds. *The Caribbean: A History of the Region and Its Peoples*. Chicago: University of Chicago Press, 2011.

Pares, Richard. *Merchants and Planters. Economic History Review* Supplement 4. Cambridge: Cambridge University Press [published for the *Economic History Review*], 1960.

———. *Yankees and Creoles: The Trade between North America and the West Indies before the American Revolution*. Cambridge, MA: Harvard University Press, 1956.

Paul, Jean Éric. *La décote de la gourde face au dollar: Quelques pistes pour sortir du marasme économique actuel*. Port-au-Prince: C3 Editions, 2016.

Peabody, Sue. "'A Dangerous Zeal': Catholic Missions to Slaves in the French Antilles, 1635–1800." *French Historical Studies* 25, no. 1 (2002): 53–90.

Petitjean Roget, Jacques. *Le Gaoulé: la révolte de la Martinique en 1717*. Fort de France: Société d'histoire de la Martinique, 1966.

Pettigrew, William A. *Freedom's Debt: The Royal African Company and the Politics of the Atlantic Slave Trade, 1672–1752*. Chapel Hill: University of North Carolina Press, 2013.

Phillips, Andrew, and J. C. Sharman. *Outsourcing Empire: How Company-States Made the Modern World*. Princeton, NJ: Princeton University Press, 2020.

Pich, Roberto Hofmeister. "Alonso de Sandoval S.J. (1576/1577–1652) and the Ideology of Black Slavery: Some Theological and Philosophical Arguments." *Patristica et Mediaevalia* 36 (2015): 51–74.

Pigeaud, Fanny, and Ndongo Samba Sylla. *Africa's Last Colonial Currency: The CFA Franc Story.* Translated by Thomas Fazi. London: Pluto Press, 2021.

Pincus, Steven. "Rethinking Mercantilism: Political Economy, the British Empire, and the Atlantic World in the Seventeenth and Eighteenth Centuries." *William and Mary Quarterly* 69, no. 1 (2012): 3–34.

Pollet, Georges. *Saint-Domingue et l'autonomie, 1629–1730.* Saint-Amand, Cher (France): Imprimerie Leclerc, 1934.

Popkin, Jeremy D. *You Are All Free: The Haitian Revolution and the Abolition of Slavery.* New York: Cambridge University Press, 2010.

Porter, Catherine, Constant Méheut, Matt Apuzzo, and Selam Gebrekidan. "The Root of Haiti's Misery: Reparations to Enslavers"; "How a French Bank Captured Haiti"; "Invade Haiti, Wall Street Urged. The US Obliged."; "Demanding Reparations, and Ending up in Exile." *New York Times*, May 20, 2022.

Postma, Johannes. *The Dutch in the Atlantic Slave Trade, 1600–1815.* Cambridge: Cambridge University Press, 1990.

Powell, Lawrence N. *The Accidental City: Improvising New Orleans.* Cambridge, MA: Harvard University Press, 2012.

Pravilova, Ekaterina. *The Ruble: A Political History.* New York: Oxford University Press, 2023.

———. "Ruble's Wars." Paper presented at the European Association for Banking History "Financing Reconstruction" conference, Frankfurt, Germany, June 30, 2023.

Price, Jacob M. "Credit in the Slave Trade and Plantation Economies." In *Slavery and the Rise of the Atlantic System*, edited by Barbara L. Solow, 293–339. New York: Cambridge University Press, 1991.

Pritchard, James S. *In Search of Empire: The French in the Americas, 1670–1730.* New York: Cambridge University Press, 2004.

Quarles, Benjamin. *The Negro in the American Revolution.* Chapel Hill: University of North Carolina Press, for the Institute of Early American History and Culture, 1961.

Rey, Alain, ed. *Dictionnaire historique de la langue française.* 3 vols. Paris: Dictionnaires le Robert, 1998.

Ribero, Carlos Alberto de Moura. *Ligne de foi: la Compagnie de Jésus et l'esclavage dans le processus de formation de la société coloniale en Amérique portugaise, XVIe-XVIIe siècles.* Paris: Honoré Champion, 2009.

Richard, Robert. "À propos de Saint-Domingue: La monnaie dans l'économie coloniale (1674–1803)." *Revue d'histoire des colonies* 41, no. 142 (1954): 22–46.

Rothkrug, Lionel. *Opposition to Louis XIV: The Political and Social Origins of the French Enlightenment.* Princeton, NJ: Princeton University Press, 1965.

Rothschild, Emma. *Economic Sentiments: Adam Smith, Condorcet, and the Enlightenment.* Cambridge, MA: Harvard University Press, 2001.

Roux, Marie. *Louis XIV et les provinces conquises.* Paris: Les Éditions de France, 1938.

Rowlands, Guy. *Dangerous and Dishonest Men: The International Bankers of Louis XIV's France.* New York: Palgrave Macmillan, 2015.

———. *The Financial Decline of a Great Power: War, Influence, and Money in Louis XIV's France.* Oxford: Oxford University Press, 2012.

Roy, J.-Edmond. "Essai sur Charlevoix." In *Proceedings and Transactions of the Royal Society of Canada: Délibérations de La Société Royale Du Canada*, 3rd series, vol. 1, 3–95. Ottawa: Royal Society of Canada, 1907.

Ruderman, Anne. "Intra-European Trade in Atlantic Africa and the African Atlantic." *William and Mary Quarterly* 77, no. 2 (2020): 211–44.

Rushforth, Brett. "The Gaulet Uprising of 1710: Maroons, Rebels, and the Informal Exchange Economy of a Caribbean Sugar Island." *William and Mary Quarterly* 76, no. 1 (2019): 75–110.

Russell, Karl, Joe Rennison, and Jason Karaian. "The Dollar Is Extremely Strong, Pushing Down the World." *New York Times*, July 16, 2022.

Safieddine, Hicham. *Banking on the State: The Financial Foundations of Lebanon.* Stanford, CA: Stanford University Press, 2019.

Sahlins, Peter. *Forest Rites: The War of the Demoiselles in Nineteenth-Century France.* Cambridge, MA: Harvard University Press, 1994.

Saint-Louis, Vertus. *Mer et liberté (1492–1794).* Port-au-Prince, Haïti: Imprimeur II, 2009.

Sajó, András, ed. *Militant Democracy.* Utrecht, the Netherlands: Eleven International Publishing, 2004.

Sargent, Thomas J., and François R. Velde. *The Big Problem of Small Change.* Princeton, NJ: Princeton University Press, 2002.

Schama, Simon. *Rough Crossings: Britain, the Slaves, and the American Revolution.* New York: Ecco, 2006.

Scott, David. *Conscripts of Modernity: The Tragedy of Colonial Enlightenment.* Durham, NC: Duke University Press, 2004.

Sewell, William H. Jr. "The Capitalist Epoch." *Social Science History* 38, no. 1–2 (January 2014): 1–11.

———. "Economic Crises and the Shape of Modern History." *Public Culture* 24, no. 2 (67) (May 2012): 303–27.

———. *Logics of History: Social Theory and Social Transformation.* Chicago Studies in Practices of Meaning. Chicago: University of Chicago Press, 2005.

Schnakenbourg, Christian. *L'économie de plantation aux Antilles françaises: XVIIIè siècle.* Paris: L'Harmattan, 2020.

Sheehan, Jonathan, and Dror Wahrman. *Invisible Hands: Self-Organization and the Eighteenth Century.* Chicago: University of Chicago Press, 2015.

Shoemaker, Karl. *Sanctuary and Crime in the Middle Ages, 400–1500.* New York: Fordham University Press, 2011.

Shovlin, John. *Trading with the Enemy: Britain, France, and the 18th-Century Quest for a Peaceful World Order.* New Haven, CT: Yale University Press, 2021.

Spence, Jonathan D. *The Memory Palace of Matteo Ricci.* New York: Viking, 1984.

Stein, Robert Louis. *The French Slave Trade in the Eighteenth Century: An Old Regime Business.* Madison: University of Wisconsin Press, 1979.

Stein, Stanley J., and Barbara H. Stein. *Silver, Trade, and War: Spain and America in the Making of Early Modern Europe.* Baltimore, MD: Johns Hopkins University Press, 2000.

Stern, Philip J. *The Company-State: Corporate Sovereignty and the Early Modern Foundations of the British Empire in India.* Oxford: Oxford University Press, 2012.

Stoler, Ann Laura. *Along the Archival Grain: Epistemic Anxieties and Colonial Common Sense.* Princeton, NJ: Princeton University Press, 2010.

Sweet, John. *Bodies Politic: Negotiating Race in the American North, 1730–1830.* Baltimore, MD: Johns Hopkins University Press, 2003.

Swingen, Abigail L. *Competing Visions of Empire: Labor, Slavery, and the Origins of the British Atlantic Empire.* New Haven, CT: Yale University Press, 2015.

Tardieu, Jean-Pierre. "Los esclavos de los jesuitas del Perú en la época de la expulsión (1767)." *C.M.H.L.B. Caravelle*, no. 81 (2003): 61–109.

Taylor, Keeanga-Yahmatta. *Race for Profit: How Banks and the Real Estate Industry Undermined Black Homeownership.* Chapel Hill: University of North Carolina Press, 2019.

Te Velde, Dirk Willem. "Africa 10 Years after the Global Financial Crisis: What We've Learned." ODI Insights, September 2018. https://odi.org/en/insights/africa-10-years-after-the-global -financial-crisis-what-weve-learned/.

Tocqueville, Alexis de. *The Ancien Régime and the French Revolution*. Edited by Jon Elster. Translated by Arthur Goldhammer. New York: Cambridge University Press, 2011.

Toussaint, Eric. *Le système dette: Histoire des dettes souveraines et de leur répudiation*. Paris: Les liens qui libèrent, 2017.

Tramond, Joannès Martial Marie Hippolyte. *Les troubles de Saint-Domingue en 1722–1724*. Paris: E. Leroux, 1929.

Trouillot, Michel-Rolph. *Silencing the Past: Power and the Production of History*. Boston: Beacon Press, 1995.

Tutino, John. "Capitalism, Christianity, and Slavery: Jesuits in New Spain, 1572–1767." *Journal of Jesuit Studies* 8, no. 1 (December 2020): 11–36.

Ullrich, Volker. *Germany 1923: Hyperinflation, Hitler's Putsch, and Democracy in Crisis*. Translated by Jefferson Chase. New York: Liveright, 2023.

Van Kley, Dale K. *The Jansenists and the Expulsion of the Jesuits from France, 1757–1765*. New Haven, CT: Yale University Press, 1975.

———. "Plots and Rumors of Plots: The Role of Conspiracy in the International Campaign against the Society of Jesus, 1758–1768." In *The Jesuit Suppression on Global Context: Causes, Events, and Consequences*, edited by Jeffrey D. Burson and Jonathan Wright, 13–39. New York: Cambridge University Press, 2015.

———. *Reform Catholicism and the International Suppression of the Jesuits in Enlightenment Europe*. New Haven, CT: Yale University Press, 2018.

Velde, François R. "French Public Finance between 1683 and 1726." In *Government Debts and Financial Markets in Europe*, edited by Fausto Piola Caselli, 135–65. London: Pickering & Chatto, 2008.

———. Introduction to *Lettres sur le visa des dettes de l'État ordonné en 1721*, by François-Michel-Chrétien Deschamps, ix–lxiv. Edited by François R. Velde. Paris: Classiques Garnier, 2015.

———. "Was John Law's System a Bubble? The Mississippi Bubble Revisited." In *The Origins and Development of Financial Markets and Institutions: From the Seventeenth Century to the Present*, edited by Larry Neal and Jeremy Atack, 99–120. New York: Cambridge University Press, 2009.

Voss, Karsten. *Sklaven als Ware und Kapital: Die Plantagenökonomie von Saint-Domingue als Entwicklungsprojekt*. Munich: C. H. Beck, 2016.

Warner, Marina. *Joan of Arc: The Image of Female Heroism*. New York: Knopf, 1981.

Webb, Stephen Saunders. *Marlborough's America*. New Haven, CT: Yale University Press, 2013.

Weber, Eugene. *Europe since 1715: A Modern History*. New York: W. W. Norton, 1972.

Wennerlind, Carl. *Casualties of Credit: The English Financial Revolution, 1620–1720*. Cambridge, MA: Harvard University Press, 2011.

White, Eugene. "Making the French Pay: The Costs and Consequences of the Napoleonic Reparations." *European Review of Economic History* 5, no. 3 (2001): 337–65.

White, Gillian B. "The Recession's Racial Slant." *The Atlantic*, June 24, 2015.

Wilder, Craig Steven. "War and Priests: Catholic Colleges and Slavery in the Age of Revolution." In *Slavery's Capitalism: A New History of American Economic Development*, edited by Sven Beckert and Seth Rockman, 226–42. Philadelphia: University of Pennsylvania Press, 2016.

Winnerling, Tobias. "The Spiritual Empire of the Society of Jesus." *Itinerario* 40, special issue no. 2 (2016): 215–37.

Wood, Laurie M. *Archipelago of Justice: Law in France's Early Modern Empire*. New Haven, CT: Yale University Press, 2020.

Wright, Celeste Turner. "The Amazons in Elizabethan Literature." *Studies in Philology* 37, no. 3 (1940): 433–56.

Zabin, Serena R. *Dangerous Economies: Status and Commerce in Imperial New York*. Philadelphia: University of Pennsylvania Press, 2009.

Zacek, Natalie. "A Death in the Morning: The Murder of Daniel Parke." In *Cultures and Identities in Colonial British America*, edited by Robert Olwell and Alan Tully, 223–43. Baltimore, MD: Johns Hopkins University Press, 2006.

Zahedieh, Nuala. "Monopoly and Free Trade: Changes in the Organization of the British Slave Trade, 1660–1720." In *Shiavitù e servaggio nell'economia Europea secc. XI-XVIII/Serfdom and Slavery in the European Economy 11th–18th centuries*, edited by Simonetta Cavaciocchi, vol. 2, 651–62. Florence, Italy: Firenze University Press, 2014.

———. "The Rise of 'King Sugar' and Enslaved Labor in Early English Jamaica." *Early American Studies: An Interdisciplinary Journal* 20, no. 4 (September 2022): 576–96.

Zay, Ernest. *Histoire monétaire des colonies françaises d'après les documents officiels*. Paris: J. Montorier, 1892.

INDEX

NOTE: Figures are indicated by *f* following the page number. Note information is indicated by n and note number following the page number.

acquisitions of companies, 4, 58, 59, 60–65, 67, 74

Alexandre, 176

Amazons, 17, 97, 100–101, 137, 139, 219n75

Antigua, 22

Aranjuez, Treaty of (1777), 161

Aristide, Jean-Bertrand, 185

Artibonite plain, 106, 113, 116, 123

Artibonite River, 45, 106, 164–65

asiento licenses: British acquisition of, 11, 27–28, 206n50; French acquisition of, 34; silver and, 27, 83; System and, 54, 56; treaty necessitating, 198n10, 203n1

Baie de St. Louis, 109*f*

banks: French Royal, 4, 58, 62–63, 71–72, 73; Law's support for, 57–58; public debt and, 186–88

Barbados, 27–28

Bizoton, 221n33

Blenac, Governor, 42

Blunt, John, 70

Boismorant, 112–13

Bonaparte, Napoleon, 184, 186

Bourbon, Louis-Antoine de, 65, 154

Bourgeois, Nicolas-Louis, 88–89, 98–100, 118

Boutin, Père, 149–54, 158

Boyer, Jean-Pierre, 185–86

Britain: chartered companies of (*see* East India Company (British); Merchant Adventurers; South Sea Company); colonial rebellion against chartered companies of, 22, 23–28, 30; Glorious Revolution in, 29–30; Law in, 57, 70–71; slave trade of, 3, 11, 27–32, 35, 55–56; South Sea Bubble of, 2–3, 54–55, 66–74, 213n52

Bubble Act (Britain, 1720), 70

Canetti, Elias, 80

Cap Français (Le Cap): maps of, 45, 48–53, 49*f*–50*f*, 52*f*, 84, 126–27, 135, 136*f*; population of, 18, 42; settlement of, 18; uprisings in (*see under* company colony; marginalized people; white planters)

Capuchin missionaries, 130, 140–41, 142

Castaing, 110

Cato's Letters (Trenchard and Gordon), 69–70, 213n45

César, 176

Champflour, Maurice-César de, 116, 119–20, 124–25, 223n57

Champmeslin. *See* Desnos-Champmeslin, Charles Gilles, comte

Charlevoix, Pierre-François-Xavier de: Jesuit historical chronicles of, 129–35, 140, 213n51; on maroons, 160–61, 166; on rebels and rebellion influences, 21, 83, 85, 97–98, 100, 111–12, 118, 124–25, 131–33; on System and bubbles, 72–75

Charpentier, 119–20, 125, 133

251

Châteaumorant, Joseph-Charles Joubert de la Bastide, marquis de, Governor, 144–47, 169

Châtenoye, 85, 112

Chilly, Captain, 110

Claver, Pedro, 149

Code Noir: creditor terms in, 13, 77; enslaved assembly bans in, 170; Jesuits and, 141, 147, 151–52; manumission in, 43; maroon punishment under, 176, 186; property rules under, 186; reinstatement of, 184, 186

Colas, Denis, 170

Colas Jambes Coupées, 8, 156, 169, 176–77, 179

Colbert, Jean-Baptiste: company colony under, 14–15, 17, 20, 30, 34, 38 (*see also* Senegal Company; West Indies Company (French)); customs union by, 18; mercantilism under, 15, 66; money under, 38, 39

Colonial Pact, 19–20

colonial System. *See* System

company colony, 11–53; administration of, 14, 20, 22, 209n96; Colonial Pact on, 19–20; demographics and population in, 17–18, 41–44, 45; enslaved labor in, 12–13, 15–16, 20, 28–31, 41–44, 52–53 (*see also* enslaved persons); founding story and, 13–14; free trade vs., 5, 11–12, 23–30; maps of, 45–53, 46*f*–50*f*, 52*f*; mercantilism and, 14–16, 26–27, 28–29, 30–31, 36, 39; overview of, 11–13; rebellion against, 11–12, 16–28, 30, 48; response to rebellion in, 17, 19, 21, 22, 48; royal territorial status vs., 18; silver, gold, and money in, 11–13, 15, 22, 33–41, 38*f*, 44; slave trade and, 5, 11–13, 15–16, 20–23, 27–35, 41–42, 43–44; smuggling effects on, 11–12, 15–16, 30–35, 41; sugar revolution in, 12, 22, 43–45, 53; taxes and, 11–12, 16–17, 18–20, 22, 28–29, 30–31, 35, 40. *See also specific companies*

Company of Africa, 61

Company of China, 61, 67, 211n18

Company of Jesus, 128, 141–42, 225n3. *See also* Jesuit missionaries

Company of Saint Christophe, 14

Company of Saint-Domingue. *See* Saint-Domingue Company

Company of the East Indies, 61, 67. *See also* East India Company *entries*

Company of the Isles of America, 14

Company of the West, 58, 67

Constant, Pieter, 16

copper coins, 6, 91–92, 92*f*, 101

Costanzo Ramirez, Francisco, 169–70, 177–78

Courseul, Baron de, 125

courts, colonial, 106–7

Craggs, James, 62–63

Crawford, Thomas, 62–63, 211n21

Credit Industriel et Commercial, 187–88

criminals: forced emigration of, 58–59, 210n11; Law as, 55, 56–57

crowd movements, 80–81

Crozat, Antoine de, 58

Cul de Sac plain, 106, 113, 116, 123

Cul de Sac Treaty (1722), 104, 113–16, 117, 222n41

Curaçao, 31

d'Armenonville, Joseph Fleuriau, 83, 216n28

d'Arquian, comte (Paul François de La Grange): absence of, 83–84; accusations against, 98; on courts, 106; on demographics, 42; on marginalized people's revolt, 89–90, 92–94, 97, 100, 108, 111–12, 134–35, 218n59; on royal ordinance on money, 87–88, 90–91; on slave trade, 117

debt: contemporary conflicts with, 183–84; conversion to/from corporate equity, 58, 61–64, 71–72, 186–87; enslaved person ownership and, 13, 77–78, 186; from French wars, 2–3, 11–12, 55–56, 62; of Haiti, 2–3, 10, 91, 184–88, 234n12; Jesuit concerns for, 129; of Latin America, 187; of planters, 4, 12–13, 73–74, 77–78, 87, 119–20, 182, 186, 199n16; restoration of credibility of, 71–72; slave trade to counter, 55; System tied to, 2–3, 55–56, 58, 61–64, 71–73, 77–78 (*see also* System)

de Fer, Nicolas, 45, 48–49

Delisle, Guillaume, 48, 161–63

democracy, militant, 103, 201n34

Descopins, 120

Desnos-Champmeslin, Charles Gilles, comte: departure of, 89–90, 92, 104, 113; insurrection against Indies Company pacified by, 48, 116, 124–26, 146, 153, 156, 179; uprising in response to, 89–90, 92, 108

Dessalines, Jean-Jacques, 155

Dessalles, Adrien, 100–102

d'Ogeron, Bertrand, 16–19, 42, 204n17

Domaine d'Occident, 18–20, 35, 108, 205n24, 208n83

d'Orléans, Duc, 57, 70

Drouïllard, 120

Dubois, Père/Cardinal, 160, 165

Dubuc, Jean, 22

Du Casse, Jean-Baptiste, Governor, 31, 34

Duclos, Jean-Baptiste Dubois: experience and positions of, 89, 209n96, 216n28; on marginalized people's revolt, 89–90, 93, 97, 100, 108, 111–12, 135; military-planter state enforcement by, 170–75, 180; on money and taxes, 39–40; on royal ordinance on money, 87–88, 90–91; on slave trade, 117

East India Company (British, EIC), 15, 23–26, 30, 70

East India Company (Dutch, VOC), 24, 25

East India Company v. Sandys (1682), 24–25, 26

Eddins, Crystal, 160–61, 163, 166, 169

émotion, 80–81

Enlightenment, 67

enslaved persons: abolition of slavery of, 186; arming of, 122–23; Code Noir on (*see* Code Noir); as domestic enemies, 201n33; fugitive or escaped (*see* maroons); Jesuits as owners of, 129, 142–46; Jesuits

ministering to, 7, 9, 129, 147–54, 155, 158–60; languages of, 152–53, 229–30nn73–74; manumission of, 31, 43, 103, 122–23, 149, 156; maps of slave markets for, 52–53; marriage of, 151; under militant slavery (*see* militant slavery); money, debt, and ownership of, 5, 13, 15–16, 35, 39, 77–78, 186, 200nn21,25; plantation labor of, 12–13, 15–16, 41–42, 83; population of, 20, 43–44, 96, 152–53, 182; resistance by, 7–9, 104, 155, 157, 166–67, 170, 179–81, 183, 202n39 (*see also* maroons); riots and revolts involving, 7–8, 95–96, 112; taxes and ownership of, 13, 20, 28–29, 30, 167–68, 204n24; trade in (*see* slave trade)

exclusive privilege: of Indies Company, 5, 65–66, 86–87, 104; of Saint-Domingue Company, 211–12nn29–30. *See also* monopoly commerce

financial crises and reconstruction: bubbles in (*see* Mississippi Bubble; South Sea Bubble); System tied to (*see* System)

Fortier, 125, 223n57

Fort Saint-Louis, 45

Fourment, Captain, 93–94

France: chartered companies of (*see* company colony; *specific companies*); colonies of (*see* company colony; Guadeloupe; Louisiana; Martinique; Saint-Domingue); debt of, 2–3, 11–12, 55–56, 58, 61–64, 71–72; indemnity and reparations in, 2–3, 91, 184–88, 234n12; navy of (*see* navy, French); slave trade of (*see* slave trade); System for financial restructuring of (*see* System)

Franquenay, 21–22

free people of color and free blacks: maroon patrols by, 167, 172–73, 180; as planters, 96, 173; political mobilization of, 125; population of, 42–43, 44, 96; regulations targeting, 89, 180; riots and revolts by, 7–8, 82, 95–96; taxes for, 204n23. *See also* maroons; "negroes"

254 INDEX

free trade: company colony vs., 5, 11–12, 23–30; marginalized people's uprising over, 81; mercantilism vs., 26–27, 28–29; in slave trade, 5, 6, 11–12, 27–30, 114, 118, 126–27; white planters' demands for, 114, 118, 126–27

Frézier, Amadée-François, 48, 120–22, 161, 163

fugitive slave patrol, See *maréchaussée*

fugitive slaves. *See* maroons

Gallicanism, 133

Gaoulé revolt, 22, 93, 122, 199n18

Gobin, 18

gold: clipped or diluted coins with, 40; exchange rates and, 188; hoarding of, 15, 36–37, 39; mercantilism and, 15, 36, 39, 76; paper currency displacing, 37, 57, 76 (*see also* paper currency); valuation of, 36–37, 40–41, 76–77, 87; weight of, 40–41, 76

Gordon, Thomas, 69–70, 213n45

Grande-Rivière, 172

Grand Goâve, 45

Grenon, 82, 86–87, 115

Grotius, Hugo, 25, 26

Guadeloupe: Code Noir in, 184; as company colony, 14, 21, 31–32; missionaries on, 150, 159–60, 228n52

Guimon, 153–54

Guinea Company: acquisition of, 60, 62, 63, 65, 74; dismantling of, 28; slave trading by, 16, 27–29, 34, 60, 62, 74–75

Haiti: central bank of, 187–88; currency of, 188–89; finances and economy of, 2–3, 10, 91, 183–89, 234n12; name of, 197n2; revolution in (*see* Haitian Revolution); Saint-Domingue preceding (*see* Saint-Domingue)

Haitian Revolution: debt as fuel for, 78; Haitian history beyond, 9–10; indemnity for independence following, 2–3, 91, 184–88, 234n12; maroon resistance and, 9, 155, 181

Horsmanden, Daniel, 213n52

Ignatius, 147–48. *See also* Jesuit missionaries

indemnity, 2–3, 91, 184–88, 234n12

indentured servants, 13, 14, 39, 42–43, 77, 201n28

Indies Company: acquisitions and takeovers by, 60–65, 67, 74; advantages of in Saint-Domingue, 64–66 (*see also under* exclusive privilege); company colony under (*see* company colony); debt conversion and, 61–64, 71; demise and receivership of, 5, 71–72, 127, 213n48; headquarters of, 60, 60f, 81–82, 84, 88, 89–102; maps of facilities of, 49, 51–52, 84; marginalized people rising against, 6, 80–102, 104, 108–13; militant slavery to oppose (*see* militant slavery); monopoly of, 5, 30, 61–67, 70, 74–75, 125 (*see also* monopoly commerce); name of, 59; registration of, 86–87, 112; silver for shares of, 199n19; slave trading by, 5, 16, 60–61, 63–64, 65–67, 74–75, 83, 86, 126–27; System and, 3, 5, 54–56, 59–67, 70–72, 74–75; tax exemption for, 5, 64, 66, 74, 85–87, 107–8, 125

indigo, as money alternative, 39

indigo plantations: on Cul de Sac plain, 106; demographics and number of, 18, 20, 28, 44, 182–83; Saint-Domingue Company fostering, 35

Jamaica, 27–28, 31, 32, 180–81

Jan, Jean-Marie, 135, 137, 139–40, 150

Jansenism, 133

Jesuit missionaries, 128–54; Capuchins vs., 130, 140–41, 142; expulsion or suppression of, 9, 133, 140–41, 150, 155, 159–60; financial considerations for, 129, 137, 139–40, 141–47, 150; historical chronicles and uprising accounts by, 97–98, 128, 129–35, 140; Jansenism influence on, 133; languages in ministry of, 152–53, 229–30nn73–74; maps of compounds of, 49, 51–52, 135, 136f; militant slavery mediated by, 129; ministering to enslaved by, 7, 9, 129, 147–54, 155, 158–60; ministering to maroons by, 9, 155, 158–60; ministering to white planters by, 129, 148–50; overview of, 128–29; Protestants vs., 133, 141; refuge or sanctuary with, 92, 97, 135, 141, 226n20; revolt role of, 129, 134–35, 137–41, 138f; slavery involvement by, 128–29, 140, 142–46, 148–49; tax stance of, 129, 142, 144–46, 150; white supremacy of, 155, 157

Knight, Robert, 70

Labat, Jean-Baptiste, Père, 129
La Ferrière, Buzé de: departure of, 89–90, 92, 104, 113, 139; Jesuits and, 134–35, 139, 141; position and responsibilities of, 82, 84; uprising in response to, 85, 89–92, 97–98, 108, 110, 218n59, 221n18
La Fossette: map of, 49, 52; riot and burning of, 88, 90, 93, 94, 97
Lagrange, 177–78
Lambert, Joseph, 67, 70
Lance, Joseph Louis de la, 165
Langot, 91, 97, 100, 218n59
Larcher, Père, 149, 153
Lartigue, Jean de, 26
La Sagona: archival traces of, 81, 88–89, 91, 94; exile of, 125; Jesuits honoring, 135, 137–40, 138f; uprisings under, 81, 82, 88–89, 91, 94, 95–102, 109–11, 120, 131; wealth of, 120
Latin America, debt of, 187
Lavigne, Léonard, 39
Law, John: background and theory of, 56–58; escape of, 55, 57, 70–71; Indies Company of (see Indies Company); System of (see System)
Lebanon, finances of, 188
Le Grandhomme, 120
Lejeune, Jean, 177–79
Léogâne: as capital, 10, 106, 120; map of, 45, 107f; population of, 17, 42; representatives

from, 116; uprisings in, 82, 86, 104, 106, 115–16
Le Pers, Jean-Baptiste, 97–98, 128, 129–35, 151–52, 213n51
Lesgut, 82, 86, 108, 115
Lestrade, 177–78
letters of exchange, 77
L'Héritier de Villandon, Marie-Jeanne, 139
liberties, royal, 23–24
liberty: in military-planter state, 181; trade (see free trade)
livres, colonial, 38, 40–41
livres tournois, 37–38, 40–41, 76
Longpré, Latouche de, 22
Louisiana: administration in, 209n96; copper coins shipped to, 92; forced emigration to, 4, 58–59, 210–11nn11–12; Indies Company demise in, 127; Natchez Indians in, 127, 225n86; System and trade in, 4, 54, 58–59, 61, 75
Louverture, Toussaint, 155

Magna Carta, 25–26, 206n39
Maniel, le, 161, 164
maps: of Baie de St. Louis, 109f; of Bayaha, 164–65, 164f; of Cap Français, 45, 48–53, 49f–50f, 52f, 84, 126–27, 135, 136f; Hispaniola border lines on, 161–65, 162f, 164f; Indies Company facilities on, 49, 51–52, 84; Jesuit compounds on, 49, 51–52, 135, 136f; of Léogâne, 45, 107f; of Saint-Domingue, xivf, 45–53, 46f–50f, 52f, 84, 105f, 161–65, 162f, 164f
Marc, Pieter, 16
maréchaussée, 7–9, 156, 157, 167–69, 170–75, 177–80, 183
Margat, Jean-Baptiste, Père, 129, 134, 148–53, 157–59
marginalized people, 80–102; ambiguity of identity of rioters among, 91, 93–95; archival traces of, 1–2, 81, 88–102; conspiracy theory on, 100–101; demographics of, 41–42; forced emigration of, 56, 58–59, 79, 175, 210–11nn11–12; Jesuit

marginalized people (*continued*)
history on rebellion of, 97–98, 128, 129–35; Jesuit revolt interaction with, 129, 134–35, 137–40, 138f; La Sagona and other women leading, 81–82, 88–89, 91, 94, 96–102, 108–12 (*see also* La Sagona); money as trigger for, 6, 7, 81, 83, 85–88, 90–92, 94, 96, 101, 137, 139–40; riots and revolts by, 6, 7–8, 80–102, 104, 108–13; sedition avoidance by, 82, 94–95; ship passengers and cargo triggering revolt of, 82–86, 102; slave trade and uprising of, 83, 85, 86, 96, 101–2; white planters' revolts with, 6, 86–87, 90, 93–94, 102, 109–13. *See also* enslaved persons; free people of color and free blacks; "negroes"; vagabonds; women

maroons, 155–81; avoiding apprehension, 165–66; borders and geography aiding, 8–9, 160–66, 162f, 164f, 168, 169–70, 171–72, 177–78; context for rebellion of, 155–57; enslaved resistance and, 7–9, 155, 157, 166–67, 170, 179–81, 183, 202n39; finances and suppression of, 167–68, 170, 172–75, 177–79; Haitian Revolution and uprising of, 9, 155, 181; Jesuits ministering to, 9, 155, 158–60; legal proceedings on, 168, 175–77; liberty and, 181; *maréchaussée* and militia actions to capture/kill, 7–9, 156, 157, 167–69, 170–75, 177–80, 183; military-planter state in response to (*see* military-planter state); population of, 166, 169; terminology for, 157; white planter rebellion and, 156–57, 169, 179; white supremacy in response to, 155, 157, 165, 169, 173, 174

Martinique: as company colony, 14, 21, 22, 31–32; Jesuits on, 142; military-planter state on, 179–80, 233n53; revolts and uprisings in, 22, 44, 93, 122, 199n18; slave trade in, 21, 31–32, 33f

Massacre River, 164–65, 169, 172

Maurepas, comte de (Jean-Fréderic Phélypeaux), 42, 124, 149

mercantilism: company colony and, 14–16, 26–27, 28–29, 30–31, 36, 39; definition of, 14–15; free trade vs., 26–27, 28–29; money, gold, silver and, 15–16, 27, 36, 39, 76; slave trade and, 15–16, 27–28, 55, 66; smuggling and, 15–16, 30–31

Merchant Adventurers, 23–25

Meunier, 120, 223n59

Michel (maroon), 168–69

Michel, Père, 135, 137–40, 146, 226–27n29

militant slavery, 103–27; anonymity of uprisers in, 112, 119, 126; courts, legal system and, 106–7, 125–26; Cul de Sac Treaty reflecting, 104, 113–16, 117; debt as influence on, 119–20; geographic scope of insurrection and, 104, 105f, 106; Jesuit mediation of, 129; manumission proposed to counter, 103, 122–23, 156; marginalized people's revolt and, 6, 104, 108–13; maroon uprising and, 156; militant democracy and, 103, 201n34; military and punitive response to, 120–26, 121f; overview of, 8, 103–6; sedition and, 114–15, 119, 124; self-governance and, 104–6, 115; silver and, 104, 125, 126; slave trade demands and, 103–5, 107–8, 114, 117–19, 126–27; taxes and representation demands and, 104, 107–8, 114–17, 125, 141; terminology for, 8; white planters' revolt and, 8, 103–6, 109–27; white supremacy perpetuated by, 8, 104

military-planter state, 155–81; avoiding apprehension in, 165–66; borders and geography in, 8–9, 160–66, 162f, 164f, 168, 169–70, 171–72, 177–78; colonial administration and, 201n35; colonial influence of, 179–80; context for, 155–57; finances and taxes in, 167–68, 170, 172–75, 177–79; Jesuit ministry to maroons in, 155, 158–60; legal proceedings in, 168, 175–77; on liberty, 181; *maréchaussée* and militia actions in, 7–9, 156, 157, 167–69, 170–75, 177–80, 183; maroons and (*see* maroons); resistance and offensive action against, 155, 157, 166–67, 170, 179–81; terminology for, 9; white planter rebellion and, 156–57, 169, 179; white supremacy in, 155, 157, 165, 169, 173, 174

Misselden, Edward, 23–24, 25

Mississippi Bubble: colonial vs. metropolitan nature of, 54–55; foundations of, 199n19; legacies of, 10; reactions to bursting of, 66–69; System effects of, 2–3, 66–74

Mississippi Company: acquisition or takeover of, 58, 60; critics of and opposition to, 69; inactivity of, 4, 61, 199n13; slave trading by, 60–61. *See also* Mississippi Bubble

Mithon, Jean-Jacques, Intendant, 42, 144–47, 170

Molière, Jean Louis, 39

money: alternative or in-kind payments vs., 5, 39–40, 77, 182, 200n21; clipped or diluted coins as, 40–41; in company colony, 11–13, 15, 22, 33–41, 38f, 44; contemporary conflicts with, 183–84; copper, 6, 91–92, 92f, 101; debt to supply (*see* debt); gold (*see* gold); imperial influence on contemporary, 188; Jesuit finances and, 129, 137, 139–40, 141–47, 150; marginalized people's uprising over, 6, 7, 81, 83, 85–88, 90–92, 94, 96, 101, 137, 139–40; maroon suppression and, 167–68, 170, 172–75, 177–79; mercantilism and, 15–16, 27, 36, 39, 76; paper, 5, 37, 57–58, 61, 73, 76; plantation economy and, 12–13 (*see also* plantation economy); royal ordinance on (*see* royal ordinance on money); silver (*see* silver); slave ownership and, 5, 13, 15–16, 35, 39, 77–78, 186, 200nn21,25; tax (*see* taxes); valuation of, 5–6, 36–37, 40–41, 75–77, 80, 83, 85–87, 146–47, 218–19n61

monopoly commerce: company colony due to (*see* company colony; *specific companies*); debt conversion and, 58; definition of monopoly for, 24–25; dismantling of, 29–30; free trade vs., 5,

23–30; Jesuits and, 145; mercantilism and, 15, 26–27, 28–29; opposition to, 70, 81–82 (*see also under* company colony; marginalized people; militant slavery); prohibition of, 24–25; regulation of, 70; System based on, 58, 61–67, 70, 74–75 (*see also* System)

Montesquieu, Charles Louis de Secondat, baron de, 69, 70

Montholon, François de: Cul de Sac Treaty by, 104, 113–16; on demographics, 42; intendant responsibilities of, 89, 209n96, 216n28; military-planter state enforcement by, 177, 179; on money and taxes, 85–87, 108; on slave trade, 118, 149; uprising and revolt response of, 93, 108–16, 119–20, 122–25, 132, 137

"Monument Consecrated to Posterity in Memory of the Incredible Folly of the Twentieth Year of the Eighteenth Century" (Picart), 68–69, 68f

Moreau de Saint-Méry, Médéric Louis-Élie: on Cul de Sac Treaty, 116, 222n41; errors by, 217nn33,41, 220n7; on Indies Company privileges, 65; on Jesuits, 143; maps published by, 51; on money and taxes, 37; publication timing of, 117; on slavery, 118, 168; on uprisings and rebellions, 94, 126

Morville, Charles Jean-Baptiste Fleuriau, comte de, 124, 216n28

Natchez Indians, 127, 225n86

navy, French: company colony and, 14, 17, 21, 22; indemnity and threat of, 185; revolt response attributed to, 6, 110, 111–12, 122, 124

"negroes," 7, 81, 95–96, 112. *See also* enslaved persons; free people of color and free blacks

Neuville, Père de la, 157–58

octroi taxes, 18, 20, 22, 40, 85, 107, 125, 145, 204–5n24

258 INDEX

Padrejean, 160–61
paper currency, 5, 37, 57–58, 61, 73, 76
Paris brothers, 71
Parke, Daniel, 22, 205n30
Pétion, Alexandre, 184
Petite Anse, 51, 90, 99, 113
Petit Goâve, 10, 45, 119, 120–22, 121*f*
Phelipeau, René, 51–53
Philippe, 82–84, 86
Philippe (cashier/financial clerk), 84–85, 140
Picart, Bernard, 68–69, 70
plantation economy: debt to finance, 4,
    12–13, 77–78, 199n16; enslaved labor
    supporting, 12–13, 15–16, 41–42, 83
    (*see also* enslaved persons; slave trade);
    Jesuits in, 143–45 (*see also* Jesuit missionar-
    ies); militant slavery to secure (*see* militant
    slavery). *See also* military-planter state;
    sugar revolution
Pointis, Baron de, 34
Ponce, Nicolas, 51
Pontchartrain, 82–83, 86
Pontchartrain, Jérome de, 42
poor whites, 82, 89
Port-au-Prince: as capital, 10; map omitting,
    45, 48; population of, 18
Port-de-Paix, 17
Port-Margot, 17
Portugal: Dutch intrusion against, 25; gold
    or money of, 38, 40; slave trade in, 35,
    198n10, 203n1
Pouançay, 21–22

Raudot, Antoine-Denis, 139, 223n70
religion: Jesuit (*see* Jesuit missionaries);
    Saint-Domingue settlement and, 18;
    System opposition and, 67–68
revolts or rebellions. *See under* company
    colony; Haitian Revolution; Jesuit
    missionaries; marginalized people;
    maroons; militant slavery; military-
    planter state; System; white planters
Robineau, Antoine, 99
Robineau, Cathérine Leroy, 99

Robineau, Françoise Féron, 98–100, 102, 110,
    221n18
Robiou, 119–20, 223nn58–59
Royal African Company (RAC), 20, 27–30,
    224n85
royal liberties, 23–24
royal ordinance on money: devaluation of
    money with, 40–41, 76–77, 83, 85–87,
    90–91, 147; repeal of, 6; suspension or
    revocation of provisions of, 87–88, 125;
    text of, 195–96
Ryswick, Treaty of (1697), 34–35, 45, 161

Saint-Domingue: colonial System in
    (*see* System); as company colony
    (*see* company colony; *specific companies*);
    demographics and population of, 4,
    17–18, 41–43, 78–79, 96; disembarkations
    of enslaved persons on, 28, 29*f*, 32, 33*f*, 83
    (*see also* slave trade); founding story of,
    13–14; Jesuits on (*see* Jesuit missionaries);
    maps of (*see* maps); plantations and
    planters of (*see* militant slavery; military-
    planter state; plantation economy; sugar
    revolution; white planters); slavery on
    (*see* enslaved persons; militant slavery;
    slave trade); terminology for, 197n2
Saint-Domingue Company: acquisition of,
    4, 60, 63, 64–65; company colony under,
    11, 16, 33–35, 39; dismantling of, 35; silver
    acquisition by, 11, 33–35; slave trading by,
    4, 16, 39, 60; tax exemption of, 211n29
Sambourg, Jacques, 167
Sandys, Thomas, 24–25, 26
Sargent, Thomas, 6, 36
Sartre de Saint-Laurens, 49
seigniorage, 36–37, 76
Senegal Company, 16, 20–22, 27–28, 30,
    60–61, 67, 74
Sicard, Captain, 117
silver: clipped or diluted coins with, 40; in
    company colony, 11, 22, 33–41, 38*f*; free
    trade and access to, 5, 27; hoarding of, 15,
    36–37, 39; Indies Company shares

converted to, 199n19; Jesuit concerns over, 129, 137, 139–40, 141–47; marginalized people's uprising over, 7, 81, 83, 85–88, 90–92, 96, 101, 137, 139–40; maroon suppression costs in, 175; mercantilism and, 15, 27, 36, 39, 76; militant slavery and, 104, 125, 126; paper currency displacing, 5, 37, 57, 76 (*see also* paper currency); royal ordinance on (*see* royal ordinance on money); slave trade and, 5, 11, 33–35, 39, 60–61; valuation of, 5–6, 36–37, 40–41, 76–77, 83, 85, 87, 146–47, 218–19n61; weight of, 40–41, 76, 85, 137, 139–40

slaves. *See* enslaved persons

slave trade: *asiento* licenses in (*see asiento* licenses); banning of, 101, 186; company colony and, 5, 11–13, 15–16, 20–23, 27–35, 41–42, 43–44; death of slaves during, 83, 117; debt mitigation via, 55; demographics and growth of, 4, 43–44; free trade in, 5, 6, 11–12, 27–30, 114, 118, 126–27; Jesuit stance on, 140, 146, 148; marginalized people's uprising and, 83, 85, 86, 96, 101–2; mercantilism and, 15–16, 27–28, 55, 66; militant slavery and demands for, 103–5, 107–8, 114, 117–19, 126–27; opposition to, 67, 101; plantation economy dependence on, 12–13; silver, money and, 5, 11, 33–35, 39, 60–61, 77–78, 200nn21,25; smuggling in, 11, 16, 30–35, 41; System tied to, 3–4, 54–56, 59–67, 72, 74–75; wholesale purchases in, 117–19

smuggling: marginalized people's revolt influenced by, 109; mercantilism and, 15–16, 30–31; Saint-Domingue founding and, 12, 30; in slave trade, 11, 16, 30–35, 41; sugar revolution and, 45

Society of Jesus. *See* Company of Jesus; Jesuit missionaries

Songo, 168

Sorel, Léon de, Governor: Cul de Sac Treaty by, 104, 113–16; military-planter state enforcement by, 170–75, 177, 179; on

money and taxes, 39–40, 83, 85–87, 108; on slave trade, 118; uprising and revolt response of, 93, 108–16, 119–20, 122–25, 132, 137

South Sea Bubble, 2–3, 54–55, 66–74, 213n52

South Sea Company: critics of and opposition to, 69–70; slave trade by, 11, 27–28, 224n85; System and, 3, 54–55, 58 (*see also* South Sea Bubble)

Spain: Saint-Domingue border with, 8–9, 160–66, 162f, 164f, 168, 169–70, 171–72, 177–78; silver of, 11, 15, 22, 27, 33–36, 38–40, 38f (*see also* silver); slave trade in, 11, 27–28, 31, 34, 198n10, 203n1 (*see also asiento* licenses); War of the Spanish Succession with, 11, 20, 27, 31, 34–35

Spanish Succession, War of the, 11, 20, 27, 31, 34–35

St. Eustatius, 31–32

stock market: bubble effects on (*see* Mississippi Bubble; South Sea Bubble); System and share offerings on, 62, 67–69

sugar, as money alternative, 39, 182

sugar revolution: debt to finance, 4, 12, 182; demographics leading to, 4, 43–44, 45; economic impacts of, 182–83; foundations of, 6–10, 44–45; Haitian Revolution and, 10, 181; Jesuits in, 7, 143–45, 152; legacies of, 10, 203n44; maps showing growth with, 53; maroon uprising and, 7–9, 157, 163, 183 (*see also* military-planter state); militant slavery to protect, 8, 103–6, 126 (*see also* militant slavery); number of plantations in, 182–83; regulation of, 22; System effects on, 4, 54, 72, 182. *See also* plantation economy

System, 54–79; acquisitions and takeovers for, 4, 58, 59, 60–65, 67, 74; *asiento* licenses and, 54, 56; banks and Banque Royale in, 57–58, 62–63, 71–72, 73; colonial vs. metropolitan nature of, 54–55; critics of and rebellion against, 65, 67–71, 68f, 75–76; debt and, 2–3, 55–56, 58, 61–64, 71–73, 77–78; demographics,

260 INDEX

System (*continued*)
forced emigration and, 4, 56, 58–59, 78–79; failure of, 55, 70–74, 78–79; Indies Company and, 3, 5, 54–56, 59–67, 70–72, 74–75; Law's background and theory underlying, 56–58; Law's demise with crash of, 55, 70–71; mercantilism and, 55, 66; Mississippi and South Sea Bubble effects on, 2–3, 66–74; monetary valuation and, 75–77, 218–19n61; overview of colonial, 2–3, 54–56, 182; paper currency in, 5, 37, 57–58, 61, 73, 76; reversion to traditional financial management following, 55, 71–72; slave trade tied to, 3–4, 54–56, 59–67, 72, 74–75

takeovers, company, 58, 59. *See also* acquisitions of companies
taverns, regulation of, 88–89
taxes: capitation or head, 19, 20, 28, 117, 204nn23–24; Colonial Pact on, 19–20; company colony and, 11–12, 16–17, 18–20, 22, 28–29, 30–31, 35, 40; enslaved person ownership and, 13, 20, 28–29, 30, 167–68, 204n24; Indies Company exemption from, 5, 64, 66, 74, 85–87, 107–8; Jesuit stance on, 129, 142, 144–46, 150; maroon patrols funded by, 167–68, 173, 175; militant slavery and demands on, 104, 107–8, 114–17, 125, 141; money for, 40; monopoly exemption from, 11–12, 64, 66, 74, 85–87, 107–8, 125, 211n29; *octroi*, 18, 20, 22, 40, 85, 107, 125, 145, 204–5n24; representation and, 102, 104, 114, 116–17; riots and revolts over, 85–87, 102, 104; smuggling and avoidance of, 30–31; tax-farming companies to collect, 18–19
Tertre, Jean-Baptiste du, 129
tobacco, as money alternative, 39, 77
Tordesillas, Treaty of (1493), 59, 198n10, 203n1
Tortuga, 14, 16–17
trade: contraband (*see* smuggling); free (*see* free trade); mercantilism and, 15–16;

slave (*see* slave trade); System based on, 56, 58, 73 (*see also under* slave trade); triangle, 21–22; war and, 56
Tramond, Joannès, 128, 133
Trenchard, John, 69–70, 213n45
Trouillot, Michel-Rolph, 155
Trujillo, Rafael, 165

United Company of Merchants of England trading to the East Indies, 25
United Kingdom. *See* Britain
United States, Haiti intervention by, 187–89
unknown/unimportant people. *See* marginalized people
Utrecht, Treaty of (1713–1714), 11, 27, 28, 55, 206n50

vagabonds: forced emigration of, 4, 56, 58–59, 79, 175; *maréchaussées* and, 170–71, 175; regulations targeting, 89; riots and revolts by, 6, 8, 82, 93, 110
Velde, François, 6, 36
Vernon, Monsieur de, 115–16
Visa, 71–72

West Indies Company (Dutch), 27, 30, 32
West Indies Company (French): company colony under, 11, 14–17, 20, 30, 34; dismantling of, 17, 18; Jesuit relationship with, 144; mercantilism under, 14–16, 30; slave trading by, 16. *See also* Indies Company
white indentured servants, 13, 14, 39, 42–43, 77, 201n28
white planters: courts representing interests of, 106–7; debt of, 4, 12–13, 73–74, 77–78, 87, 119–20, 182, 186, 199n16; indemnity settling claims of, 184–86; Jesuits ministering to, 129, 148–50; military-planter state of (*see* military-planter state); Mississippi and South Sea Bubble effects on, 72–74; nonwhite planters and, 96, 173; plantation economy and (*see* plantation economy); population of,

42–43, 44; riots and revolts by, 6, 8, 86–87, 90, 93–94, 102, 103–6, 109–27, 156–57, 169, 179 (*see also under* company colony; militant slavery); slavery under (*see* enslaved persons; militant slavery; slave trade); sugar revolution and (*see* sugar revolution); taxes paid by (*see* taxes)

whites, poor, 82, 89

white supremacy: Jesuit ministry tinged with, 155, 157; militant slavery to perpetuate, 8, 104; in military-planter state, 155, 157, 165, 169, 173, 174

white women: forced emigration of, 4, 59, 79, 210–11nn11–12; population of, 17, 42–43; riots and revolts by, 6, 7–8, 81–82, 88, 91, 93–102, 108–12 (*see also* La Sagona); shipment of for marriage, 17

Wilson, Edward, 57, 71

women: as Amazons, 17, 97, 100–101, 137, 139, 219n75; of color, 42–43, 98 (*see also* enslaved persons); population of, 17, 42; riots and revolts by, 6, 7–8, 81–82, 88, 91, 93–102, 108–12 (*see also* La Sagona); white (*see* white women)

A NOTE ON THE TYPE

This book has been composed in Arno, an Old-style serif typeface in the classic Venetian tradition, designed by Robert Slimbach at Adobe.

GPSR Authorized Representative: Easy Access System Europe - Mustamäe tee 50, 10621 Tallinn, Estonia, gpsr.requests@easproject.com

www.ingramcontent.com/pod-product-compliance
Lightning Source LLC
Jackson TN
JSHW022149240525
84171JS00002B/5/J